BARKHAM BURROUGHS' ENCYCLOPAEDIA OF ASTOUNDING FACTS AND USEFUL INFORMATION CONTAINS KNOWLEDGE OF SOLID VALUE AND PRACTICAL UTILITY FOR EVERY HOUSEHOLD, INCLUDING A REMEDY FOR EVERY ILL, A SOLUTION FOR EVERY DIFFICULTY, AND AN ANSWER FOR EVERY QUESTION.

DID YOU KNOW ...

- A firkin of butter weighs 56 lbs
- Admirals earn $13,000 per annum
- Gold is worth $20 an ounce
- A barrel of pork weighs 56 lbs
- Wrought iron melts at 3980°
- Cathedral at Cologne is the highest building in the world
- Average duration of human life is 31 years
- The word "and" appears in the Old Testament 35,543 times
- In 70 years a good eater consumes 30 railway baggage cars full of food

DISCOVER ...

- How to remove freckles
- How to measure corn in the crib
- How to tell any person's age
- About the "dark day" in New England
- Odd facts about shoes
- Blunders and absurdities in art
- The remarkable story of Charlie Ross
- The language of flowers
- The dangers of celluloid
- Hints to young housewives
- Fingernails as an indication of character
- The cure for scurf in the head

See page 1 for complete contents

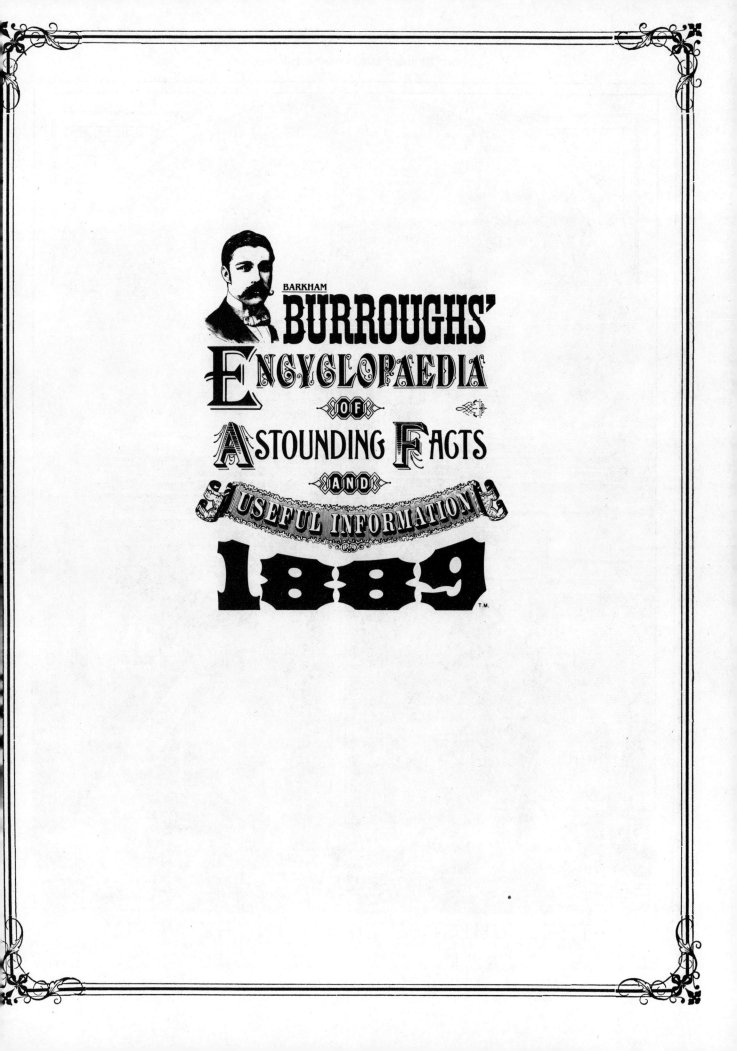

THE HIGHEST BUILDINGS IN THE WORLD.

1. An imaginary tower, 1000 feet high. 2. Cathedral at Cologne, 501 feet. 3. Pyramid of Cheops, 480 feet. 4. Strasbourg Cathedral, 468 feet. 5. St. Peter's, Rome, 457 feet. 6. Pyramid of Cephren, 454 feet. 7. St. Paul's, London, 365 feet. 8. Capitol at Washington, 287 feet. 9. Trinity Church, N, Y., 286 feet. 10. Bunker Hill Monument, 221 feet. 11. St. Mark's, Philadelphia, 150 feet.

BARKHAM

BURROUGHS'
ENCYCLOPAEDIA
OF
ASTOUNDING FACTS
AND
USEFUL INFORMATION
1889
T.M.

BONANZA BOOKS
NEW YORK

This 1989 edition is published by Bonanza Books, distributed by Crown
Publishers, Inc., 225 Park Avenue South, New York, New York 10003, by
arrangement with Brayden Books.

Manufactured in the United States of America

Design: Miggs Burroughs
Inspiration: Mimi Burroughs
Determination: Brady Burroughs
Education: Bernard Burroughs
Fortification: Esta Burroughs
Imagination: Tracy Burroughs

Library of Congress Cataloging-in-Publication Data

Burroughs, Barkham, d. 1952.
    [Encyclopaedia of astounding facts and useful information, 1889]
    Barkham Burroughs' encyclopaedia of astounding facts and useful
    information, 1889.
       p.   cm.
    Reprint. Originally published in 1889.
    ISBN 0-517-67950-7
    1. Handbooks, vade-mecums, etc.   I. Title.
AG106.B87   1989
031'.02—dc 19   89-533
                                                                 CIP

h g f e d c b a

For Melba Conner

CONTENTS

NOTE: As an exact reproduction of the 1889 edition, all the
eccentricities of the original language, typesetting and
printing have been left intact for your appreciation.

Foreword

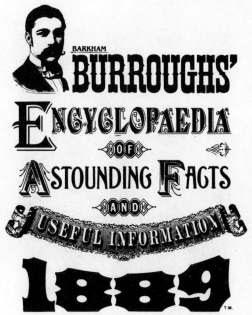

BARKHAM BURROUGHS'
ENCYCLOPAEDIA
OF
ASTOUNDING FACTS
AND
USEFUL INFORMATION
1889™.

President Harrison valued him as an intrepid Rear-Admiral. The Postmaster General and a grateful public recognized him as the inventor of the "modern-day" return address; and to those who were fortunate enough to own a copy of this incredible encyclopaedia, he was the best friend a Victorian household ever had.

Although I was only six when he died in 1952, at age 87, I remember Barkham Burroughs, my Father's Father's Father to be a gentle and fun-loving old man who was always ready for a rough and tumble game of skittles on the drawing room floor. Years later I began to realize that for all his acclaim my Great Grandfather had not been as happy as he appeared to some admiring eyes. Despair over a succession of failed romances, questionable business affairs and a bout with shingles late in life, lead to a grim dependence on "Briarwood Tonic", a patented medicine of his own creation.

Inspite of the less attractive details, I accept his past as part of my own and I am proud to be the Great Grandson of a young man who, in 1889, without benefit of a formal education or personal computer, compiled and published this remarkable volume of curiosities. Now, almost 100 years later, it is my pleasure to introduce this entertaining and informative treasure to the high-tech households of the 1980's.

Miggs Burroughs — Westport, Connecticut

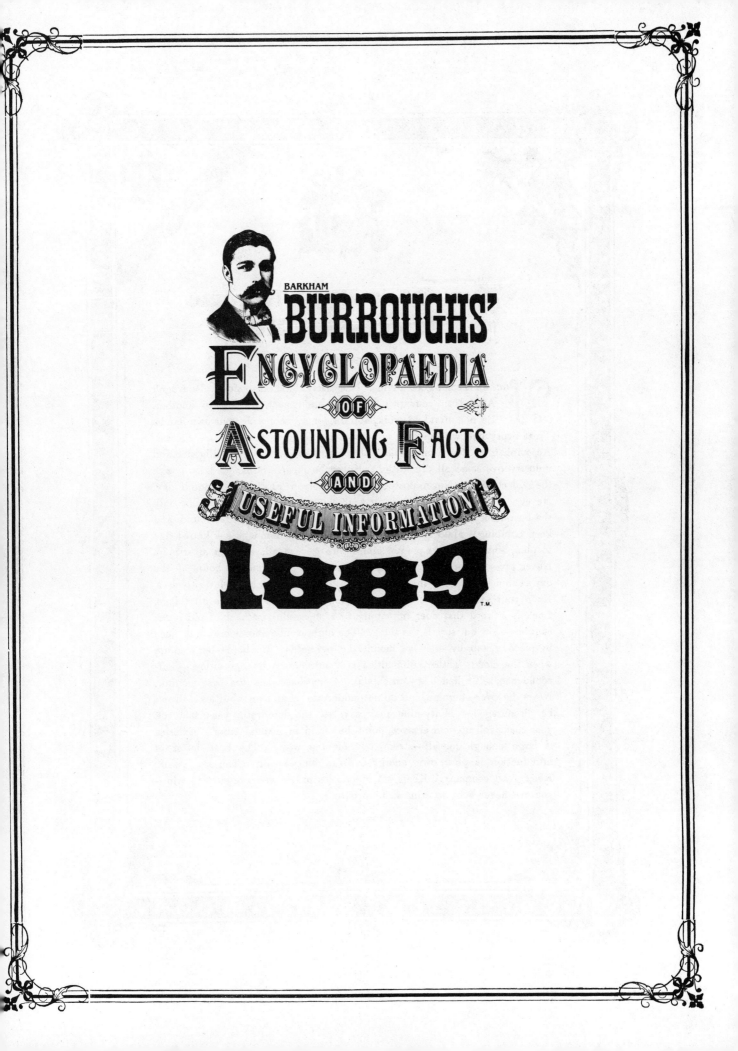

How Poor Boys Become Successful Men.

You want some good advice. Rise early. Be abstemious. Be frugal. Attend to your own business and never trust it to another. Be not afraid to work, and diligently, too, with your own hands. Treat every one with civility and respect. Good manners insure success. Accomplish what you undertake. Decide, then persevere. Diligence and industry overcome all difficulties. Never be mean—rather give than take the odd shilling. Never postpone till to-morrow what can be done to-day. Never anticipate wealth from any source but labor. Honesty is not only the best policy, but the only policy. Commence at the first round and keep climbing. Make your word as good as your bond. Seek knowledge to plan, enterprise to execute, honesty to govern all. Never overtrade. Never give too large credit. Time is money. Reckon the hours of the day as so many dollars, the minutes as so many cents. Make few promises. Keep your secrets. Live within your income. Sobriety above all things. Luck is a word that does not apply to a successful man. Not too much caution—slow but sure is the thing. The highest monuments are built piece by piece. Step by step we mount the pyramids. Be bold—be resolute when the clouds gather, difficulties are surmounted by opposition. Self-confidence, self-reliance is your capital. Your conscience the best monitor. Never be over-sanguine, but do not underrate your own abilities. Don't be discouraged. Ninty-nine may say no, the hundreth, yes: take off your coat: roll up your sleeves, don't be afraid of manual labor! America is large enough for all—strike out for the west. The best letter of introduction is your own energy. Lean on yourself when you walk. Keep good company. Keep out of politics unless you are sure to win— you are never sure to win, so look out.

THE Art of Penmanship

How to Become a Handsome Writer.

THE subject of the importance of good writing is as broad as its use. Reaching out in every direction, and pervading every corner of civilized society, from the humblest up to the highest employments, it is a servant of man, second only in importance to that of speech itself. In the world of business its value is seen, from the simplest record or memorandum, up to the parchment which conveys a kingdom. Without it, the wheels of commerce could not move a single hour. At night it has recorded the transactions of the Bank of England during the day; of London; of the whole world.

Through the art of writing, the deeds of men live after them, and we may surround ourselves with the companionship of philosophers, scientists, historians, discoverers and poets; and their discoveries, and reasonings and imaginings become ours. In the amenities of social life, through the medium of the pen, heart speaks to heart, though ocean rolls between. Thoughts of tenderness and affection live when we are gone, and words and deeds of kindness are not preserved by monuments alone. What fountains of grief or joy have been opened in the hearts of those who have read the records of the pen! The pen has recorded the rapturous emotions of love reciprocated. The pen has written the message of sadness which has covered life's pilgrimage with gloom. The pen has traced the record of noble and useful lives, spent in humanity's cause. The songs of the poet, the beautiful tints of his imagination, the flights of the orator in the realms of fancy, and the facts of history, would all perish as the dew of morning, without this noble art of writing.

As a means of livelihood, there is perhaps no other department of education which affords such universal and profitable employment, as writing. From the mere copyist, up to the practical accountant, and onward into that department of penmanship designated as a fine art, the remuneration is always very ample, considering the time and effort required in its acquisition.

Teachers, editors, farmers, doctors and all persons should possess a practical and substantial knowledge of writing, and should be ready with the pen. Business men must of course be ready writers, and hence, in a treatise on business, designed for the education and advancement of the youth of the country, it seems eminently fitting to first make the way clear to a plain, practical handwriting.

Neatness and accuracy should characterize the hand-writing of every one. Botch-work and bungling are inexcusable, as well in writing as in the transaction of business. No person has a right to cause a tinge of shame to their correspondent, by sending a letter addressed in a stupid and awkward manner, nor to consume the time of another in deciphering the illegible hooks and scrawls of a message. Every one should have the ambition to *write* respectably as well as to *appear* respectable on any occasion.

MATERIALS USED IN WRITING.

Having a suitable desk or table, arranged with reference to light, in order to learn to write, it is necessary to be provided with proper materials. Writing materials are so abundant and so cheap in these times that no excuse is afforded for using an inferior or worthless quality. The materials consist of *Pens, Ink* and *Paper.*

PENS.

Steel pens are considered the best. Gold pens have the advantage of always producing the same quality of writing, while steel pens, new or old, produce finer or courser lines. Notwithstanding this advantage in favor of the gold pen, steel pens adhere to the paper, and produce a better line. The pen should be adapted to the hand of the writer. Some persons require a coarse pen, and some fine. Elastic pens in the hand of one writer may produce the best results, while a less flexible pen may suit the hand of others best. Pens are manufactured of almost an infinite grade and quality, in order to suit the requirements of all. About the only rule that can be given in selecting pens, is to write a few lines, or a page, with each of the pens on trial, and then compare the writing. If it be shaded too heavily, select a less flexible pen, if the hair lines are too delicate, select a coarser pen.

INK.

Black ink is always preferable. That which is free from sediment and flows well, should be selected. Use an inkstand with broad base as being less liable to upset. With persons in learning to write it is perhaps best to have a quality of ink which is perfectly black when put on the paper, in order that they may see the results of their labor at once. Business men and accountants prefer a fluid ink, however, which, although not black at first, continues to grow black, and becomes a very bright and durable black, notwithstanding the action of light and heat. Avoid the use of fancy colored inks, especially the more gaudy, such as blue, red or green, in writing all documents which you desire to command attention and respect.

PAPER.

There are almost as many grades of paper to be found in the stationery stores, as there are of pens. For practicing penmanship, nothing is more suitable than foolscap, which may be easily sewed into book-form, with cover of some different color, and thus serves every requirement. The paper should have a medium surface, neither rough and coarse, or too fine and glazed. Have a few extra sheets beside the writing book, for the purpose of practicing the movement exercises and testing the pens. Be provided at all times with a large-sized blotter, and when writing, keep this under the hand. Do not attempt to write with a single sheet of paper on a bare table or desk; there should be many sheets of paper underneath, in order to make an elastic surface.

STUDY WITH PRACTICE.

Aimless, indifferent, or careless practice, never made a good writer, and never will. In order to succeed in this, as in other things, there must be will and determination to succeed, and then persevering and studious effort. Study the models until their forms are fixed in the mind.

Study gives form

No one can execute that which he does not clearly conceive. The artist must first see the picture on the white canvas, before he can paint it, and the sculptor must be able to see in the rough and uninviting stone, the outlines of the beautiful image which he is to carve. In writing, a clear idea of the formation of the different letters, and their various proportions, must become familiar by proper study, examination and analysis. Study precedes practice. It is, of course, not necessary, nor even well, to undertake the mastery of all the forms in writing, by study, until some have been executed. It is best that each form should, as it is taken up, be first measured and analyzed and then practiced at once.

Practice gives grace

It is the act which crowns the thought. After study, careful and earnest practice can hardly fail to make a good writer of any one. Some persons secure a good style of penmanship with less labor than others, and attain to the elegant, and beautiful formation. But it is only fair to presume that no greater diversity of talent exists in this direction than in the study of other things. All do not learn arithmetic or history with like ease, but no one will assert that all who will, may not learn arithmetic or history. And so, all who will put forth the proper exertion in study and practice may learn to write a good business style, while many of the number will attain to the elegant. The conditions of practice in writing are, *Position of the Body, Position of the Hand and Pen, and Movement.*

POSITION of BODY.

SITTING squarely fronting the desk, with feet placed firmly on the floor, and both arms on the desk, is, as a rule, the best position for practice in writing, or correspondence. The right side, may, however, be placed to the desk, with the right arm, only, resting thereon, and some persons prefer this position. Avoid crossing the feet, sitting on the edge of the chair, or assuming any careless attitude. The body should be erect, but slightly inclined forward, in order that the eye may follow the pen closely. This position will never cause curvature of the spine. The body should never be allowed to settle down into a cramped and unhealthy position with the face almost on the paper. By thus compressing the lungs and the digestive organs **they** are soon injured, and if the stomach lose its tone, the eyesight is impaired, there is such a close sympathy between these organs of the body. The practice of writing should be, and properly is, a healthful exercise, and injurious effects result only from improper positions of the body, at variance with good writing as well as good health.

When wearied by sitting and the effort at writing, lay aside paper and pen, arise from the chair, and take exercise and rest by walking about the room or in the open air. Then come back refreshed, and vigorous, for the practice of writing.

In general, the light should fall on the paper from the left side, thus enabling a writer to clearly see the ruled lines, and render the labor of writing easier and more rapid. If one writes left-handed, of course he will sit so as to get his light from the right side, or over the right shoulder.

SHADING.

As a beautifier of the handwriting, by causing a diversity of light and shade among the letters, shading has its value; but in the practical handwriting for business purposes, it should, as a rule, be classed with flourishing, and left out. Requiring time and effort, to bring down the shades on letters, business men, clerks and telegraph operators find a uniform and regular style of writing, without shade, the best, even though it may not be as artistic.

UNIFORMITY.

A most necessary element in all good penmanship is uniformity. In the slope of the letters and words which form a written page there must be no disagreement. With the letters leaning about in various directions, writing is presented in its most ridiculous phase. Uniformity in the size of letters, throughout the written page; how greatly it conduces to neatness and beauty. All letters resting on the line, and being of uniform hight, adds another condition towards good penmanship. This essential element of uniformity may be watched and guarded closely and cultivated by any learner in his own practice.

SLANT OF WRITING.

As said before, it matters not so much what angle of slant is adopted in writing, provided it is made uniform, and all letters are required to conform exactly to the same slant. Writing which is nearest perpendicular is most legible, and hence is preferable for business purposes. The printed page of perpendicular type; how legible it is. But for ease in execution, writing should slant. It follows then that writing should be made as perpendicular as is consistent with ease of execution. The slant of writing should not be less than sixty degrees from the horizontal.

Position Body While Standing.

THE practical book-keeper finds it advantageous to do his writing while standing; in fact, where large books are in use, and entries are to be transferred from one to another, the work of the book-keeper can hardly be performed otherwise than in a standing position, free to move about his office. Cumbrous books necessitate a different position at the desk, from that of the correspondent, or the learner. Since large books must lie squarely on the desk, the writer, in order to have the proper position thereto, must place his left side to the desk. The body thus has the same relative position, as if squarely fronting the desk with the paper or book placed diagonally. In other words, the writer, while engaged in writing in large, heavy books, must adjust himself to the position of the books. Should the correspondent or bill clerk perform his work while standing, he would assume the same as the sitting position—squarely fronting the desk.

LEGIBILITY.

Children, in learning to write, are apt to sacrifice all other good qualities of beauty, regularity and grace, for the quality of legibility, or plainness. With some older persons this legibility is considered of very little consequence, and is obscured by all manner of meaningless flourishes, in which the writer takes pride. In the estimation of the business man, writing is injured by shades and flourishes. The demand of this practical time is a plain, regular style that can be written rapidly, and read at a glance.

FINISH.

By a careless habit, which many persons allow themselves to fall into, they omit to attend to the little things in writing. Good penmanship consists in attention to small details, each letter and word correctly formed, makes the beautiful page. By inattention to the finish of one letter, or part of a letter of a word, oftentimes the word is mistaken for another, and the entire meaning changed. Particular attention should be devoted to the finish of some of the small letters, such as the dotting of the i, or crossing of the t. Blending the lines which form a loop, often causes the letter to become a stem, similar to the t or d, or an e to become an i. In many of the capital letters, the want of attention to the finish of the letter converts it into another or destroys its identity, such, for instance, as the small cross on the capital F, which, if left off, makes the letter a T. The W often becomes an M, or *vice versa*, and the I a J. Mistakes in this regard are more the result of carelessness and inattention than anything else. By careful practice a person will acquire a settled habit of giving a perfection to each letter and word, and then it is no longer a task, but is performed naturally and almost involuntarily, while the difference in the appearance of the written page, as well as the exactness and certainty of the meaning conveyed, may be incalculably great.

While practicing penmanship, or while endeavoring to correct a careless habit in writing, the mind must be upon the work in hand, and not be allowed to wander into fields of thought or imagination; by thus confining the attention, any defect or imperfection in the formation of letters may be soon mastered or corrected.

Position of the Hand and Pen.

THE right arm should rest on the muscles just below the elbow, and wrist should be elevated so as to move free from paper and desk. Turn the hand so that the wrist will be level, or so that the back of the hand will face the ceiling. The third and fourth fingers turned slightly underneath the hand will form its support, and the pen, these fingers and the muscles of the arm near the elbow form the only points of rest or contact on desk or paper. The pen should point over the shoulder, and should be so held that it may pass the root of the nail on the second finger, and about opposite the knuckle of the hand. An unnatural or cramped position of the hand, like such a position of the body, is opposed to good writing, and after many years of observation and study, all teachers concur in the one position above described, as being the most natural, easy and graceful for the writer, and as affording the most freedom and strength of movement.

Avoid getting the hand in an awkward or tiresome position, rolling it over to one side, or drawing the fore finger up into a crooked shape. Hold the pen firmly but lightly, not with a grip as if it were about to escape from service. Do not say, "I can't" hold the pen correctly. Habits are strong, but will may be stronger, and if you hold the pen correctly in spite of old habits, for a few lessons, all will then be easy, and

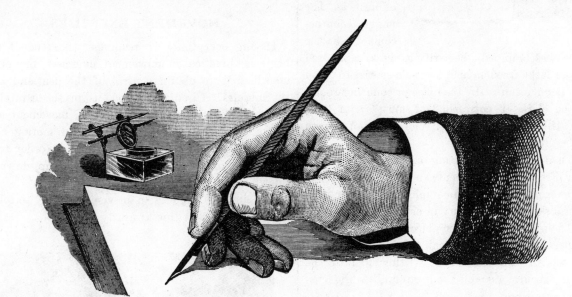

the pen will take its position at each writing exercise, with no effort whatever. Everything being in readiness, and the proper position assumed, the writer must now obtain complete control of hand and pen, by practice in movement.

RAPIDITY.

One of the essentials of a practical business style of writing must be rapidity of execution, in order to be of any avail in the necessities and press of a business position. The demand of the merchant is, that his clerk shall not only write well, but with rapidity, and the volume of letters to be answered, bills to be made out, or items to be entered on the books of account, compel the clerk to move the pen with dexterity and rapidity, as well as skill. While there is great diversity among persons as to the rapidity as well as quality of their penmanship, some being naturally more alert and active than others, yet by securing the proper position of the hand, arm and body, favorable to ease and freedom of execution, then following this with careful practice in movement, until all the varied motions necessary in writing are thoroughly mastered, the person may, with suitable effort, acquire the quality of rapidity in writing, gradually increasing the speed until the desired rate is accomplished.

BEAUTY.

In the handwriting, as in other things, beauty is largely a matter of taste and education. To the man of business, the most beautiful handwriting is that which is written with ease, and expresses plainly and neatly the thought of the writer. To the professional or artistic taste, while such a hand may be regarded as "a good business hand," it would not be considered as beautiful, because it conforms to no rule as to proportion, shade, and spacing. In the practical art of writing, it is not very unfair to measure its beauty largely by its utility.

MOVEMENT.

INGER movement, or writing by the use of the fingers as the motive power, is entirely inadequate to the requirements of business. The fingers soon become tired, the hand becomes cramped, the writing shows a labored effort, and lacks freedom and ease so essential to good business penmanship. In the office or counting-room, where the clerk or correspondent must write from morning till night, the finger movement of course cannot be used.

What is designated by writing teachers as the Whole Arm, or Free Arm Movement, in which the arm is lifted free from the desk and completes the letter with a dash or a swoop, is necessary in ornamental penmanship and flourishing, but has no place in a practical style of business writing. The man of business would hardly stop, in the midst of his writing, to raise the arm, and execute an "off-hand capital," while customers are waiting.

But adapted to the practical purposes of business is the *muscular movement*, in which the arm moves freely on the muscles below the elbow, and in cases of precise writing, or in the more extended letters, such as f, is assisted by a slight movement of the fingers. The third and fourth fingers may remain stationary on the paper, and be moved from time to time, or between words, where careful and accurate writing is desired, but in more rapid, free and flowing penmanship, the fingers should slide over the paper.

MOVEMENT EXERCISES.

Having everything in readiness, the student may begin his practice on movement exercises, the object of which is to obtain control of the pen and train the muscles. Circular motion, as in the capital O, reversed as in the capital W, vertical movement as in f, long s and capital J, and the lateral motion as in small letters, must each be practiced in order to be able to move the pen in any direction, up, down, or sidewise.

The simplest exercise in movement. Try to follow around in the same line as nearly as possible. Do not shade.

The same exercise, only with ovals drawn out and and slight shade added to each down stroke

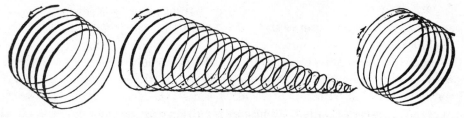

Sides of ovals should be even, forming as nearly a straight line as possible. Reverse the movement as in third form.

The following three exercises embrace the essential elements in capital letters, and should at first be made large for purposes of movement:

Capital O, down strokes parallel.

Capital stem. Down stroke a compound curve. Shade low. Finish with a dash.

Capital loop. Curves parallel. First curve highest.

Having succeeded to some extent with these exercises, the learner may next undertake the vertical movement. In order to obtain the lateral movement, which enables one to write long words without lifting the pen, and move easily and gracefully across the page, exercises like the following should be practiced·

Down strokes straight.   Even and resting on line.

In all movement exercises the third and fourth fingers should slide on the paper, and the finger movement should be carefully avoided. The different movements having been practiced, they may now be combined in various forms

Lateral and rolling movement combined. Vertical movement and rolling movement combined.   Do not shade the circles. Lines should be parallel.

Movement exercises may be multiplied almost indefinitely by studying the forms used in writing and their combinations. Repeating many of the small letters, such as m, u, e, r, s, a, d, h and c, also capitals D, J, P, etc., forms an excellent exercise for the learner.

PRINCIPLES IN WRITING.

In order to enable the learner to examine, analyze and criticise his writing, the following principles are given as his standards of measurements and form. By combining them in various ways the essential part of all letters in the alphabet may be formed.

The principles must be first carefully studied, and separated into the primary lines which compose them and the form of each principle well understood. The student may then form a scale like the one following, by dividing the distance between the blue lines on the paper into four equal spaces, with a lightly ruled line.   The letters of the small alphabet should then be placed in the scale and the hight of each letter fixed in the mind.

Notice that the contracted letters, or those which occupy only one space, as a, m, n, o, s, v, w and e, and that part of d, g, h, q and y, found in the first space, are all well rounded and developed.   These letters and parts of letters, found in the first space, form the essential part of all writing, and therefore deserve especial care. Also notice that the loop letters, above the line, such as b, f, h, k and l, extend two and one-half spaces above the blue line, while the loop below the line, such as g, f, j, q, y and z, extend one and one-half spaces below the blue line, thus two and one-half and one and one-half making the four spaces of the scale, and the upper loops on one line will just meet the lower loops of the line above, but never conflict, to the destruction of neat body writing.   Notice the type of the printer.   The extensions above the shorter letters are quite insignificant, and are only used to save the letter from resembling some other letter of the alphabet.   They never conflict, and how legible they are.

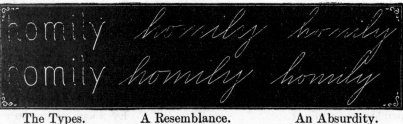

The Types.   A Resemblance.   An Absurdity.

Besides, to make long loops, requires more time, and more power with the pen, while shorter loops are in every way easier to acquire, quicker, and better.   Telegraph operators, some of whom are among our best business penmen, make all extended letters very short, while accountants, and business men, favor the style of short loops, well developed letters, and small capitals.

Apply the principles.   Observe regularity.   Muscular movement.

Down strokes straight.   Up strokes curved.

Principle No. 1.   Well formed loop.

These exercises should be practiced with the muscular movement, until they can be made with regularity and ease.

4th principle.   Let 3d and 4th fingers slide.   Notice the top.

O closed at top.   No retracing.

Two spaces high.   Down stroke straight.

A rule in writing may be laid down, that all small letters should commence on the blue line, and end one space high.

Discover the principles.   Avoid retracing.

ggggg ggggg gggg ggggg ggggg

Notice form.   In w, last part narrow.   Make without raising the pen.

v vvvvvvv w wwwwwwwwww x xxxxxxxx

Extend two spaces above the line, and one below.

p p ppppp pump paper prepared pen

Retracing is an error.   The only exception to this is in d, t, p and x, where it becomes necessary.

b b b blending blooming k k kick kicking

hurt hint hand heart head hundred hhh

f find fund fame flame flowers fumigate

Upper loops have their crossing at the hight of one space, while lower loops cross at the blue line.

y your youth y j journey joining rejoicing

fs effs efffs assure z zone zone zenith zzzz

t tune time tanner drum dime tttdddd

Place the capital letters on the scale, analyze them according to principles 6, 7 and 8, and notice their relative proportions.

A B C D E F G H I J K L M

N O P Q R S T U V W X Y Z

In order to practice capital letters to advantage, as well as to study them, collect in a group or family all those letters which have some one form or principle as an essential part.   Take first the 6th principle, or oval, and we group the letters as follows:

O A C E P B R

The excellence of an oval depends largely on its fullness and roundness.   No corners or flat **sides.**

Down strokes parallel.   Capital D is a Capital O with a knot on the lower corner.

O Olean Orleans Ohio Delia David Dahlia

C Church Currency C E E Elucidate Economy

P Prince Prayer P B Began R Raymond R

The letters in which the capital stem, or 7th principle, forms a leading part, may be grouped as follows:

H K F T S L I

In the H and K, the capital stem is almost straight on the down stroke, in the F and T it is little more of a wave line, and in S and L the line is much of a compound or double curve.

H Hand Hunter Hinder K Kingdom Ky.

F Famine Fremont T Tenement Troy

S Sumpter St. L Larimore G Grammar

The capital I, and also the J, which is a modified I, are sometimes classed among the capital stem letters, from the resemblance of the I to this principle in all but the top.

Independence Jamestown Inkerman Judgment

The capital loop, or 8th principle, is found as an essential element in

M N X W Q Z V U Y

In the capital loop, or 8th principle, another oval may be made within the large turn at the top, but for practical purposes the letter is perhaps better without it, and may be simplified even more, as in the N below.

M Monumental N Nathaniel X Xenophon

W Writing Q Quay Quack Z Z Zones Z Z

V Value Valuable U Union Y Youthful

FIGURES.

Make figures small, neat, and of form exact. Each figure must show for itself, and cannot be known by those which precede or follow it, as is the case with letters. The common tendency is to make figures too large and coarse. Mind the ovals in figures and have them full and round. The chief excellence of the zero lies in its roundness; the 3, 5, 6 or 9, without care in making the ovals, may degenerate into a straight line, or simply a meaningless hook, which it would hardly be safe to use in expressing sums of money, ordering goods, or the transaction of other business.

1 2 3 4 5 6 7 8 9 0 $ ¢ # % % 1 2 3 4 5 6 7 8 9 0

COPIES FOR PRACTICE.

Having proceeded thus far in the study and practice of writing, and having obtained the proper control of the pen through the movement exercises, all that is necessary now in order to secure a good handwriting, is continued and well-directed practice.

$1100ᵒᵒ/₁₀₀   *Chicago, Jan. 10, /80.*

Due Henry Harrington, or order, Eleven
Hundred Dollars in Merchandise, value rec'd
No. 43.   *Newton P. Kelley, Sr.*

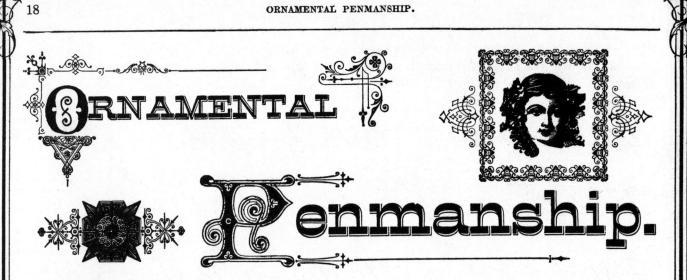

Ornamental Penmanship.

CHARMING and fascinating are the graceful and harmonious curves produced, when, wielded by some trained and skillful hand, the pen becomes an instrument of beauty. As by the power of speech, men may pass from the common tone of conversation up to the melodious strains of music, or may soar in flights of oratory into the sublime, until the multitude is entranced; so the capabilities of the pen are not limited to the common uses of life, but may take on forms of beauty in elegant outlines of bird, or landscape, or graceful swan or bounding stag.

Ornamental writing is not a practical art, and has no connection whatever with the practical business of life. It is in the realm of poetry. The imagery of graceful outlines must first be seen by a poetic imagination. While the great masses may acquire a good style of plain, practical penmanship, few have the necessary conception of mind, combined with the skill and dexterity of hand to become successful ornamental penmen.

The ornamental pages which follow are given, not as models for imitation or practice by the learner, but merely to show the possibilities of the pen in the hand of a master, and as a fitting closing to this, our chapter on penmanship.

To any one who may have an artistic quality of mind, and delights in beautiful lines and harmonious curves, these pages of ornamental penmanship will serve as models for practice and imitation, and every attempt at such an exercise as the one on this, or the following pages, will give greater strength and freedom of movement, and better command of the pen, so that it will conduce to an easy, flowing and elegant style of plain business writing, while affording a most pleasant and profitable employment in the cultivation of the taste.

Various beautiful designs or pictures may be made with the pen, in the hands of one that possesses the skill of a penman and the eye of an artist.

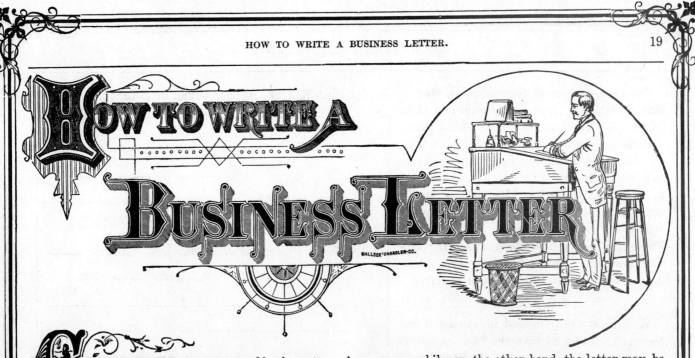

How to Write a Business Letter

CONSIDERING the vast amount of business transacted by correspondence between the parties, Letter Writing seems only second in importance to book-keeping. The merchant of the smaller cities or towns, perhaps in the far west, desires to order articles of merchandise from the wholesale house in New York or Boston. Possibly a remittance is to be sent. It may be that an error has occurred and needs correction. Credit is to be asked, references given, and a multitude of other matters call for adjustment through correspondence. To write every conceivable variety and shade of meaning, expressing the proper thought in the most fitting and appropriate language, is indeed a rare and valuable accomplishment. And when the proper language takes on the graceful and business like

air of the well written letter, with its several parts harmoniously arranged, it is a combination of brain and skill which can hardly be overestimated.

This subject, therefore, naturally divides itself into two parts: *The Mechanical Structure*, and the *Literature of a Letter*. The former of these being the less difficult will be first considered.

THE STRUCTURE OF A BUSINESS LETTER,

Consists in the arrangement of its several parts, with a view to the most harmonious effect. Excellent penmanship is very desirable, but not absolutely essential. The penmanship may indeed be poor, but the arrangement of the several parts of the letter, the neatness, and finish, may be such as to give it an attractive appearance, while on the other hand, the letter may be clothed in the most elegant penmanship, and yet the construction be such as to stamp its author as a careless and indifferent person, devoid of precision and order.

No one great thing, but many little things carefully watched, and attentively practiced, make up the structure and dress of a business letter, and give it a business-like air. The penmanship should be a neat, strong hand, very plain and legible, and devoid of all flourish.

PAPER AND ENVELOPE.

The paper and envelopes used in business correspondence should be of a good, durable quality, and a white color is preferable. Cheap materials are not only unsatisfactory to the writer, but may give the reader an unfavorable impression, which would be an injury far exceeding the cost of the best stationery for a life time. Persons form impressions from very little things sometimes.

The size of a letter sheet in business correspondence should be about 8 x 10 inches. This sheet affords a sufficient space for a communication of ordinary length to be written on one side only, which is essential in case the letter is copied in a letter press. A sheet of paper, note size, (5 x 8) is oftentimes used for brief communications of no special importance, and not designed to be filed for future reference. Among professional men the commercial note sheet is more extensively used, but with business men the letter size is considered preferable.

The envelope should correspond in size to that of the letter sheet, and should be a trifle longer than one-half the length of the sheet. Thus in a sheet eight by ten inches, one-half the length of the sheet is five inches, and this requires the length of the envelope to be about five and a quarter inches. Its width is usually about three inches. Avoid the use of fancy colored and fancy shaped paper and envelopes. These may not be objectional in social correspondence among ladies, but the gravity of business affairs does not admit of such display.

THE HEADING.

With most firms engaged in business it has become a custom to have the business advertisement placed at the head of the letter page, together with street, number and city. Thus leaving only the date to be inserted to complete the heading.

In case the heading of the letter is to be entirely written, it should be placed so as to occupy the right hand half of the first two lines at the top of the page. If, however, the letter is to be a very brief one, occupying only three or four lines, the heading may then be placed lower down on the sheet, so as to bring the body of the letter about the center of the sheet.

Writing from a large city the heading should contain the street and number. Your correspondent, in directing his answer will rely on the address given in the heading of your letter. Never be guilty of the blunder committed by ignorant persons of placing a part of the heading under the signature.

965 Market Street,

Philadelphia, June 10, 1882.

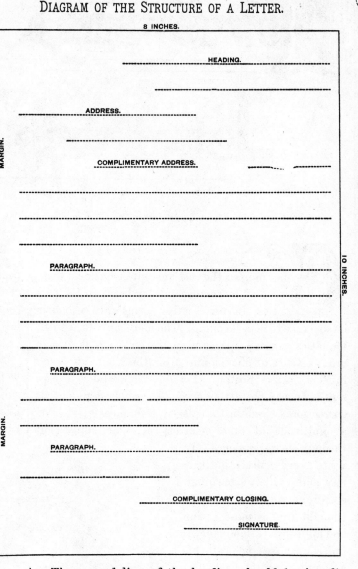

DIAGRAM OF THE STRUCTURE OF A LETTER.

The second line of the heading should begin a little farther to the right than the first line, as seen above.

If the writer has a box at the Post Office and wishes his mail delivered there, he may head his letter, as on the following page:

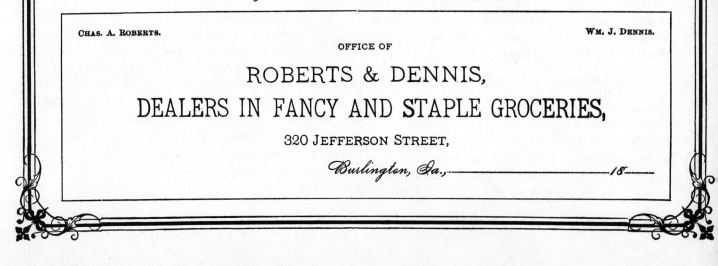

CHAS. A. ROBERTS.   WM. J. DENNIS.

OFFICE OF

ROBERTS & DENNIS,

DEALERS IN FANCY AND STAPLE GROCERIES,

320 JEFFERSON STREET,

Burlington, Ia., ———————— *18*———

P. O. Box 3587,

New York, May 16, 1882.

Writing from the principal cities of the United States it is not necessary to make the name of the state a part of the heading, as that is supposed to be known and understood, but with smaller cities the name of the state also, should be given. Thus, there is a Quincy in Illinois, and also in Massachusetts, and unless the state were mentioned a person answering a letter from Quincy, would not know which state to direct his reply to. In writing from an obscure town or village, not only the state should be given, but the county as well.

Ottawa, LaSalle County, Ill.,

December 20, 1882.

The punctuation of the heading and other parts of the letter, is of great importance in the estimation of cultivated persons, and something which can be learned by a little attention on the part of anyone, in examining the forms here given.

MARGIN.

A margin three-quarters of an inch in width should be left, on the side of the letter, as shown in the diagram. This is convenient for any mark or memorandum which your correspondent may desire to make concerning anything contained in the letter, but its greater value lies in the open, airy, and cheerful dress which it imparts to the letter. A margin too narrow conveys the idea of stinginess, as if to economize paper, while an irregular or zigzag margin conveys the idea of carelessness or want of precision. On a sheet of note paper the margin may be only one-half inch in width, thus making its width proportionate to the size of the sheet.

ADDRESS.

On the next line below the heading, that is the third line from the top of the sheet, and beginning at the left margin, should be placed the *Address*, which consists of the name of the person to whom the letter is written, together with his titles, if any, and his place of residence or business. The letter is not complete without all this, in the estimation of the business man. It does not fully explain itself, if the place of residence is not down as well as the name, and in preserving a letter press copy, this is quite essential for future reference.

Messrs. Samuel Bliss & Co,

Reading, Pa.

Gentlemen:

Or if the letter is written to a person living or doing business in a large city, thus:

Mr. James M. Cummings,

645 Broadway, New York.

Sir:

The names and residence should not be allowed to extend further to the right than about the center of the sheet, thus leaving an open space between this and the heading of your letter. In case the names or place of residence should be so long as to require it, they may be placed thus:

Messrs. Richards, Shaw, Fitch

& Winslow, Chicago.

Gentlemen:

The words *Dear Sir* or *Gentlemen* are sometimes placed farther to the left, as in the above example, but most business men in their correspondence place this complimentary address with reference to the words above them, about three-quarters of an inch farther to the right, as shown below.

William H. Nelson, Esq.,

177 Erie St., Boston.

Dear Sir:

The custom of placing the address beneath the body instead of at the beginning of the letter, is not much in vogue in business circles in this country, most business men preferring to place the name and address at the head of the sheet, and then write at it as if they were talking to the person himself. When, however, the address is placed below the letter it should occupy the same position as to the margin, etc., as if placed at the beginning. The custom is borrowed from the English, and its use is confined mostly to government officials and professional men.

BODY OF THE LETTER.

This constitutes the written message. It should begin on the same line with the words *Dear Sir*, or

Gentlemen, leaving after these words a small space. In case the place of residence or business is not written in the address, then the complimentary address of *Dear Sir* or *Gentlemen* will be placed on the next line under the name, or fourth line from the top of the sheet, and the letter will begin on the fifth line from the top, thus ·

Mr. Henry L. Dunham,

 Dear Sir :

   In answer to your esteemed favor

Sometimes for the sake of convenience, and the saving of time and labor, the letter head has printed in the left corner, above the address, a blank form of memorandum as follows:

Referring to }   **OR,**   In reply to }
yours of..... }   your favor of....., }

and after this introduction the writer is able speedily to get at the marrow of his letter, without acknowledging the receipt of a former communication.

The body of the letter should be divided into as many paragraphs as there are distinct subjects in the letter, or a new paragraph should be commenced at every change of the subject. The habit which some persons have of tacking one subject to the end of another, and thus making a letter one continuous paragraph of mixed up information, instructions and requests, is extremely objectionable. It destroys the force of what is said, instead of fixing each thought clearly on the mind of the reader; it leaves him confused, and he reads a second time and tries to get his ideas fixed and systematized, or he throws aside the letter until he has more time in which to study it and get the meaning clear.

If the letter is long and is really concerning only one subject, then it may properly be divided into paragraphs by separating the different divisions of the subject, and giving a paragraph to each. These should be arranged in their logical order. Wherever the letter is to contain numerous paragraphs to avoid omitting any of the items, it is best to jot them down on a slip of paper, then embody them in the letter in their natural order.

The first word of each paragraph should be indented, or moved in from the margin, usually about the width of the margin. Thus if the margin is three-fourths of an inch in width, the paragraph should begin three-fourths of an inch from the margin. Some writers, however, prefer to commence the first word of the paragraph an inch from the margin, and it is really not so essential what the distance is, as that it should be uniform, and all the paragraphs begin alike. A little attention is necessary here. In ordering goods make each article a separate paragraph.

COMPLIMENTARY CLOSING AND SIGNATURE.

The complimentary closing consists of such words as *Yours truly*, *Respectfully*, etc., and should be placed on the next line beneath the last one occupied by the body of the letter, commencing a little to the right of the middle. The signature should be placed underneath the words of respect, and begin still a little farther to the right. Thus the conclusion of the letter will correspond in position and arrangement with the heading.

  Yours truly,

    John Maynard.

The language of the complimentary closing should be governed by the relation between the parties, and should correspond with the complimentary address. The first letter between strangers should commence with *Sir* and end with the word *Respectfully*. After the exchange of a few letters and a sort of business acquaintance may be said to exist between the correspondents, then *Dear Sir*, and *Yours truly*, may properly be introduced. A little more cordial would be such a conclusion as the following:

  Yours very truly,

    Arnold, Constable & Co.

The man of business is apt, however, to have one stereotyped beginning and ending to all his letters, and seldom stops to discriminate between strangers and old customers in this respect. Often the conclusion may be connected to the closing paragraph with perfect grace and ease thus:

  Hoping to receive the goods without delay, I remain,

  Respectfully,

    Henry P. Bowen.

In the signature of a letter, especial care should be exercised. Bear in mind that names of persons are not governed by the rules of spelling, and words which precede or follow, proper names will not aid us in deciphering them if they are poorly written.

A MODEL BUSINESS LETTER.

146 S. Tenth Street,
Cincinnati, March 11, 1884.

Messrs. Arnold, Constable & Co.,
Broadway & 19th Sts., New York.

Gentlemen: Inclosed please find New York Exchange in settlement of your Invoice of the 1st inst. less Cash discount.

Amount of Invoice, $325.80
Cash discount 5%, 16.29
Draft inclosed $309.51.

The goods have been received, and are very satisfactory in both quality and price. You may expect another order soon.

Yours truly,
James G. Wilson

The young person who would learn to write a good business letter, should, with pen, ink and suitable paper, sit down and practice faithfully after the above model. Write and re-write it a dozen times or more, until your letter resembles it closely. Then take any of the models for letters given near the close of this chapter, and with this matter, write a letter which will conform with the foregoing model in appearance and dress. Write the same matter over again, and improve it in its defects. Criticise each line and word. See that no words or letters are omitted, and that the punctuation is according to the models in this book. Eliminate all ungainly letters, shorten the loops, see that each letter rests on the line, and that, withal your page is clean and regular.

The person who will thus devote a little earnest study and practice, may early acquire the valuable accomplishment of writing a pleasing business letter, so far as the mechanical structure goes.

ADDRESSING THE ENVELOPE.

After the letter is finished, and while it yet lies open before you, the Envelope should be addressed. As before stated, the directions on the envelope must conform to the address at the beginning of the letter, hence the necessity for addressing the envelope before the letter is folded.

The first line of the address of the envelope should consist of the name of the person or firm to whom the letter is written, together with any appropriate titles, and should be written across or a little below the middle of the envelope, but never above it, beginning near the left edge. The space between this first line and the bottom of the envelope should be about equally divided among the other lines, each of which begins still farther to the right than the one above, thus:

Messrs. Arnold, Constable & Co.,
Cor. Broadway & 19th Sts.,
New York City.

When writing to a person in a large city the number and street should be a part of the address, and may be placed as in the above form, or in the left hand lower corner as follows:

Lewis N. Taylor, Esq.,
Chicago,
118 Wabash Ave.　　　Ill.

In case the letter is addressed in care of any one this should be placed in the lower left corner. If a letter of introduction, the words *Introducing Mr. John Smith,* or similar words, should be placed in this corner.

Letters addressed to small towns or villages should bear the name of the county as follows:

Mr. Henry H. Chambers,
Washington,
Porter County,
Fla.

Or the name of the county may be placed in the lower left corner. The Post Office box number is usually placed in the lower left corner.

FOLDING A LETTER.

Having written an excellent letter, and faultlessly addressed the envelope, all may be easily stamped as unbusiness-like, and spoiled, by improperly performing so simple a part as the folding. Remember that excellent rule that, whatever is worth doing should be well done.

With the letter sheet lying before you, turn the bottom edge up so that it lies along with the top edge, thus making a fold in the middle, which press down with the thumb nail or with a paper folder. Then fold the right edge over so that it falls two-thirds the distance across the sheet, and press down the edge. Next fold the left edge of the sheet over to the right, breaking the fold at the edge of the part folded over just before.

In case a check, note, draft, bill or currency is to be sent by letter, it should be placed on the upper half of the sheet as it lies open, and then the letter should be folded the same as if it were not there. This will fold the paper or document in the letter so that it will be difficult to extract it while being transmitted in the mails, and so that it will not be dropped or lost in opening the letter.

The letter is now folded so that it will be of equal thickness in every part of the envelope. Insert the last broken or folded edge in the envelope first, with the original edges of the sheet at the end of the envelope which the stamp is on; when taken from the envelope the letter will then be proper side up.

THE LITERATURE OF A LETTER.

To be able to compose a letter requires more ability than to give it the proper arrangement and mechanical dress. A mind well stored with useful knowledge as well as command of language, is necessary in writing a letter on general subjects. The strictly business letter requires a thorough understanding of the facts concerning which the letter is written, and these facts to be set forth in plain and unmistakable language. All display of rhetoric or flourish of words is entirely out of place in the sober, practical letter of business. The proper use of capital letters, punctuation, and correct spelling are essential to the well written letter, and with a little care and striving may be easily acquired.

ARRANGEMENT OF ITEMS.

As stated before, each item or subject in a letter should be embraced in a separate paragraph. These should be arranged in the order in which they would naturally come, either in point of time, importance, or as regards policy. Never begin a letter abruptly with a complaint, but rather bring in all unpleasant subjects toward the close. If an answer to a letter of inquiry, take up the questions as they are asked, indicate first what the question is, and then state clearly the answer. The first paragraph should acknowledge the receipt of the communication now to be answered, giving date and indicating its nature and contents, thus:

Your letter of the 10th instant concerning damaged goods is received, etc.

The closing paragraph usually begins with such words as *Hoping, Trusting, Awaiting, Thanking,* or similar expressions, and is complimentary in its tone and designed as a courtesy.

BREVITY.

Business letters should be brief and to the point. The best letter states clearly all the facts in the fewest words. Brevity is not inconsistent with a long letter, as so much may need to be said as to require a long letter, but all repetitions, lengthy statements and multiplication of words should be avoided. Use short sentences, and make every word mean something. Short sentences are more forcible, and more easily understood or remembered, than long drawn out utterances.

STYLE.

Sty'e refers to the tone, air, or manner of expression. Dignity and strength should characterize the style of the business letter. No ornament of expression or eloquence of language is necessary or appropriate in a correspondence between business men. Come to your meaning at once. State the facts. Let every sentence bristle with points.

The successful business man must possess energy, decision, and force, and these qualities should be conspicuous in his correspondence in order to command respect. Never use loose or slang expressions. The business man should be a *gentleman*. Indulge in no display of superior knowledge or education, but temper each paragraph with respect and deference to others. The learner who would aspire to write a good letter, should, after having finished his attempt, go over each sentence carefully and wherever the pronoun I occurs, modify the expression so as to leave this out.

ORDERING GOODS.

In ordering goods of any kind, care should be used to state very explicitly the color, size, quality, and quantity of the articles desired. If manufactured goods, the name of the manufacturer, or his trade mark or brand should be given. Also state when you desire the goods shipped and in what way. If by freight or express, state what Freight line or Express Company.

SENDING MONEY BY LETTER.

Paper currency should seldom be trusted to pass through the mails, as the liability to loss is too great. Better send draft or P. O. money order, and in every case the amount of the remittance should be stated in the letter, and also whether by draft or otherwise sent. The letter may become important evidence in regard to payment at some future time.

INSTRUCTIONS.

In giving instructions to agents, manufacturers and others, let each order occupy a separate paragraph. State in unmistakable language the instructions desired to be conveyed. If possible a diagram or plan should be enclosed in the letter. Cautions and complaints, if any, should be clearly set forth in paragraphs near the close of the letter.

A DUNNING LETTER.

State when the debt was contracted, its amount, the fact of it having been long past due, the necessity for immediate payment, and any other facts depending on the peculiarities of the case, which it may seem best to make use of, such as promises to pay, which have not been met; the inconvenience as well as injury and distrust caused by such irregularities, etc.

LETTERS OF INTRODUCTION.

Be just and truthful, avoiding any stereotyped form in letters of introduction. Never give a letter of introduction unless you have entire confidence in the person to whom it is given; it may reflect on your character or be used against you. Be very guarded that no expressions may be construed into a letter of credit, thus making the writer liable for payment. Use no unfounded statements or assertions, over-estimating your friend, as these may prove untrue.

Willing to extend a favor to a friend by giving a letter of introduction, do not be guilty of introducing him to any one in whom he may not place confidence, as he might be a loser by such.

Form of a Letter Ordering Goods.

128 Jackson Street,
RICHMOND, VA., May 24, 18—.
Messrs. JONES & SMITH,
867 Market St., Philadelphia.
Gentlemen: Please ship me by Fast Freight as soon as possible the following goods:
3 hhds. N. O. Molasses.
1 bbl. Granulated Sugar.
5 chests English Breakfast Tea.
2 sacks Mocha Coffee, wanted not ground.
5 boxes Colgate's Toilet Soap.
I will remit the amount of the invoice immediately upon the receipt of the goods.
Yours respectfully,
JAMES C. ADAMS.

Ordering Goods and Enclosing Price.

RICHMOND, IND., Dec. 29, 18—.
Messrs. MARSHALL FIELD & CO.,
Chicago, Ill.
Gentlemen: Please forward me by American Express at once
1 Lancaster Spread,	$3.50
12 yds. Gingham, small check. (15c.)	1.80
3 doz. Napkins ($3.00),	9.00
	$14.30

For which I inclose P. O. Money order.
Hoping to receive the goods without delay, I am,
Respectfully,
WILLIAM L. MILLER.

Desiring to Open an Account.

DAYTON, OHIO, Oct. 12, 18—
Messrs. HOLMES & WILSON,
Detroit, Mich.
Gentlemen: Having recently established myself in the retail Hardware trade in this city, with fair prospects of success, and being in need of new goods from time to time, would like to open an account with your highly respectable house.

My capital is small, but I have the satisfaction of knowing that what little I possess is the fruit of my own industry and saving. I can refer you to the well known firm of Smith, Day & Co., of this city, as to my character and standing.

Should my reference prove satisfactory, please forward me at once by U. S. Express,
2 Butchers' Bow Saws,

½ doz. Mortise Locks, with Porcelain Knobs.
2 kegs 8d Nails,
and charge to my account.
Hoping that my order may receive your usual prompt attention, I am,
Yours respectfully,
HENRY M. BARROWS.

Letter of Credit.

LEXINGTON, KY., June 25, 18—.
Messrs. DODGE, MANOR & DEVOE,
New York City.
Gentlemen: Please allow the bearer of this, Mr. James Curtis, a credit for such goods as he may select, not exceeding One Thousand dollars, and if he does not pay for them, I will.
Please notify me in case he buys, of the amount, and when due, and if the account is not settled promptly according to agreement, write me at once.
Yours truly,
HIRAM DUNCAN.

Inclosing an Invoice.

125 Lake Street,
CHICAGO, Nov. 15, 18—.
SAMUEL D. PRENTICE, Esq.,
Vevay, Ind.
Dear Sir: Inclosed please find invoice of goods amounting to $218.60, shipped you this day by the B. & O. Express, as per your order of the 11th inst.
Hoping that the goods may prove satisfactory, and that we may be favored with further orders, we remain,
Yours truly,
SIBLEY, DUDLEY & CO.

Letter of Introduction.

168 Olive Street,
ST. LOUIS, June 4, 18—.
HENRY M. BLISS, Esq.,
Boston.
Dear Sir: This will introduce to you the bearer, Mr. William P. Hainline, of this city who visits Boston, for the purpose of engaging in the Hat, Cap and Fur trade.
He is a young man of energy and ability, and withal, a gentlemen in every sense.
Any assistance you may render him by way of introduction to your leading merchants or otherwise, in establishing his new enterprise will be duly appreciated by both himself and
Yours truly,
JAMES W. BROOKING.

Inclosing Remittance.

MILWAUKEE, WIS., Feb. 18, 18—.
Messrs. ARNOLD, CONSTABLE & CO.,
New York.
Gentlemen: The goods ordered of you on the 3d inst. have been received and are entirely satisfactory in both quality and price.
Enclosed please find New York exchange for $816.23, the amount of your bill.
Thanking you for your promptness in filling my order, I am,
Yours respectfully,
HENRY GOODFELLOW.

Inclosing Draft for Acceptance.

NEW YORK, Aug. 8, 18—.
Messrs. WEBSTER & DUNN,
Cairo, Ill.
Gentlemen: Inclosed we hand you Draft at 30 days for acceptance for $928.15, the amount of balance due from you to us to the present date.
We shall feel obliged by your accepting the same, and returning it by due course of mail.
Awaiting further favors, we are,
Very truly yours,
DODGE, HOLMES & CO.

Inclosing a Statement of Account.

CHICAGO, March 1, 18—.

Messrs. CHASE & HOWARD,
South Bend, Ind.

Gentlemen: Inclosed please find a statement of your account for the past three months, which we believe you will find correct.

We shall feel obliged by your examining the same at your earliest convenience, and shall be happy to receive your check for the amount or instructions to draw on you in the ordinary course.

We are, gentlemen,
Yours truly,
J. V. FARWELL & CO.

A Dunning Letter.

DENVER, COL., June 30, 18—.

JAMES C. ADAMS, Esq.,
Great Bend, Kansas.

Dear Sir: Allow me to remind you that your account with me has been standing for several months unsettled.

I should not even now have called your attention to it, were it not that in a few days I must meet a heavy bill, and must rely in part on your account to furnish me the means.

I would, therefore, esteem it a great favor if you would let me have either the whole, or at least the greater part of your account in the course of a week or ten days.

Thanking you for past favors, I remain, Sir,
Yours truly,
A. R. MORGAN.

An Application for a Situation in Business.

Paste the Advertisement at the head of the sheet, and write as follows:

124 Fayette Street,
SYRACUSE, N. Y., Sept. 17, 18—

H. JOURNAL OFFICE,
City.

Dear Sir: In reply to the above advertisement I would respectfully offer my services.

I am 19 years of age, have a good education, and have had some experience in business, having assisted my father in his grocery store. I am not afraid of work, and never allow myself to be idle when there is work to be done. I can refer you as to my character, to Mr. J. H. Trout, president of the Gas Company, who has known me all my life.

In reference to salary, I leave that with you, but feel certain that I could earn five dollars per week for you.

Hoping to have the pleasure of an interview, I remain,
Respectfully,
HENRY OTIS.

Asking Permission to Refer to a Person.

SYRACUSE, N. Y., Sept. 17, 18—.

J. H. TROUT, Esq.,
Dear Sir:

I beg to inform you that in applying for a situation this morning, advertised in the *Journal*, I took the liberty of using your name as a reference.

The length of time I have been honored with your acquaintance, and the words of encouragement which you have given me heretofore, lead me to hope you would speak favorably in this instance, adding this to the numerous obligations already conferred upon
Your obedient servant,
HENRY OTIS.

Inquiring as to Business Prospects.

NEWARK, OHIO, June 15, 18—

Mr. J. D. SHAYLOR,
Denver, Col.

My Dear Sir: As I told you a year ago, I have been thinking seriously of disposing of my small business here and locating in some live and promising city out west, where I can grow up with the country as you are doing.

Will you have the kindness to sit down and write me at your convenience, full information in regard to the prospects of business, price of rents, cost of living, etc., in your city, and any other information, especially in regard to the hardware trade.

If you will thus kindly give me the facts on which I can base a calculation, and all is favorable, I will probably visit Denver this fall, and eventually become your neighbor.

Yours very truly,
J. C. GOODRICH.

Letter of Recommendation.

GRAND HAVEN, Mich., May 17, 18—.

TO WHOM IT MAY CONCERN:

Mr. Henry McPherson, who is now leaving our employ, has been in our office for the past two years, during which time he has faithfully attended to his duties, proving himself to be industrious and thoroughly reliable. He is a good penman, correct accountant, and acquainted with correspondence.

We shall at any time cheerfully respond to all applications we may have regarding his character and abilities, and wish him every success.

Yours truly,
WOOD & HILL.

Notice of Dissolution of a Partnership.

DAVENPORT, IA., Dec. 10, 18—.

JAS. L. BINGHAM & CO.,
Cedar Rapids, Ia.

Gentlemen: On the 1st of January next the partnership for the past ten years existing between Geo. H. Clark and Henry Webster, wholesale grocers in this City, will expire by limitation of the contract.

The firm takes this opportunity to thank its customers and friends for their generous patronage and support, whereby the business of the house grew to such large proportions.

After the first of January the business will be carried on at the old stand, Nos. 76 and 78 Main St., by Henry Webster and Cyrus D. Bradford, under the firm name of Webster & Bradford. We are, gentlemen,
Your obedient servants,
CLARK & WEBSTER.

Recommending a Successor in Business.

CINCINNATI, OHIO, Dec. 15, 18—.

TO THE PUBLIC:

It is with some feeling of regret that we announce our retirement from the business on the beginning of the new year. Our stock and premises will then be transferred to Messrs. Franklin and Warren, whom we cheerfully present to your notice, and feel it our duty to recommend them for a continuance of that liberal confidence and patronage which you have bestowed on us during the past twenty years.

Both these young gentlemen have been clerks of ours for several years past, and are in every way efficient and capable to continue the business.

We are
Respectfully,
JOHNSON & FOX.

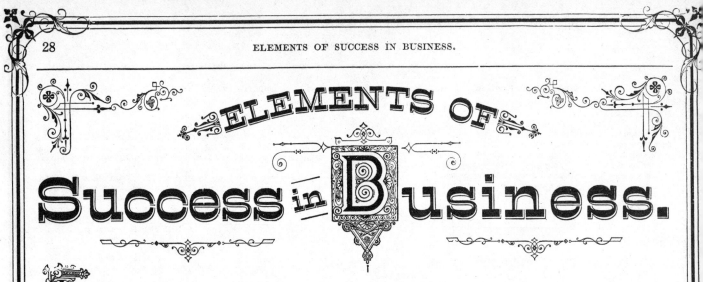

ELEMENTS OF Success in Business.

IN ORDER to succeed in business life, it is necessary to cultivate and develop certain qualities and traits of character. These are a portion of the capital of the successful man, and a more essential portion than money or goods.

HONESTY.

"Sharp practice" may bring a temporary gain but in the long run of life that man will be far ahead who deals squarely and honestly at all times. A thoroughly honest clerk will command a higher salary than one of equivocal habits, while the merchant who has a reputation for honesty and truthfulness in regard to the quality and value of his goods, will on this account be favored with a considerable custom. The business man whose "word is as good as his bond" can, in any emergency, control large amounts of capital, the use of which brings him a rich return, while the man who sells his neighbor's good opinion for a temporary gain, will find that he

COUNSEL AND ADVICE.

has discounted his future success, by taking an advantage at the cost of ten times its value.

INDUSTRY.

No other quality can take the place of this, and no talents of mind, however excellent, will bring success without labor; persistent, systematic labor. The young man who expects to find some royal road to success with little or no effort, or who imagines that his mental abilities will compensate for a lack of application, cheats and ruins himself. Horace Greeley probably never said a grander thing than this:

"The saddest hour in any man's career is that wherein he, for the first time, fancies there is an easier way of gaining a dollar than by squarely earning it," and Horace Greeley was himself an example of success through industry.

It is not genius, but the great mass of average people, who *work*, that make the successes in life. Some toil with the brain, and others toil with the hand, but all must toil. Industry applies to hours in business and out of business. It means not only to perform all required work promptly, but to occupy spare moments usefully, not to idle evenings, and to rise early in the morning.

An employe should not confine himself to his mere obligatory duties. He should be ready to work sometimes over hours or in other departments if it is desired of him. Willingness to *work* is one of the finest qualities in a character, and will compensate for many other deficiencies.

MEMORY.

This faculty, always so useful, is pre-eminently so to the business man. It must be both retentive and quick. By proper training this faculty may be so cultivated that names, dates and events to a surprising number may be readily recalled. The ability to greet a customer by calling him by name is considered very valuable in any class of business. It makes a very agreeable impression when a man who has not seen us but once or twice, and who is not expecting us, meets us promptly as we enter his store, with, " Why, Mr. ——, how do you do? Glad to see you. When did you leave Newark?" We feel as if we had occupied that man's thoughts since we saw him before. He appreciates us, and we feel like patronizing him. Whereas, on the other hand to meet a customer with a blank, inquiring expression, and greet him with, "Your face is familiar, but I can't recall your name," is unpleasant and tends to drive away custom. Every hotel keeper knows the value of this greeting of customers.

Facts, figures and dates are very necessary to remember in business, and these often form the basis of a business transaction or venture by which large profits are made. Superior ability in remembering prices and their fluctuations has been the secret of more than one brilliant success.

Desultory reading injures the memory, while close application to a subject, recalling the various points therein, tends greatly to improve this faculty. The clerk or employe in receiving instructions from his principal should endeavor to impress every point clearly on his mind, and retain them there until they are carried out in action. Carelessness and forgetfulness often causes the discharge of otherwise worthy and competent young persons, as employers do not like to repeat their orders.

PROMPTNESS.

A very essential element in the character of the business man is promptness. Filling all engagements at exactly the appointed time, answering letters or forwarding goods with promptness, the man of business finds that much more can be accomplished and with far greater accuracy, than by a loose system of putting off till tomorrow, or according to convenience. Not only so, but competition in business is such that the merchant or tradesman who does not deal with promptness can hardly expect to hold his custom. Young men starting out in the world should form the resolution of doing everything on time. Better to be ahead in the performance of duties than behind. This promptness then acts as a stimulant in itself, and is oftentimes the means of winning success in an enterprise.

A thing that is worth the doing, ought to be done quickly when the time is ripe for it. A prompt man or woman is valued, as he respects his word and has due regard for the convenience of others.

EXECUTIVE ABILITY.

Wavering, timid and uncertain, the man without executive ability never achieves distinction in active life. Intelligence to decide on any measure, firmness in adhering to the decision, and force of will in carrying it out, constitute executive ability, and are as essential to the business man as his stock in trade.

The timid man never makes up his mind until after the opportunity is past, or decides, then recalls his decision, and feels incapable of promptly estimating all the facts in the case. This weakness is oftentimes natural, but more frequently it is a bad habit which should be broken up.

Rashness is to decide and act without taking the trouble to weigh intelligently the facts in the case. This is inexcusable folly, and always brings serious trouble sooner or later.

Through executive ability the labor or services of one man may be made to produce largely, or without proper direction such services may be almost worthless; and in the case of many employes under one executive head, the results of this combined labor may be great success, or where executive ability is wanting, a great failure.

The successful farmer, merchant, manufacturer, banker, and professional man must have this combination of ability, firmness, and will power.

PERSEVERANCE.

Those who put their minds on their work, whatever kind that may be, and persist in its thorough execution; who get interested in something for their own advancement, that they may become more capable as men and women of sense and tact; such persons have a lively appreciation of the fact that success is never more certain to be gained by any other course.

These people have a just pride in learning the best methods of giving expression to the faculties and powers they possess, and which they desire to make the most of. It is incumbent that they do all in their power for their own and other people's good. Feeling this, an ever present incentive keeps them employed, and they are never idle.

If one does not succeed from persisting in doing the best he knows how, he may conclude that the ministry of failure is better for him than any worldly success would be.

CIVILITY.

Good behavior is an essential element of our civilization. It should be displayed every day through courteous acts and becoming manners.

Politeness is said to be the poetry of conduct; and like poetry, it has many qualities. Let not your politeness be too florid, but of that gentle kind which indicates a refined nature.

In his relations with others, one should never forget his good breeding. It is a general regard for the feelings of others that springs from the absence of all selfishness. No one should behave in the presence of others as though his own wishes were bound to be gratified or his will to control.

In the more active sphere of business, as in the larger localities where there is close competition, the small merchant frequently outstrips his more powerful rival by one element of success, which may be added to any stock without cost, but cannot be withheld without loss. That element is civility. A kind and obliging manner carries with it an indescribable charm. It must not

be a manner that indicates a mean, groveling, time-serving spirit, but a plain, open, and agreeable demeanor that seems to desire to oblige for the pleasure of doing so, and not for the sake of squeezing an extra penny out of a customer's purse.

INTEGRITY.

The sole reliance of a business man should be in the integrity of his transactions, and in the civility of his demeanor. He should make it the interest and the pleasure of a customer to come to his office or store. If he does this, he will form the very best "connections," and so long as he continues this system of business, they will never desert him.

No real business man will take advantage of a customer's ignorance, nor equivocate nor misrepresent. If he sells goods, he will have but one price and a small profit. He will ere long find all the most profitable customers—the cash ones—or they will find him.

If such a man is ever deceived in business transactions, he will never attempt to save himself by putting the deception upon others; but submit to the loss, and be more cautious in future. In his business relations, he will stick to those whom he finds strictly just in their transactions, and shun all others even at a temporary disadvantage.

The word of a business man should be worth all that it expresses and promises, and all engagements should be met with punctilious concern. An indifferent or false policy in business is a serious mistake. It is fatal to grasp an advantage at ten times its cost; and there is nothing to compensate for the loss of a neighbor's confidence or good will.

The long-established customs and forms of business, which in these times are assumed to be legitimate, already have within them enough of the elements of peculiarity, commonly termed "tricks of trade," or, in the sense of any particular business, "tricks of the trade." Therefore it does not behoove any active man to make gratuitous additions of a peculiar nature to the law of business. On the contrary, all should strive to render business transactions less peculiar than they are.

ECONOMY.

One may rest in the assurance that industry and economy will be sure to tell in the end. If in early life these habits become confirmed, no doubt can exist as to the ultimate triumph of the merchant in attaining a competency.

There should be no antagonism between economy and a generous business policy. Narrow selfishness is to be avoided in the use of money or means. In buying goods, one should not take advantage of another's necessities to beat him down to a figure which leaves him little or no profit, perhaps a loss, because he must

have money. This is against manhood and is a ruinous policy, because it tends to picayunishness and chicanery. A sacred regard for the principles of justice forms the basis of every transaction, and regulates the conduct of the upright man of business.

If economy is wealth, it is not so because of a niggardly and parsimonious policy. Perhaps the simplest, fewest and best rules for economical business are these, by observance of which a noted merchant amassed a large fortune: 1. Obtain the earliest and fullest information possible in regard to the matter in hand. 2. Act rapidly and promptly upon it. 3. Keep your intentions and means secret. 4. Secure the best employes you can obtain, and reward them liberally.

Proprietors of institutions will early discover that order, and neatness, are necessary as economical agents in prosecuting a successful business. And the youth who would grow up to become well-to-do, to gain complete success, to be a valuable member and assume a position in society, should take pains to acquire habits of cleanliness, of order, and of business.

To this effect each one may early learn the simple rules of health and good order by paying reasonable attention to those so-called minor details, which pertain to the well-being of the person, and which must be faithfully observed in order to avoid failure and win success.

A person, young or old, in or out of business, may keep a memorandum-book in his pocket, in which he notes every particular relative to appointments, addresses, and petty cash matters. An accurate account of personal expenses should be kept, which should be balanced each week. By this means each individual will be more careful and economical in his expenditures, and generally live within his income. He must be reasonable in spending, or his memorandum or record-book, if it be honestly kept, will stand to his discredit.

A well-kept memorandum-book is often very useful, as it is very convenient, and sometimes serves to settle a troublesome query, arising in other minds, by which the possessor is absolved from the prejudice of doubt. Young people who expect to labor with their hands for what they have of this world's goods, or rise by their own efforts, should by all means acquire habits of economy, learn to save, form correct habits, and no time will be required overcoming these. So surely as they do this, so surely will they be in a situation to ask no special favors. Every man wants to learn to look out for himself and rely upon himself. Every man needs to feel that he is the peer of every other man, and he cannot do it if he is penniless. Money is power, and those who have it exert a wider influence than the destitute. Hence it should be the ambition of all young men to acquire it, as well as to store their minds with useful knowledge.

GETTING A SITUATION.

In seeking a situation, it is always best to appear in person if practicable. A business man who requires the services of a salesman or clerk, a bookkeeper, stenographer, or some one to remain in his employ a considerable time, usually prefers to see an applicant and have a few words with him about the work that is to be done.

If an application has to be made by letter, it should be done in the handwriting of the applicant. It may be brief, and should include references.

It is best for a young man to learn a trade. In this country the trades offer more stable means of subsistence than do other departments of active life. His knowledge of a trade will form no bar to any effort he may afterward make to rise to a higher or more congenial calling.

When a position has been obtained by an applicant, he should at once proceed to render himself indispensable to his employer by following up the details of his work in a conscientious and agreeable manner. Thus he will gain confidence and grow in favor with men who are quick to recognize merit, and who respond to that which contributes to the success of a meritorious man.

There is always room in every business for an honest, hard-worker. It will not do to presume otherwise; nor should one sit down to grumble or concoct mischief. The most perilous hour of one's life is when he is tempted to despond. He who loses his courage loses all. There are men in the world who would rather work than be idle at the same price. Imitate them. Success is not far off. An honorable and happy life is before you. Lay hold of it.

THE desire to accumulate property is one of the noblest that nature has implanted in man, and it is through the successful results of this desire, we are enabled to point with unerring certainty to the disembarking line, which so surely characterizes the advanced, educated, refined and civilized man from that of the wild savage, whose highest desire is to slay and rob his fellow men, and proudly exhibit their scalps, or the plunder he has acquired, as evidence of his cunning or courage.

It is through this inborn desire to accumulate that man is willing to labor, toil, suffer, and forego present gratifications for the hope of future greater satisfactions; that has resulted in the building and equiping the mighty ships of commerce, whose white, spreading canvas dots every sea where commerce may be known, or where the interests of God's creatures may best be served. It is through this desire, coupled with unremitting toil, that we owe everything of permanent enjoyment, of enlightenment and of prosperity.

The millions of dollars of paper money which is handled every day as the natural fruit of toil and saving through the many and diversified transactions in the vast, illimitable and ever rapidly developing field of commerce, is but the representative of ownership of property.

If this representative is what it purports on its face to be, each and every one who receives it in exchange for services or commodities, owns not merely a piece of paper, with designs, words and promises printed or engraved thereon, but an interest or an undivided whole in a farm, a block of buildings or a store well stocked with merchandise, which, in his estimation, at least, is more desirable to him than the labor or commodity for

which he has voluntarily made the exchange; but, if on the contrary, it is other than what it purports on its face to be, he finds that he is the owner of a piece of paper whose value is *nil*.

There is, at the present writing, 1884, nearly eight hundred million dollars of paper currency in the United States, consisting of greenbacks and national currency, a great portion of which is in actual circulation, and it has been estimated by eminent authorities who occupy positions of trust in the various departments through which the financial machinery of this vast sea of paper money is daily circulated, that there is in circulation nearly one-fifth of this amount in counterfeit money, or about one hundred and sixty million dollars; and not one dollar of this counterfeit money owes its circulation to any excellence of the work in its manufacture, but wholly to the general ignorance of those who handle it, as to what is required to constitute a genuine bill. The time will come when the United States will redeem all of its issue of paper money, when those who are holding any of this counterfeit money will have to stand the loss to the extent of the sum in their possession.

To all of those who are willing to take a small portion of their time each day for a few weeks in learning just what it takes to constitute a genuine bill, there need be no necessity of ever losing anything by counterfeiters, as it is impossible for them to make bills which will in any way approach the beauty and exactness of the genuine ones. There is not at the present time, nor has there ever been in the past, nor will there ever be in the future, a counterfeit bill made that cannot be detected at sight; and the positive knowledge of how to know at all times when a bill is genuine and when not is within the reach of all those who may have the privilege of reading the following information or infallible rules with a genuine desire to be benefited thereby.

DEVICES AND FRAUDS.

Various devices are resorted to by a numerous gang or body of persons, to get on in the world without turning their attention to legitimate and useful employments.

This class includes many that are not engaged in the practice of counterfeiting and putting forth bad money, but who make themselves felt in various ways through vain tricks and schemes, which are, to all intents and purposes, frauds.

Business men are generally apt at detecting and turning off petty schemes, but they find it best to have the means with which they may deal successfully as against regular swindlers, forgers and counterfeiters.

COUNTERFEIT AND GENUINE WORK.

As indicated above, counterfeit notes are issued and put into the channels of circulation in abundance every year by those engaged in the practice of counterfeiting. These notes are often such good imitations of the genuine that it is quite difficult to discern the difference.

That he may protect himself, each business man should have some definite knowledge of a genuine bank-note.

The engraving of a genuine bank note, in most all of

DETECTING COUNTERFEIT MONEY.

its parts, is done by machinery, and it is more exact and perfect. On the contrary, most all parts of counterfeit notes are done by hand.

Counterfeiters cannot afford to purchase machinery, such as is used for the production of genuine notes. The cost of such machinery is between $100,000, and $150,000, and if it were in wrong hands it would be always liable to seizure and confiscation.

In order to prevent the forgery of bank-notes, a great deal of ingenuity and art has been expended on their production. The principal features of the manufacture are described as a peculiar kind of paper and water mark; an elaborate design, printed with a peculiar kind of ink, and certain private marks, known only by the bank officials.

The work of counterfeiters can never equal that of the makers of genuine notes, whose skill and facilities for producing the highest grade of work known to the art, are the best that the world affords.

Unless one is somewhat learned as to the quality of engraving, that he may be able to distinguish a fine specimen of the art when he sees it, he is likely to become a victim of the counterfeiter's operations.

LATHE WORK.

When the genuineness of a bank-note is doubted, the Lathe Work on the note should first be closely scrutinized. The several letters of denomination, circles, ovals, and shadings between and around the letters in the words, etc., are composed of numberless extremely fine lines — inclusive of lines straight, curved and network. These are all regular and unbroken, never running into each other, and may be traced throughout with a magnifying glass.

Without the skill or machinery, by which the genuine is produced, the same quality of work cannot be done. Therefore, in a counterfeit, the lines are imperfect, giving the paper a dull or hazy aspect, that may be all the better appreciated by comparing it with the genuine. The lines in the counterfeit will be found now and then irregular in size, and broken; not uniform in course, sometimes heavy, sometimes light; no two stamps or dies on the same note being exactly alike.

The fine, uniform, shade-lines, with which the letters on the genuine are embellished, are wrought by a machine that cannot be reproduced by counterfeiters, nor used for other than legitimate purposes, by authority.

GEOMETRICAL LATHE.

The fine line is the characteristic of the various and beautiful figures which are seen on a genuine note. This line is produced by what is called the Geometrical Lathe. The patterns made by the geometrical lathe are of every variety of form. They are not engraved directly upon the bank-note plate, but on pieces of soft steel plate, which are afterwards hardened. The impressions are then transferred to a soft steel roller, which, in its turn, is also hardened, and the impressions remain there, in relief. This roller is then capable of transferring the same designs to the bank-note plate, by means of the transfer press.

In counterfeit engraving, the design is made directly upon the plate, and not by transfer, as in the produc-

tion of plates for genuine notes. The essential difference between the two methods of production is, the
counterfeit is made by hand, and is inexact and imperfect, while the genuine is made on geometrical principles, and is therefore exact, artistic and beautiful.

In all the government issues the geometric lathe
work is liberally used. This should be studied carefully, as it constitutes the chief test of genuineness.

Fine lines, of unerring exactness, never broken, are
seen on the genuine medallion heads, or shields, upon
which the designation of the note is sometimes stamped.
This nicety cannot be given by hand, or with the use
of imperfect machinery. By close scrutiny
the lines will be found to break off in
the pattern, or appear forked, irregular in
size, and not well defined throughout.

On most counterfeits the vignettes are not
well engraved, and the portraits have a dull
appearance; the letters are usually wanting
in clearness; the printing is sometimes faulty,
by which some features of the note are
obscured.

RULING ENGINE WORK.

In Ruling Engine Work, as it is called,
the fine line is present, also. The engraving
is produced and transferred in the same way
as the geometrical lathe work. In this they
are parallel and not in circles. Those which
constitute the shading of letters are so fine
that they form a perfectly even gray shade.
They may be printed so that the shading
will appear darker, but the aspect will be
uniform. The spaces between lines are
exact, whether the lines be horizontal or
diagonal. The lines are also made crooked
or wave-like, not absolutely parallel. Ruling engine work is generally used for shading of names of banks, and also for the
names of town, state, etc.

VIGNETTES.

While lathe work and that of the ruling
engine are invariably machine work, and therefore
cannot be successfully reproduced by counterfeiters,
the Vignettes are chiefly the work of the hands. In
all genuine work they are made by first class artists,
who are well paid for their services, and who therefore
have no incentive to exercise their skill for illegitimate
purposes.

Sometimes water and sky are done with the ruling

engine, and when they are, no counterfeiter can successfully imitate them. Fine vignettes are seldom seen
on counterfeit notes. If the lathe and ruling engine
work be genuine, an ordinary vignette cannot make a
note counterfeit, and if that be counterfeit, no vignette
can make the note genuine.

The vignettes on genuine notes are executed by men
at the head of their vocation, and are very life-like and
beautiful. Counterfeit vignettes usually have a sunken
and lifeless appearance. Genuine vignettes, as seen
upon government issues, consist of out-door scenes,
portraits, historical pictures, and allegorical figures.

They are all exceedingly beautiful, and it is
not likely that such work will ever be successfully imitated.

SOLID PRINT.

The lettering, or solid print, in genuine
work is done by a first-class artist, who
makes that kind of work his exclusive concern. The name of the engraving company
is always engraved with great pains and is
very accurate. It will be seen on the upper
and lower margin of the note. This, in
counterfeits, is not quite uniform or even.
The words "one dollar," as on the one dollar greenbacks, are to be considered as a
sample of solid print.

BANK-NOTE PAPER.

Bank-notes are printed upon paper composed of linen, the quality of which is not
always the same, and it varies in thickness.
Therefore, the paper is not always a sure
test, but it is important. The manufacture
of this paper is a profound secret, as carefully
kept as the combinations to the great
vaults where the government's millions lie
awaiting further river and harbor bills. It
is made only at the Dalton mill, which dates
back almost to colonial days. What its
combinations are nobody knows except those
intimately connected with its manufacture. The secret
of the paper-making is jealously guarded, as is also the
paper itself. From the moment it is made until it gets
into the treasury vaults it is carefully guarded. It
goes there in small iron safes, the sheets carefully
counted, and all precautions against its loss being taken
both by the government officials and by the express
companies which carry it.

COUNTERFEIT SIGNATURES.

Sometimes genuine notes are stolen before they are signed; then the only thing about them made counterfeit is the signatures. Those who are familiar with the signatures of the officers of the bank where notes are purloined, may not be lead into error, as such signatures usually appear more or less cramped or unsteady; but there is no sure protection against a counterfeit of this kind for those who do not have special knowledge of the signatures.

ALTERED BANK-NOTES.

Bank-notes are altered in two ways, namely: raising the denomination, and changing the name of a broken to that of a responsible bank.

First, in altering a note, it is scraped until thin; then figures of larger denomination are pasted over. A pasted note may be detected by holding it up to the light, when the pasted parts will appear darker, as they are thicker.

Second, the denomination of a note is raised by taking out a low one with an acid, and printing in a higher one with a counterfeit stamp. The ink used in genuine bank-note printing is a peculiar kind, and not easily to be obtained by counterfeiters; therefore, their printing will not appear as clear and bright as that of the government, which is done with ink of the

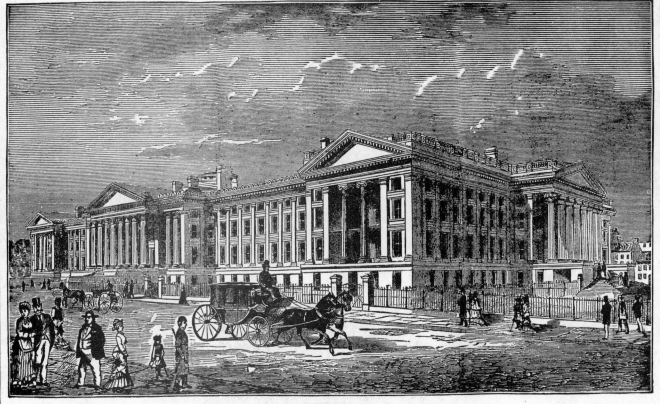

UNITED STATES TREASURY BUILDING, WASHINGTON, D. C.

finest quality. If the ink is black, it gives a clear and glossy impression, without any of that smutty appearance, as is sometimes seen in counterfeit bank-notes. It is almost impossible to imitate the green ink that is used by the government, and it is nearly as difficult to imitate the red and other colors. Counterfeit inks look dull and muddy, while genuine inks have a glossy appearance.

In the case of a note altered by the use of acid, it may be noticed that the acid, by spreading more than was intended by the counterfeiter, has injured parts of other letters, and the paper will appear more or less stained by the acid.

COMPARING AND EXAMINING NOTES.

A counterfeit should be compared with one that is genuine, in order to familiarize one's self with the distinguishing features which have already been indicated.

It is best to acquire the habit of giving each note as received a searching glance, turning it over to see the back, and if there be any defect, it will probably catch the eye. If there be the least suspicion, a critical examination of all its parts should be made.

In case of doubt, the lathe work should be carefully examined, and it may be compared with a perfectly good bill; then examine the shading around the letters, and search for any sign of alteration in the title or denomination of the note. If there are any medallion heads or shields, notice the lines; if there is any red letter work, designed to appear on both sides, look at the character of the work on the face, then turn the note and examine the back. If the printing is not exactly alike on both sides, but varies in any part the note is counterfeit. Then observe the vignettes and portraits, to see whether their style and perfection compare well with the work on genuine notes. Then examine the solid print and engravers' names, as well as the printing, ink, and paper. By such thorough examination, one can hardly be at a loss to determine the status of the note.

Good magnifying glasses are necessary, in most instances, to bring out the fine lines on bank-notes. Sometimes a microscope of great power is required to discern the genuine line.

PIECING, ETC.

Counterfeiters sometimes make ten bills of nine by what is termed piecing. Thus, a counterfeit note is cut into ten pieces by the counterfeiter, and these pieces are used in piecing nine genuine bills, from each of which a piece has been cut. The nine genuine pieces, thus obtained, are then pasted together, and with the tenth counterfeit piece added, make a tenth bill, which is the gain.

Piecing bank-bills is not a very successful practice. One who possesses such information as here given, can readily detect the difference between the counterfeit and the genuine. This difference is, however, made less apparent by the counterfeiter, who defaces the counterfeit part, so as to give the note a worn appearance.

Counterfeiting is rendered very difficult in consequence of the remarkable excellence of the work on the government and national currency, as also from the difficulty of imitating the green. But this currency, if successfully imitated by counterfeiters, will repay large outlay and care, as the greenbacks pass anywhere in the nation, and a counterfeit may be carried to other states or sections as it becomes known in any particular locality. National bank currency may be counterfeited by preparing a plate, and then with simple change in the name of the bank the counterfeit can be adapted to the various towns where banks are located. This much is written, not to lessen the value of or confidence in the issues of the government, but to admonish the public against the dangers of a false security.

HOW TO ADVERTISE.

EMBRACING RULES, SUGGESTIONS, AND PRACTICAL HINTS ON THIS IMPORTANT SUBJECT.

VOLUMES might be written on the necessity of, and the various methods employed for, advertising. Many prosperous men owe their success in life to judicious and liberal advertising. In this age of strong competition in the various avenues of trade, he who does not advertise his wares will probably be outdone by a more ambitious dealer, with perhaps a poorer article, who advertises liberally. People go where they are invited, and the merchant who advertises freely, places his store and windows in attractive order, and leaves the door open, will do far more business than he who does not cater to the public, is indifferent about appearances, gruff, and complaining of hard times.

Horace Greeley laid it down as a rule that a merchant should advertise equal to his rent. This, like all good rules, ought to have exceptions. An old and well established business would not require so much, while a new enterprise would require more than this amount expended judiciously in advertising. The merchant should decide at the beginning of the year about what amount he may expend in advertising during the year, and then endeavor to place that amount in the best possible manner before the public.

An advertiser should not be discouraged too soon. Returns are often slow and inadequate. Time is required to familiarize the public with a new article or new name. Some men have given up in despair, when just on the eve of reaping a harvest of success by this means. Many of the most prosperous and wealthy business men in this country have at times been driven hard to meet their advertising bills, but they knew that this was their most productive outlay, and by persistently continuing it they weathered the storm.

NEWSPAPER ADVERTISING.

Select the newspaper which circulates among the class of persons desired to reach. Do not advertise a special article or business designed for a limited class of customers, in a general newspaper. Almost all trades and occupations in these latter days have their special journals, and these afford the best means of reaching that class of persons. The purpose of the advertiser then should be to discover, first, the character of a paper's circulation, and second, the extent of its circulation. On these two essentials may then be based an estimate of its value as an advertising medium. The character of a paper's circulation is easily determined by the quality of the reading matter which the paper contains, and the general tone imparted to it by its conductors. The extent of a paper's circulation bears chiefly on the rates of advertising, which, other things being equal, should have a direct ratio to it. The extent of circulation is a matter of almost constant misrepresentation on the part of publishers or their agents.

As a rule, the most prominent and costly part of the paper is the best. In country weeklies the "local items," or next to them, is preferable. In city journals containing a large amount of reading matter, a well displayed advertisement on the outside pages is perhaps the best for most classes of business.

Place the advertisement before the public at the proper time, just when people are beginning to feel the need of such as the article advertised, as furs, when winter sets in. An advertisement may, however, profitably be kept before the public constantly, and increased or diminished as occasion requires.

CIRCULARS.

There are many well established firms who will not advertise in the newspapers at all. They believe that the same amount of money spent in circulars, catalogues, etc., sent direct to the persons whom they desire to reach, pays better than newspaper advertising. This is more direct, and affords the advertiser the opportunity of setting forth his claims more fully. Circulars, cards, catalogues, etc., also afford a means for the display of taste in their typographical arrangement and appearance, and often times this has as much to do in making an impression on the person who receives it, as the reading matter contained therein. The printed circular goes out to the public as the representative of the house; it should, therefore, in order to command attention and respect, have about it an air of appropriateness and attraction. Such a circular will perhaps be carefully preserved for years, while another which was of not enough importance, apparently, to the proprietor or firm issuing it, to command their taste and skill, will soon be thrown aside as of no importance to the person receiving it.

Several circulars must often be sent in order to command the attention and secure the custom of a person. Where circulars referring to the same article are repeatedly sent out, the attention of the person who receives them is likely to be arrested at last, and his response may be made in the form of an order.

Perhaps thereafter he becomes a constant customer, buying himself, and recommending his friends to do likewise.

CHARTS, CALENDARS, ETC.

An important idea in advertising is to enlist the services of others, by making it to their interest to advertise your business. This is often done by sending out charts, calendars, etc., containing useful information, together with the advertisement. These, when properly arranged and prepared in an attractive manner, will be placed in a conspicuous place in the store, office, or home of the person receiving them. Railway, insurance, and other corporations have vied with each other in the elegance and attractiveness of their charts, etc., until they have gone into the fine arts, and spared no expense to captivate the public.

LETTERS.

More effectual than circulars, and nearest a personal interview, is a personal letter. As an advertisement the letter impresses itself upon the mind of the person receiving it, in an unusual way. A prominent firm employed clerks, and had written several thousand letters, at many times the cost of printed circulars, which they mailed throughout the country, calling especial attention to their line of goods. Even the two cent postage stamp, and the envelope being sealed, impresses the person receiving it with the thought that it is of importance, and one of the largest dry goods houses in Chicago, when issuing any circular which they regard as special, seal the envelope and place a two cent stamp thereon. They consider that this gives their circulars a preference over ordinary printed matter. Certain it is, that the public accept advertisements largely at the value and importance attached to them by their owners.

DRUMMERS AND AGENTS.

Personal effort exceeds all other means of advertising, and competition in many branches of business has become so strong in these times, and the facilities for travel so excellent, that large numbers of solicitors and agents traverse the country. Good personal address, a thorough understanding of the business, a knowledge of human nature, together with social qualities, constitute a good drummer.

HOW TO WRITE AN ADVERTISEMENT.

Before writing an advertisement, one should always place before his mind what is the most important thing to impress upon the public. If he is advertising an article of established trade, it is the name and location of the house selling it which must be the more prominent, or at least equally so with any other part; but if he be introducing some new article, or seeking to extend the sale of something little known or rare, these items are of far less importance, and the name of the article itself should be more prominent. The advertisement should be so constructed as to claim the attention of the reader, and retain that attention until he has read it through. "Excite but never satisfy," is the principle pursued by many successful advertisers.

The advertisement should never contain anything repugnant to refined taste, and nothing grotesque or ridiculous. The most meaning should be condensed into the fewest possible words. The wording should often be changed, and an attractive typography should be used. It is well to choose an attractive heading, followed by fairly spaced paragraphs, with appropriate sub-heads.

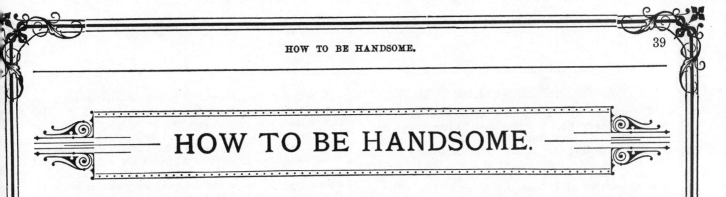

HOW TO BE HANDSOME.

Where is the woman who would not be beautiful? If such there be—but no, she does not exist. From that memorable day when the Queen of Sheba made a formal call on the late lamented King Solomon until the recent advent of the Jersey Lily, the power of beauty has controlled the fate of dynasties and the lives of men. How to be beautiful, and consequently powerful, is a question of far greater importance to the feminine mind than pre-destination or any other abstract subject. If women are to govern, control, manage, influence and retain the ador-ation of husbands, fathers, brothers, lovers or even cousins, they must look their prettiest at all times.

All women cannot have good features, but they can look well, and it is possible to a great extent to correct deform-ity and develop much of the figure. The first step to good looks is good health, and the first element of health is cleanliness. Keep clean—wash freely, bathe regularly. All the skin wants is leave to act, and it takes care of itself. In the matter of baths we do not strongly advocate a plunge in ice-cold water; it takes a woman with clear grit and a strong constitution to endure it. If a hot bath be used, let it come before retiring, as there is less danger of taking cold afterwards; and, besides, the body is weakened by the ablution and needs immediate rest. It is well to use a flesh-brush, and afterwards rinse off the soap-suds by briskly rubbing the body with a pair of coarse toilet gloves. The most important part of a bath is the drying. Every part of the body should be rubbed to a glowing red-ness, using a coarse crash towel at the finish. If sufficient friction can not be given, a small amount of bay rum applied with the palm of the hand will be found effica-cious. Ladies who have ample leisure and who lead me-thodical lives, take a plunge or sponge bath three times a week, and a vapor or sun bath every day. To facilitate this very beneficial practice, a south or east apartment is desirable. The lady denudes herself, takes a seat near the window, and takes in the warm rays of the sun. The effect is both beneficial and delightful. If, however, she be of a restless disposition, she may dance, instead of basking, in the sunlight. Or, if she be not fond of danc-ing, she may improve the shining hours by taking down her hair and brushing it, using sulphur water, pulverized borax dissolved in alcohol, or some similar dressing. It would be surprising to many ladies to see her carefully wiping the separate locks on a clean, white towel until the dust of the previous day is entirely removed. With such care it is not necessary to wash the head, and the hair under this treatment is invariably good.

One of the most useful articles of the toilet is a bottle of ammonia, and any lady who has once learned its value will never be without it. A few drops in the water takes the place of the usual amount of soap, and cleans out the pores of the skin as well as a bleach will do. Wash the face with a flesh-brush, and rub the lips well to tone their color. It is well to bathe the eyes before putting in the spirits, and if it is desirable to increase their brightness, this may be done by dashing soapsuds into them. Always rub the eyes, in washing, toward the nose. If the eye-brows are inclined to spread irregularly, pinch the hairs together where thickest. If they show a tendency to meet, this contact may be avoided by pulling out the hairs every morning before the toilet.

The dash of Orientalism in costume and lace now turns a lady's attention to her eyelashes, which are worthless if not long and drooping. Indeed, so prevalent is the desire for this beautiful feature that hair-dressers and ladies' artists have scores of customers under treatment for invig-orating their stunted eyelashes and eyebrows. To obtain these fringed curtains, anoint the roots with a balsam made of two drachms of nitric oxid of mercury mixed with one of leaf lard. After an application wash the roots with a camel's hair brush dipped in warm milk. Tiny scissors are used, with which the lashes are carefully but slightly trimmed every other day. When obtained, refrain from rubbing or even touching the lids with the finger-nails. There is more beauty in a pair of well-kept eyebrows and full, sweeping eyelashes than people are aware of, and a very inattractive and lusterless eye assumes new beauty when it looks out from beneath elongated fringes. Many ladies have a habit of rubbing the corners of their eyes to remove the dust that will frequently accumulate there. Unless this operation is done with little friction it will be found that the growth of hair is very spare, and in that case it will become necessary to pencil the barren corners. Instead of putting cologne water on the handkerchief, which has come to be con-sidered a vulgarism among ladies of correct tastes, the per-fume is spent on the eyebrows and lobes of the ears.

If commenced in youth, thick lips may be reduced by compression, and thin linear ones are easily modified by suction. This draws the blood to the surfaces, and pro-duces at first a temporary and, later, a permanent inflation. It is a mistaken belief that biting the lips reddens them. The skin of the lips is very thin, rendering them extremely susceptible to organic derangement, and if the atmosphere does not cause chaps or parchment, the result of such harsh treatment will develop into swelling or the for-mation of scars. Above all things, keep a sweet breath.

Everybody can not have beautiful hands, but there is no plausible reason for their being ill kept. Red hands may be overcome by soaking the feet in hot water as often as possible. If the skin is hard and dry, use tar or oat-meal soap, saturate them with glycerine, and wear gloves in bed. Never bathe them in hot water, and wash no oftener than is necessary. There are dozens of women with soft, white hands who do not put them in water once a month. Rubber gloves are worn in making the toilet, and they are cared for by an ointment of glycerine and rubbed dry with chamois-skin or cotton flannel. The same treatment is not unfrequently applied to the face with the most successful results. If such methods are used, it would be just as well to keep the knowledge of it from the gentlemen. We know of one beautiful lady who has not washed her face for three years, yet it is always clean, rosy, sweet and kissable. With some of her other secrets she gave it to her lover for safe keeping. Unfortunately, it proved to be her last gift to that gentle-man, who declared in a subsequent note that "I can not reconcile my heart and my manhood to a woman who can get along without washing her face."

SOME OF THE SECRETS OF BEAUTY.

There is as much a "fashion" in complexion as there is in bonnets or boots. Sometimes nature is the mode, sometimes art. Just now the latter is in the ascendant, though, as a rule, only in that inferior phase which has not reached the "concealment of art"—the point where extremes meet and the perfection of artifice presents all the appearance of artlessness. No one of an observant turn of mind, who is accustomed to the sight of English maids and matrons, can deny that making-up, as at present practiced, partakes of the amateurish element. Impossible reds and whites grow still more impossibly red and white from week to week under the unskilled hands of the wearer of "false colors," who does not like to ask for advice on so delicate a subject, for, even were she willing to confess to the practice, the imputation of experience conveyed in the asking for counsel might be badly received, and would scarcely be in good taste.

The prevalent and increasing short-sightedness of our times is, perhaps, partly the cause of the excessive use of rouge and powder. The wielder of the powder puff sees herself afar off, as it were. She knows that she cannot judge of the effect of her complexion with her face almost touching its reflection in the glass, and, standing about a yard off, she naturally accentuates her roses and lilies in a way that looks very pleasing to her, but is rather startling to any one with longer sight. Nor can she tone down her rouge with the powdered hair that softened the artificial coloring of her grandmother when she had her day. Powder is only occasionally worn with evening dress, and it is by daylight that those dreadful bluish reds and whites look their worst.

On the other hand, there are some women so clever at making up their faces that one feels almost inclined to condone the practice in admiration of the result. These are the small minority, and are likely to remain so, for their secret is of a kind unlikely to be shared. The closest inspection of these cleverly managed complexions reveals no trace of art.

Notwithstanding the reticence of these skilled artists, an occasional burst of confidence has revealed a few of their means of accomplishing the great end of looking pretty. "Do you often do that?" said one of those clever ones, a matron of 37, who looked like a girl of 19, to a friend who was vigorously rubbing her cheeks with a coarse towel after a plentiful application of cold water.

"Yes, every time I come in from a walk, ride or drive. Why?"

"Well, no wonder you look older than you are. You are simply wearing your face out!"

"But I must wash?"

"Certainly, but not like that. Take a leaf out of my book; never wash you face just before going out into the fresh air, or just after coming in. Nothing is more injurious to the skin. Come to the glass. Do you notice a drawn look about your eyes and a general streakiness in the cheeks? That is the result of your violent assault upon your complexion just now. You look at this moment ten years older than you did twenty minutes ago in the park."

"Well, I really do. I look old enough to be your mother; but then, you are wonderful. You always look so young and fresh!"

"Because I never treat my poor face so badly as you do yours. I use rain-water, and if I cannot get that, I have the water filtered. When I dress for dinner I always wash my face with milk, adding just enough hot water to make it pleasant to use. A very soft sponge and very fine towel take the place of your terrible huckaback arrangement."

Two or three years ago a lady of Oriental parentage on her father's side spent a season in London society. Her complexion was brown, relieved by yellow, her features large and irregular, but redeemed by a pair of lovely and expressive eyes. So perfect was her taste in dress that she always attracted admiration wherever she went. Dressed in rich dark brown or dullest crimsons or russets, so that no one ever noticed much what she wore, she so managed that suggestions and hints—no more—of brilliant amber or promegranate scarlet should appear just where they imparted brilliancy to her deep coloring, and abstract the yellow from her skin. A knot of old gold satin under the rim of her bonnet, another at her throat, and others in among the lace at her wrists, brightened up the otherwise subdued tinting of her costume, so that it always looked as though it had been designed expressly for her by some great colorist. Here rouge was unnecessary. The surroundings were arranged to suit the complexion, instead of the complexion to suit the surroundings. There can be no doubt as to which is the method which best becomes the gentlewoman.

In addition to the disagreeable sensation of making-up, it must be remembered that the use of some of the white powders eventually destroys the texture of the skin, rendering it rough and coarse. Rimmel, the celebrated perfumer, in his "Book of Perfumes," says that rouge, being composed of cochineal and saffron, is harmless, but that white cosmetics consist occasionally of deleterious substances which may injure the health. He advises actors and actresses to choose cosmetics, especially the white, with the greatest care, and women of the world, who wish to preserve the freshness of their complexion, to observe the following recipe: Open air, rest, exercise and cold water.

In another part of this pleasant book the author says that *schonada*, a cosmetic used among the Arabs, is quite innocuous and at the same time effectual. "This cream, which consists of sublimated benzoin, acts upon the skin as a slight stimulant, and imparts perfectly natural colors during some hours without occasioning the inconveniences with which European cosmetics may justly be reproached." It is a well-known fact that bismuth, a white powder containing sugar of lead, injures the nerve-centers when constantly employed, and occasionally causes paralysis itself.

In getting up the eyes, nothing is injurious that is not dropped into them. The use of *kohl* or *kohol* is quite harmless, and, it must be confessed, very effective when applied—as the famous recipe for salad dressing enjoins with regard to the vinegar—by the hand of a miser. Modern Egyptian ladies make their *kohol* of the smoke produced by burning almonds. A small bag holding the bottle of *kohol*, and a pin, with a rounded point with which to apply it, form part of the toilet paraphernalia of all the beauties of Cairo, who make the immense mistake of getting up their eyes in an exactly similar manner, thus trying to reduce the endless variety of nature to one common pattern, a mistake that may be accounted for by the fact that the Arabs believe *kohol* to be a sovereign specific against ophthalmia. Their English sisters often make the same mistake without the same excuse. A hairpin steeped in lampblack is the usual method of darkening the eyes in England, retribution following sooner or later in the shape of a total loss of the eyelashes. Eau de Cologne is occasionally dropped into the eyes, with the effect of making them brighter. The operation is painful, and it is said that half a dozen drops of whisky and the same quantity of Eau de Cologne, eaten on a lump of sugar, is quite as effective.

HIGH-HEELED BOOTS.

A lady looks infinitely taller and slimmer in a long dress than she does in a short costume, and there is always a way of showing the feet, if desired, by making the front quite short, which gives, indeed, a more youthful appearance to a train dress. The greatest attention must, of course, be paid to the feet with these short dresses, and I may here at once state that high heels are absolutely forbidden by fashion. Doctors, are you content? Only on cheap shoes and boots are they now made, and are only worn by common people. A good bootmaker will not make high heels now, even if paid double price to do so. Ladies —that is, real ladies—now wear flat-soled shoes and boots, *a la* Cinderella. For morning walking, boots or high Moliere shoes are worn.

If you wear boots you may wear any stockings you like, for no one sees them. But if you wear shoes you must adapt your stockings to your dress. Floss silk, Scotch thread, and even cotton stockings are worn for walking, silk stockings have returned into exclusively evening wear. Day stockings should be of the same color as the dress, but they may be shaded, or stripped, or dotted, just as you please. White stockings are absolutely forbidden for day wear—no one wears them—no one dares wear them under fashion's interdiction.

HOW TO APPEAR GRACEFUL IN WALKING.

The whole secret of standing and walking erect consists in keeping the chin well away from the breast. This throws the head upward and backward, and the shoulders will naturally settle backward and in their true position. Those who stoop in walking generally look downward. The proper way is to look straight ahead, upon the same level with your eyes, or if you are inclined to stoop, until that tendency is overcome, look rather above than below the level. Mountaineers are said to be as "straight as an arrow," and the reason is because they are obliged to look upward so much. It is simply impossible to stoop in walking if you will heed and practice this rule. You will notice that all round-shouldered persons carry the chin near the breast and pointed downward. Take warning in time, and heed grandmother's advice, for a bad habit is more easily prevented than cured. The habit of stooping when one walks or stands is a bad habit and especially hard to cure.

- - - MULTUM IN PARVO. - - -

HISTORY OF THE BIBLES OF THE WORLD.

The Bibles of the world are the koran of the Mohammedans, the tripitaka of the Buddhists, the five kings of the Chinese, the three vedas of the Hindoos, the zendavesta of the Parsees and the scriptures of the Christians. The koran, says the Chicago Times, is the most recent, dating from the seventh century after Christ. It is a compound of quotations from both the Old and the New Testaments and from the talmud. The tripitaka contain sublime morals and pure aspirations. Their author lived and died in the sixth century before Christ.

The sacred writings of the Chinese are called the five kings, the word "king" meaning web of cloth. From this it is presumed that they were originally written on five rolls of cloth. They contain wise sayings from the sages on the duties of life, but they can not be traced further back than the eleventh century before our era. The vedas are the most ancient books in the language of the Hindoos, but they do not, according to late commentators, antedate the twelfth before the Christian era. The zendavesta of the Parsees, next to our Bible, is reckoned among scholars as being the greatest and most learned of the sacred writings. Zoroaster, whose sayings it contains, lived and worked in the twelfth century before Christ. Moses lived and wrote the pentateuch 1,500 years before the birth of Jesus, therefore that portion of our Bible is at least 300 years older than the most ancient of other sacred writings. The eddas, a semi-sacred work of the Scandinavians, was first given to the world in the fourteen century A. D.

PRECIOUS STONES.

ARRANGED ACCORDING TO COLOR AND IN ORDER OF HARDINESS.

Limpid.—Diamond, Sapphire, Topaz, Rock-Crystal.
Blue.—Sapphire, Topaz, Indicolite, Turquoise, Spinel, Aquamarine, Kaynite.
Green.—Oriental Emerald, Chrysoberyl, Amazon Stone, Malachite, Emerald, Chrysoprase, Chrysolite.
Yellow.—Diamond, Topaz, Fire-Opal.
Red.—Sapphire-Ruby, Spinel-Ruby, Rubellite, Garnet, Brazilian-Topaz, Hyacinth, Carnelian.
Violet.—Oriental-Amethyst, Amethyst.
Black and Brown.—Diamond, Tourmaline, Hyacinth, Garnet.

HOW TO MEASURE CORN IN THE CRIB.

Rule: 1st. Measure the length, breadth and height of the crib inside the rail; multiply them together and divide by two, the result is the number of bushels of shelled corn.

2d. Level the corn so that it is of equal depth throughout, multiply the length, breath and depth together, and this product by four, and cut off one figure to the right of the product; the other will represent the number of bushels of shelled corn.

3d. Multiply length by height, and then by width, add two ciphers to the result and divide by 124; this gives the number of bushels of ear corn.

HOME DRESSMAKING.

The art of dressmaking in America has been of late years so simplified that almost anyone with a reasonable degree of executive ability can manufacture a fashionable costume by using an approved pattern and following the directions printed upon it, selecting a new pattern for each distinct style; while in Europe many ladies adhere to the old plan of cutting one model and using it for everything, trusting to personal skill or luck to gain the desired formation. However, some useful hints are given which are well worth offering after the paper pattern has been chosen.

The best dressmakers here and abroad use silk for lining, but nothing is so durable or preserves the material as well as a firm slate twill. This is sold double width and should be laid out thus folded : place the pattern upon it with the upper part towards the cut end, the selvedge for the fronts. The side pieces for the back will most probably be got out of the width, while the top of the back will fit in the intersect of the front. A yard of good stuff may be often saved by laying the pattern out and well considering how one part cuts into another. Prick the outline on to the lining ; these marks serve as a guide for the tacking.

In forming the front side plaits be careful and do not allow a fold or crease to be apparent on the bodice beyond where the stitching commences. To avoid this, before beginning stick a pin through what is to be the top of the plait. The head will be on the right side, and holding the point, one can begin pinning the seam without touching the upper part of the bodice. To ascertain the size of the buttonholes put a piece of card beneath the button to be used and cut it an eighth of an inch on either side beyond. Having turned down the piece in front on the buttonhole side run a thread a sixteenth of an inch from the extreme edge, and again another the width of the card. Begin to cut the first buttonhole at the bottom of the bodice; and continue at equal distances. The other side of the bodice is left wide enough to come well under the buttonholes. The buttonholes must be laid upon it and a pin put through the center of each to mark where the button is to be placed. In sewing on the buttons put the stiches in horizontally; if perpendicularly they are likely to pucker that side of the bodice so much that it will be quite drawn up, and the buttons will not match the buttonholes.

A WOMAN'S SKIRTS.

Observe the extra fatigue which is insured to every woman in merely carrying a tray upstairs, from the skirts of the dress. Ask any young women who are studying to pass examinations whether they do not find loose clothes a *sine qua non* while poring over their books, and then realize the harm we are doing ourselves and the race by habitually lowering our powers of life and energy in such a manner. As a matter of fact it is doubtful whether any persons have ever been found who would say that their stays were at all tight ; and, indeed, by a muscular contraction they can apparently prove that they are not so by moving them about on themselves, and thus probably believe what they say. That they are in error all the same they can easily assure themselves by first measuring round the waist outside the stays; then take them off, let them measure while they take a deep breath, with the tape merely laid on the body as if measuring for the quantity of braid to go round a dress, and mark the result. The injury done by stays is so entirely internal that it is not strange that the maladies caused by wearing them should be attributed to every reason under the sun except the true one, which is, briefly, that all the internal organs, being by them displaced, are doing their work imperfectly and under the least advantageous conditions; and are, therefore, exactly in the state most favorable to the development of disease, whether hereditary or otherwise.— *Macmillan's Magazine.*

TO MAKE THE SLEEVES.

As to sleeves. Measure from the shoulder to the elbow and again from elbow to the wrist. Lay these measurements on any sleeve patterns you may have, and lengthen and shorten accordingly. The sleeve is cut in two pieces, the top of the arm and the under part, which is about an inch narrower than the outside. In joining the two together, if the sleeve is at all tight, the upper part is slightly fulled to the lower at the elbow. The sleeve is sown to the armhole with no cordings now, and the front seam should be about two inches in front of the bodice.

Bodices are now worn very tight-fitting, and the French stretch the material well on the cross before beginning to cut out, and in cutting allow the lining to be slightly pulled, so that when on, the outside stretches to it and insures a better fit. An experienced eye can tell a French-cut bodice at once, the front side pieces being always on the cross. In dress cutting and fitting, as in everything else, there are failures and discouragements, but practice overrules these little matters, and "trying again" brings a sure reward in success.

A sensible suggestion is made in regard to the finish in necks of dresses for morning wear. Plain colors have rather a stiff appearance, tulle or crepe lisse frilling are expensive and frail, so it is a good idea to purchase a few yards of really good washing lace, about an inch and a half in depth; quill or plait and cut into suitable lengths to tack around the necks of dresses. This can be easily removed and cleaned when soiled. A piece of soft black Spanish lace, folded loosely around the throat close to the frillings, but below it, looks very pretty; or you may get three yards of scarf lace, trim the ends with frillings, place it around the neck, leaving nearly all the length in the right hand, the end lying upon the left shoulder being about half a yard long. Wind the larger piece twice around the throat, in loose, soft folds, and festoon the other yard and a half, and fasten with brooch or flower at the side.—*Philadelphia Times.*

DISCOVERY OF GOLD IN CALIFORNIA.

It was on the 19th day of January, 1848, that James W. Marshall, while engaged in digging a race for a saw-mill at Coloma, about thirty-five miles eastward from Sutter's Fort, found some pieces of yellow metal, which he and the half-dozen men working with him at the mill supposed to be gold. He felt confident that he had made a discovery of great importance, but he knew nothing of either chemistry or gold-mining, so he could not prove the nature of the metal nor tell how to obtain it in paying quantities. Every morning he went down to the race to look for the bits of metal; but the other men at the mill thought Marshall was very wild in his ideas, and they continued their labors in building the mill, and in sowing wheat and planting vegetables. The swift current of the mill-race washed away a considerable body of earthy matter, leaving the coarse particles of gold behind; so Marshall's collection of specimens continued to accumulate, and his associates began to think there might be something in his gold mines after all. About the middle of February, a Mr. Bennett, one of the party employed at the mill, went to San Francisco for the purpose of learning whether this metal was precious, and there he was introduced to Isaac Humphrey, who had washed for gold in Georgia. The experienced miner saw at a glance that he had the true stuff before him, and, after a few inquiries, he was satisfied that the diggings must be rich. He made immediate preparation to visit the mill, and tried to persuade some of his friends to go with him; but they thought it would be only a waste of time and money, so he went with Bennett for his sole companion.

He arrived at Coloma on the 7th of March, and found the work at the mill going on as if no gold existed in the neighborhood. The next day he took a pan and spade, and washed some of the dirt in the bottom of the mill-race in places where Marshall had found his specimens, and, in a few hours, Humphrey declared that these mines were far richer than any in Georgia. He now made a rocker and went to work washing gold industriously, and every day yielded to him an ounce or two of metal. The men at the mill made rockers for themselves, and all were soon busy in search of the yellow metal. Everything else was abandoned; the rumor of the discovery spread slowly. In the middle of March Pearson B. Reading, the owner of a large ranch at the head of the Sacramento valley, happened to visit Sutter's Fort, and hearing of the mining at Coloma, he went thither to see it. He said that if similarity of formation could be taken as a proof, there must be gold mines near his ranch; so, after observing the method of washing, he posted off, and in a few weeks he was at work on the bars of Clear Creek, nearly two hundred miles northwestward from Coloma. A few days after Reading had left, John Bidwell, now representative of the northern district of the State in the lower House of Congress, came to Coloma, and the result of his visit was that, in less than a month, he had a party of Indians from his ranch washing gold on the bars of Feather River, twenty-five miles northwestward from Coloma. Thus the mines were opened at far distant points.

The first printed notice of the discovery of gold was given in the California newspaper published in San Francisco on the 15th of March. On the 29th of May the same paper, announcing that its publication would be suspended, says: "The whole country, from San Francisco to Los Angeles, and from the seashore to the base of the Sierra Nevada, resound the sordid cry of *gold! gold! gold!* while the field is left half planted, the house half built and everything neglected but the manufacture of pick and shovels, and the means of transportation to the spot where one man obtained one hundred and twenty-eight dollars' worth of the real stuff in one day's washing; and the average for all concerned, is twenty dollars per diem."

The first to commence quartz mining in California were Capt. Wm. Jackson and Mr. Eliason, both Virginians, and the first machine used was a Chilian mill.

The Reid Mine, in North Carolina, was the first gold mine discovered and worked in the United States, and the only one in North America from which, up to 1825, gold was sent to the Mint.

HOW TO MAKE ARTIFICIAL GOLD.

The following oroid or imitation gold is sometimes sold for the genuine article which it closely resembles. Pure copper, 100 parts by weight, is melted in a crucible, and then 6 parts of magnesia, 3.6 of sal-ammoniac, 1.8 of quicklime and 9. of tartar are added separately and gradually in the form of powder. The whole is then stirred for about half an hour, and 17 parts of zinc or tin in small grains are thrown in and thoroughly mixed. The cruicible is now covered and the mixture kept melted for half an hour longer, when it is skimmed and poured out.

Any imitation of gold may be detected by its weight, which is not one-half of what it should be, and by its dissolving in nitric acid while pure gold is untouched.

HOW TO TELL ANY PERSON'S AGE.

There is a good deal of amusement in the following magical table of figures. It will enable you to tell how old the young ladies are. Just hand this table to a young lady, and request her to tell you in which column or columns her age is contained, and add together the figures at the top of the columns in which her age is found, and you have the great secret. Thus, suppose her age to be 17, you will find that number in the first and fifth columns; add the first figures of these two columns.

Here is the magic table:

1	2	4	8	16	32
3	3	5	9	17	33
5	6	6	10	18	34
7	7	7	11	19	35
9	10	12	12	20	36
11	11	13	13	21	37
13	14	14	14	22	38
15	15	15	15	23	39
17	18	20	24	24	40
19	19	21	25	25	41
21	22	22	26	26	42
23	23	23	27	27	43
25	26	28	28	28	44
27	27	29	29	29	45
29	30	30	30	30	46
31	31	31	31	31	47
33	34	36	40	48	48
35	35	37	41	49	49
37	38	38	42	50	50
39	39	39	43	51	51
41	42	44	44	52	52
43	43	45	45	53	53
45	46	46	46	54	54
47	47	47	47	55	55
49	50	52	56	56	56
51	51	53	57	57	57
53	54	54	58	58	58
55	55	55	59	59	59
57	58	60	60	60	60
59	59	61	61	61	61
61	62	62	62	62	62
63	63	63	63	63	63

WHAT THE WHITE HOUSE COSTS.

Salary of President, $50,000; additional appropriations are about $75,000. A total of $125,000. The President has the following corps of assistants: Private Secretary, $3,250; Assistant Private Secretary, $2,250; Stenographer, $1,800; five Messengers, $1,200 each, $6,000; Steward—; two Doorkeepers, $1,200 each, $2,400; two Ushers, $1,200, $1,400, $2,600; Night Usher, $1,200; Watchman, $900, and a few other minor clerks and telegraph operators.

SUNDRIES.—Incidental expenses, $8,000; White House repairs—carpets and refurnishing, $12,500; fuel, $2,500; green-house, $4,000; gas, matches and stable, $15,000.

These amounts, with others of minor importance, consume the entire appropriations.

BUSINESS LAW.

Ignorance of the law excuses no one. It is a fraud to conceal a fraud. The law compels no one to do impossibilities. An agreement without consideration is void. Signatures made with a lead pencil are good in law. A receipt for money paid is not legally conclusive. The acts of one partner bind all the others. Contracts made on Sunday cannot be enforced. A contract made with a minor is void. A contract made with a lunatic is void. Principals are responsible for the acts of their agents.

Agents are responsible to their principals for errors. Each individual in a partnership is responsible for the whole amount of the debts of the firm. A note given by a minor is void. Notes bear interest only when so stated. It is legally necessary to say on a note "for value received." A note drawn on Sunday is void. A note obtained by fraud, or from a person in a state of intoxication, cannot be collected. If a note be lost or stolen, it does not release the maker; he must pay it. An endorser of a note is exempt from liability if not served with notice of its dishonor within twenty-four hours of its non-payment.

ITEMS WORTH REMEMBERING.

A sun bath is of more worth than much warming by the fire.

Books exposed to the atmosphere keep in better condition than if confined in a book-case. Pictures are both for use and ornament. They serve to recall pleasant memories and scenes; they harmonize with the furnishing of the rooms. If they serve neither of these purposes they are worse than useless; they only help fill space which would look better empty, or gather dust and make work to keep them clean.

A room filled with quantities of trifling ornaments has the look of a bazaar and displays neither good taste nor good sense. Artistic excellence aims to have all the furnishings of a high order of workmanship combined with simplicity, while good sense understands the folly of dusting a lot of rubbish.

A poor book had best be burned to give place to a better, or even to an empty shelf, for the fire destroys its poison, and puts it out of the way of doing harm.

Better economize in the purchasing of furniture or carpets than scrimp in buying good books or papers.

Our sitting-rooms need never be empty of guests or our libraries of society if the company of good books is admitted to them.

REMARKABLE CALCULATIONS REGARDING THE SUN.

The sun's average distance from the earth is about 91,500,000 miles. Since the orbit of the earth is elliptical, and the sun is situated at one of its foci, the earth is nearly 3,000,000 miles further from the sun in aphelion than in perihelion. As we attempt to locate the heavenly bodies in space, we are immediately startled by the enormous figures employed. The first number, 91,500,000 miles, is far beyond our grasp. Let us try to comprehend it. If there were air to convey a sound from the sun to the earth, and a noise could be made loud enough to pass that distance it would require over fourteen years for it to come to us. Suppose a railroad could be built to the sun. An express train traveling day and night at the rate of thirty miles an hour, would require 341 years to reach its destination. Ten generations would be born and would die; the young men would become gray haired, and their great-grandchildren would forget the story of the beginning of that wonderful journey, and could find it only in history, as we now read of Queen Elizabeth or of Shakespeare; the eleventh generation would see the solar depot at the end of the route. Yet this enormous distance of 91,500,000 miles is used as the unit for expressing celestial distances—as the foot-rule for measuring space; and astronomers speak of so many times the sun's distance as we speak of so many feet or inches.

SIGNS OF STORMS APPROACHING.—A ring around the sun or moon stands for an approaching storm, its near or distant approach being indicated by its larger or smaller circumference. When the sun rises brightly and immediately afterward becomes veiled with clouds, the farmer distrusts the day. Rains which begin early in the morning often stop by nine in place of "eleven," the hour specified in the old saw, "If it rains before seven."

On a still, quiet day, with scarcely the least wind afloat, the ranchman or farmer can tell the direction of impending storm by cattle sniffing the air in the direction whence it is coming. Lack of dew in summer is a rain sign. Sharp white frosts in autumn and winter precede damp weather, and we will stake our reputation as a prophet that three successive white frosts are an infallible sign of rain. Spiders do not spin their webs out of doors before rain. Previous to rain flies sting sharper, bees remain in their hives or fly but short distances, and almost all animals appear uneasy.

HOW TO DISTINGUISH GOOD MEAT FROM BAD MEAT.

1st. It is neither of a pale pink color nor of a deep purple tint, for the former is a sign of disease, and the latter indicates that the animal has not been slaughtered, but has died with the blood in it, or has suffered from acute fever.

2d. It has a marked appearance from the ramifications of little veins of fat among the muscles.

3d. It should be firm and elastic to the touch and should scarcely moisten the fingers—bad meat being wet and sodden and flabby with the fat looking like jelly or wet parchment.

4th. It should have little or no odor, and the odor should not be disagreeable, for diseased meat has a sickly cadaverous smell, and sometimes a smell of physic. This is very discoverable when the meat is chopped up and drenched with warm water.

5th. It should not shrink or waste much in cooking.

6th. It should not run to water or become very wet on standing for a day or two, but should, on the contrary, dry upon the surface.

7th. When dried at a temperature of 212 deg., or thereabouts, it should not lose more than from 70 to 74 per cent. of its weight, whereas bad meat will often lose as much as 80 per cent. The juice of the flesh is alkaline or neutral to test paper.

RAILROADS IN FINLAND.

People who think of Finland as a sub-arctic country of bleak and forbidding aspect may be surprised to hear that several railroads have already made a large part of the region accessible. A new line, 160 miles long, has just been opened to the heart of the country in the midst of great forests and perhaps the most wonderful lake region in the world. Sportsmen are now within less than a day's journey from St. Petersburg of central Finland, where there is the best of hunting and fishing and twenty hours of sunlight every summer day. The most unique of railroads, however, is still the little line in Norway, north of the arctic circle, carrying the product of far northern mines to the sea, and famous as the only railroad that has yet invaded the polar regions.

COMPARATIVE SIZE OF THE ARK AND THE GREAT EASTERN.

The following comparison between the size of Noah's ark and the Great Eastern, both being considered in point of tonnage, after the old law for calculating the tonnage of a vessel, exhibits a remarkable similarity. The cubit of the Bible, according to Sir Isaac Newton, is 20½ inches, or, to be exact, 20.625 inches. Bishop Wilkins makes the cubit 20.88 inches. According to Newton the dimensions of the ark were: Length between perpendiculars, 515.62 feet; breadth, 84.94 feet; depth, 51.56 feet; keel, or length for tonnage, 464.08 feet. Tonnage, according to old law, 18,231 58-94. The measurements of the ark, according to Wilkins' calculations were: Length, 54700 feet; breadth, 91.16 feet; depth, 54.70 feet; keel, 492.31 feet. Tonnage, 21,761. Notice how surprisingly near the Great Eastern came to being constructed after the same plan: Length, 680 feet; breadth, 83 feet; depth, 60 feet; keel, 630 feet. Tonnage, 23,092.

FINGER NAILS AS AN INDICATION OF CHARACTER.

A white mark on the nail bespeaks misfortune.

Pale or lead-colored nails indicate melancholy people.

Broad nails indicate a gentle, timid, and bashful nature.

Lovers of knowledge and liberal sentiments have round nails.

People with narrow nails are ambitious and quarrelsome.

Small nails indicate littleness of mind, obstinacy and conceit.

Choleric, martial men, delighting in war, have red and spotted nails.

Nails growing into the flesh at the points or sides indicate luxurious tastes.

People with very pale nails are subject to much infirmity of the flesh and persecution by neighbors and friends.

DANGERS OF CELLULOID.

A curious accident, which happened recently in Paris, points out a possible danger in the wearing of combs and bracelets of celluloid. A little girl sat down before the fire to prepare her lessons. Her hair was kept back by a semi-circle comb of celluloid. As her head was bent forward to the fire this became warm, and suddenly burst into flames. The child's hair was partly burned off, and the skin of the head was so injured that several months after, though the burn was healed, the cicatrix formed a white patch on which no hair would grow. The burning point of celluloid is about 180 degrees, and the comb worn by the girl had attained that heat as it was held before the fire.

ODD FACTS ABOUT SHOES.

Grecian shoes were peculiar in reaching to the middle of the legs.

The present fashion of shoes was introduced into England in 1633.

In the ninth and tenth centuries the greatest princes of Europe wore wooden shoes.

Slippers were in use before Shakespeare's time, and were originally made "rights" and "lefts."

Shoes among the Jews were made of leather, linen, rush or wood; soldiers' shoes were sometimes made of brass or iron.

In the reign of William Rufus of England, in the eleventh century, a great beau, "Robert, the Horned," used shoes with sharp points, stuffed with tow, and twisted like rams' horns.

The Romans made use of two kinds of shoes—the solea, or sandal, which covered the sole of the foot, and was worn at home and in company, and the calceus, which covered the whole foot and was always worn with the toga when a person went abroad.

In the reign of Richard II., shoes were of such absurd length as to require to be supported by being tied to the knees with chains, sometimes of gold and silver. In 1463 the English parliament took the matter in hand and passed an act forbidding shoes with spikes more than two inches in length being worn and manufactured.

TABLE SHOWING THE AVERAGE VELOCITIES OF VARIOUS BODIES.

A man walks 3 miles per hour or 4 feet per second.
A horse trots 7 "   "   10 "   "
A horse runs 20 "   "   29 "   "
Steamboat runs 20 "   "   26 "   "
Sailing vessel runs 10 miles per hour or 14 feet per second.
Rapid rivers flow 3 "   "   4 "   "
A moderate wind blows 7 miles per hour or 10 feet per second.
A storm moves 36 "   "   52 "   "
A hurricane moves 80 "   "   117 "   "
A rifle ball 1000 "   "   1466 "   "
Sound 743 "   "   1142 "   "
Light, 192,000 miles per second.
Electricity, 288,000 miles per second.

QUANTITY OF OIL REQUIRED FOR DIFFERENT COLORS.

Heath & Miligan quote the following figures. They are color manufacturers:

100 parts (weight)	White Lead	require	12	parts of oil.
" "	Zinc White	"	14	"
" "	Green Chrome	"	15	"
" "	Chrome Yellow	"	19	"
" "	Vermilion	"	25	"
" "	Light Red	"	31	"
" "	Madder Lake	"	62	"
" "	Yellow Ochre	"	66	"
" "	Light Ochre	"	72	"
" "	Camels Brown	"	75	"
" "	Brown Manganese	require	87	parts of oil.
" "	Terre Verte	"	100	"
" "	Parisian Blue	"	106	"
" "	Burnt Terreverte	"	112	"
" "	Berlin Blue	"	112	"
" "	Ivory Black	"	112	"
" "	Cobalt	"	125	"
" "	Florentine Brown	"	150	"
" "	Burnt Terra Sienna	"	181	"
" "	Raw Terra Sienna	"	140	"

According to this table, a hundred parts of the quick drying white lead are ground with 12 parts of oil, and on the other hand slow drying ivory black requires 112 parts of oil.

PAINTING.

1 gallon Priming Color will cover 50 superficial yards.
" White Zinc " 50 "
" White Paint " 44 "
" Lead Color " 50 "
" Black Paint " 50 "
" Stone Color " 44 "
" Yellow Paint " 44 "
" Blue Color " 45 "
" Green Paint " 45 "
" Bright Emerald Green will cover 25 superficial yards.
" Bronze Green will cover 45 superficial yards.

One pound of paint will cover about four superficial yards the first coat, and about six yards each additional coat.

RAPID PROCESS OF MARKING GOODS AT ANY DESIRED PER CENT. PROFIT.

Retail merchants, in buying goods by wholesale, buy a great many articles by the dozen, such as boots and shoes, hats and caps, and notions of various kinds; now the merchant, in buying, for instance, a dozen hats, knows exactly what one of these hats will retail for in the market where he deals; and unless he is a good accountant, it will often take him some time to determine whether he can afford to purchase the dozen hats and make a living profit by selling them by the single hat; and in buying his goods by auction, as the merchant often does, he has not time to make the calculation before the goods are bid off. He therefore loses the chance of making good bargains by being afraid to bid at random, or if he bids, and the goods are cried off, he may have made a poor bargain by bidding thus at a venture. It then becomes a useful and practical problem to determine instantly what per cent. he would gain if he retailed the hat at a certain price, to tell what an article should retail for to make a profit of 20 per cent.

Rule.—Divide what the articles cost per dozen by 10, which is done by removing the decimal point one place to the left.

For instance, if hats cost $17.50 per dozen, remove the decimal point one place to the left, making $1.75, what they should be sold for apiece to gain 20 per cent. on the cost. If they cost $31.00 per dozen, they should be sold at $3.10 apiece, etc.

THE SEVEN WONDERS OF THE WORLD.

Pyramids of Egypt.
Tower, Walls and Terrace Hanging Gardens of Babylon.
Statue of Jupiter Olympus, on the Capitoline Hill, at Rome.
Temple of Diana, at Ephesus.
Pharos, or watch-tower, at Alexandria, Egypt.
Colossus of Rhodes, a statue 105 feet high; overthrown by an earthquake 224 B. C.
Mausoleum at Halicarnassus, a Grecian-Persian city in Asia Minor.

HEAT AND COLD.

Degrees of heat above zero at which substances melt:—Wrought iron, 3,980 degrees; cast iron, 3,479; platinum, 3,080; gold, 2,590; copper, 2,548; steel, 2,500; glass, 2,377; brass, 1,900; silver, 1,250; antimony, 951; zinc, 740; lead, 594; tin, 421; arsenic, 365; sulphur, 226; beeswax, 151; gutta percha, 145; tallow, 97; lard, 95; pitch, 91; ice, 33.

Degrees of heat above zero at which substances boil:—Ether, 98 degrees; alcohol, 173; water, 212; petroleum, 306; linseed oil, 640; blood heat, 98; eggs hatch, 104.

QUANTITY OF SEED TO AN ACRE.

Wheat, 1½ to 2 bu.; rye, 1½ to 2 bu.; oats, 3 bu.; barley, 2 bu.; buckwheat, ½ bu.; corn, broadcast, 4 bu.; corn, in drills, 2 to 3 bu.; corn, in hills, 4 to 8 qts.; broom corn, ¼ bu.; potatoes, 10 to 15 bu.; rutabagas, ¾ lbs.; millet, ¼ bu.; clover, white, 4 qts.; clover, red, 8 qts.; timothy, 6 qts.; orchard grass, 2 qts.; red top, 1 to 2 pks.; blue grass, 2 bu.; mixed lawn grass, ½ bu.; tobacco, 2 ozs.

SOLUBLE GLASS FOR FLOORS.

Instead of the old-fashioned method of using wax for polishing floors, etc., soluble glass is now employed to great advantage. For this purpose the floor is first well cleaned, and then the cracks well filled up with a cement of water-glass and powdered chalk or gypsum. Afterward, a water-glass of 60° to 65°, of the thickness of syrup, is applied by means of a stiff brush. Any desired color may be imparted to the floor in a second coat of the water-glass, and additional coats are to be given until the requisite polish is obtained. A still higher finish may be given by pummicing off the last layer, and then putting on a coating of oil.

DURABILITY OF A HORSE.

A horse will travel 400 yards in 4½ minutes at a walk, 400 yards in 2 minutes at a trot, and 400 yards in 1 minute at a gallop. The usual work of a horse is taken at 22,500 lbs. raised 1 foot per minute, for 8 hours per day. A horse will carry 250 lbs. 25 miles per day of 8 hours. An average draught-horse will draw 1,600 lbs. 23 miles per day on a level road, weight of wagon included. The average weight of a horse is 1,000 lbs.; his strength is equal to that of 5 men. In a horse mill moving at 3 feet per second, track 25 feet diameter, he exerts with the machine the power of 4½ horses. The greatest amount a horse can pull in a horizontal line is 900 lbs.; but he can only do this momentarily, in continued exertion, probably half of this is the limit. He attains his growth in 5 years, will live 25, average 16 years. A horse will live 25 days on water, without solid food, 17 days without eating or drinking, but only 5 days on solid food, without drinking.

A cart drawn by horses over an ordinary road will travel 1.1 miles per hour of trip. A 4-horse team will haul from 25 to 36 cubic feet of lime stone at each load. The time expended in loading, unloading, etc., including delays, averages 35 minutes per trip. The cost of loading and unloading a cart, using a horse cram at the quarry, and unloading by hand, when labor is $1.25 per day, and a horse 75 cents, is 25 cents per perch=24.75 cubic feet. The work done by an animal is greatest when the velocity with which he moves is ⅛ of the greatest with which he can move when not impeded, and the force then exerted .45 of the utmost force the animal can exert at a dead pull.

COMPARATIVE COST OF FREIGHT BY WATER AND RAIL.

It has been proved by actual test that a single tow-boat can transport at one trip from the Ohio to New Orleans 29,000 tons of coal, loaded in barges. Estimating in this way the boat and its tow, worked by a few men, carries as much freight to its destination as 3,000 cars and 100 locomotives, manned by 600 men, could transport.

HINTS TO YOUNG HOUSEWIVES.

Glycerine does not agree with a dry skin.

If you use powder always wash it off before going to bed.

When you give your cellar its spring cleaning, add a little copperas water and salt to the whitewash.

A little ammonia and borax in the water when washing blankets keeps them soft and prevents shrinkage.

Sprinkling salt on the top and at the bottom of garden walls is said to keep snails from climbing up or down.

For relief from heartburn or dyspepsia, drink a little cold water in which has been dissolved a teaspoonful of salt.

For hoarseness, beat a fresh egg and thicken it with fine white sugar. Eat of it freely and the hoarseness will soon be relieved.

If quilts are folded or rolled tightly after washing, then beaten with a rolling pin or potato masher, it lightens up the cotton and makes them seem soft and new.

Chemists say that it takes more than twice as much sugar to sweeten preserves, sauce, etc., if put in when they begin to cook as it does to sweeten after the fruit is cooked.

Tar may be removed from the hands by rubbing with the outside of fresh orange or lemon peel and drying immediately. The volatile oils dissolve the tar so that it can be rubbed off.

Moths or any summer flying insects may be enticed to destruction by a bright tin pan half filled with kerosene set in a dark corner of the room. Attracted by the bright pan, the moth will meet his death in the kerosene.

It may be worth knowing that water in which three or four onions have been boiled, applied with a gilding brush to the frames of pictures and chimney glasses, will prevent flies from lighting on them and will not injure the frames.

SUPERSTITIONS REGARDING BABIES.

It is believed by many that if a child cries at its birth and lifts up only one hand, it is born to command. It is thought very unlucky not to weigh the baby before it is dressed. When first dressed the clothes should not be put on over the head, but drawn on over the feet, for luck. When first taken from the room in which it was born it must be carried up stairs before going down, so that it will rise in the world. In any case it must be carried up stairs or up the street, the first time it is taken out. It is also considered in England and Scotland unlucky to cut the baby's nails or hair before it is twelve months old. The saying:

Born on Monday, fair in the face;
Born on Tuesday, full of God's grace;
Born on Wednesday, the best to be had;
Born on Thursday, merry and glad;
Born on Friday, worthily given;
Born on Saturday, work hard for a living;
Born on Sunday, shall never know want,

is known with various changes all over the Christian world; one deviation from the original makes Friday's child "free in giving." Thursday has one very lucky hour just before sunrise.

The child that is born on the Sabbath day
Is bonny and good and gay,

While

He who is born on New Year's morn
Will have his own way as sure as you're born.

And

He who is born on Easter morn
Shall never know care, or want, or harm.

SECRET ART OF CATCHING FISH.

Put the oil of rhodium on the bait, when fishing with a hook, and you will always succeed.

TO CATCH FISH.

Take the juice of smallage or lovage, and mix with any kind of bait. As long as there remain any kind of fish within yards of your hook, you will find yourself busy pulling them out.

CERTAIN CURE FOR DRUNKENNESS.

Take of sulphate of iron 5 grains, magnesia 10 grains, peppermint water 11 drachms, spirits of nutmeg 1 drachm. Administer this twice a day. It acts as a tonic and stimulant and so partially supplies the place of the accustomed liquor, and prevents that absolute physical and moral prostration that follows a sudden breaking off from the use of stimulating drinks.

LADIES' STAMPING POWDER.

For use in stamping any desired pattern upon goods for needle work, embroidery, etc. Draw pattern upon heavy paper, and perforate with small holes all the lines with some sharp instrument, dust the powder through, remove the pattern and pass a warm iron over the fabric, when the pattern will become fixed. Any desired color can be used, such as Prussian blue, chrome green, yellow, vermilion, etc. Fine white rosin, 2 ounces; gum sandarach, 4 ounces; color, 2 ounces. Powder very fine, mix, and pass through a sieve.

SALARIES OF THE UNITED STATES OFFICERS, PER ANNUM.

President, Vice-President and Cabinet.—President, $50,000; Vice-President, $8,000; Cabinet Officers, $8,000 each.

United States Senators.—$5,000, with mileage.

Congress.—Members of Congress, $5,000, with mileage.

Supreme Court.—Chief Justice, $10,500; Associate Justices, $10,000.

Circuit Courts.—Justices of Circuit Courts, $6,000.

Heads of Departments.—Supt. of Bureau of Engraving and Printing, $4,500; Public Printer, $4,500; Supt. of Census, $5,000; Supt. of Naval Observatory, $5,000; Supt. of the Signal Service, $4,000; Director of Geological Surveys, $6,000; Director of the Mint, $4,500; Commissioner of General Land Office, $4,000; Commissioner of Pensions, $3,600; Commissioner of Agriculture, $3,000; Commissioner of Indian Affairs, $3,000; Commissioner of Education $3,000; Commander of Marine Corps, $3,500; Supt. of Coast and Geodetic Survey, $6,000.

United States Treasury.—Treasurer, $6,000; Register of Treasury, $4,000; Commissioner of Customs, $4,000.

Internal Revenue Agencies.—Supervising Agents, $12 per day; 34 other agents, per day, $6 to $8.

Postoffice Department, Washington.—Three Assistant Postmaster-Generals, $3,500; Chief Clerk, $2,200.

Postmasters.—Postmasters are divided into four classes. First class, $3,000 to $4,000 (excepting New York City, which is $8,000); second class, $2,000 to $3,000; third class, $1,000 to $2,000; fourth class, less than $1,000. The first three classes are appointed by the President, and confirmed by the Senate; those of fourth class are appointed by the Postmaster-General.

Diplomatic appointments.—Ministers to Germany, Great Britain, France and Russia, $17,500; Ministers to Brazil, China, Austria-Hungary, Italy, Mexico, Japan and Spain, $12,000; Ministers to Chili, Peru and Central Amer., $10,000; Ministers to Argentine Confederation, Hawaiian Islands, Belgium, Hayti, Columbia, Netherlands, Sweden, Turkey and Venezuela, $7,500; Ministers to Switzerland, Denmark, Paraguay, Bolivia and Portugal, $5,000; Minister to Liberia, $4,000.

Army Officers.—General, $13,500; Lieut.-General, $11,000; Major-General, $7,500; Brigadier-General, $5,500; Colonel, $3,500; Lieutenant-Colonel, $3,000; Major, $2,500; Captain, mounted, $2,000; Captain, not mounted, $1,800; Regimental Adjutant, $1,800; Regimental Quartermaster, $1,800; 1st Lieutenant, mounted, $1,600; 1st Lieutenant, not mounted, $1,500; 2d Lieutenant, mounted, $1,500; 2d Lieutenant, not mounted, $1,400; Chaplain, $1,500.

Navy Officers.—Admiral, $13,000; Vice-Admiral, $9,000; Rear-Admirals, $6,000; Commodores, $5,000; Captains, $45,000; Commanders, $3,500; Lieut.-Commanders, $2,800; Lieutenants, $2,400; Masters, $1,800; Ensigns, $1,200; Midshipmen, $1,000; Cadet Midshipmen, $500; Mates, $900; Medical and Pay Directors and Medical and Pay Inspectors and Chief Engineers, $4,400; Fleet Surgeons, Fleet Paymasters and Fleet Engineers, $4,400; Surgeons and Paymasters, $2,800; Chaplains, $2,500.

CHRONOLOGY OF IMPORTANT EVENTS.

BEFORE CHRIST.

The Deluge..2348
Babylon built.......................................2247
Birth of Abraham...................................1993
Death of Joseph....................................1635
Moses born..1571
Athens founded.....................................1556
The Pyramids built.................................1250
Solomon's Temple finished.........................1004
Rome founded..753
Jerusalem destroyed.................................587
Babylon taken by Jews...............................538
Death of Socrates...................................400
Rome taken by the Gauls.............................835
Paper invented in China.............................170
Carthage destroyed..................................146
Cæsar landed in Britain..............................55
Cæsar killed...44
Birth of Christ.......................................0

AFTER CHRIST.

Death of Augustus................................... 14
Pilate, governor of Judea........................... 27
Jesus Christ crucified.............................. 33
Claudius visited Britain............................ 43
St. Paul put to death............................... 67
Death of Josephus................................... 93
Jerusalem rebuilt...................................131
The Romans destroyed 580,000 Jews and banished the
    rest from Judea................................135
The Bible in Gothic.................................373
Horseshoes made of iron.............................481
Latin tongue ceased to be spoken 580
Pens made of quills.................................635
Organs used...660
Glass in England....................................663
Bank of Venice established.........................1157
Glass windows first used for lights................1180
Mariner's compass used.............................1200
Coal dug for fuel..................................1234
Chimneys first put to houses 1236
Spectacles invented by an Italian..................1240
The first English House of Commons... 1258
Tallow candles for lights..........................1290
Paper made from linen..............................1302
Gunpowder invented.................................1340
Woolen cloth made in England.......................1341
Printing invented..................................1436
The first almanac..................................1470
America discovered.................................1492
First book printed in England......................1507
Luther began to preach.............................1517
Interest fixed at ten per cent. in England.........1547
Telescopes invented 1549
First coach made in England........................1564
Clocks first made in England.......................1568
Bank of England incorporated.......................1594
Shakespeare died...................................1616
Circulation of the blood discovered................1619
Barometer invented 1623
First newspaper....................................1629
Death of Galileo...................................1643
Steam engine invented..............................1649
Great fire in London...............................1666
Cotton planted in the United States................1759
Commencement of the American war...................1775
Declaration of American Independence...............1776
Recognition of American Independence 1782
Bank of England suspended cash payment.............1791
Napoleon I. crowned emperor 1804
Death of Napoleon..................................1820
Telegraph invented by Morse........................1832
First daguerreotype in France......................1839
Beginning of the American civil war................1861
End of the American civil war......................1865
Abraham Lincoln died...............................1865
Great Chicago Fire.................................1871
Jas. A. Garfield died..............................1881

INTERESTING FACTS ABOUT OUR BODIES.

The weight of the male infant at birth is 7 lbs. avoirdupois; that of the female is not quite 6½ lbs. The maximum weight (140½ lbs.) of the male is attained at the age of 40; that of the female (nearly 124 lbs.) is not attained until 50; from which ages they decline afterward, the male to 127¼ lbs., the female to 100 lbs., nearly a stone. The full-grown adult is 20 times as heavy as a new-born infant. In the first year he triples his weight, afterwards the growth proceeds in geometrical progression, so that if 50 infants in their first year weigh 1,000 lbs., they will in the second weigh 1,210 lbs.; in the third 1,331; in the fourth 1464 lbs.; the term remaining very constant up to the ages of 11-12 in females, and 12-13 in males, where it must be nearly doubled; afterwards it may be continued, and will be found very nearly correct up to the age of 18 or 19, when the growth proceeds very slowly. At an equality of age the male is generally heavier than the female. Towards the age of 12 years only an individual of each sex has the same weight. The male attains the maximum weight at about the age of 40, and he begins to lose it very sensibly toward 60. At 80 he loses about 13.2328 lbs., and the stature is diminished 2.756 inches. Females attain their maximum weight at about 50. The mean weight of a mature man is 104 lbs., and of an average woman 94 lbs. In old age they lose about 12 or 14 lbs. Men weigh most at 40, women at 50, and begin to lose weight at 60. The mean weight of both sexes in old age is that which they had at 19.

When the male and female have assumed their complete development they weigh almost exactly 20 times as much as at birth, while the stature is about 3½ times greater.

Children lose weight during the first three days after birth; at the age of a week they sensibly increase; after one year they triple their weight; then they require six years to double their weight, and 13 to quadruple it.

It has been computed that nearly two years' sickness is experienced by every person before he is 70 years old, and therefore that 10 days per annum is the average sickness of human life. Till 40 it is but half, and after 50 it rapidly increases. The mixed and fanciful diet of man is considered the cause of numerous diseases from which animals are exempt. Many diseases have abated with changes of diet, and others are virulent in particular countries, arising from peculiarities.

Human Longevity.—Of 100,000 male and female children, in the first month they are reduced to 90,396, or nearly a tenth. In the second, to 87,936. In the third, to 86,175. In the fourth, to 84,720. In the fifth, to 83,571. In the sixth, to 82,526, and at the end of the first year to 77,528, the deaths being 2 to 9. The next four years reduce the 77,528 to 62,448, indicating 37,552 deaths before the completion of the fifth year.

At 25 years the 100,000 are half, or 49,995; at 52, one-third. At 58½, a fourth, or 25,000; at 67, a fifth; at 76, a tenth, or 10,000; at 81, a twentieth, or 5,000; and ten attain 100. Children die in large proportions because their diseases cannot be explained, and because the organs are not habituated to the functions of life. The mean of life varies in different countries from 40 to 45. A generation from father to son is about 30 years; of men in general five-sixths die before 70, and fifteen-sixteenths before 80. After 80 it is rather endurance than enjoyment. The nerves are blunted, the senses fail, the muscles are rigid, the softer tubes become hard, the memory fails, the brain ossifies, the affections are buried, and hope ceases. The remaining one-sixteenth die at 80; except a one-thirty-third, at 90. The remainder die from inability to live, at or before 100.

About the age of 36 the lean man usually becomes fatter and the fat man leaner. Again, between the years of 43 and 50 his appetite fails, his complexion fades, and his tongue is apt to be furred on the least exertion of body or mind. At this period his muscles become flabby, his joints weak; his spirits droop, and his sleep is imperfect and unrefreshing. After suffering under these complaints a year, or perhaps two, he starts afresh with renewed vigor, and goes on to 61 or 62, when a similar change takes place, but with aggravated symptoms. When these grand periods have been successively passed, the gravity of incumbent years is more strongly marked, and he begins to boast of his age.

In Russia, much more than in any other country, instances of longevity are numerous, if true. In the report of the Holy Synod, in 1827, during the year 1825, and only among the Greek religion, 848 men had reached upward of 100 years of age; 32 had passed their 120th year, 4 from 130 to 135. Out of 606,818 men who died in 1826, 2,765 were above 90; 1,432 above 95, and 848 above 100 years of age. Among this last number 88 were above 115; 24 more than 120; 7 above 125, and one 130. Riley asserts that Arabs in the Desert live 200 years.

On the average, men have their first-born at 30 and women at 28. The greatest number of deliveries take place between 25 and 35. The greatest number of deliveries take place in the winter months, and in February, and the smallest in July, i. e., to February, as 4 to 5 in towns and 3 to 4 in the country. The night births are to the day as 5 to 4.

Human Strength.—In Schulze's experiments on human strength, he found that men of five feet, weighing 126 lbs., could lift vertically 156 lbs. 8 inches; 217 lbs. 1.2 inches. Others, 6.1 feet, weighing 183 lbs., 156 lbs. 13 inches, and 217 lbs. 6 inches; others 6 feet 3 inches, weighing 158 lbs., 156 lbs. 16 inches, and 217 lbs. 9 inches. By a great variety of experiments he determined the mean human strength at 30 lbs., with a velocity of 2.5 feet per second; or it is equal to the raising half a hogshead 10 feet in a minute.

RULES FOR SPELLING.

Words ending in e drop that letter before the termination *able*, as in move, movable; unless ending in *ce* or *ge*, when it is retained, as in change, changeable, etc.

Words of one syllable, ending in a consonant, with a single vowel before it, double the consonants in derivatives; as, ship, shipping, etc. But if ending in a consonant with a double vowel before it, they do not double the consonant in derivatives; as, troop, trooper, etc.

Words of more than one syllable, ending in a consonant preceded by a single vowel, and accented on the last syllable, double that consonant in derivatives; as, commit, committed; but except chagrin, chagrined.

All words of one syllable ending in l, with a single vowel before it, have ll at the close; as mill, sell.

All words of one syllable ending in l, with a double vowel before it, have only one l at the close; as mail, sail.

The words foretell, distill, instill and fulfill, retain the ll of their primitives. Derivatives of dull, skill, will and full also retain the ll when the accent falls on these words; as dullness, skillfull, willfull, fullness.

Words of more than one syllable ending in l have only one l at the close; as delightful, faithful; unless the accent falls on the last syllable; as befall, etc.

Words ending in l, double the letter in the termination ly.

Participles ending in ing, from verbs ending in e, lose the final e; as have, having; make, making, etc; but verbs ending in ee retain both; as see, seeing. The word dye, to color, however, must retain the e before ing.

All verbs ending in ly, and nouns ending in ment, retain the e final of the primitives; as brave, bravely; refine, refinement; except words ending in dge; as, acknowledge, acknowledgment.

Nouns ending in y, preceded by a vowel, form their plural by adding s; as money, moneys; but if y is preceded by a consonant, it is changed to ies in the plural; as bounty, bounties.

Compound words whose primitives end in y, change the y into i; as beauty, beautiful.

THE USE OF CAPITALS.

Every entire sentence should begin with a capital.

Proper names, and adjectives derived from these, should begin with a capital.

All appellations of the Deity should begin with a capital.

Official and honorary titles should begin with a capital.

Every line of poetry should begin with a capital.

Titles of books and the heads of their chapters and divisions are printed in capitals.

The pronoun I and the exclamation O are always capitals.

The days of the week and the months of the year begin with capitals.

Every quotation should begin with a capital letter.

Names of religious denominations begin with capitals.

In preparing accounts each item should begin with a capital.

Any word of very special importance may begin with a capital.

TWENTY CHOICE COURSE DINNER MENUS.

1. Rice Soup, Baked Pike, Mashed Potatoes, Roast of Beef, Stewed Corn, Chicken Fricassee, Celery Salad, Compote of Oranges, Plain Custard, Cheese, Wafers, Coffee.

2. Mutton Soup, Fried Oysters, Stewed Potatoes, Boiled Corn Beef, Cabbage, Turnips, Roast Pheasants, Onion Salad, Apple Pie, White Custard, Bent's Water Crackers, Cheese, Coffee.

3. Oyster Soup, Roast Mutton, Baked Potatoes, Breaded Veal Cutlets, Tomato Sauce, Baked Celery, Cabbage Salad, Apple Custard, Sponge Cake, Cheese, Coffee.

4. Macaroni Soup, Boiled Chicken, with Oysters, Mutton Chops, Creamed Potatoes, Stewed Tomatoes, Pickled Beets, Peaches and Rice, Plain Cake, Cheese, Coffee.

5. Tapioca Soup, Boiled Halibut, Duchesse Potatoes, Roast Beef Tongue, Canned Peas, Baked Macaroni, with Gravy, Fried Sweet Potatoes, Beet Salad, Cornstarch Pudding, Jelly Tarts, Cheese, Wafers, Coffee.

6. Vegetable Soup, Boiled Trout, Oyster Sauce, Roast Veal, with Dressing, Boiled Potatoes, Stewed Tomatoes, Corn, Egg Salad, Snow Cream, Peach Pie, Sultana Biscuit, Cheese, Coffee.

7. Potato Soup, Oyster Patties, Whipped Potatoes, Roast Mutton, with Spinach, Beets, Fried Parsnips, Egg

Sauce, Celery Salad, Boiled Custard, Lemon Tarts, White Cake, Cheese, Coffee.

8. Veal Soup, Boiled Shad, Caper Sauce, Porterhouse Steak, with Mushrooms, Pigeon Pie, Mashed Potatoes, Pickles, Rice Sponge Cakes, Cheese, Canned Apricots with Cream, Coffee.

9. Giblet Soup, Scalloped Clams, Potato Cakes, Lamb Chops, Canned Beans, Tomatoes, Sweet Potatoes, Salmon Salad, Charlotte Russe, Apricot Tarts, Cheese, Coffee.

10. Vermicelli Soup, Fried Small Fish, Mashed Potatoes, Roast Beef, Minced Cabbage, Chicken Croquettes, Beet Salad, Stewed Pears, Plain Sponge Cake, Cheese, Coffee.

11. Oxtail Soup, Fricasseed Chicken with Oysters, Breaded Mutton Chops, Turnips, Duchesse Potatoes, Chow-chow Salad, Chocolate Pudding, Nut Cake, Cheese, Coffee.

12. Barley Soup, Boiled Trout, Creamed Potatoes, Roast Loin of Veal, Stewed Mushrooms, Broiled Chicken, Lettuce Salad, Fig Pudding, Wafers, Cheese, Coffee.

13. Noodle Soup, Salmon, with Oyster Sauce, Fried Potatoes, Glazed Beef, Boiled Spinach, Parsnips, with Cream Sauce, Celery, Plain Rice Pudding, with Custard Sauce, Current Cake, Cheese, Coffee.

14. Lobster Soup, Baked Ribs of Beef, with Browned Potatoes, Boiled Duck, with Onion Sauce, Turnips, Stewed Tomatoes, Lettuce, Delmonico Pudding, Cheese, Sliced Oranges, Wafers, Coffee.

15. Chicken Broth, Baked Whitefish, Boiled Potatoes, Canned Peas, Mutton Chops, Tomatoes, Beets, Celery Salad, Apple Trifle, Lady Fingers, Cheese, Coffee.

16. Sago Soup, Boiled Leg of Mutton, Caper Sauce, Stewed Potatoes, Canned Corn, Scalloped Oysters, with Cream Sauce, Celery and Lettuce Salad, Marmalade Fritters, Apple Custard, Cheese Cakes, Coffee.

17. Vegetable Soup, Broiled Shad, Lyonnaise Potatoes, Pork Chops, with Sage Dressing, Parsnip Fritters, Macaroni and Gravy, Cauliflower Salad, Rhubarb Tarts, Silver Cake, Cheese, Coffee.

18. Chicken Soup, with Rice, Codfish, Boiled, with Cream Sauce, Roast Veal, Tomatoes, Oyster Salad, Boiled Potatoes, Asparagus, Orange Jelly, White Cake, Cheese, Coffee.

19. Macaroni Soup, Fried Shad, Tomato Sauce, Roast Mutton, Mashed Potatoes, Boiled Tongue, with Mayonnaise Dressing, Fried Parsnips, Canned Beans, Lemon Puffs, Cheese Cakes, Fruit, Coffee.

20. Scotch Broth, Baked Halibut, Boiled Potatoes, Breaded Mutton Chops, Tomato Sauce, Spinach, Bean Salad, Asparagus and Eggs, Peach Batter Pudding, with Sauce, Wafers, Cheese, Coffee.

TERMS USED IN MEDICINE.

Anthelmintics are medicines which have the power of destroying or expelling worms from the intestinal canal.

Antiscorbutics are medicines which prevent or cure the scurvy.

Antispasmodics are medicines given to relieve spasm, or irregular and painful action of the muscles or muscular fibers, as in Epilepsy, St. Vitus' Dance, etc.

Aromatics are medicines which have a grateful smell and agreeable pungent taste.

Astringents are those remedies which, when applied to the body, render the solids dense and firmer.

Carminatives are those medicines which dispel flatulency of the stomach and bowels.

Cathartics are medicines which accelerate the action of the bowels, or increase the discharge by stool.

Demulcents are medicines suited to prevent the action of acrid and stimulating matters upon the mucous membranes of the throat, lungs, etc.

Diaphoretics are medicines that promote or cause perspirable discharge by the skin.

Diuretics are medicines which increase the flow of urine by their action upon the kidneys.

Emetics are those medicines which produce vomiting.

Emmenagogues are medicines which promote the menstrual discharge.

Emollients are those remedies which, when applied to the solids of the body, render them soft and flexible.

Errhines are substances which, when applied to the lining membrane of the nostrils, occasion a discharge of mucous fluid.

Epispastices are those which cause blisters when applied to the surface.

Escharotics are substances used to destroy a portion of the surface of the body, forming sloughs.

Expectorants are medicines capable of facilitating the excretion of mucous from the chest.

Narcotics are those substances having the property of diminishing the action of the nervous and vascular systems, and of inducing sleep.

Rubefacients are remedies which excite the vessels of the skin and increase its heat and redness.

Sedatives are medicines which have the power of allaying the actions of the systems generally, or of lessening the exercise of some particular function.

Sialagogues are medicines which increase the flow of the saliva.

Stimulants are medicines capable of exciting the vital energy, whether as exerted in sensation or motion.

Tonics are those medicines which increase the tone or healthy action, or strength of the living system.

RULES FOR THE PRESERVATION OF HEALTH.

Pure atmospheric air is composed of nitrogen, oxygen and a very small proportion of carbonic acid gas. Air once breathed has lost the chief part of its oxygen, and acquired a proportionate increase of carbonic acid gas. Therefore, health requires that we breathe the same air once only.

The solid part of our bodies is continually wasting and requires to be repaired by fresh substances. Therefore, food, which is to repair the loss, should be taken with due regard to the exercise and waste of the body.

The fluid part of our bodies also wastes constantly; there is but one fluid in animals, which is water. Therefore, water only is necessary, and no artifice can produce a better drink.

The fluid of our bodies is to the solid in proportion as nine to one. Therefore, a like proportion should prevail in the total amount of food taken.

Light exercises an important influence upon the growth and vigor of animals and plants. Therefore, our dwellings should freely admit the sun's rays.

Decomposing animal and vegetable substances yield various noxious gases, which enter the lungs and corrupt the blood. Therefore, all impurities should be kept away from our abodes, and every precaution be observed to secure a pure atmosphere.

Warmth is essential to all the bodily functions. Therefore, an equal bodily temperature should be maintained by exercise, by clothing or by fire.

Exercise warms, invigorates and purifies the body; clothing preserves the warmth the body generates; fire imparts warmth externally. Therefore, to obtain and preserve warmth, exercise and clothing are preferable to fire.

Fire consumes the oxygen of the air, and produces noxious gases. Therefore, the air is less pure in the presence of candles, gas or coal fire, than otherwise, and the deterioration should be repaired by increased ventilation.

The skin is a highly-organized membrane, full of minute pores, cells, blood-vessels, and nerves; it imbibes moisture or throws it off according to the state of the atmosphere or the temperature of the body. It also "breathes," like the lungs (though less actively). All the internal organs sympathize with the skin. Therefore, it should be repeatedly cleansed.

Late hours and anxious pursuits exhaust the nervous system and produce disease and premature death. Therefore, the hours of labor and study should be short.

Mental and bodily exercise are equally essential to the general health and happiness. Therefore, labor and study should succeed each other.

Man will live most happily upon simple solids and fluids, of which a sufficient but temperate quantity should be taken. Therefore, over-indulgence in strong drinks, tobacco, snuff, opium, and all mere indulgences, should be avoided.

Sudden alternations of heat and cold are dangerous (especially to the young and the aged). Therefore, clothing, in quantity and quality, should be adapted to the alternations of night and day, and of the seasons. And therefore, also, drinking cold water when the body is hot, and hot tea and soups when cold are productive of many evils.

Never visit a sick person (especially if the complaint be of a contagious nature) with an empty stomach, as this disposes the system more readily to receive the contagion. And in attending a sick person, place yourself where the air passes from the door or window to the bed of the diseased; not between the diseased person and any fire that is in the room, as the heat of the fire will draw the infectious vapor in that direction.

MOTHER SHIPTON'S PROPHECY.—The lines known as "Mother Shipton's Prophecy" were first published in England in 1485, before the discovery of America, and, of course, before any of the discoveries and inventions mentioned therein. All the events predicted have come to pass except that in the last two lines.

Carriages without horses shall go,
And accidents fill the world with woe
Around the world thoughts shall fly
In the twinkling of an eye.
Waters shall yet more wonders do,
Now strange, yet shall be true.
The world upside down shall be,
And gold be found at root of tree.
Through hills man shall ride,
And no horse nor ass be at his side.
Under water man shall walk,
Shall ride, shall sleep, shall talk.
In the air men shall be seen
In white, in black, in green.
Iron in the water shall float,
As easy as a wooden boat.

Gold shall be found 'mid stone,
In a land that's now unknown.
Fire and water shall wonders do,
England shall at last admit a Jew.
And this world to an end shall come
In eighteen hundred and eighty-one.

CAPTAIN KIDD, a notorious American pirate, was born about 1650. In 1696 he was entrusted by the British Government with the command of a privateer, and sailed from New York, for the purpose of suppressing the numerous pirates then infesting the seas. He went to the East Indies, where he began a career of piracy, and returned to New York in 1698 with a large amount of booty. He was soon after arrested, sent to England for trial, and executed in 1701.

VALUE OF OLD AMERICAN COINS.—1793—Half cent, 75 cents; one cent, $2. 1794—Half cent, 20 cents, one cent, 10 cents; five cents, $1.25; fifty cents, $3; one dollar, $10. 1795—Half cent, 5 cents; one cent, 5 cents; five cents, 25 cents; fifty cents, 55 cents; one dollar, $1.25. 1796—Half cent, $5; one cent, 10 cents; five cents $1; ten cents, 50 cents; twenty-five cents, $1; fifty cents, $10; one dollar, $1.50. 1797—Half cent, 5 cents; one cent, 5 cents; five cents, 50 cents; ten cents, $1; fifty cents, $10; one dollar, $1.50. 1798—One cent, 5 cents; ten cents, $1; one dollar, $1.50. 1799—One cent, $5; one dollar, $1.60. 1800—Half cent, 5 cents; one cent, 3 cents; five cents, 25 cents; ten cents 1; one dollar, $1.10. 1801—One cent, 3 cents; five cents, $1; ten cents, $1; fifty cents, $2; one dollar, $1.25. 1802—Half cent, 50 cents; one cent, 2 cents; ten cents, $1; fifty cents, $2; one dollar, $1.25. 1803—Half cent, 2 cents; one cent, 2 cents; five cents, $10; ten cents, 1; one dollar, $1.10. 1804—Half cent, 2 cents; one cent, $2; five cents, 75 cents; ten cents, $2; twenty-five cents, 75 cents; one dollar, $100. 1805—Half cent, 2 cents; one cent, 3 cents; five cents, $1.50; ten cents, 25 cents. 1806—Half cent, 2 cents; one cent, 3 cents. 1807—Half cent, 2 cents; one cent, 3 cents; ten cents, 25 cents. 1808—Half cent, 2 cents; one cent, 5 cents. 1809—Half cent, 1 cent; one cent, 25 cents; ten cents, 50 cents. 1810—Half cent, 5 cents; one cent, 5 cents. 1811—Half cent, 25 cents; one cent, 10 cents; ten cents, 50 cents. 1812—One cent, 2 cents. 1813—One cent, 5 cents. 1815—Fifty cents, $5. 1821—One cent, 5 cents. 1822—Ten cents, $1. 1823—One cent, 5 cents; twenty-five cents, $10. 1824—Twenty-five cents, 40 cents. 1825—Half cent, 2 cents. 1826—Half cent, 2 cents; one cent, 50 cents. 1827—One cent, 3 cents; twenty-five cents, $10. 1828—Half cent, 1 cent; twenty-five cents, 30 cents. 1829—Half cent, 2 cents. 1830—Half cent, 2 cents. 1832-'33-'34—Half cent, 2 cents. 1835—Half cent, 1 cent. 1836—Fifty cents, $3; one dollar, $3. 1838—Ten cents, 25 cents. 1839—One dollar, $10. 1846—Five cents, 50 cents. 1849-'50—Half cent, 5 cents. 1851—Half cent, 1 cent; twenty-five cents, 30 cents; one dollar, $10.90. 1852—Twenty-five cents, 30 cents; fifty cents, $2; one dollar, $10. 1853—Half cent, 1 cent; twenty cents (with no arrows), $2.50; one dollar, $1.25. 1854—Half cent, 2 cents; one dollar, $2. 1855-'57—Half cent, 5 cents; one dollar, $1.50. 1856—Half cent, 5 cents; one dollar, $1.50. 1858—One dollar, $10. 1863-'4-'5—Three cents, 25 cents. 1866—Half cent, 6 cents; three cents, 25 cents; five cents, 10 cents; twenty-five cents, 30 cents. 1867—Three cents, 25 cents; five cents, 10 cents. 1868-'9—Three cents, 25 cents. 1870—Three cents, 15 cents. 1871—Two cents, 10 cents; three cents, 25 cents. 1873—Two cents, 50 cents; three cents, 50 cents. 1877-'8—Twenty cents, $1.50. These prices are for good ordinary coins without holes. Fine specimens are worth more.

LEANING TOWER OF PISA.—The leaning tower of Pisa was commenced in 1152, and was not finished till the fourteenth century. The cathedral to which this belongs was erected to celebrate a triumph of the Pisans in the harbor of Palermo in 1063, when allied with the Normans to drive the Saracens out of Sicily. It is a circular building, one hundred feet in diameter and 179 feet in extreme height, and has fine mosaic pavements, elaborately carved columns, and numerous bas-reliefs. The building is of white marble. The tower is divided into eight stories, each having an outside gallery of seven feet projection, and the topmost story overhangs the base about sixteen feet, though, as the center of gravity is still ten feet within the base, the building is perfectly safe. It has been supposed that this inclination was intentional, but the opinion that the foundation has sunk is no doubt correct. It is most likely that the defective foundation became perceptible before the tower had reached one-half its height, as at that elevation the unequal length of the columns exhibits an endeavor to restore the perpendicular, and at about the same place the walls are strengthened with iron bars.

What causes the water to flow out of an artesian well?—The theoretical explanation of the phenomenon is easily understood. The secondary and tertiary geological formations often present the appearance of immense basins, the boundary or rim of the basin having been formed by an upheaval of adjacent strata. In these formations it often happens that a porous stratum, consisting of sand, sandstone, chalk or other calcareous matter, is included between two impermeable layers of clay, so as to form a flat porus U tube, continuous from side to side of the valley, the outcrop on the surrounding hills forming the mouth of the tube. The rain filtering down through the porous layer to the bottom of the basin forms there a subterranean pool, which, with the liquid or semi-liquid column pressing upon it, constitutes a sort of huge natural hydrostatic bellows. Sometimes the pressure on the superincumbent crust is so great as to cause an upheaval or disturbance of the valley. It is obvious, then, that when a hole is bored down through the upper impermeable layer to the surface of the lake, the water will be forced up by the natural law of water seeking its level to a height above the surface of the valley, greater or less, according to the elevation of the level in the feeding column, thus forming a natural mountain on precisely the same principle as that of most artificial fountains, where the water supply comes from a considerable height above the jet.

HOW MANY CUBIC FEET THERE ARE IN A TON OF COAL.—There is a difference between a ton of hard coal and one of soft coal. For that matter, coal from different mines, whether hard or soft, differs in weight, and consequently in cubic measure, according to quality. Then there is a difference according to size. To illustrate, careful measurements have been made of Wilkesbarre anthracite, a fine quality of hard coal, with the following results:

Size of coal.	Cubic feet in ton of 2,240 lbs.	Cubic feet in ton of 2,000 lbs.
Lump	33.2	28.8
Broken	33.9	30.3
Egg	34.5	30.8
Stone	34.8	31.1
Chestnut	35.7	31.9
Pea	36.7	32.8

For soft coal the following measures may be taken as nearly correct; it is simply impossible to determine any exact rule, even for bituminous coal of the same district: Briar Hill coal, 44.8 cubic feet per ton of 2,240 pounds; Pittsburgh, 47.8; Wilmington, Ill., 47; Indiana block coal, 42 to 43 cubic feet.

The dimensions of the great wall of China and of what it is built.—It runs from a point on the Gulf of Liantung, an arm of the Gulf of Pechili in Northeastern China, westerly to the Yellow River; thence makes a great bend to the south for nearly 100 miles, and then runs to the northwest for several hundred miles to the Desert of Gobi. Its length is variously estimated to be from 1,250 to 1,500 miles. For the most of this distance it runs through a mountainous country, keeping on the ridges, and winding over many of the highest peaks. In some places it is only a formidable rampart, but most of the way it is composed of lofty walls of masonry and concrete, or impacted lime and clay, from 12 to 16 feet in thickness, and from 15 to 30 or 35 feet in height. The top of this wall is paved for hundreds of miles, and crowned with crenallated battlements, and towers 30 to 40 feet high. In numerous places the wall climbs such steep declivities that its top ascends from height to height in flights of granite steps. An army could march on the top of the wall for weeks and even months, moving in some places ten men abreast.

Limits of Natural Vision.—This question is too indefinite for a specific answer. The limits of vision vary with elevation, conditions of the atmosphere, intensity of illumination, and other modifying elements in different cases. In a clear day an object one foot above a level plain may be seen at the distance of 1.31 miles; one ten feet high, 4.15 miles; one twenty feet high, 5.86 miles; one 100 feet high, 13.1 miles; one a mile high, as the top of a mountain, 95.23 miles. This allows seven inches (or, to be exact, 6.99 inches) for the curvature of the earth, and assumes that the size and illumination of the object are sufficient to produce an image. Five miles may be taken as the extreme limit at which a man is visible on a flat plain to an observer on the same level.

THE NIAGARA SUSPENSION BRIDGE.—For seven miles below the falls, Niagara river flows through a gorge varying in width from 200 to 400 yards. Two miles below the falls the river is but 350 feet wide, and it is here that the great suspension bridge, constructed in 1855 by Mr. Roebling, crosses the gorge, 245 feet above the water. The length of the span, from tower to tower, is 821 feet, and the total length of the bridge is 2,220 feet. The length of the span, which is capable of sustaining a strain of 10,000 tons, is 821 feet from tower to tower, and the total length of the bridge is 2,220 feet. It is used both for railway and wagon traffic, the wagon-road and foot-way being directly under the railway bed. There is another suspension bridge across the Niagara river at a distance of only about fifty rods from the falls, on the American side. This is only for carriages and foot travel. It was finished in 1869. It is 1,190 feet long from cliff to cliff, 1,268 feet from tower to tower, and 190 feet above the river, which at this point is a little over 900 feet in width.

THE SPEED OF SOUND.—It has been ascertained that a full human voice, speaking in the open air, calm, can be heard at a distance of 460 feet; in an observable breeze a, powerful human voice with the wind is audible at a distance of 15,840 feet; the report of a musket, 16,000 feet; a drum, 10,560 feet; music, a strong brass band, 15,840 feet; very heavy cannonading, 575,000 feet, or 90 miles. In the Arctic regions conversation has been maintained over water a distance of 6,766 feet. In gases the velocity of sound increases with the temperature; in air this increase is about two feet per second for each degree centigrade. The velocity of sound in oxygen gas at zero C. is 1,040 feet; in carbonic acid, 858 feet; in hydrogen, 4,164 feet. In 1827 Colladon and Sturm determined experimentally the velocity of sound in fresh water; the experiment was made in the Lake of Geneva, and it was found to be 4,174 feet per second at a temperature of 15 degrees C.

The velocity of sound in alcohol at 20 degrees C. is 4,218 feet; in ether at zero, 3,801; in sea water at 20 degrees C., 4,768. By direct measurements, carefully made, by observing at night the interval which elapses between the flash and report of a cannon at a known distance, the velocity of sound has been about 1,090 per second at the temperature of freezing water.

DESCRIPTION OF THE YELLOWSTONE PARK.—The Yellowstone National Park extends sixty-five miles north and south, and fifty-five miles east and west, comprising 3,575 square miles, and is all 6,000 feet or more above sea-level. Yellowstone Lake, twenty miles by fifteen, has an altitude of 7,788 feet. The mountain ranges which hem in the valleys on every side rise to the height of 10,000 to 12,000 feet, and are always covered with snow. This great park contains the most striking of all the mountains, gorges, falls, rivers and lakes in the whole Yellowstone region. The springs on Gardiner's River cover an area of about one square mile, and three or four square miles thereabout are occupied by the remains of springs which have ceased to flow. The natural basins into which these springs flow are from four to six feet in diameter and from one to four feet in depth. The principal ones are located upon terraces midway up the sides of the mountain. The banks of the Yellowstone River abound with ravines and canons, which are carved out of the heart of the mountains through the hardest of rocks. The most remarkable of these is the canon of Tower Creek and Column Mountain. The latter, which extends along the eastern bank of the river for upward of two miles, is said to resemble the Giant's Causeway. The canon of Tower Creek is about ten miles in length and is so deep and gloomy that it is called "The Devil's Den." Where Tower Creek ends the Grand Canon begins. It is twenty miles in length, impassable throughout, and inaccessible at the water's edge, except at a few points. Its rugged edges are from 200 to 500 yards apart, and its depth is so profound that no sound ever reaches the ear from the bottom. The Grand Canon contains a great multitude of hot springs of sulphur, sulphate of copper, alum, etc. In the number and magnitude of its hot springs and geysers, the Yelowstone Park surpasses all the rest of the world. There are probably fifty geysers that throw a column of water to the height of from 50 to 200 feet, and it is stated that there are not fewer than 5,000 springs; there are two kinds, those depositing lime and those depositing silica. The temperature of the calcareous springs is from 160 to 170 degrees, while that of the others rises to 200 or more. The principal collections are the upper and lower geyser basins of the Madison River, and the calcareous springs on Gardiner's River. The great falls are marvels to which adventurous travelers have gone only to return and report that they are parts of the wonders of this new American wonderland.

DESIGNATIONS OF GROUPS OF ANIMALS.—The ingenuity of the sportsman is, perhaps, no better illustrated than by the use he puts the English language to in designating particular groups of animals. The following is a list of the terms which have been applied to the various classes:

A covey of partidges, A nide of pheasants, A wisp of snipe, A flight of doves or swallows, A muster of peacocks, A siege of herons, A building of rooks, A brood of grouse, A plump of wild fowl, A stand of plovers, A watch of nightingales, A clattering of choughs, A flock of geese, A herd or bunch of cattle, A bevy of quails, A cast of hawks, A trip of dottrell, A swarm of bees, A school of whales, A shoal of herrings, A herd of swine, A skulk of foxes, A pack of wolves, A drove of oxen, A sounder of hogs, A troop of monkeys, A pride of lions, A sleuth of bears, A gang of elk.

THE BUNKER HILL MONUMENT.—The monument is a square shaft, built of Quincy granite, 221 feet high, 31 feet square at the base and 15 at the top. Its foundations are inclosed 12 feet under ground. Inside the shaft is a round, hollow cone, 7 feet wide at the bottom and 4 feet 2 inches at the top, encircled by a winding staircase of 224 stone steps, which leads to a chamber immediately under the apex, 11 feet in diameter. The chamber has four windows, which afford a wide view of the surrounding country, and contains two cannons, named respectively Hancock and Adams, which were used in many engagements during the war. The corner-stone of the monument was laid on the fiftieth anniversary of the battle, June 17, 1825, by Lafayette, who was then visiting America, when Webster pronounced the oration. The monument was completed, and June 17, 1843, was dedicated, Webster again delivering the oration.

THE SEVEN WISE MEN OF GREECE.—The names generally given are Solon, Chilo, Pittacus, Bias, Periander (in place of whom some give Epimenides), Cleobulus, and Thales. They were the authors of the celebrated mottoes inscribed in later days in the Delphian Temple. These mottoes were as follows:

"Know thyself."—Solon.
"Consider the end."—Chilo.
"Know thy opportunity."—Pittacus.
"Most men are bad."—Bias.
"Nothing is impossible to industry."—Periander.
"Avoid excesses."—Cleobulus.
"Suretyship is the precursor of ruin."—Thales.

FIRST STEAMBOAT ON THE MISSISSIPPI.—Nicholas J. Roosevelt was the first to take a steamboat down the great river. His boat was built at Pittsburgh, in the year 1811, under an arrangement with Fulton and Livingston, from Fulton's plans. It was called the "New Orleans," was about 200 tons burden, and was propelled by a stern-wheel, assisted, when the wind was favorable, by sails carried on two masts. The hull was 138 feet long, 30 feet beam, and the cost of the whole, including engines, was about $40,-000. The builder, with his family, an engineer, a pilot, and six "deck hands," left Pittsburgh in October, 1811, reaching Louisville in about seventy hours (steaming about ten miles an hour), and New Orleans in fourteen days, steaming from Natchez.

THE EXPLORATIONS OF FREMONT.—Among the earliest efforts of Fremont, after he had tried and been sickened by the sea, were his experiences as a surveyor and engineer on railroad lines from Charleston to Augusta, Ga., and Charleston to Cincinnati. Then he accompanied an army detachment on a military reconnoissance of the mountainous Cherokee country in Georgia, North Carolina and Tennessee, made in the depth of winter. In 1838-9 he accompanied M. Nicollet in explorations of the country between the Missouri and the British line, and his first detail of any importance, after he had been commissioned by President Van Buren, was to make an examination of the river Des Moines, then on the Western frontier. In 1841 he projected his first trans-continental expedition, and left Washington May 2, 1842, and accomplished the object of his trip, examined the South Pass, explored the Wind River mountains, ascended in August, the highest peak of that range, now known as Fremont's Peak, and returned, after an absence of four months. His report of the expedition attracted great attention in the United States and abroad. Fremont began to plan another and a second expedition. He determined to extend his explorations across the continent; and in May, 1843, commenced his journey with thirty-nine men, and September 6, after traveling over 1,700 miles, arrived at the Great Salt Lake; there made some important discoveries, and then pushed on to the upper Columbia, down whose valley he proceeded to Fort Vancouver, near its mouth. On Nov. 10, he set out to return East, selecting a southeasterly course, leading from the lower part of the Columbia to the upper Colorado, through an almost unknown region, crossed by high and rugged mountains. He and his party suffered incredible hardships in crossing from the Great Basin to Sutter's Fort on the Sacramento; started from there March 24, proceeded southward, skirted the western base of the Sierra Nevada, crossed that range through a gap, entered the Great Basin; again visited the Great Salt Lake, from which they returned through the South Pass to Kansas, in July, 1844, after an absence of fourteen months. In the spring of 1845 Fremont set out on a third expedition to explore the Great Basin and the maritime region of Oregon and California; spent the summer examining the headwaters of the rivers whose springs are in the grand divide of the continent; in October camped on the shores of the Great Salt Lake: proceeded to explore the Sierra Nevada, which he again crossed in the dead of winter; made his way into the Valley of the San Joaquin; obtained permission, at Monterey, from the Mexican authorities there, to proceed with his expedition, which permission was almost immediately revoked, and Fremont peremptorily ordered to leave the country without delay, but he refused, and a collision was imminent, but was averted, and Fremont proceeded toward San Joaquin. Near Tlamath Lake, Fremont met, May 9, 1846, a party in search of him, with dispatches from Washington, ordering him to watch over the interests of the United States in California, as there was reason to believe that province would be transferred to Great Britain. He at once returned to California; General Castro was already marching against our settlements; the settlers rose in arms, flocked to Fremont's camp, and, with him as leader, in less than a month, all Northern California was freed from Mexican authority; and on July 4 Fremont was elected Governor of California by the American settlers. Later came the conflict between Commodore Stockton and General Kearney; and Fremont resigned his commission as Lieutenant-Colonel, to which he had been promoted. In October, 1848, he started across the continent on a fourth expedition, outfitted at his own expense, to find a practicable route to California. In attempting to cross the great Sierra, covered with snow, his guide lost his way, and the party encountered horrible suffering from cold and hunger, a portion of them being driven to cannibalism; he lost all his animals (he had 120 mules when he started), and one-third of his men (he had thirty-three) perished, and he had to retrace his steps to Santa Fe. He again set out, with thirty men, and, after a long search, discovered a secure route, which led to the Sacramento, where he arrived in the spring of 1849. He led a fifth expedition across the continent in 1853, at his own expense, and found passes through the mountains in the line of latitude 38 deg., 39 min., and reached California after enduring great hardships; for fifty days his party lived on horse-flesh, and for forty-eight hours at a time without food of any kind. These are the barest outlines of five expeditions of which many volumes have been written, but will hint at Fremont's work in the West which entitled him to the name of the "Pathfinder."

CHINESE PROVERBS.—The Chinese are indeed remarkably fond of proverbs. They not only employ them in conversation—and even to a greater degree than the Spaniards, who are noted among Europeans for the number and excellence of their proverbial sayings—but they have a practice of adorning their reception rooms with these sententious bits of wisdom, inscribed on decorated scrolls or embroidered on rich crapes and brocades. They carve them on door-posts and pillars, and emblazon them on the walls and ceilings in gilt letters. The following are a few specimens of this sort of literature: As a sneer at the use of unnecessary force to crush a contemptible enemy, they say: "He rides a fierce dog to catch a lame rabbit." Similar to this is another, "To use a battle-ax to cut off a hen's head." They say of wicked associates: "To cherish a bad man is like nourishing a tiger; if not well-fed he will devour you." Here are several others mingling wit with wisdom: "To instigate a villain to do wrong is like teaching a monkey to climb trees;" "To catch fish and throw away the net," which recalls our saying, "Using the cat's paw to pull the chestnuts out of the fire;" "To climb a tree to catch a fish" is to talk much to no purpose; "A superficial scholar is a sheep dressed in a tiger's skin;" "A cuckoo in a magpie's nest," equivalent to saying, "he is enjoying another's labor without compensation;" "If the blind lead the blind they will both fall into the pit;" "A fair wind raises no storm;" "Vast chasms can be filled, but the heart of man is never satisfied;" "The body may be healed, but the mind is incurable;" "He seeks the ass, and lo! he sits upon him;" "He who looks at the sun is dazzled; he who hears the thunder is deafened," i. e., do not come too near the powerful; "Prevention is better than cure;" "Wine and good dinners make abundance of friends, but in adversity not one of them is to be found." "Let every man sweep the snow from before his own door, and not trouble himself about the frost on his neighbor's tiles." The following one is a gem of moral wisdom: "Only correct yourself on the same principle that you correct others, and excuse others on the same principles on which you excuse yourself." "Better not be, than be nothing." "One thread does not make a rope; one swallow does not make a summer." "Sensuality is the chief of sins, filial duty the best of acts." "The horse's back is not so safe as the buffalo's"—the former is used by the politician, the latter by the farmer. "Too much lenity multiplies crime." "If you love your son give him plenty of the rod; if you hate him cram him with dainties." "He is my teacher who tells me my faults, he my enemy who speaks my virtues." Having a wholesome dread of litigation, they say of one who goes to law, "He sues a flea to catch a bite." Their equivalent for our "coming out at the little end of the horn" is, "The farther the rat creeps up (or into) the cow's horn, the narrower it grows." The truth of their saying that "The fame of good deeds does not leave a man's door, but his evil acts are known a thousand miles off," is illustrated in our own daily papers every morning. Finally, we close this list with a Chinese proverb which should be inscribed on the lintel of every door in Christendom: "The happy-hearted man carries joy for all the household."

MASON AND DIXON'S LINE.—Mason and Dixon's line is the concurrent State line of Maryland and Pennsylvania. It is named after two eminent astronomers and mathemeticians, Charles Mason and Jeremiah Dixon, who were sent out from England to run it. They completed the survey between 1763 and 1767, excepting thirty-six miles surveyed in 1782 by Colonel Alex. McLean and Joseph Neville. It is in the latitude of 39 deg. 43 min. 26.3 sec.

GREAT FIRES OF HISTORY.—The loss of life and property in the willful destruction by fire and sword of the principal cities of ancient history—Nineveh, Babylon, Persepolis, Carthage, Palmyra, and many others—is largely a matter of conjecture. The following is a memorandum of the chief conflagrations of the current era:

In 64, A. D., during the reign of Nero, a terrible fire raged in Rome for eight days, destroying ten of the fourteen wards. The loss of life and destruction of property is not known.

In 70, A. D., Jerusalem was taken by the Romans and a large part of it given to the torch, entailing an enormous destruction of life and property.

In 1106 Venice, then a city of immense opulence, was almost wholly consumed by a fire, originating in accident or incendiarism.

In 1212 the greater part of London was burned.

In 1666 what is known as the Great Fire of London raged in the city from September 2 to 6, consuming 13,200 houses, with St. Paul's Church, 86 parish churches, 6 chapels, the Guild Hall, the Royal Exchange, the Custom House, 52 companies halls, many hospitals, libraries and other public edifices. The total destruction of property was estimated at $53,652,500. Six lives were lost, and 436 acres burnt over.

In 1679 a fire in Boston burned all the warehouses, eighty dwellings, and vessels in the dock-yards; loss estimated at $1,000,000.

In 1700 a large part of Edinburgh was burned; loss unknown.

In 1728 Copenhagen was nearly destroyed; 1,650 houses burned.

In 1736 a fire in St. Petersburg burned 2,000 houses.

In 1729 a fire in Constantinople destroyed 12,000 houses, and 7,000 people perished. The same city suffered a conflagration in 1745, lasting five days; and in 1750 a series of three appalling fires: one in January, consuming 10,000 houses; another in April destroying property to the value of $5,000,000, according to one historian, and according to another, $15,000,000; and in the latter part of the year another, sweeping fully 10,000 houses more out of existence. It seemed as if Constantinople was doomed to utter annihilation.

In 1751 a fire in Stockholm destroyed 1,000 houses and another fire in the same city in 1759 burned 250 houses with a loss of $2,420,000.

In 1752 a fire in Moscow swept away 18,000 houses, involving an immense loss.

In 1758 Christiania suffered a loss of $1,250,000 by conflagration.

In 1760 the Portsmouth (England) dock yards were burned, with a loss of $2,000,000.

In 1764 a fire in Konigsburg, Prussia, consumed the public buildings, with a loss of $3,000,000; and in 1769 the city was almost totally destroyed.

In 1763 a fire in Smyrna destroyed 2,600 houses, with a loss of $1,000,000; in 1772 a fire in the same city carried off 3,000 dwellings and 3,000 to 4,000 shops, entailing a loss of $20,000,000; and in 1796 there were 4,000 shops, mosques, magazines, etc., burned.

In 1776, six days after the British seized the city, a fire swept off all the west side of New York city, from Broadway to the river.

In 1771 a fire in Constantinople burned 2,500 houses; another in 1778 burned 2,000 houses; in 1782 there were 600 houses burned in February, 7,000 in June, and on August 12 during a conflagration that lasted three days, 10,000 houses, 50 mosques, and 100 corn-mills, with a loss of 100 lives. Two years later a fire, on March 13, destroyed two-thirds of Pera, the loveliest suburb of Constantinople, and on August 5 a fire in the main city, lasting twenty-six hours, burned 10,000 houses. In this same fire-scourged city, in 1791, between March and July, there were 32,000 houses burned, and about as many more in 1795; and in 1799 Pera was again swept with fire, with a loss of 13,000 houses, including many buildings of great magnificence.

In 1784 a fire and explosion in the dock yards, Brest, caused a loss of $5,000,000.

But the greatest destruction of life and property by conflagration, of which the world has anything like accurate records, must be looked for within the current century. Of these the following is a partial list of instances in which the loss of property amounted to $3,000,000 and upward:

Dates. Cities.	Property destroyed.
1802—Liverpool	$5,000,000
1803—Bombay	3,000,600
1805—St. Thomas	30,000,000
1808—Spanish Town	7,500,000
1812—Moscow, burned five days; 30,800 houses destroyed	150,000,000
1816—Constantinople, 12,000 dwellings, 3,000 shops	......
1820—Savannah	4,000,000
1822—Canton nearly destroyed	......
1828—Havana, 350 houses	......
1835—New York ("Great Fire")	15,000,000
1837—St. Johns, N. B.	5,000,000
1838—Charleston, 1,158 buildings	3,000,000
1841—Smyrna, 12,000 houses	......
1842—Hamburg, 4,219 buildings, 100 lives lost	35,000,000
1845—New York, 35 persons killed	7,500,000
1845—Pittsburgh, 1,100 buildings	10,000,000
1845—Quebec, May 28, 1,650 dwellings	3,750,000
1845—Quebec, June 28, 1,300 dwellings	......
1846—St. Johns, Newfoundland	5,000,000
1848—Constantinople, 2,500 buildings	15,000,000
1848—Albany, N. Y., 600 houses	3,000,000
1849—St. Louis	3,000,000
1851—St. Louis, 2,500 buildings	11,000,000
1851—St. Louis, 500 buildings	3,000,000
1851—San Francisco, May 4 and 5, many lives lost	10,000,000
1851—San Francisco, June	3,000,000
1852—Montreal, 1,200 buildings	5,000,000
1861—Mendoza destroyed by eartquake and fire, 10,000 lives lost	......
1862—St. Petersburg	5,000,000
1862—Troy, N. Y., nearly destroyed	......
1862—Valparaiso almost destroyed	......
1864—Novgorod, immense destruction of property	......
1865—Constantinople, 2,800 buildings burned	......
1866—Yokohama, nearly destroyed	......
1865—Carlstadt, Sweden, all consumed but Bishop's residence, hospital and jail; 10 lives lost	......
1866—Portland, Me., half the city	11,000,000
1866—Quebec, 2,500 dwellings, 17 churches	......
1870—Constantinople, Pera, suburb	26,000,000
1871—Chicago—250 lives lost, 17,430 buildings burned, on 2,124 acres	192,000,000
1871—Paris, fired by the Commune	160,000,000
1872—Boston	75,000,000
1873—Yeddo, 10,000 houses	......
1877—Pittsburgh, caused by riot	3,260,000
1877—St. Johns, N. B., 1,650 dwellings, 18 lives lost	12,500,000

From the above it appears that the five greatest fires on record, reckoned by destruction of property, are:

Chicago fire, of Oct. 8 and 9, 1871	$192,000,000
Paris fires, of May, 1871	160,000,000
Moscow fire, of Sept. 14-19, 1812	150,000,000
Boston fire, Nov. 9-10, 1872	75,000,000
London fire, Sept. 2-6, 1666	53,652,500
Hamburg fire, May 5-7, 1842	35,000,000

Taking into account, with the fires of Paris and Chicago, the great Wisconsin and Michigan forest fires of 1871, in which it is estimated that 1,000 human beings perished and property to the amount of over $3,000,000 was consumed, it is plain that in the annals of conflagrations that year stands forth in gloomy pre-eminence.

WEALTH OF THE UNITED STATES PER CAPITA.—The following statistics represent the amount of taxable property, real and personal, in each State and Territory, and also the amount per capita:

	Total.	Per capita.
Maine	$235,978,716	362.09
New Hampshire	164,755,181	474.81
Vermont	86,806,755	261,24
Massachusetts	1,584,756,802	888.77
Rhode Island	252,536,673	913.23
Connecticut	327,177,385	525.41
New Jersey	572,518,361	506.06
New York	2,651,940,000	521.74
Pennsylvania	1,683,459,016	393.08
Delaware	59,951,643	408.92
Maryland	497,307,675	533.07
District of Columbia	99,401,787	845.08
Virginia	308,455,135	203.92
West Virginia	139,622,705	225.75
North Carolina	156,100,202	111.52
South Carolina	153,560,135	154.24
Georgia	239,472,599	155.82
Florida	30,938,309	114.80
Alabama	122,867,228	97.32
Mississippi	110,628,129	97.76
Louisiana	160,162,439	170.39
Texas	320,364,515	201.26
Arkansas	86,409,364	176.71
Kentucky	350,563,971	212.63
Tennessee	211,778,538	137.30
Ohio	1,534,360,508	479.77
Indiana	727,815,131	367.89
Illinois	786,616,394	255.24
Michigan	517,666,359	316.23
Wisconsin	438,971,751	333.69
Iowa	398,671,251	245.39
Minnesota	258,028,687	330.48
Missouri	432,795,801	245.72
Kansas	160,891,689	161.52
Nebraska	90,585,782	200.23
Colorado	74,471,693	383.22
Nevada	29,291,459	470.40
Oregon	52,522,084	300.52
California	584,578,036	676.05
Arizona	9,270,214	229.23
Dakota	20,321,530	150.33
Idaho	6,440,876	197.51
Montana	18,609,802	475.23
New Mexico	11,362,406	95.04
Utah	24,775,279	172.09
Washington	23,810,603	316.98
Wyoming	13,621,829	655,24
Total	$16,902,993,543	337.00

TABLE FOR MEASURING AN ACRE.—To measure an acre in rectangular form is a simple question in arithmetic. One has only to divide the total number of square yards in an acre, 4,840, by the number of yards in the known side or breadth to find the unkown side in yards. By this process it appears that a rectangular strip of ground—

5 yards wide by 968 yards long is 1 acre.
10 yards wide by 484 yards long is 1 acre.
20 yards wide by 242 yards long is 1 acre.
40 yards wide by 121 yards long is 1 acre.
80 yards wide by 60½ yards long is 1 acre.
70 yards wide by 69½ yards long is 1 acre.
60 yards wide by 80⅔ yards long is 1 acre.

THE LANGUAGE OF GEMS.—The language of the various precious stones is as follows:

Moss Agate—Health, prosperity and long life.
Amethyst—Prevents violent passions.
Bloodstone—Courage, wisdom and firmness in affection.
Chrysolite—Frees from evil passions and sadness.
Emerald—Insures true love, discovers false.
Diamonds—Innocence, faith and virgin purity, friends.
Garnet—Constancy and fidelity in every engagement.
Opal—Sharpens the sight and faith of the possessor.
Pearl—Purity; gives clearness to physical and mental sight.
Ruby—Corrects evils resulting from mistaken friendship.
Sapphire—Repentance; frees from enchantment.
Sardonyx—Insures conjugal felicity.
Topaz—Fidelity and friendship; prevents bad dreams.
Turquoise—Insures prosperity in love.

GREAT SALT LAKE AND THE DEAD SEA.—Great Salt Lake is a shallow body of water, its average depth being but a little more than three feet, while in many parts it is much less. The water is transparent, but excessively salt; it contains about 22 per cent of common salt, slightly mixed with other salts, and forming one of the purest and most concentrated brines in the world. Its specific gravity is 1.17. The water is so buoyant that a man may float in it at full length upon his back, having his head and neck, his legs to the knee, and both arms to the elbow, entirely out of water. If he assumes a sitting posture, with his arms extended, his shoulders will rise above the water. Swimming, however, is difficult as the lower limbs tend to rise above the surface, and the brine is so strong that to swallow even a very little of it will cause strangulation. The waters of the Dead Sea, on the other hand, are nearly black, and contain much sulphur and bitumen, as well as salt. It is also very deep, varying from thirteen feet near the south end of the lake to more than 1,300 feet in the northern part. Its buoyancy is quite equal to that of Great Salt Lake, for travelers say that a man can float prone upon the surface for hours without danger of sinking, and in a sitting position is held breast-high above the water.

SOME FAMOUS WAR SONGS.—The slavery war developed several Union song-writers whose stirring verses have kept on singing themselves since the close of that great struggle. Two among them are best remembered nowadays, both men who wrote the words and composed the music to their own verses. Chicago lays claim to one, Dr. George F. Root, and Boston to the other, Henry C. Work. The song "Marching Through Georgia," as every one knows, was written in memory of Sherman's famous march from Atlanta to the sea, and words and music were the composition of Henry C. Work, who died not many months ago (in 1884). The first stanza is as follows:

Bring the good old bugle, boys, we'll sing another song—
Sing it with spirit that will start the world along—
Sing it as we used to sing it, fifty thousand strong,
While we were marching through Georgia.

Chorus—
"Hurrah! hurrah! we bring the jubilee!
Hurrah! hurrah! the flag that makes you free!"
So we sang the chorus from Atlanta to the sea,
While we were marching through Georgia.

Among the other songs of Work the following are best known: "Kingdom Coming," or "Say, Darkey, Hab You Seen de Massa?" "Babylon is Fallen," "Grafted into the Army" and "Corporal Schnapps." This record would be incomplete were we to fail to mention some of the many ringing songs of George F. Root, songs which have made the name of Root famous in thousands upon thousands of households in the West. Some of these songs are: "Battle Cry of Freedom," "Tramp, Tramp, Tramp," "On, on, on, the Boys Came Marching," "Just Before the Battle, Mother," "Just After the Battle," "Lay Me Down and Save the Flag," "Stand Up for Uncle Sam, My Boys." The well known song, "Wrap the Flag Around Me, Boys," was composed by R. Stewart Taylor, and "When Johnny Comes Marching Home" by Louis Lambert.

THE COST OF ROYALTY IN ENGLAND.—Her Majesty:

Privy purse.................................£60,000	
Salaries of household................131,260	
Expenses of household.............172,500	
Royal bounty, etc....................13,200	
Unappropriated.....................8,040——	
	£385,000
Prince of Wales...............................	40,000
Princess of Wales............................	10,000
Crown Princess of Prussia.....................	8,000
Duke of Edinburgh............................	25,000
Princess Christian of Schleswig-Holstein.......	6,000
Princess Louise (Marchioness of Lorne).........	6,000
Duke of Connaught..........................	25,000
Duke of Albany..............................	25,000
Duchess of Cambridge.......................	6,000
Duchess of Mecklenburg-Strelitz.............	3,000
Duke of Cambridge..........................	12,000
Duchess of Teck............................	5,000

SOME GREAT RIVERS.—From Haswell's little work for engineers and mechanics the following figures are taken, showing the lengths of the largest rivers on the various continents:

EUROPE.		SOUTH AMERICA.	
Name.	Miles.	Name.	Miles.
Volga, Russia........	2,500	Amazon and Beni....	4,000
Danube..............	1,800	Platte..............	2,700
Rhine...............	840	Rio Madeira.........	2,300
Vistula.............	700	Rio Negro...........	1,650
ASIA.		Orinoco.............	1,600
Yeneisy and Selenga..	3,580	Uruguay............	1,100
Kiang..............	3,290	Magdalena...........	900
Hoang Ho...........	3,040	**NORTH AMERICA.**	
Amoor..............	2,500	Mississippi and Mis-	
Euphrates...........	1,900	souri..............	4,300
Ganges.............	1,850	Mackenzie..........	2,800
Tigris..............	1,160	Rio Bravo..........	2,300
AFRICA.		Arkansas...........	2,070
Nile...............	3,240	Red River..........	1,520
Niger..............	2,400	Ohio and Alleghany..	1,480
Gambia.............	1,000	St. Lawrence.......	1,450

The figures as to the length of the Nile are estimated. The Amazon, with its tributaries (including the Rio Negro and Madeira), drains an area of 2,330,000 square miles; the Mississippi and Missouri, 1,726,000 square miles; the Yeneisy (or Yenisei, as it is often written) drains about 1,000,000 square miles; the Volga, about 500,000. In this group of great rivers the St. Lawrence is the most remarkable. It constitutes by far the largest body of fresh water in the world. Including the lakes and streams, which it comprises in its widest acceptation, the St. Lawrence covers about 73,000 square miles; the aggregate, it is estimated, represents not less than 9,000 solid miles—a mass of water which would have taken upward of forty years to pour over Niagara at the computed rate of 1,000,000 cubic feet in a second. As the entire basin of this water system falls short of 300,000 square miles, the surface of the land is only three times that of the water.

HOW THE UNITED STATES GOT ITS LANDS.—The United States bought Louisiana, the vast region between the Mississippi River, the eastern and northern boundary of Texas (then belonging to Spain), and the dividing ridge of the Rocky Mountains, together with what is now Oregon, Washington Territory, and the western parts of Montana and Idaho, from France for $11,250,000. This was in 1803. Before the principal, interest, and claims of one sort and another assumed by the United States were settled, the total cost of this "Louisiana purchase," comprising, according to French construction and our understanding, 1,171,931 square miles, swelled to $23,500,-000, or almost $25 per section—a fact not stated in cyclopedias and school histories, and therefore not generally understood. Spain still held Florida and claimed a part of what we understood to be included in the Louisiana purchase—a strip up to north latitude 31—and disputed our boundary along the south and west, and even claimed Oregon. We bought Florida and all the disputed land east of the Mississippi and her claim to Oregon, and settled our southwestern boundary dispute for the sum of $6,500,000. Texas smilingly proposed annexation to the United States, and this great government was "taken in" December 29, 1845, Texas keeping her public lands and giving us all her State debts and a three-year war (costing us $66,000,000) with Mexico, who claimed her for a runaway from Mexican jurisdiction. This was a bargain that out-yankeed the Yankees, but the South insisted on it and the North submitted. After conquering all the territory now embraced in New Mexico, a part of Colorado, Arizona, Utah, Nevada and California, we paid Mexico $25,000,000 for it—$15,000,000 for the greater part of it and $10,000,000 for another slice, known as the "Gadsden purchase." In 1867 we bought Alaska from Russia for $7,200,000. All the several amounts above named were paid long ago. As for all the rest of our landed possessions, we took them with us when we cut loose from mother Britain's apron string, but did not get a clear title until we had fought ten years for it—first in the Revolutionary War, costing us in killed 7,343 reported—besides the unreported killed—and over 15,000 wounded, and $135,193,103 in money; afterward in the War of 1812-15, costing us in killed 1,877, in wounded 3,737, in money $107,159,003. We have paid everybody but the Indians, the only real owners, and, thanks to gunpowder, sword, bayonet, bad whisky, small-pox, cholera and other weapons of civilization, there are not many of them left to complain. Besides all the beads, earrings, blankets, pots, kettles, brass buttons, etc., given them for land titles in the olden times, we paid them, or the Indian agents, in one way and another, in the ninety years from 1791 to 1881, inclusive, $193,672,697.31, to say nothing of the thousands of lives sacrificed and many millions spent in Indian wars, from the war of King Philip to the last fight with the Apaches.

ILLUSTRIOUS MEN AND WOMEN.—It is not likely that any two persons would agree as to who are entitled to the first fifty places on the roll of great men and great women. Using "great" in the sense of eminence in their professions, of great military commanders the following are among the chief: Sesostris, the Egyptian conqueror, who is represented as having subdued all Asia to the Oxus and the Ganges, Ethiopia, and a part of Europe; Cyrus the Great; Alexander the Great; Hannibal; Che-Hwanti, who reduced all the kingdoms of China and Indo-China to one empire, and constructed the Great Wall; Cæsar; Genghis Khan, the Tartar chief, who overran all Asia and a considerable part of Europe; Napoleon Bonaparte; Ulysses S. Grant, and General Von Moltke. Among the most illustrious benefactors of mankind, as statesmen, lawgivers and patriots, stand Moses, David, Solon, Numa Pompilius, Zoroaster, Confucius, Justinian, Charlemagne, Cromwell, Washington and Lincoln. Eminent among the philosophers, rhetoricians and logicians stand Socrates, Plato, Aristotle, Seneca, the two Catos, and Lord Bacon; among orators, Pericles, Demosthenes, Cicero, Mirabeau, Burke, Webster and Clay; among poets, Homer, Virgil, Dante, Milton, and Shakespeare; among painters and sculptors, Phidias, Parrhasius, Zenxis, Praxiteles, Scopas, Michael Angelo, Raphael and Rubens; among philanthropists, John Howard; among inventors, Archimedes, Watt, Fulton, Arkwright, Whitney and Morse; among astronomers, Copernicus, Galileo, Tycho Brahe, Newton, La Place and the elder Herschel. Here are sixty names of distinguished men, and yet the great religious leaders, excepting Moses and Zoroaster, have not been named. Among these stand Siddhartha or Buddha, Mahomet, Martin Luther, John Knox and John Wesley. Then the great explorers and geographers of the world have not been noticed, among whom Herodotus, Strabo, Pliny, Vasco de Gama, Columbus and Humboldt barely lead the van.

Of eminent women there are Seling, wife of the Emperor Hwang-ti, B. C. 2637, who taught her people the art of silk-raising and weaving; Semiramis, the Assyrian Queen; Deborah, the heroic warrior prophetess of the Israelites; Queen Esther, who, with the counsel of her cousin, Mordecai, not only saved the Jews from extermination, but lifted them from a condition of slavery into prosperity and power; Dido, the founder of Carthage; Sappho, the eminent Grecian poetess; Hypatia, the eloquent philosopher; Mary, the mother of Christ; Zenobia, Queen of Palmyra; the mother of St. Augustine; Elizabeth of Hungary; Queen Elizabeth of England; Queen Isabella of Spain; the Empress Maria Theresa; Margaret the Great of Denmark; Catherine the Great of Russia, Queen Victoria; Florence Nightingale; Mme. de Stael; Mrs. Fry, the philanthropist; among authoresses, Mrs. Hemans, Mrs. Sigourney, Mrs. Browning, "George Sand," "George Eliot," and Mrs. Stowe; and among artists, Rosa Bonheur, and our own Harriet Hosmer.

THE SUEZ CANAL.—The Suez Canal was begun in 1,858 and was formally opened in November, 1869. Its cost, including harbors, is estimated at $100,000,000. Its length is 100 miles, 75 of which were excavated; its width is generally 325 feet at the surface, and 75 feet at the bottom, and its depth 26 feet. The workmen employed were chiefly natives, and many were drafted by the Khedive. The number of laborers is estimated at 30,000. The British government virtually controls the canal as it owns most of the stock.

SENDING VESSELS OVER NIAGARA FALLS.—There have been three such instances. The first was in 1827. Some men got an old ship—the Michigan—which had been used on lake Erie, and had been pronounced unseaworthy. For mere wantonness they put aboard a bear, a fox, a buffalo, a dog and some geese and sent it over the cataract. The bear jumped from the vessel before it reached the rapids, swam toward the shore, and was rescued by some humane persons. The geese went over the falls, and came to the shore below alive, and, therefore, became objects of great interest, and were sold at high prices to visitors at the Falls. The dog, fox, and buffalo were not heard of or seen again. Another condemned vessel, the Detroit, that had belonged to Commodore Perry's victorious fleet, was started over the cataract in the winter of 1841, but grounded about midway in the rapids, and lay there till knocked to pieces

by the ice. A somewhat more picturesque instance was the sending over the Canada side of a ship on fire. This occurred in 1837. The vessel was the Caroline, which had been run in the interest of the insurgents in the Canadian rebellion. It was captured by Colonel McNabb, an officer of the Canada militia, and by his orders it was set on fire then cut loose from its moorings. All in flames, it went glaring and hissing down the rapids and over the precipice, and smothered its ruddy blaze in the boiling chasm below. This was witnessed by large crowds on both sides of the falls, and was described as a most magnificent sight. Of course there was no one on board the vessel.

OLD TIME WAGES IN ENGLAND.—The following rates of daily wages "determined" by the Justices of Somerset, in 1685, answer this question very fairly. Somerset being one of the average shires of England. The orthography is conformed to original record:

	s.	d.
Mowers per diem, findeing themselves	1	2
Mowers at meate and drinke	0	7
Men makeing hay per diem, findeing themselves	0	10
Men at meate and drinke	0	6
Women makeing hay	0	7
Women at meate and drinke	0	4
Men reapeing corne per diem, findeing themselves	1	2
Men reapinge corne at meate and drinke	0	8
Moweing an acre of grasse, findeing themselves	1	2
Moweing an acre of grasse to hay	1	6
Moweing an acre of barley	1	1
Reapeinge and bindeinge an acre of wheate	3	0
Cuttinge and bindeinge an acre of beanes and hookinge	2	0

The shilling is about 24 cents and the penny 2 cents.

DECLARATION OF INDEPENDENCE SIGNERS.—The following is the list of names appended to that famous document, with the colony which each represented in Congress:

New Hampshire—Josiah Bartlett; William Whipple, Matthew Thornton.

Massachusetts—John Hancock, John Adams, Samuel Adams, Robert Treat Paine.

Rhode Island—Elbridge Gerry, Stephen Hopkins, William Ellery.

Connecticut—Roger Sherman, Samuel Huntington, William Williams, Oliver Wolcott.

New York—William Floyd, Philip Livingston, Francis Lewis, Lewis Morris.

New Jersey—Richard Hockton, John Witherspoon, Francis Hopkinson, John Hart, Abraham Clark.

Pennsylvania—Robert Morris, Benjamin Rush, Benjamin Franklin, John Morton, George Clymer, James Smith, George Taylor, James Wilson, George Ross.

Delaware—Cæsar Rodney, George Reed, Thomas McKean.

Maryland—Samuel Chase, Thomas Stone, William Paca, Charles Carroll, of Carrollton.

Virginia—George Wythe, Richard Henry Lee, Thomas Jefferson, Benjamin Harrison, Thomas Nelson, Jr., Francis Lightfoot Lee, Carter Braxton.

North Carolina—William Hooper, Joseph Hewes, John Penn.

South Carolina—Edward Rutledge, Thomas Heyward, Jr., Thomas Lynch, Jr., Arthur Middleton.

Georgia—Button Gwinntet, Lyman Hall, George Walton.

LIFE OF ETHAN ALLEN.—Colonel Ethan Allan was captured in an attack upon Montreal, September 25, 1775. He was sent as prisoner to Great Britain, ostensibly for trial, but in a few months was sent back to America, and confined in prison ships and jails at Halifax and New York till May 3, 1778, when he was exchanged. During most of his captivity he was treated as a felon and kept heavily ironed, but during 1777 was allowed restricted liberty on parole. After his exchange he again offered his services to the patriot army, but because of trouble in Vermont was put in command of the militia in that State. The British authorities were at that time making especial efforts to secure the allegiance of the Vermonters, and it was owing to Allen's skillful negotiations that the question was kept open until the theater of war was changed, thus keeping the colony on the American side, but avoiding the attacks from the British that would certainly have followed an open avowal of their political preferences. Allen died at Burlington, Vt., February 13, 1789.

BURIAL CUSTOMS.—Among the early Christians the dead were buried with the face upward and the feet toward the east, in token of the resurrection at the coming again of the Sun of Righteousness. It cannot be said, however, that the custom was first used by the Christians. It was in practice among early pagan nations also, and is regarded as a survival of the ideas of the fire-worshipers. The sun, which was the impersonation of deity to many primitive races, had his home in their mythology in the east, and out of respect for him the dead were placed facing this quarter, among certain tribes always in a sitting posture. It may also be remarked that among other races the position was reversed, the dead body being placed with its feet toward the west, because the region of sunset was the home of the departed spirits.

THE SURRENDER OF LEE TO GRANT.—The surrender of General Lee was made at the house of a farmer named McLean, in Appomattox village, that house having been selected by General Lee himself at General Grant's request for the interview. General Grant went thither, and was met by General Lee on the threshold. The two went into the parlor of the house, a small room, containing little furnishing but a table and several chairs. About twenty Union officers besides General Grant were present, among them the members of the General's staff. The only Confederate officer with General Lee was Colonel Marshall, who acted as his secretary. General Lee, as well as his aid, was in full uniform, and wore a burnished sword which was given him by the State of Virginia; General Grant was in plain uniform, without a sword. After a brief conversation, relative to the meeting of the two generals while soldiers in Mexico, General Lee adverted at once to the object of the interview by asking on what terms the surrender of his army would be received. General Grant replied that officers and men must become prisoners of war, giving up of course all munitions, weapons and supplies, but that a parole would be accepted. General Lee then requested that the terms should be put in writing, that he might sign them. General Badeau says that while General Grant was writing the conditions of surrender he chanced to look up and his eye caught the glitter of General Lee's sword, and that this sight induced him to insert the provision that the "officers should be allowed to retain their side-arms, horses and personal property." This historian thinks that General Lee fully expected to give up his sword, and that General Grant omitted this from the terms of surrender out of consideration for the feelings of a soldier. Badeau says that General Lee was evidently much touched by the clemency of his adversary in this regard. The Confederate chief now wrote his acceptance of the terms offered and signed them. He further requested that the cavalry and artillery soldiers might be allowed to retain their horses as well as the officers, to which General Grant consented, and asked that a supply train left at Danville might be allowed to pass on, as his soldiers were without food. The reply

of General Grant to this was an order that 25,000 rations should be immediately issued from the commissariat of the National army to the Army of Northern Virginia. The formal papers were now drawn up and signed, and the interview which ended one of the greatest wars of modern times was over.

COLORED POPULATION AT EACH CENSUS.—The following will show the white and colored population of the United States, from 1790 to 1880, inclusive:

Year.	White.	Colored.	
		Free.	Slaves.
1790	3,172,006	59,527	697,681
1800	4,306,446	108,435	893,602
1810	5,862,073	186,446	1,191,362
1820	7,862,166	223,634	1,538,022
1830	10,538,378	319,599	2,009,043
1840	14,195,805	386,293	2,487,355
1850	19,553,068	434,495	3,204,313
1860	26,922,537	488,070	3,953,760
1870	33,589,377	4,880,009	None.
1880	43,402,970	6,580,973	None.

ARCTIC EXPLORATIONS.—From 1496 to 1857 there were 134 voyages and land journeys undertaken by governments and explorers of Europe and America to investigate the unknown region around the North Pole. Of these, sixty-three went to the northwest, twenty-nine via Behring Straits, and the rest to the northeast or due north. Since 1857 there have been the notable expeditions of Dr. Hayes, of Captain Hall, those of Nordenskjold, and others sent by Germany, Russia and Denmark; three voyages made by James Lamont, of the Royal Geographical Society, England, at his own expense; the expeditions of Sir George Nares, of Leigh Smith, and that of the ill-fated Jeannette; the search expeditions of the Tigress, the Juniata, and those sent to rescue Lieutenant Greely; further, all the expeditions fitted out under the auspices of the Polar Commission—in which the Greely expedition was included—and a number of minor voyages, making a sum total of some sixty exploring journeys in these twenty-seven years.

THE BATTLE OF WATERLOO.—The battle of Waterloo was fought June 18, 1815, between the allied British, Netherland and German troops under Wellington and the French under Napoleon. On June 16 Napoleon had attacked the Prussians under Blucher at Ligny and forced them to retreat toward Wavre, and Marshal Ney at the same time attacked the British and Dutch forces at Quatre Bras, but was forced to retire after an engagement of five hours. Napoleon's object, however, which was to prevent a union of the Prussians with Wellington's main army, was partially gained. The latter commander, having learned the next morning of Blucher's repulse, moved on to Waterloo expecting that the Prussian commander, according to previous arrangement, would join him there as speedily as possible. On June 17 Napoleon also moved toward Waterloo with the main body of his army, having directed Marshal Grouchy with 34,000 men and ninety-six guns to pursue Blucher's command toward Wavre. Both armies bivouacked on the field of Waterloo, and the next morning Napoleon, confident that Grouchy would prevent the arrival of the Prussians, delayed attack until the ground should become dry, a heavy shower having fallen on the day previous. The forces under Wellington occupied a semi-circular ridge a mile and a half in length, and the French were on an opposite ridge, the two being separated by a valley about 500 yards wide. The plan of Napoleon was to turn the allied left, force it back upon center, and gain possession of the enemy's line of retreat. To draw off Wellington's attention to his right, French troops were sent about 11 o'clock to attack the chateau of Houguemont, which the English had fortified. After a fight of more than two hours this was still in the possession of its defenders. About 1 o'clock a Prussian corps under Bulow was seen approaching on the French right, and Napoleon, finding it necessary to send 10,000 men to check their advance, was obliged to change the plan of battle. He therefore ordered a fierce attack upon the allied center. Wellington massed his troops there, and the battle was obstinately maintained for five hours, with varying success to the participants, both commanders hourly expecting re-enforcements. Wellington was waiting for Blucher and Napoleon for Grouchy. The French at last were gaining ground; the allied troops in the center were wavering under Ney's impetuous onslaughts, General Durutte had forced back the left, and Bulow's troops on the right had been forced to yield the position they had taken. Now, however, there were rumors that Blucher's army was approaching and the allies again rallied. At 7 o'clock Napoleon, despairing of the approach of Grouchy, determined to decide the day by a charge of the Old Guard, which had been held in reserve. At this stage the advance of Prussian horse on the allied left forced back General Durutte's troops, and the Old Guard formed in squares to cover this retreat. Ney's division surrounded, made a gallant struggle—their brave leader still unwounded, though five horses had been shot under him, heading them on foot, sword in hand—but were forced to give way. The Old Guard held their ground against overwhelming numbers. Finally, when five squares were broken, the Emperor gave the order to "fall back." The cry "The Guard is repulsed" spread consternation through the French army and threatened to turn retreat into precipitate flight. Napoleon, seeing this, reformed the Guard in order to give a rallying point for the fugitives. Failing in this, he declared that he would die within the square, but Marshal Soult hurried him away. The heroic band, surrounded, was bidden to surrender. "The Old Guard dies, but never surrenders" is the reply popularly attributed to General Cambronne, and with the cry of "Vive l'Empereur!" the remnant of the Guard made a last charge upon the enemy and perished almost to a man. The forces of Blucher being now upon the field, the rout of the French was complete, and the Prussians pursued the fleeing troops, capturing guns and men. There is no doubt that the failure of Grouchy to come upon the field caused Napoleon to lose his last great battle. It was subsequently asserted that this marshal was bribed, but there seems to be no real foundation for so base a charge. The trouble was that he had been ordered by Napoleon to follow the Prussians toward Wavre and thought it necessary to follow the strict letter of his instructions. Before he reached the village the main body of the Prussian force was on its way to Waterloo, but one division had been left there to occupy his attention. Engaged in skirmishing with this, he paid no attention to the advice of his subordinate generals who, hearing the terrible cannonading at Waterloo, besought him to go to the aid of the army there. Napoleon believing that he was either holding back Blucher's forces or was hotly pursuing them, did not recall him to the main army, and the decisive battle was lost. Grouchy was summoned before a council of war, but the court declared itself incompetent to decide his case, and nothing further came of it.

OUR NATIONAL CEMETERIES. — National Cemeteries for soldiers and sailors may be said to have originated in 1850, the army appropriation bill of that year appropriating money for a cemetery near the City of Mexico, for the interment of the remains of soldiers who fell in the Mexican War. The remains of Federal soldiers and sailors who fell in the war for the Union have been buried in seventy-eight cemeteries exclusive of those interred elsewhere, a far greater number. In the subjoined list are given the names and locations of the National Cemeteries with the number therein buried, known and unknown. We have no means of knowing what cemeteries also contain the bodies of Southern soldiers:

	Known.	Unkn'n.
Cypress Hill, N. Y.	3,675	76
Woodlawn, Elmira, N. Y.	3,096	.....
Beverly, N. J.	142	7
Finn's Point, N. J.	....	2,644
Gettysburg, Pa.	1,967	1,608
Philadelphia, Pa.	1,880	28
Annapolis, Md.	2,289	197
Antietam, Md.	2,853	1,811
London Park, Baltimore, Md.	1,627	166
Laurel, Baltimore, Md.	232	6
Soldiers' Home, D. C.	5,313	288
Battle, D. C.	13	.....
Grafton, W. Va.	634	620
Arlington, Va.	11,911	4,349
Alexandria, Va.	3,434	124
Ball's Bluff, Va.	1	24
Cold Harbor, Va.	672	1,281
City Point, Va.	3,779	1,374
Culpepper, Va.	454	910
Danville, Va.	1,171	155
Fredericksburg, Va.	2,487	12,770
Fort Harrison, Va.	239	575
Glendale, Va.	233	961
Hampton, Va.	4,868	494
Poplar Grove, Va.	2,197	3,993
Richmond, Va.	841	5,700
Seven Pines Va.	150	1,208
Staunton, Va.	233	520
Winchester, Va.	2,094	2,361
Yorktown, Va.	748	1,434
Newbern, N. C.	2,174	1,077
Raleigh, N. C.	625	553
Salisbury, N. C.	94	12,032
Wilmington, N. C.	710	1,398
Beaufort, S. C.	4,748	4,493
Florence, S. C.	199	2,799
Andersonville, Ga.	12,878	959
Marietta, Ga.	7,182	2,963
Barrancas, Fla.	791	657
Mobile, Ala.	751	112
Corinth, Miss.	1,788	3,920
Natchez, Miss.	308	2,780
Vicksburg, Miss.	3,896	12,704
Alexandria, La.	534	772
Baton Rouge, La.	2,468	495
Chalmette, La.	6,833	5,675
Port Hudson, La.	596	3,218
Brownsville, Texas	1,409	1,379
San Antonio, Texas	307	167
Fayetteville, Ark.	431	781
Fort Smith, Ark.	706	1,152
Little Rock, Ark.	3,260	2,337
Chattanooga, Tenn.	7,993	4,963
Fort Donelson, Tenn.	158	511
Knoxville, Tenn.	2,089	1,046
Memphis, Tenn.	5,159	8,817
Nashville, Tenn.	11,824	4,692
Pittsburg Landing, Tenn.	1,229	2,361
Stone River, Tenn.	3,820	2,314
Camp Nelson, Ky.	2,477	1,165
Cave Hill, Louisville, Ky.	3,342	583
Danville, Ky.	346	12
Lebanon, Ky.	591	277

	Known.	Unkn'n.
Lexington, Ky......................	824	105
Logan's, Ky.......................	345	366
Crown Hill, Indianapolis, Ind..........	686	36
New Albany, Ind....................	2,138	676
Camp Butler, Ill...................	1,007	355
Mound City, Ill....................	2,505	2,721
Rock Island, Ill...................	280	9
Jefferson Barracks, Mo..............	8,569	2,906
Jefferson City, Mo.................	348	412
Springfield, Mo....................	845	713
Fort Leavenworth, Kas..............	821	913
Fort Scott, Kas....................	388	161
Keokuk, Iowa.....................	610	21
Fort Gibson, I. T..................	212	2,212
Fort McPherson, Neb...............	149	291
City of Mexico, Mexico..............	254	750

THE CATACOMBS OF PARIS.—The so-called catacombs of Paris were never catacombs in the ancient sense of the word, and were not devoted to purposes of sepulture until 1784. In that year the Council of State issued a decree for clearing the Cemetery of the Innocents, and for removing its contents, as well as those of other graveyards, into the quarries which had existed from the earlier times under the city of Paris and completely undermined the southern part of the city. Engineers and workmen were sent to examine the quarries and to prop up their roofs lest the weight of buildings above should break them in. April 7, 1786, the consecration of the catacombs was performed with great solemnity, and the work of removal from the cemeteries was immediately begun. This work was all performed by night; the bones were brought in funeral cars, covered with a pall, and followed by priests chanting the service of the dead, and when they reached the catacombs the bones were shot down the shaft. As the cemeteries were cleared by order of the government, their contents were removed to this place of general deposit, and these catacombs further served as convenient receptacles for those who perished in the revolution. At first the bones were heaped up without any kind of order except that those from each cemetery were kept separate, but in 1810 a regular system of arranging them was commenced, and the skulls and bones were built up along the wall. From the main entrance to the catacombs, which is near the barriers d' Enfer, a flight of ninety steps descends, at whose foot galleries are seen branching in various directions. Some yards distant is a vestibule of octagonal form, which opens into a long gallery lined with bones from floor to roof. The arm, leg and thigh bones are in front, closely and regularly piled, and their uniformity is relieved by three rows of skulls at equal distances. Behind these are thrown the smaller bones. This gallery conducts to several rooms resembling chapels, lined with bones variously arranged. One is called the "Tomb of the Revolution," another the "Tomb of Victims," the latter containing the relics of those who perished in the early period of the revolution and in the "Massacre of September." It is estimated that the remains of 3,000,000 human beings lie in this receptacle. Admission to these catacombs has for years been strictly forbidden on account of the unsafe condition of the roof. They are said to comprise an extent of about 3,250,000 square yards.

HISTORY OF THE TELEPHONE.—The principle of the telephone, that sounds could be conveyed to a distance by a distended wire, was demonstrated by Robert Hook in 1667, but no practical application was made of the discovery until 1821, when Professor Wheatstone exhibited his "Enchanted Lyre," in which the sounds of a music-box were conveyed from a cellar to upper rooms. The first true discoverer of the speaking telephone, however, was Johann Philipp Reis, a German scientist and professor in the institute at Friedrichsdorf. April 25, 1861, Reis exhibited his telephone at Frankfort. This contained all the essential features of the modern telephone, but as its commercial value was not at all comprehended, little attention was paid to it. Reis, after trying in vain to arouse the interest of scientists in his discovery, died in 1874, without having reaped any advantage from it, and there is no doubt that his death was hastened by the distress of mind caused by his continual rebuffs. Meanwhile, the idea was being worked into more practical shape by other persons, Professor Elisha Gray and Professor A. G. Bell, and later by Edison. There is little doubt that Professor Gray's successful experiments considerably antedated those of the others, but Professor Bell was the first to perfect his patent. February 12, 1877, Bell's articulating telephone was tested by experiments at Boston and Salem, Mass., and was found to convey sounds distinctly from one place to the other, a distance of eighteen miles. This telephone was exhibited widely in this country and in Europe during that year, and telephone companies were established to bring it into general use. Edison's carbon "loud-speaking" telephone was brought out in 1878. It is not worth while to go into details of the suits on the subject of priority of invention. The examiner of patents at Washington, July 21, 1883, decided that Professor Bell was the first inventor, because he was the first to complete his invention and secure a full patent. Since 1878 there have been many improvements in the different parts of the telephone, rendering it now nearly perfect in its working.

SECESSION AND READMISSION OF REBEL STATES.—

	Seceded.	Readmitted.
South Carolina........	Dec. 20, 1860.	June 11, 1868.
Mississippi............	Jan. 9, 1861.	Feb. 3, 1870.
Alabama..............	Jan. 11, 1861.	June 11, 1868.
Florida...............	Jan. 11, 1861.	June 11, 1868.
Georgia..............	Jan. 19, 1861.	April 20, 1870.
Louisiana.............	Jan. 26, 1861.	June 11, 1868.
Texas................	Feb. 1, 1861.	Mar. 15, 1870.
Virginia	April 16, 1861.	Jan. 15, 1870.
Arkansas.............	May 6, 1861.	June 20, 1868.
North Carolina........	May 21, 1861.	June 11, 1868.
Tennessee	June 24, 1861.	July, 1866.

THE EARTHQUAKE OF 1811–12.—The earthquake shocks felt on the shores of the Lower Mississippi in the years 1811-12 are recorded as among the most remarkable phenomena of their kind. Similar instances where earth disturbances have prevailed, severely and continuously, far from the vicinity of a volcano, are very rare indeed. In this instance, over an extent of country stretching for 300 miles southward from the mouth of the Ohio river, the ground rose and sank in great undulations, and lakes were formed and again drained. The shocks were attended by loud explosions, great fissures—generally traveling from northeast to southwest, and sometimes more than half a mile in length—were opened in the earth, and from these openings mud and water were thrown often to the tops of the highest trees. Islands in the Mississippi were sunk, the current of the river was driven back by the rising of its bed, and overflowed the adjacent lands. More than half of New Madrid county was permanently submerged. The inhabitants noticed that these earth movements were sometimes vertical and sometimes horizontal, the former being by far the most serious in their effects. These disturbances ceased March 26, 1812, simultaneously with the great earthquake which destroyed the city of Caracas, South America.

THE DARK DAY IN NEW ENGLAND.—On May 19, 1780, there was a remarkable darkening of the sky and atmosphere over a large part of New England, which caused much alarm among those who witnessed it. The darkness began between ten and eleven o'clock on the day named, and continued in some places through the entire day, and was followed by an unusually intense degree of blackness during the ensuing night. This phenomenon extended from the northeastern part of New England westward as far as Albany, and southward to the coast of New Jersey. The most intense and prolonged darkness, however, was confined to Massachusetts, especially to the eastern half of the State. It came up from the southwest, and overhung the country like a pall. It was necessary to light candles in all the houses, and thousands of good people, believing that the end of all things terrestrial had come, betook themselves to religious devotions. One incident of the occasion has been woven into verse with excellent effect by the poet Whittier. The Connecticut Legislature was in session on that day, and as the darkness came on and grew more and more dense, the members became terrified, and thought that the day of judgment had come; so a motion was made to adjourn. At this, a Mr. Davenport arose and said: "Mr. Speaker, it is either the day of judgment, or it is not. If it is not, there is no need of adjourning. If it is, I desire to be found doing my duty. I move that candles be brought and that we proceed to business." Mr. Davenport's suggestion was taken, candles were brought in, and business went on as usual. As to the explanation of this phenomenon, scientists have been much puzzled. It was plain from the falling of the barometer that the air was surcharged with heavy vapor. The darkness then, it might be said, was only the result of a dense fog, but the question of the cause of so remarkable a fog was still unanswered. Omitting this unascertained primary cause, then, Professor Williams, of Harvard College, who subsequently made a thorough investigation of the matter, gave it as his opinion that this unprecedented quantity of vapor had gathered in the air in layers so as to cut off the rays of light, by repeated refraction, in a remarkable degree. He thought that the specific gravity of this vapor must have been the same as that of the air, which caused it to be held so long in suspension in the atmosphere. In this case the extent of the darkness would coincide with the area of the vapor, and it would continue until a change in the gravity of the air caused the vapors to ascend or descend. In some places when the darkness cleared it was as if the vapor was lifted and borne away by the wind like a dark pall, and in others, after a period of intense darkness the atmosphere gradually lightened again. In our day, a phenomenon of this kind would be thoroughly investigated to its most remote possible cause; but then owing to the sparse settlement of the country and the difficulties of travel, the investigation of distant causes could not be made. Large fires may have prevailed that spring in the forests of Western New York and Pennsylvania—a region then an absolute wilderness—the smoke of which was borne through the upper regions of the atmosphere, to fall when it came to a locality of less buoyant air, down to the lower strata. We say these fires may have recently preceded this day, and served as its sufficient cause, but we have only presumptive evidence that they did occur. Had Professor Williams entertained a supposition of the previous existence of such fires, he had then no means of verifying it, and long before the advent of railroads and telegraphs, or even of stage lines, the scientific theories of the dark day had passed from the general memory.

A SHORT HISTORY OF THE LIBERTY BELL.—In 1751 the Pennsylvania Assembly authorized a committee to procure a bell for their State House. November 1st of that year an order was sent to London for "a good bell of about 2,000 pounds weight." To this order were added the following directions: "Let the bell be cast by the best workmen and examined carefully before it is shipped, with the following words well shaped in large letters around it, viz.: 'By order of the Assembly of the Province of Pennsylvania, for the State House, in the city of Philadelphia, 1752.' And underneath, 'Proclaim Liberty Through All the Land Unto All the Inhabitants Thereof. —Levit. xxv. 10.'" In due time, in the following year, the bell reached Philadelphia, but when it was hung, early in 1753, as it was being first rung to test the sound, it cracked without any apparent reason, and it was necessary to have it recast. It was at first thought to be necessary to send it back to England for the purpose, but some "ingenious workmen" in Philadelphia wished to do the casting and were allowed to do so. In the first week of June, 1753, the bell was again hung in the belfry of the State House. On July 4, 1776, it was known throughout the city that the final decision on the question of declaring the colonies independent of Great Britain was to be made by the Continental Congress, in session at the State House. Accordingly the old bellman had been stationed in the belfry on that morning, with orders to ring the bell when a boy waiting at the door of the State House below should signal to him that the bill for independence had been passed. Hour after hour the old man stood at his post. At last, at 2 o'clock, when he had about concluded that the question would not be decided on that day at least, the watchman heard a shout from below, and looking down saw the boy at the door clapping his hands and calling at the top of his voice: "Ring! ring!" And he did ring, the story goes, for two whole hours, being so filled with excitement and enthusiasm that he could not stop. When the British threatened Philadelphia, in 1777, the precious bell was taken down and removed to the town of Bethlehem for safety. In 1778 it was returned to the State House and a new steeple built for it. Several years after it cracked, for some unknown reason, under a stroke of the clapper, and its tone was thus destroyed. An attempt was made to restore its tone by sawing the crack wider, but without success. This bell was sent to New Orleans during the winter to be exhibited in the World's Fair there. The Pullman Company gave one of their handsomest cars for the transit. It was in the charge of three custodians appointed by the Mayor of Philadelphia, who did not leave it night or day, and guarded it as fully as possible against accident. A pilot engine preceded the train carrying the bell over the entire route. It left Philadelphia Jan. 24, 1885, and returned in June.

THE ANTARCTIC POLAR REGIONS.—The climate of the southern polar regions is much more severe than that at the north pole, the icefields extending 10 degrees nearer the equator from the south than from the north. Within the arctic circle there are tribes of men living on the borders of the icy ocean on both the east and west hemispheres, but within the antarctic all is one dreary, uninhabitable waste. In the extreme north the reindeer and the musk-ox are found in numbers, but not a single land quadruped exists beyond 50 degrees of southern latitude. Flowers are seen in summer by the arctic navigator as far as 78 degrees north, but no plant of any description, not even a moss or a lichen, has been observed beyond Cockburn Island, in 64 degrees 12 minutes south latitude. In Spitzbergen, 79 degrees north, vegetation ascends the mountain slopes to a height of 3,000 feet, but on every land within or near the antarctic circle the snow-line descends to the water's edge. The highest latitude ever reached at the south is 78 degrees 10 minutes, while in the north navigators have penetrated to 84 degrees. The reason for this remarkable difference is the predominance of large tracts of land in the northern regions, while in the south is a vast expanse of ocean. In the north continental masses form an almost continuous belt around the icy sea, while in the southern hemisphere the continents taper down into a broad extent of frigid waters. In the north the plains of Siberia and of the Hudson's Bay territories, warmed by the sunbeams of summer, become at that season centers of radiating heat, while the antarctic lands, of small extent, isolated in the midst of a polar ocean and chilled by cold sea winds, act at every season as refrigerators of the atmosphere. Further in the north the cold currents of the polar sea, having but two openings of any extent through which they can convey drift ice, have their chilly influence confined to comparatively narrow limits, but the cold currents of the antarctic seas have scope to branch out freely on all sides and carry their ice even into temperate waters. Finally, at the northern hemisphere, the Gulf Stream conveys warmth even to the shores of Spitzbergen and Nova Zembla, while on the opposite regions of the globe no traces of warm currents have been observed beyond 55 degrees of south latitude.

THE LANGUAGE USED BY CHRIST.—The language used by Christ was the Aramaic, the dialect of Northern Syria. The Israelites were much in contact with Aramæan populations, and some words from that tongue became incorporated into the Hebrew at a very early date. At the time of Hezekiah, Aramaic had become the official language of both Judea and Assyria; that is, the language spoken at the courts. After the fall of Samaria the Hebrew inhabitants of Northern Israel were largely carried into captivity, and their place was taken by colonists from Syria, who probably spoke Aramaic as their mother tongue. The fall of the Jewish Kingdom hastened the decay of Hebrew as a spoken language—not that the captives forgot their own language, as is generally assumed, but after the return to Judea the Jews found themselves, a people few in number, among a large number of surrounding populations using the Aramaic tongue. When the latest books of the Old Testament were written, Hebrew, though still the language of literature, had been supplanted by Aramaic as the language of common life. From that time on the former tongue was the exclusive property of scholars, and has no history save that of a merely literary language.

HOW ANCIENT TEMPLES AND PYRAMIDS WERE BUILT.—This is beyond modern conjecture, so imperfect is our understanding of the extent of the mechanical knowledge of the ancients. Their appliances are believed to have been of the simplest order, and their implements exceedingly crude, and yet they were able to convey these enormous blocks of stones for vast distances, over routes most difficult, and having accomplished this, to raise them to great height, and fit them in place without the aid of either cement or mortar to cover up the errors of the stone-cutter. How all this was done is one of the enigmas of modern science. It has been generally believed that inclined planes of earth were used to enable the workmen to raise the huge stones to their places, the earth being cleared away afterward. But it is possible that the ancients had a more extended knowledge of mechanical powers than we usually give them credit for, and that they made use of machinery very like that employed by moderns for lifting great weights. Large cavities are found in some of the stones in the pyramids, which may have been worn by the foot of a derrick turning in them. That there were enormous numbers of men employed in the building of these ancient structures is well known; these results of their great aggregated strength we see, but they left no record of the means by which this strength was focused and brought most effectually to bear on their mighty tasks.

THE FIRST ATLANTIC CABLE.—As early as 1842 Professor Morse declared a submarine cable connection between America and Europe to be among the possibilities, but no attempt toward this great achievement was made until 1854, when Cyrus Field established a company, which secured the right of landing cables in Newfoundland for fifty years. In 1858 soundings between Ireland and Newfoundland were completed, showing a maximum depth of 4,400 meters. Having succeeded in laying a cable between Nova Scotia and Newfoundland, Mr. Field secured the co-operation of English capitalists in his enterprise. The laying of the cable was begun August 7, 1857, from the port of Valencia, Ireland, but on the third day it broke, and the expedition had to return. Early in the following year another attempt was made. The cable was laid from both ends at the same time, was joined in mid-ocean, but in lowering it was broken. Again, in the same year, the attempt was made, and this time connection was successfully made. The first message over the line was sent August 7, 1858. The insulation of this cable, however, was defective, and by September 4th had quite failed. Some time was now spent in experiments, conducted by scientists, to secure a more perfect cable. A new company was formed, and in 1865 the work again began. The Great Eastern was employed to lay the cable, but when it was partly laid serious defects in the line were discovered and in repairing these it broke. The apparatus for recovering the wire proving insufficient the vessel returned to England. A new company, called the Anglo-American, was formed in 1866, and again the Great Eastern was equipped for the enterprise. The plan of the new expedition was not only to lay a new cable, but also to take up the end of the old one and join it to a new piece, thus obtaining a second telegraph line. The vessel sailed from Valencia July 13, 1866, and July 27 the cable was completely laid to Heart's Content, Newfoundland, and a message announcing the fact sent over the wire to Lord Stanley. Queen Victoria sent a message of congratulation to President Buchanan on the 28th. September 2d the lost cable of 1865 was recovered and its laying completed at Newfoundland September 8, 1866.

ENGRAVING ON EGGS.—The art of engraving on eggs is very puzzling to the uninitiated, but in reality it is very simple. It merely consists in writing upon the egg-shell with wax or varnish, or simply with tallow, and then immersing the egg in some weak acid, such, for example, as vinegar, dilute hydrochloric acid, or etching liquor. Wherever the varnish or wax has not protected the shell, the lime of the latter is decomposed and dissolved in the acid, and the writing or drawing remains in relief. In connection with this art a curious incident is told in history. In the month of August, 1808, at the time of the Spanish war, there was found in a church in Lisbon an egg, on which was plainly foretold the utter destruction of the French, who then had control of the city. The story of the wonderful prophecy spread through the town, causing the greatest excitement among the superstitious populace, and a general uprising was expected. This, however, the French commander cleverly thwarted by causing a counter-prophecy, directly denying the first, to be engrossed on several hundred eggs, which were then distributed in various parts of the city. The astonished Portuguese did not know what to think of this new phenomenon, but its "numerousness," if we may so call it, caused it to altogether outweigh the influence of the first prediction, and there were no further symptoms of revolt against the French.

CAYENNE PEPPER.—The name of the plant genus from which cayenne pepper is obtained is capsicum, a name also given to the product of the plant. This genus belongs to the solanaceæ, or night shade family, and has no relation to the family piperaceæ, which produces the shrub yielding black pepper. The plant which yields cayenne pepper is identical with the common red pepper of our gardens. It is an annual, a native of tropical countries, where it thrives luxuriantly even in the dryest soils, but it is also cultivated in other parts of the world. It grows to the height of two or three feet, and bears a fruit in the shape of a conical pod or seed-vessel, which is green when immature, but bright scarlet or orange when ripe. This pod, with its seeds, has a very pungent taste, and is used when green for pickling, and when ripe and dried is ground to powder to make cayenne pepper, or is used for medicine. This powder has a strongly stimulating effect, and is believed to aid digestion. It is also employed externally to excite the action of the skin.

THE BIG TREES OF CALIFORNIA.—There are several groves of Big Trees in California, the most famous of which are the Calaveras grove and the Mariposa grove. The Calaveras grove occupies what may be described as a band or belt 3,200 feet long and 700 in width. It is between two slopes, in a depression in the mountains, and has a stream winding through it, which runs dry in the summer time. In this grove the Big Trees number ninety-three, besides a great many smaller ones, which would be considered very large if it were not for the presence of these monarchs of the forest. Several of the Big Trees have fallen since the grove was discovered, one has been cut down, and one had the bark stripped from it to the height 116 feet from the ground. The highest now standing is the "Keystone State," 325 feet high and 45 feet in circumference; and the largest and finest is the "Empire State." There are four trees over 300 feet in height, and 40 to 61 feet in circumferenbe. The tree which was cut down occupied five men twenty-two days, which would be at the rate of one man 110 days, or nearly four months' work, not counting Sundays. Pump augers were used for boring through the giant. After the trunk was severed from the stump it required five men with immense wedges for three days to topple it over. The bark was eighteen inches thick. The tree would have yielded more than 1,000 cords of four-foot wood and 100 cords of bark, or more than 1,100 cords in all. On the stump of the tree was built a house, thirty feet in diameter, which the Rev. A. H. Tevis, an observant traveler, says contains room enough in square feet, if it were the right shape, for a parlor 12x16 feet, a dining-room 10x12, a kitchen 10x12, two bed-rooms 10 feet square each, a pantry 4x8, two clothes-presses 1½ feet deep and 4 feet wide, and still have a little to spare! The Mariposa grove is part of a grant made by Congress to be set apart for public use, resort and recreation forever. The area of the grant is two miles square and comprises two distinct groves about half a mile apart. The upper grove contains 365 trees, of which 154 are over fifteen feet in diameter, besides a great number of smaller ones. The average height of the Mariposa trees is less than that of the Calaveras, the highest Mariposa tree being 272 feet; but the average size of the Mariposa is greater than that of Calaveras. The "Grizzly Giant," in the lower grove, is 94 feet in circumference and 31 feet in diameter; it has been decreased by burning. Indeed, the forests at times present a somewhat unattractive appearance, as, in the past, the Indians, to help them in their hunting, burned off the chaparral and rubbish, and thus disfigured many of these splendid trees by burning off nearly all the bark. The first branch of the "Grizzly Giant" is nearly two hundred feet from the ground and is six feet in diameter. The remains of a tree, now prostrate, indicate that it had reached a diameter of about forty feet and a height of 400 feet; the trunk is hollow and will admit of the passage of three horsemen riding abreast. There are about 125 trees of over forty feet in circumference. Besides these two main groves there are the Tolumne grove, with thirty big trees; the Fresno grove, with over eight hundred spread over an area of two and a half miles long and one to two broad; and the Stanislaus grove, the Calaveras group, with from 700 to 800. There should be named in this connection the petrified forest near Calitoga, which contains portions of nearly one hundred distinct trees of great size, scattered over a tract of three or four miles in extent; the largest of this forest is eleven feet in diameter at the base and sixty feet long. It is conjectured that these prostrate giants were silicified by the eruption of the neighboring Mount St. Helena, which discharged hot alkaline waters containing silica in solution. This petrified forest is considered one of the great natural wonders of California.

HISTORY OF THE CITY OF JERUSALEM.—The earliest name of Jerusalem appears to have been Jebus, or poetically, Salem, and its king in Abraham's time was Melchizedek. When the Hebrews took possession of Canaan, the city of Salem was burned, but the fortress remained in the hands of the Jebusites till King David took it by storm and made it the capital of his kingdom. From that time it was called Jerusalem. During the reigns of David and Solomon it attained its highest degree of power. When ten of the Jewish tribes seceded under Jeroboam they made Shechem (and later Samaria) the capital of their kingdom of Israel, and Jerusalem remained the capital of the smaller but more powerful kingdom of Judah. The city was taken by Shishak, King of Egypt, in 971 B. C., was later conquered and sacked by Joash, King of Israel, and in the time of Ahaz, the King of Syria came against it with a large force, but could not take it. The city was besieged in Hezekiah's reign, by the army of Sennacherib, King of Assyria, but was saved by the sudden destruction of the invading army. After the death of Josiah, the city was tributary for some years to the King of Egypt, but was taken after repeated attempts by the Babylonians under Nebuchadnezzar in 586 B. C., and was left a heap of ruins. The work of rebuilding it began by order of King Cyrus about 538 B. C., who allowed the Jewish people who had been carried into captivity to return for this purpose. From this time Jerusalem enjoyed comparative peace for several hundred years and grew to be an important commercial city. When Alexander invaded Syria it submitted to him without resistance. After his death it belonged for a time to Egypt and in 198 B. C., passed with the rest of Judea under the rule of Syria. Antiochus the Great ruled it with mildness and justice, but the tyranny of his son, Antiochus Epiphanes, brought about the revolt, headed by the Maccabees, through which Jerusalem gained a brief independence. In 63 B. C., Pompey the Great took the city, demolished the walls and killed thousands of the people, but did not plunder it. However, nine years later Crassus robbed the temple of all its treasures. The walls were soon after rebuilt under Antipater, the Roman procurator, but when Herod came to rule over the city with the title of King, given him by the Roman Senate, he was resisted and only took possession after an obstinate siege, which was followed by the massacre of great numbers of the people. Herod improved and enlarged the city, and restored the temple on a more magnificent scale than in Solomon's time. Jerusalem is said at this time to have had a population of over 200,000. This period of wealth and prosperity was also rendered most memorable for Jerusalem by the ministry and crucifixion of Christ. About A. D. 66, the Jews, goaded to desperation by the tranny of the Romans, revolted, garrisoned Jerusalem, and defeated a Roman army sent against them. This was the beginning of the disastrous war which ended with the destruction of the city. It was taken by Titus, in the year 70, after a long siege, all the inhabitants were massacred, or made prisoners, and the entire city left a heap of ruins. The Emperor Hadrian built on the site of Jerusalem a Roman city, under the name of Elia Capitolina, with a temple of Jupiter, and Jews were forbidden to enter the city under pain of death. Under Constantine it was made a place of pilgrimage for Christians, as the Emperor's mother, Helena, had with much pains located the various sites of events in the history of Christ. The Emperor Julian, on the contrary, not only allowed the Jews to return to their city, but also made an attempt, which ended in failure, to rebuild their temple. In 614 the Persian Emperor Chosroes invaded the Roman empire. The Jews joined his army, and after conquering the northern part of Palestine, the united forces laid siege to and took Jerusalem. The Jews wreaked vengeance on the Christians for what they had been forced to endure, and 20,000 people were massacred. The Persians held rule in the city for fourteen years; it was then taken by the Romans again, but in 636 the Caliph Omar beseiged it. After four months the city capitulated. It was under the rule of the Caliphs for 400 years, until the Seljuk Turks in 1077 invaded Syria and made it a province of their empire. Christian pilgrims had for many years kept up the practice of visiting tne tomb of Christ, as the Caliphs did not interfere with their devotions any further than by exacting a small tribute from each visitor. But the cruelties practiced upon the pilgrims by the Turks were many, and report of them soon roused all Europe to a pitch of indignation, and brought about that series of holy wars, which for a time restored the holy sepulcher into Christian hands. Jerusalem was stormed and taken July 15, 1099, and 50,000 Moslems were slaughtered by their wrathful Christian foes. The new sovereignty was precariously maintained until 1187, when it fell before the power of Saladin. Jerusalem, after a siege of twelve days, surrendered. Saladin, however, did not put his captives to death, but contented himself with expelling them from the city. Jerusalem passed into the hands of the Franks by treaty, in 1229, was retaken by the Moslems in 1239, once more restored in 1243, and finally conquered in 1244 by a horde of Kharesmian Turks. In 1517 Palestine was conquered by Sultan Selin I., and since then has been under the rule of the Ottoman Empire, except for a brief period—from 1832 to 1840, when it was in the hands of Mahomet Ali, Pasha of Egypt, and his son Ibrahim had his seat of government in Jerusalem.

THE BLACK DEATH.—This great plague, known as the "Black Death," was the most deadly epidemic ever known. It is believed to have been an aggravated outburst of the Oriental plague, which from the earliest records of history has periodically appeared in Asia and Northern Africa. There had been a visitation of the plague in Europe in 1342; the Black Death, in terrible virulence, appeared in 1348–9; it also came in milder form in 1361–2, and again in 1369. The prevalence and severity of the pestilence during this century is ascribed to the disturbed conditions of the elements that preceded it. For a number of years Asia and Europe had suffered from mighty earthquakes, furious tornadoes, violent floods, clouds of locusts darkening the air and poisoning it with their corrupting bodies. Whether these natural disturbances were the cause of the plague is not certainly known, but many writers on the subject regard the connection as both probable and possible. The disease was brought from the Orient to Constantinople, and early in 1347 appeared in Sicily and several coast towns of Italy. After a brief pause the pestilence broke out at Avignon in January, 1348; advanced thence to

Southern France, Spain and Northern Italy. Passing through France and visiting, but not yet ravaging, Germany, it made its way to England, cutting down its first victims at Dorset, in August, 1348. Thence it traveled slowly, reaching London early in the winter. Soon it embraced the entire kingdom, penetrating to every rural hamlet, so that England became a mere pest-house. The chief symptoms of the disease are described as "spitting, in some cases actual vomiting, of blood, the breaking out of inflammatory boils in parts, or over the whole of the body, and the appearance of those dark blotches upon the skin which suggested its most startling name. Some of the victims died almost on the first attack, some in twelve hours, some in two days, almost all within the first three days." The utter powerlessness of medical skill before the disease was owing partly to the physicians' ignorance of its nature, and largely to the effect of the spirit of terror which hung like a pall over men's minds. After some months had passed, the practice of opening the hard boils was adopted, with very good effect, and many lives were thus saved. But the havoc wrought by the disease in England was terrible. It is said that 100,000 persons died in London, nearly 60,000 in Norwich, and proportionate numbers in other cities. These figures seem incredible, but a recent writer, who has spent much time in the investigation of records, asserts that at least half the population, or about 2,500,000 souls, of England perished in this outbreak. The ravages of the pestilence over the rest of the world were no less terrible. Germany is said to have lost 1,244,434 victims; Italy, over half the population. On a moderate calculation, it may be assumed that there perished in Europe during the first appearance of the Black Death, fully 25,000,000 human beings. Concerning the Orient we have less reliable records, but 13,000,000 are said to have died in China, and 24,000,000 in the rest of Asia and adjacent islands. The plague also ravaged Northern Africa, but of its course there little is known. The horrors of that dreadful time were increased by the fearful persecutions visited on the Jews, who were accused of having caused the pestilence by poisoning the public wells. The people rose to exterminate the hapless race, and killed them by fire and torture wherever found. It is impossible for us to conceive of the actual horror of such times.

MIGHTY HAMMERS.—An authority on scientific subjects give the weights of the great hammers used in the iron works of Europe, and their date of manufacture, as follows: At the Terni Works, Italy, the heaviest hammer weighs 50 tons, and was made in 1873; one at Alexandrovski, Russia, was made the following year of like weight. In 1877, one was finished at Creusot Works, France, weighing 80 tons; in 1885, one at the Cockerill Works, Belgium, of 100 tons, and in 1886, at the Krupp Works, Essen, Germany, one of 150 tons. The latter being the heaviest hammer in the world.

ASSASSINATION OF PRESIDENT GARFIELD.—July 2, 1881, at 9:25 A. M., as President Garfield was entering the Baltimore & Potomac Railroad depot at Washington, preparatory to taking the cars for a two weeks' jaunt in New England, he was fired upon and severely wounded by Charles Jules Guiteau, a native of Illinois, but of French descent. The scene of the assassination was the ladies' reception-room at the station. The President and Mr. Blaine, arm in arm, were walking slowly through the aisle between two rows of benches on either side of the room; when Guiteau entered by a side door on the left of the gentlemen, passed quickly around the back of the benches till directly behind the President, and fired the shot that struck his arm. Mr. Garfield walked about ten feet to the end of the aisle, and was in the act of turning to face his assailant when the second shot struck him in the small of the back, and he fell. The assassin was immediately seized and taken to jail. The wounded president was conveyed in an ambulance to the White House. As he was very faint, the first fear was of internal hemorrhage, which might cause speedy death. But as he rallied in a few hours, this danger was thought to be averted and inflammation was now feared. But as symptoms of this failed to appear, the surgeons in attendance concluded that no important organ had been injured, that the bullet would become encysted and harmless, or might possibly be located and successfully removed. By the 10th of July, the reports were so favorable, that the president's recovery was regarded as certain, and public thanksgivings were offered in several of the States, by order of the governors, for his deliverance. The first check in the favorable symptoms occurred on July 18, and July 23 there was a serious relapse, attended with chills and fever. The wound had been frequently probed but without securing any favorable result. The induction balance was used to locate the ball, and was regarded as a success, though subsequently its indications were known to have been altogether erroneous. The probings, therefore, in what was assumed to be the track of the ball, only increased the unfavorable symptoms. During the entire month of August these reports were alternately hopeful and discouraging, the dangerous indications being generally on the increase. By August 25, his situation was understood to be very critical, though an apparent improvement on the 26th and 28th again aroused hope. At his own earnest desire the president was removed, September 6, to Elberon Park, near Long Branch, N. J., in the hope that the cooler air of the seaside might renew his strength more rapidly. However, the improvement hoped for did not appear. On September 16, there was a serious relapse, with well-marked symptoms of blood poisoning, and September 19 the president died. A post-mortem examination showed that the ball, after fracturing one of the ribs, had passed through the spinal column, fracturing the body of one of the vertebra, driving a number of small fragments of bone into the soft parts adjacent, and lodging below the pancreas, where it had become completely encysted. The immediate cause of death was hemorrhage from one of the small arteries in the track of the ball, but the principal cause was the poisoning of the blood from suppuration.

COINS OF FOREIGN COUNTRIES.—The following carefully prepared summary indicates the coins in use in the various countries, taking their names in alphabetical order·

Argentine Republic—Gold coins: 20 peso piece, $19.94; 10 pesos, $9.97; 5 pesos, $4.98. Silver: 1 peso, 99 cents. The copper coin of the country is the centisimo, 100 of which make a peso or dollar.

Austria—Gold coins: 8 gulden piece, $3.86; 4 gulden, $1.93. Silver: Marie Theresa thaler, $1.02; 2 gulden, 96 cents; 1 gulden, 48 cents; ¼ gulden, 12 cents; 20 kreutzer, 10 cents; 10 kreutzer, 5 cents. Of the small copper coin current, known as the kreutzer, 100 make a gulden.

Brazil—Gold coins: 20 milrei piece, $10.91; 10 milreis, $5.45. Silver: 2 milreis, $1.09; 1 milreis, 55 cents; ½ milreis, 27 cents. The Portuguese rei is used for copper money, worth about ⅕ of a cent.

Chili—Gold coin: 10 pesos (or 1 condor), $9.10; 5 pesos, $4.55; 2 pesos, $1.82. Silver; 1 peso, 91 cents; 50 centavos, 45 cents; 20 centavos 18 cents; 10 centavos, 9 cents; 5 centavos, 4 cents. The copper coin is 1 centavo, 100th of a peso.

Colombia—Gold coins: Twenty peso piece, $19.30; 10 pesos, $9.65; 5 pesos, $4.82; 2 pesos, $1.93. Silver: 1 peso, 96 cents; 20 centavos, 19 cents; 10 centavos, 10 cents; 5 centavos, 5 cents. The copper centavo of Colombia is identical in value with our cent. (The currency of Coloumbia is also used in Venezuela.)

Denmark—Gold coins: Twenty kroner piece, $5.36; 10 kroner, $2.68. Silver: Two kroner, 53 cents; 1 krone, 27 cents; 50 ore, 13 cents; 40 ore, 10 cents; 25 ore, 6½ cents; 10 ore, 2½ cents. One hundred of the copper ore make one krone.

France—Gold coins: One hundred franc piece, $19.30; 50 francs, $9.65; 20 francs, $3.85; 10 francs, 1.93; 5 francs, 96 cents. Silver: Five francs, 96 cents; 2 francs, 38 cents; 1 franc, 19 cents; 50 centimes, 10 cents; 20 centimes, 4 cents. The copper coins are the sou, worth about 9½ mills, and the centime, 2 mills.

Germany—Gold coins: Twenty-mark piece, $4.76; 10 marks, $2.38; 5 marks, $1.19. Silver: Five marks, $1.19; 2 marks, 48 cents; 1 mark 24 cents; 50 pfennige, 12 cents; 20 pfennige, 5 cents. One hundred copper pfennige make one mark.

Great Britain—Gold coins: Pound or sovereign, $4.86; guinea, $5.12. Silver: Five shillings or crown, $1.25; half crown, 62½ cents; shilling, 25 cents; sixpence, 12½ cents. Also a three-penny piece and a four-penny piece, but the latter is being called in, and is nearly out of circulation. The copper coins of Great Britain are the penny, half-penny and farthing.

India—Gold coins: Thirty rupees or double mohur, $14.58; 15 rupees or mohur, $7.29; 10 rupees, $4.86; 5 rupees, $2.43. Silver: One rupee, 48 cents, and coins respectively of the value of one-half, one-fourth and one-eighth rupee. In copper there is the pie, one-fourth of a cent; the pice, ¾ of a cent; the ana, 3 cents.

Japan—Gold coins: Twenty yen, $19.94; 10 yen, $9.97; 5 yen, $4.98; 2 yen, $1.99; 1 yen, 99 cents. Silver: The 50, 20, 10 and 5 sen pieces, answering respectively to 50, 20, 10 and 5 cents. In copper there is the sen, answering to 1 cent.

Mexico—Gold coins: Sixteen dollar piece, $15.74; 8 dollars, $7.87; 4 dollars, $3.93; 2 dollars, $1.96; 1 dollar 98 cents. Silver: 1 dollar, 98 cents; 50-cent piece, 49 cents; 25 cents, 24 cents. The Mexican cent, like our own, equals one-hundreth of a dollar.

Netherlands—Gold coins: Ten-guilder piece, $4.02; 5 guilders, $2.01. Silver: 2½ guilders, $1; 1 guilder, 40 cents; half-guilder, 20 cents; 25 cents, 10 cents; 10 cents, 4 cents; 5 cents, 2 cents. The Dutch copper cent is one-hundreth of the guilder.

Peru—Gold coins: Twenty-sol piece, $19.30; 10 sol, $9.65; 5 sol, $4.82; 2 sol, $1.93; 1 sol, 96 cents. Silver: 1 sol, 96 cents; 50 centesimos, 48 cents; 20, 10 and 5 centesimos, worth respectively 19, 10 and 5 cents. It will be noted that the Peruvian coinage is almost identical with that of Colombia. It is also used in Bolivia.

Portugal—Gold coins: Crown, $10.80; half-crown, $5.40; one-fifth crown, $2.16; one-tenth crown, $1.08. These gold pieces are also known respectively as 10, 5, 2 and 1 dollar pices. The silver coins are the 500, 200, 100 and 5 reis coins, worth respectively 54, 21, 11 and 5 cents. One thousand reis are equal to one crown.

Russia—Gold coins: Imperial or 10-ruble piece, $7.72; 5 rubles, $3.86; 3 rubles, $2.31. Silver: ruble, 77 cents; half-ruble, 38 cents; quarter-ruble, 19 cents; 20 copecks, 15 cents; 10 copecks, 7 cents; 5 copecks, 4 cents; 100 copecks are worth 1 ruble.

Turkey—Gold coins: Lira or medjidie, $4.40; half-lira, $2.20; quarter-lira, $1.10. The silver unit is the piastre, worth 4 cents of our currency, and silver coins of 1, 2, 5, 10 and 20 piastres are current.

The currency of Denmark is also in use in Norway and Sweden, these three countries forming the Scandinavian

Union. Belgium, France, Greece, Italy, Roumania, Servia, Spain and Switzerland are united in the Latin Union, and use the French coinage. The units in the different States are, it is true, called by different names; as in France, Belgium and Switzerland, franc and centime; in Italy, lira and centesimo; in Greece, drachm and lepta; in Roumania, lei and bani; in Servia, dinar and para; in Spain, peseta and centesimo; but in all cases the value is the same.

The similarity in the coinage of different countries is worth notice. A very slight change in the percentage of silver used would render the half-guilder of Austria, the krone of the Scandinavian Union, the franc of the Latin Union, the mark of Germany, the half-guilder of Holland, the quarter-ruble of Russia, the 200-reis piece of Portugal, the 5-piastre piece of Turkey, the half-milreis of Brazil and the half-rupee of India, all interchangeable with the English shilling, and all of them about the value of the quarter-dollar of North and South American coinage. With the exception of Brazil, the other South American States, as well as Mexico and the Central American countries, are all rapidly approximating a uniform coinage, which the needs of commerce will unquestionably soon harmonize with that of the United States. Curiously enough, the great force that is assimilating the alien branches of the human race is not Christianity but trade.

A HISTORY OF THE PANIC OF 1857.—The cause of the panic of 1857 was mainly the rage for land speculation which had run through the country like an epidemic. Paper cities abounded, unproductive railroads were opened, and to help forward these projects, irresponsible banks were started, or good banks found themselves drawn into an excessive issue of notes. Every one was anxious to invest in real estate and become rich by an advance in prices. Capital was attracted into this speculation by the prospect of large gains, and so great was the demand for money that there was a remarkable advance in the rates of interest. In the West, where the speculative fever was at its highest, the common rates of interest were from 2 to 5 per cent. a month. Everything was apparently in the most prosperous condition, real estate going up steadily, the demand for money constant, and its manufacture by the banks progressing successfully, when the failure of the "Ohio Life and Trust Company," came, August 24, 1857, like a thunderbolt from a clear sky. This was followed by the portentous mutterings of a terrible coming storm. One by one small banks in Illinois, Ohio, and everywhere throughout the West and South went down. September 25–26 the banks of Philadelphia suspended payment, and thus wrecked hundreds of banks in Pennsylvania, Maryland and adjoining States. October 13–14, after a terrible run on them by thousands of depositors, the banks of New York suspended payment. October 14 all the banks of Massachusetts went down, followed by a general wreckage of credit throughout New England. The distress which followed these calamities was very great, tens of thousands of workmen being unemployed for months. The New York banks resumed payment again December 12, and were soon followed by the banks in other cities. The darkest period of the crisis now seemed past, although there was much heartrending suffering among the poor during the winter which followed. The commercial reports for the year 1857 showed 5,123 commercial failures, with liabilities amounting to $291,-750,000.

THE HISTORY OF PLYMOUTH ROCK.—A flat rock near the vicinity of New Plymouth is said to have been the one on which the great body of the Pilgrims landed from the Mayflower. The many members of the colony, who died in the winter of 1620–21, were buried near this rock. About 1738 it was proposed to build a wharf along the shore there. At this time there lived in New Plymouth an old man over 90 years of age named Thomas Faunce, who had known some of the Mayflower's passengers when a lad, and by them had been shown the rock on which they had landed. On hearing that it was to be covered with a wharf the old man wept, and it has been said that his tears probably saved Plymouth Rock from oblivion. After the Revolution it was found that the rock was quite hidden by the sand washed upon it by the sea. The sand was cleared away, but in attempting to take up the rock it was split in two. The upper half was taken to the village and placed in the town square. In 1834 it was removed to a position in front of Pilgrim Hall and enclosed in an iron railing. In September, 1880, this half of the stone was taken back to the shore and reunited to the other portion. A handsome archway was then built over the rock, to protect it in part from the depredations of relic hunters.

GRANT'S TOUR AROUND THE WORLD.—General Grant embarked on a steamer at the Philadelphia wharf for his tour around the world May 17, 1877. He arrived at Queenstown, Ireland, May 27. Thence he went to Liverpool, Manchester, and on to London. He remained in that city several weeks, and was made the recipient of the most brilliant social honors. July 5th he went to Belgium, and thence made a tour through Germany and Switzerland. He then visited Denmark, and August 25 returned to Great Britain, and until October spent the time in visiting the various cities of Scotland and England. October 24th he started for Paris, where he remained a month, then went on to Lyons, thence to Naples, and subsequently with several friends he made a trip on the Mediterranean, visiting the islands of Sicily, Malta and others. Thence going to Egypt, the pyramids and other points of note were visited, and a journey made up the Nile as far as the first cataract. The programme of travel next included a visit to Turkey and the Holy Land, whence, in March, the party came back to Italy through Greece, revisited Naples, went to Turin and back to Paris. After a few weeks spent in the social gayeties of that city, the Netherlands was chosen as the next locality of interest, and The Hague, Rotterdam, and Amsterdam were visited in turn. June 26, 1878, the General and his party arrived in Berlin. After staying there some weeks they went to Christiana and Stockholm, then to St. Petersburg, Moscow and Warsaw, and back over German soil to Vienna. Another trip was now made through Switzerland, and, then returning to Paris, a start was made for a journey through Spain and Portugal, in which Victoria, Madrid, Lisbon, Seville and other important towns were visited. A trip was also made from Cadiz to Gibraltar by steamer. After another brief visit to Paris, General Grant went to Ireland, arriving at Dublin January 3, 1879; visited several points of interest in that country, then, by way of London and Paris, went to Marseilles, whence he set sail by way of the Mediterranean Sea and the Suez Canal for India. He reached Bombay February 13th. Thence visited Allahabad, Agra and rode on an elephant to Amber; also went to Benares, Delhi, Calcutta and Rangoon, spent a week in Siam, then went by steamer to China. After spending some time at Canton, Pekin and other places he went to Japan for a brief visit. He went to Nagasaki, Tokio and Yokahama, and at last, September 3, 1879, set sail from Tokio on his return to the United States. September 20th he arrived in the harbor of San Francisco. After some weeks spent in visiting the points of interest in California and Oregon he returned to his home in the Eastern States.

HISTORY OF VASSAR COLLEGE.—Vassar College is on the east bank of the Hudson, near Poughkeepsie, N. Y. It was founded in 1861. In that year Matthew Vassar, a wealthy brewer of Poughkeepsie, gave to an incorporated board of trustees the sum of $408,000 and 200 acres of land for the endowment of a college for women. The building was constructed from plans approved by him, at a cost of about $200,000. The college was opened in September, 1865, with eight professors and twenty other instructors, and 300 students. The first president of the college was Professor Milo P. Jewett; the second Dr. John H. Raymond; the third, the Rev. Samuel Caldwell. The college has a fine library, with scientific apparatus and a museum of natural history specimens.

THE ORIGIN OF CHESS.—So ancient is chess, the most purely intellectual of games, that its origin is wrapped in mystery. The Hindoos say that it was the invention of an astronomer, who lived more than 5,000 years ago, and was possessed of supernatural knowledge and acuteness. Greek historians assert that the game was invented by Palamedes to beguile the tedium of the siege of Troy. The Arab legend is that it was devised for the instruction of a young despot by his father, a learned Brahmin, to teach the youth that a king, no matter how powerful, was dependent upon his subjects for safety. The probability is that the game was the invention of some military genius for the purpose of illustrating the art of war. There is no doubt that it originated in India, for a game called by the Sanscrit name of Cheturanga—which in most essential points strongly resembles modern chess, and was unquestionably the parent of the latter game—is mentioned in Oriental literature as in use fully 2,000 years before the Christian area. In its gradual diffusion over the world the game has undergone many modifications and changes, but marked resemblances to the early Indian game are still to be found in it. From India, chess spread into Persia, and thence into Arabia, and the Arabs took it to Spain and the rest of Western Europe.

THE DARK AGES.—The Dark Ages is a name often applied by historians to the Middle Ages, a term comprising about 1,000 years, from the fall of the Roman Empire in the fifth century to the invention of printing in the fifteenth. The period is called "dark" because of the generally depraved state of European society at this time, the subserviency of men's minds to priestly domination, and the general indifference to learning. The admirable civilization that Rome had developed and fostered, was swept out of existence by the barbarous invaders from Northern Europe, and there is no doubt that the first half of the medieval era, at least, from the year 500 to 1000, was one of the most brutal and ruffianly epochs in history. The principal characteristics of the middle ages were the feudal system and the papal power. By the first the common people were ground into a condition of almost hopeless slavery, by the second the evolution of just and equitable governments by the ruling classes was rendered impossible through the intrusion of the pontifical authority into civil affairs. Learning did not wholly perish, but it betook itself to the seclusion of the cloisters. The monasteries were the resort of many earnest scholars, and there were prepared the writings of historians, metaphysicians and theologians. But during this time man lived, as the historian Symonds says, "enveloped in a cowl." The study of nature was not only ignored but barred, save only as it ministered in the forms of alchemy and astrology to the one cardinal medieval virtue—credulity. Still the period saw many great characters and events fraught with the greatest importance to the advancement of the race.

THE GREATEST DEPTH OF THE OCEAN EVER MEASURED.—The deepest verified soundings are those made in the Atlantic Ocean, ninety miles off the island of St. Thomas, in the West Indies, 3,875 fathoms, or 23,250 feet. Deeper water has been reported south of the Grand Bank of Newfoundland, over 27,000 feet in depth, but additional soundings in that locality did not corroborate this. Some years ago, it was claimed that very deep soundings, from 45,000 to 48,000 feet, had been found off the coast of South America, but this report was altogether discredited on additional investigation in these localities. The ship Challenger, which in 1872–74 made a voyage round the globe for the express purpose of taking deep sea soundings in all the oceans, found the greatest depth touched in the Pacific Ocean less than 3,000 fathoms, and the lowest in the Atlantic 3,875 fathoms, as given above.

THE ARMY OF THE REVOLUTION.—It is not positively known how many men from the colonies served in the war. The official tabular statement indicates a total of recorded years of enlistment and not a total of the men who served. Hence, a man who served from April 19, 1775, until the formal cessation of hostilities, April 19, 1783, counted as eight men in the aggregate. In this basis of enlisted years, the following table gives the contributions of the various States: New Hampshire, 12,497; Massachusetts, 69,907; Rhode Island, 5,908; Connecticut, 31,939; New York, 17,781; New Jersey, 10,726; Pennsylvania, 25,-678; Delaware, 2,386; Maryland, 13,912; Virginia, 26,-678; North Carolina, 7,263; South Carolina, 6,417; Georgia, 2,679; Total, 233,771.

THE WORLD'S DECISIVE BATTLES.—The fifteen decisive battles of the world from the fifth century before Christ to the beginning of the nineteenth century of the present era, are as follows:

The battle of Marathon, in which the Persian hosts were defeated by the Greeks under Miltiades, B. C. 490.

The defeat of the Athenians at Syracuse, B. C. 413.

The battle of Arbela, in which the Persians under Darius were defeated by the invading Greeks under Alexander the Great, B. C. 331.

The battle of the Metaurus, in which the Carthaginian forces under Hasdrubal were overthrown by the Romans, B. C. 207.

Victory of the German tribes under Arminius over the Roman legions under Varus, A. D. 9. (The battle was fought in what is now the province of Lippe, Germany, near the source of the river Ems.)

Battle of Chalons, where Attila, the terrible King of the Huns, was repulsed by the Romans under Aetius, A. D. 451.

Battle of Tours, in which the Saracen Turks invading Western Europe were utterly overthrown by the Franks under Charles Martel, A. D. 732.

Battle of Hastings, by which William the Conqueror became the ruler of England, Oct. 14, 1066.

Victory of the French under Joan of Arc over the English at Orleans, April 29, 1429.

Defeat of the Spanish Armada by the English naval force, July 29 and 30, 1588.

Battle of Blenheim, in which the French and Bavarians were defeated by the allied armies of Great Britain and Holland under the Duke of Marlborough, Aug. 2, 1704.

Battle of Pultowa, the Swedish army under Charles XII, defeated by the Russians under Peter the Great, July 8, 1709.

Victory of the American army under General Gates over the British under General Burgoyne at Saratoga, Oct. 17, 1777.

Battle of Valmy, where the allied armies of Prussia and Austria were defeated by the French under Marshal Kellerman, Sept. 20, 1792.

Battle of Waterloo, the allied forces of the British and Prussians defeated the French under Napoleon, the final overthrow of the great commander, June 18, 1815.

These battles are selected as decisive, because of the important consequences that followed them. Few students of history, probably, would agree with Prof. Creasy, in restricting the list as he does. Many other conflicts might be noted, fraught with great importance to the human race, and unquestionably "decisive" in their nature; as, for instance, the victory of Sobieski over the Turkish army at Vienna, Sept. 12, 1683. Had the Poles and Austrians been defeated there, the Turkish general might readily have fulfilled his threat "to stable his horses in the Church of St. Peter's at Rome," and all Western Europe would, no doubt, have been devastated by the ruthless and bloodthirsty Ottomans. Of important and decisive battles since that of Waterloo we may mention in our own Civil War those of Gettysburg, by which the invasion of the North was checked, and at Chattanooga, Nov. 23 and 25, 1863, by which the power of the Confederates in the southwest received a deadly blow.

THE WANDERING JEW.—There are various versions of the story of "The Wandering Jew," the legends of whom have formed the foundation of numerous romances, poems and tragedies. One version is that this person was a servant in the house of Pilate, and gave the Master a blow as He was being dragged out of the palace to go to His death. A popular tradition makes the wanderer a member of the tribe of Naphtali, who, some seven or eight years previous to the birth of the Christ-child left his father to go with the wise men of the East whom the star led to the lowly cot in Bethlehem. It runs, also, that the cause of the killing of the children can be traced to stories this person related when he returned to Jerusalem of the visit of the wise men, and the presentation of the gifts they brought to the Divine Infant, when He was acknowledged by them to be the king of the Jews. He was lost sight of for a time, when he appeared as a carpenter who was employed in making the cross on which the Saviour was to be lifted up into the eyes of all men. As Christ walked up the way to Calvary, He had to pass the workshop of this man, and when He reached its door, the soldiers, touched by the sufferings of the Man of Sorrows, besought the carpenter to allow Him to rest there for a little, but he refused, adding insult to a want of charity. Then it is said that Christ pronounced his doom, which was to wander over the earth until the second coming. Since that sentence was uttered, he has wandered, courting death, but finding it not, and his punishment becoming more unbearable as the generations come and go. He is said to have appeared in the sixteenth, seventeenth, and even as recently as the eighteenth century, under the names of Cartaphilus, and Ahasuerus, by which the Wandering Jew has been known. One of the legends described him as a shoemaker of Jerusalem, at whose door Christ desired to rest on the road to Calvary, but the man refused, and the sentence to wander was pronounced.

SOME MEMORABLE DARK DAYS.—During the last hundred years there have been an unusually large number of dark days recorded. As has been suggested by several writers, this may have been the result of the careful scientific observations of modern times, as well as of the frequency of these phenomena. The dark day in the beginning of this century about which so much has been said and written occurred Oct. 21, 1816. The first day of the same month and year is also represented as "a close dark day." Mr. Thomas Robie, who took observations at Cambridge, Mass., has this to offer in regard to the phenomenon: "On Oct. 21 the day was so dark that people were forced to light candles to eat their dinners by; which could not be from an eclipse, the solar eclipse being the fourth of that month." The day is referred to by another writer as "a remarkable dark day in New England and New York," and it is noted, quaintly by a third, that "in October, 1816, a dark day occurred after a severe winter in New England." Nov. 26, 1816, was a dark day in London, and is described "in the neighborhood of Walworth and Camberwell so completely dark that some of the coachmen driving stages were obliged to get down and lead their horses with a lantern." The famous dark day in America was May 19, 1780. The phenomenon began about 10 o'clock in the forenoon. The darkness increased rapidly, and "in many places it was impossible to read ordinary print." There was widespread fear. Many thought that the Day of Judgment was at hand. At that time the Legislature of Connecticut was in session at Hartford. The House of Representatives, being unable to transact their business, adjourned. A proposal to adjourn the council was under consideration. When the opinion of Colonel Davenport was asked, he answered: "I am against an adjournment. The day of judgment is approaching or it is not. If it is not, there is no cause for adjournment; if it is, I choose to be found doing my duty. I wish, therefore, that candles may be brought." In Whittier's "Tent on the Beach" is given a beautiful poetical version of this anecdote. It is suggested by several authorities that the cause of the dark day in 1780 should be attributed simply to the presence of ordinary clouds of very unusual volume and density. These instances are, of course, grouped with phenomena of which not a great deal is known, and can in no way be classed with those occurrances occasioned by the smoke from extensive forest fires, volcanic eruptions, or fogs.

THE REMARKABLE STORY OF CHARLIE ROSS.—Charlie Ross was the son of Christian K. Ross of Germantown, Pa., and at the time of his disappearance was a little over 4 years of age. The child and a brother 6 years old were playing July 1, 1874, in the streets of Germantown, when a couple of men drove up in a buggy and persuaded the children, with promises of toys and candies, to get in and ride with them in the vehicle. After driving around the place for a little time, the older brother, Walter Ross, was put out of the conveyance, and the strangers gave him 25 cents, telling him to go to a store near at hand and buy some candy and torpedoes for himself and Charlie. Walter did as he was told, but when he came out of the store the men with Charlie and the vehicle had disappeared. It was believed at first by the relatives and friends of the missing boy that he would be returned in a short time, as they supposed he might have been taken by some drunken men. Time passed, however, but no trace of the child had been discovered. In a few weeks a letter was received by Mr. Ross to the effect that if he would pay $20,000 his son would be returned, but that the parent need not search for Charlie, as all efforts to find the abducted boy or his captors would only be attended with failure; and it was stated that if this amount was not paid, Charlie would be killed. The father answered this and a long correspondence ensued, while the search was prosecuted in all directions. Mr. Ross wanted the child delivered at the time the money was paid, but to this the abductors refused to agree. It is stated that more than $50,000 were expended to recover the child. At one time two gentlemen were two days in Fifth Avenue Hotel, New York, with the $20,000 ransom money to be given to the child-thieves, but they did not appear. The search was continued, and the officers of the law were looking up any and all evidence, until they had located the two men. These were found Dec. 4, 1874, committing a burglary in the house of Judge Van Brunt, Bay Ridge, L. I.; the burglary was discovered, the burglars seen and shot by persons residing in an adjoining residence. One of the men was killed instantly, the other lived several hours, and confessed that he and his companion had abducted Charlie Ross, but that the dead thief, Mosher by name, was the one who knew where the boy was secreted. Walter Ross identified the burglars as the men who had enticed him and Charlie into the buggy. There the case rested. No new fact has been developed. The missing child has never been found. Many times have children been reported who resembled Charlie, and Mr. Ross has traveled far and near in his endless search, only to return sadly and report that his boy was still missing. No case in recent years has excited such universal sympathy as that of Charlie Ross.

THE BLUE LAWS ON SMOKING.—There were some very stringent laws in Massachusetts against the use of tobacco in public, and while the penalties were not so heavy, yet they were apparently rigidly enforced for a time. We quote from a law passed in October, 1632, as follows: "It is ordered that noe person shall take any tobacco publiquely, under paine of punishment; also that every one shall pay 1d. for every time hee is convicted of takeing tobacco in any place, and that any Assistant shall have power to receave evidence and give order for levyeing of it, as also to give order for the levyeing of the officer's charge. This order to begin the 10th of November next." In September, 1634, we discover another law on the same article: "Victualers, or keepers of an Ordinary, shall not suffer any tobacco to be taken in their howses, under the penalty of 5s. for every offence, to be payde by the victuler, and 12d. by the party that takes it. Further, it is ordered, that noe person shall take tobacco publiquely, under the penalty of 2s. 6d., nor privately, in his owne house, or in the howse of another, before strangers, and that two or more shall not take it togeather, anywhere, under the aforesaid penalty for every offence." In November, 1637, the record runs: "All former laws against tobacco are repealed, and tobacco is sett at liberty;" but in September, 1638, "the [General] Court, finding that since the repealing of the former laws against tobacco, the same is more abused then before, it hath therefore ordered, that no man shall take any tobacco in the fields, except in his journey, or at meale times, under paine of 12d. for every offence; nor shall take any tobacco in (or so near) any dwelling house, barne, corne or hay rick, as may likely indanger the fireing thereof, upon paine of 10s. for every offence; nor shall take any tobacco in any inne or common victualing house, except in a private roome there, so as neither the master of the same house nor any other guests there shall take offence thereat, which if they do, then such person is fourthwith to forbeare, upon paine of 12s. 6d. for every offence. Noe man shall kindle fyre by gunpowder, for takeing tobacco, except in his journey, upon paine of 12d. for every offence."

THE REMARKABLE CAVES—WYANDOTTE AND MAMMOTH.—Wyandotte Cave is in Jennings township, Crawford county, Ind., near the Ohio river. It is a rival of the great Mammoth Cave in grandeur and extent. Explorations have been made for many miles. It excels the Mammoth Cave in the number and variety of its stalagmites and stalactites, and in the size of several of its chambers. One of these chambers is 350 feet in length, 245 feet in height, and contains a hill 175 feet high, on which are three fine stalagmites. Epsom salts, niter and alum have been obtained from the earth of the cave. The Mammoth Cave is in Edmondson county, near Green River, about seventy-five miles from Louisville. Its entrance is reached by passing down a wild, rocky ravine through a dense forest. The cave extends some nine miles. To visit the portions already traversed, it is said, requires 150 to 200 miles of travel. The cave contains a succession of wonderful avenues, chambers, domes,

abysses, grottoes, lakes, rivers, cataracts and other marvels, which are too well known to need more than a reference. One chamber—the Star—is about 500 feet long, 70 feet wide, 70 feet high, the ceiling of which is composed of black gypsum, and is studded with innumerable white points, that by a dim light resemble stars, hence the name of the chamber. There are avenues one and a half and even two miles in length, some of which are incrusted with beautiful formations, and present the appearance of enchanted palace halls. There is a natural tunnel about three-quarters of a mile long, 100 feet wide, covered with a ceiling of smooth rock 45 feet high. There is a chamber having an area of from four to five acres, and there are domes 200 and 300 feet high. Echo River is some three-fourths of a mile in length, 200 feet in width at some points, and from 10 to 30 in depth, and runs beneath an arched ceiling of smooth rock about 15 feet high, while the Styx, another river, is 450 feet long, from 15 to 40 feet wide, and from 30 to 40 feet deep, and is spanned by a natural bridge. Lake Lethe has about the same length and width as the river Styx, varies in depth from 3 to 40 feet, lies beneath a ceiling some 90 feet above its surface, and sometimes rises to a height of 60 feet. There is also a Dead Sea, quite a somber body of water. There are several interesting caves in the neighborhood, one three miles long and three each about a mile in length.

THE SOUTH SEA BUBBLE.—The "South Sea Bubble," as it is generally called, was a financial scheme which occupied the attention of prominent politicians, communities, and even nations in the early part of the eighteenth century. Briefly the facts are: In 1711 Robert Hartley, Earl of Oxford, then Lord Treasurer, proposed to fund a floating debt of about £10,000,000 sterling, the interest, about $600,000, to be secured by rendering permanent the duties upon wines, tobacco, wrought silks, etc. Purchasers of this fund were to become also shareholders in the "South Sea Company," a corporation to have the monopoly of the trade with Spanish South America, a part of the capital stock of which was to be the new fund. But Spain, after the treaty of Utrecht, refused to open her commerce to England, and the privileges of the "South Sea Company" became worthless. There were many men of wealth who were stockholders, and the company continued to flourish, while the ill success of its trading operations was concealed. Even the Spanish War of 1718 did not shake the popular confidence. Then in April, 1720, Parliament, by large majorities in both Houses, accepted the company's plan for paying the national debt, and after that a frenzy of speculation seized the nation, and the stock rose to £300 a share, and by August had reached £1,000 a share. Then Sir John Blunt, one of the leaders, sold out, others followed, and the stock began to fall. By the close of September the company stopped payment and thousands were beggared. An investigation ordered by Parliament disclosed much fraud and corruption, and many prominent persons were implicated, some of the directors were imprisoned, and all of them were fined to an aggregate amount of £2,000,000 for the benefit of the stockholders. A great part of the valid assets was distributed among them, yielding a dividend of about 33 per cent.

AREA OF NORTH AMERICA.—The following figures show the extent of the United States as compared with the British possessions in North America: United States, 3,602,884 square miles. British possessions—Ontario, 121,260; Quebec, 210,020; Nova Scotia, 18,670; New Brunswick, 27,037; British Columbia, 233,000; Manitoba, 16,000; N. W. and Hudson Bay Territories, 2,206,725; Labrador and Arctic Ocean Islands, make a total of 3,500,-000.

HOUSEHOLD RECIPES

MISCELLANEOUS.

Axle Grease.—1. Water, 1 gallon; soda, $\frac{1}{3}$ pound; palm oil, 10 pounds. Mix by heat, and stir till nearly cold.

2. Water, rape oil, of each 1 gallon; soda, $\frac{1}{3}$ pound; palm oil, $\frac{1}{4}$ pound.

3. Water, 1 gallon; tallow, 3 pounds; palm oil, 6 pounds; soda, $\frac{1}{2}$ pound. Heat to 210 deg. Fahrenheit and stir until cool.

4. Tallow, 8 pounds; palm oil, 10 pounds; plumbago, 1 pound. Makes a good lubricator for wagon axles.

How to Shell Beans Easy.—Pour upon the pods a quantity of scalding water, and the beans will slip very easily from the pod. By pouring scalding water on apples the skin may be easily slipped off, and much labor saved.

How to Clean Bed-Ticks.—Apply Poland starch, by rubbing it on thick with a cloth. Place it in the sun. When dry, rub it if necessary. The soiled part will be clean as new.

How to Wash Carpets.—Shake and beat it well; lay it upon the floor and tack it firmly; then with a clean flannel wash it over with a quart of bullock's gall mixed with three quarts of soft, cold water, and rub it off with a clean flannel or house-cloth. Any particular dirty spot should be rubbed with pure gall.

How to Clean Carpets.—Before proceeding to sweep a carpet a few handfuls of waste tea-leaves should be sprinkled over it. A stiff hair broom or brush should be employed, unless the carpet is very dirty, when a whisk or carpet-broom should be used, first followed by another made of hair, to take off the loose dust. The frequent use of a stiff carpet-broom soon wears off the beauty of the best carpet. An ordinary clothes brush is best adapted for superior carpets. When carpets are very dirty they should be cleaned by shaking and beating.

Beat it well with a stick in the usual manner until all the dust is removed, then take out the stains, if any, with lemon or sorrel-juice. When thoroughly dry rub it all over with the crumb of a hot wheaten loaf, and if the weather is very fine, let hang out in the open air for a night or two. This treatment will revive the colors, and make the carpet appear equal to new.

How to Remove Spots on Carpets.—A few drops of carbonate of ammonia, and a small quantity of warm rain water, will prove a safe and easy antacid, etc., and will change, if carefully applied, discolored spots upon carpets, and indeed, all spots, whether produced by acids or alkalies. If one has the misfortune to have a carpet injured by whitewash, this will immediately restore it.

How to Remove Ink Spots on Carpets.—As soon as the ink has been spilled, take up as much as you can with a sponge, and then pour on cold water repeatedly, still taking up the liquid; next rub the place with a little wet oxalic acid or salt of sorrel, and wash it off immediately with cold water, and then rub on some hartshorn.

Cleaning and Scouring of Cloth.—The common method of cleaning cloth is by beating and brushing, unless when very dirty, when it undergoes the operation of scouring. This is best done on the small scale, as for articles of wearing apparel, etc., by dissolving a little curd soap in water, and after mixing it with a little ox-gall, to touch over all the spots of grease, dirt. etc., with it, and to rub them well with a stiff brush, until they are removed, after which the article may be well rubbed all over with a brush or sponge dipped into some warm water, to which the previous mixture and a little more ox-gall has been added. When this has been properly done, it only remains to thoroughly rinse the article in clean water until the latter passes off uncolored, when it must be hung up to dry. For dark colored cloths the common practice is to add some Fuller's-earth to the mixture of soap and gall. When nearly dry the nap should be laid right and the article carefully pressed, after which a brush, moistened with a drop or two of olive oil, is passed several times over it, which will give it a superior finish.

Cloth may also be cleaned in the dry way, as follows: First remove the spots, as above, and when the parts have dried, strew clean, damp sand over it, and beat it in with a brush, after which brush the article with a hard brush when the sand will readily come out, and bring the dirt with it. Black cloth which is very rusty should receive a coat of reviver after drying, and be hung up until the next day, when it may be pressed and finished off as before. Scarlet cloth requires considerable caution. After being thoroughly rinsed, it should be repeatedly passed through cold spring water, to which a tablespoonful or two of solution of tin has been added. If much faded, it should be dipped in a scarlet dye-bath. Buff cloth is generally cleansed by covering it with a paste made with pipe-clay and water, which, when dry; is rubbed and brushed off.

Renovation of Cloth.—The article undergoes the process of scouring before described, and, after being well rinsed and drained, it is put on a board, and the threadbare parts rubbed with a half-worn hatter's card, filled with flocks, or with a teazle or a prickly thistle, until a nap is raised. It is next hung up to dry, the nap laid the right way with a hard brush, and finished as before. When the cloth is much faded, it is usual to give it a dip, as it is called, or to pass it through a dye-bath, to freshen up the color.

How to Revive the Color of Black Cloth.—If a coat, clean it well, then boil from two to four ounces of logwood in your copper, or boiler, for half an hour; dip your coat in warm water, and squeeze it as dry as you can; then put it into the copper and boil it for half an hour. Take it out, and add a piece of green copperas, about the size of a horse-bean; boil it another half hour, then draw it, and hang it in the air for an hour or two; take it down, rinse it in two or three cold waters; dry it, and let it be well brushed with a soft brush, over which a drop or two of the oil of olives has been rubbed, then stroke your coat regularly over.

How to Restore Crape.—Skimmed milk and water, with a little bit of glue in it, made scalding hot, is excellent to restore rusty Italian crape. If clapped and pulled dry like muslin, it will look as good as new; or, brush the veil till all the dust is removed, then fold it lengthwise, and roll it smoothly and tightly on a roller. Steam it till it is thoroughly dampened, and dry on the roller.

How to Cleanse Feather Beds.—When feather beds become soiled and heavy they may be made clean and light by being treated in the following manner: Rub them over with a stiff brush, dipped in hot soap-suds. When clean lay them on a shed, or any other clean place where the rain will fall on them. When thoroughly soaked let them dry in a hot sun for six or seven successive days, shaking them up well and turning them over each day. They should be covered over with a thick cloth during the night; if exposed to the night air they will become damp and mildew. This way of washing the bed-ticking and feathers makes them very fresh and light, and is much easier than the old-fashioned way of emptying the beds and washing the feathers separately, while it answers quite as well. Care must be taken to dry the bed perfectly before sleeping on it. Hair mattresses that have become hard and dirty can be made nearly as good as new by ripping them, washing the ticking, and picking the hair free from bunches and keeping it in a dry, airy place several days. Whenever the ticking gets dry fill it lightly with the hair, and tack it together.

How to Cut Up and Cure Pork.—Have the hog laid on his back on a stout, clean bench; cut off the head close to the base. If the hog is large, there will come off a considerable collar, between head and shoulders, which, pickled or dried, is useful for cooking with vegetables. Separate the jowl from the face at the natural joint; open the skull lengthwise and take out the brains, esteemed a luxury. Then with a sharp knife remove the back-bone the whole length, then the long strip of fat underlying it, leaving about one inch of fat covering the spinal column.

The leaf lard, if not before taken out for the housewife's convenience, is removed, as is also the tenderloin—a fishy-shaped piece of flesh—often used for sausage, but which makes delicious steak. The middling or sides are now cut out, leaving the shoulders square-shaped and the hams pointed, or they may be rounded to your taste. The spareribs are usually wholly removed from the sides, with but little meat adhering. It is the sides of small, young hogs cured as hams that bear the name of breakfast bacon. The sausage meat comes chiefly in strips from the backbone, part of which may also be used as steak. The lean trimmings from about the joints are used for sausage, the fat scraps rendered up with the backbone lard.

The thick part of the backbone that lies between the shoulders, called griskin or chine, is separated from the tapering, bony part, called backbone by way of distinction, and used as flesh. The chines are smoked with jowls, and and used in late winter or spring.

When your meat is to be pickled it should be dusted lightly with saltpetre sprinkled with salt, and allowed to drain twenty-four hours; then plunge it into pickle, and keep under with a weight. It is good policy to pickle a portion of the sides. They, after soaking, are sweeter to cook with vegetables, and the grease fried from them is much more useful than that of smoked meat.

If your meat is to be dry salted, allow one teaspoonful of pulverized saltpetre to one gallon of salt, and keep the mixture warm beside you. Put on a hog's ear as a mitten, and rub each piece of meat thoroughly. Then pack skin

side down, ham upon ham, side upon side, strewing on salt abundantly. It is best to put large and small pieces in different boxes for the convenience of getting at them to hang up at the different times they will come into readiness. The weather has so much to do with the time that meat requires to take salt that no particular time can be specified for leaving it in.

The best test is to try a medium-sized ham; if salt enough, all similar and smaller pieces are surely ready, and it is well to remember that the saltness increases in drying.

Ribs and steaks should be kept in a cold, dark place, without salting, until ready for use. If you have many, or the weather is warm, they keep better in pickle than dry salt. Many persons turn and rub their meat frequently. We have never practiced this, and have never lost any.

When the meat is ready for smoking, dip the hocks of the joints in ground black pepper and dust the raw surface thickly with it. Sacks, after this treatment, may be used for double security, and I think bacon high and dry is sweeter than packed in any substance. For sugar-cured hams we append the best recipe we have ever used, though troublesome.

English Recipe for Sugar-Curing Hams.—So soon as the meat comes from the butcher's hand rub it thoroughly with the salt. Repeat this four days, keeping the meat where it can drain. The fourth day rub it with saltpetre and a handful of common salt, allowing one pound of saltpetre to seventy pounds of meat. Now mix one pound of brown sugar and one of molasses, rub over the ham every day for a fortnight, and then smoke with hickory chips or cobs. Hams should be hung highest in meat-houses, because there they are less liable to the attacks of insects, for insects do not so much infest high places—unlike human pests.

Pickle.—Make eight gallons of brine strong enough to float an egg; add two pounds of brown sugar or a quart of molasses, and four ounces of saltpetre; boil and skim clean, and pour cold on your meat. Meat intended for smoking should remain in pickle about four weeks. This pickle can be boiled over, and with a fresh cup of sugar and salt used all summer. Some persons use as much soda as saltpetre. It will correct acidity, but we think impairs the meat.

Washing Preparation.—Take a ¼ of a pound of soap, a ¼ of a pound of soda, and a ¼ of a pound of quicklime. Cut up the soap and dissolve it in 1 quart of boiling water; pour 1 quart of boiling water over the soda, and 3 quarts of boiling water upon the quicklime. The lime must be quick and fresh; if it is good it will bubble up on pouring the hot water upon it. Each must be prepared in separate vessels. The lime must settle so as to leave the water on the top perfectly clear; then strain it carefully (not disturbing the settlings) into the washboiler with the soda and soap; let it scald long enough to dissolve the soap, then add 6 gallons of soap water. The clothes must be put to soak over night, after rubbing soap upon the dirtiest parts of them. After having the above in readiness, wring out the clothes which have been put in soak, put them on to boil, and let each lot boil half an hour; the same water will answer for the whole washing. After boiling each lot half an hour drain them from the boiling water put them in a tub and pour upon them two or three pailsful of clear, hot water; after this they will want very little rubbing; then rinse through two waters, blueing the last. When dried they will be a beautiful white. After washing the cleanest part of the white clothes, take two pails of the suds in which they have been washed, put it over the fire and scald, and this will wash all the flannels and colored clothes without any extra soap. The white flannels, after being well washed in the suds, will require to be scalded by turning on a teakettle of boiling water.

HOW TO DESTROY HOUSEHOLD PESTS

How to Destroy Ants.—Ants that frequent houses or gardens may be destroyed by taking flower of brimstone half a pound and potash four ounces; set them in an iron or earthen pan over the fire till dissolved and united; afterward beat them to a powder, and infuse a little of this powder in water; and wherever you sprinkle it the ants will die or fly the place.

How to Destroy Black Ants.—A few leaves of green wormwood, scattered among the haunts of these troublesome insects, is said to be effectual in dislodging them.

How to Destroy Red Ants.—The best way to get rid of ants, is to set a quantity of cracked walnuts or shellbarks on plates, and put them in the closet or places where the ants congregate. They are very fond of these, and will collect on them in myriads. When they have collected on them make a general *auto-da-fe*, by turning nuts and ants together into the fire, and then replenish the plates with fresh nuts. After they have become so thinned off as to cease collecting on plates, powder some camphor and put in the holes and crevices, whereupon the remainder of them will speedily depart. It may help the process of getting them to assemble on shell-barks, to remove all edibles out of their way for the time.

How to Destroy Black Bees.—Place two or three shallow vessels—the larger kind of flower-pot saucers will do—half filled with water, on the floors where they assemble, with strips of cardboard running from the edge of the vessel to the floor, at a gentle inclination; these the unwelcome guests will eagerly ascend, and so find a watery grave.

How to Destroy Bed-Bugs.—1. When they have made a lodgement in the wall, fill all the apertures with a mixture of soft soap and Scotch snuff. Take the bedstead to pieces, and treat that in the same way. 2. A strong decoction of red pepper applied to bedsteads will either kill the bugs or drive them away. 3. Put the bedstead into a close room and set fire to the following composition, placed in an iron pot upon the hearth, having previously closed up the chimney, then shut the door, let them remain a day: Sulphur nine parts; saltpetre, powdered, one part. Mix. Be sure to open the door of the room five or six hours before you venture to go into it a second time. 4. Rub the bedstead well with lampoil; this alone is good, but to make it more effectual, get ten cents worth of quicksilver and add to it. Put it into all the cracks around the bed, and they will soon disappear. The bedsteads should first be scalded and wiped dry, then put on with a feather. 5. Corrosive sublimate, one ounce; muriatic acid, two ounces; water, four ounces; dissolve, then add turpentine, one pint; decoction of tobacco, one pint. Mix. For the decoction of tobacco boil one ounce of tobacco in a ½ pint of water. The mixture must be applied with a paint brush. This wash is deadly poison. 6. Rub the bedsteads in the joints with equal parts of spirits of turpentine and kerosene oil, and the cracks of the surbase in rooms where there are many. Filling up all the cracks with hard soap is an excellent remedy.

March and April are the months when bedsteads should be examined to kill all the eggs. 7. Mix together two ounces spirits of turpentine, one ounce corrosive sublimate, and one pint alcohol. 8. Distilled vinegar, or diluted good vinegar, a pint; camphor one-half ounce; dissolve. 9. White arsenic, two ounces; lard, thirteen ounces; corrosive sublimate, one-fourth ounce; venetian red, one-fourth ounce. (Deadly poison.) 10. Strong mercurial ointment, one ounce; soft soap one ounce; oil of turpentine, a pint. 11. Gasoline and coaloil are both excellent adjuncts, with cleanliness, in ridding a bed or house of these pests.

How to Destroy Caterpillars.—Boil together a quantity of rue, wormwood, and any cheap tobacco (equal parts) in common water. The liquid should be very strong. Sprinkle it on the leaves and young branches every morning and evening during the time the fruit is ripening.

How to Destroy Cockroaches and Beetles.—1. Strew the roots of black hellebore, at night, in the places infested by these vermin, and they will be found in the morning dead or dying. Black hellebore grows in marshy grounds, and may be had at the herb shops. 2. Put about a quart of water sweetened with molasses in a tin wash basin or smooth glazed china bowl. Set it at evening in a place frequented by the bugs. Around the basin put an old piece of carpet that the bugs can have easy access to the top. They will go down in the water, and stay till you come. 3. Take pulverized borax, 4 parts, flour 1 part, mix intimately and distribute the mixture in cupboards which are frequented by the roaches, or blow it, by means of a bellows, into the holes or cracks that are infested by them. 4. By scattering a handful of fresh cucumber parings about the house. 5. Take carbonic acid and powdered camphor in equal parts; put them in a bottle; they will become fluid. With a painter's brush of the size called a sash-tool, put the mixture on the cracks or places where the roaches hide; they will come out at once. Then kill. 6. Mix up a quantity of fresh burned plaster of paris (gypsum, such as is used for making molds and ornaments), with wheat flour and a little sugar, and distribute on shallow plates and box boards, and place in the corners of the kitchen and pantry, where they frequent. In the darkness they will feast themselves on it. Whether it interferes with their digestion or not, is difficult to ascertain, but after three or four nights renewal of the preparation, no cockroaches will be found on the premises.

How to Destroy Crickets.—Sprinkle a little quicklime near to the cracks through which they enter the room. The lime may be laid down overnight, and swept away in the morning. In a few days they will most likely all be destroyed. But care must be taken that the children do not meddle with the lime, as a very small portion of it, getting into the eye, would prove exceedingly hurtful. In case of such an accident the best thing to do would be to wash the eye with vinegar and water.

How to get Rid of Fleas.—Much of the largest number of fleas are brought into our family circles by pet dogs and cats. The oil of pennyroyal will drive these insects off; but a cheaper method, where the herb flourishes, is to throw your cats and dogs into a decoction of it once a week. When the herb cannot be got, the oil can be procured. In this case, saturate strings with it and tie them around the necks of the dogs and cats. These applications should be repeated every twelve or fifteen days. Mint, freshly cut, and hung round a bedstead, or on the furniture, will prevent annoyance from bed insects; a few drops of essential oil of lavender will be more efficacious.

How to Destroy Flies.—1. Take an infusion of quassia, one pint; brown sugar, four ounces, ground pepper, two ounces. To be well mixed together, and put in small shallow dishes where required. 2. Black pepper (powdered), one drachm; brown sugar, one drachm; milk or cream, two drachms. Mix, and place it on a plate or saucer where the flies are most troublesome. 3. Pour a little simple oxymel (an article to be obtained at the druggists), into a common tumbler glass, and place in the glass a piece of cap paper, made into the shape of the upper part of a funnel, with a hole at the bottom to admit the flies. Attracted by the smell, they readily enter the trap in swarms, and by the thousands soon collected prove that they have not the wit or the disposition to return. 4. Take some jars, mugs, or tumblers, fill them half full with soapy water; cover them as jam-pots are covered, with a piece of paper, either tied down or tucked under the rim. Let this paper be rubbed inside with wet sugar, molasses, honey, or jam, or any thing sweet; cut a small hole in the center, large enough for a fly to enter. The flies settle on the top, attracted by the smell of the bait; they then crawl through the hole, to feed upon the sweets beneath. Meanwhile the warmth of the weather causes the soapy water to ferment, and produces a gas which overpowers the flies, and they drop down into the vessel. Thousands may be destroyed this way, and the traps last a long time.

Fly Paper.—Melt resin, and add thereto while soft, sufficient sweet oil, lard, or lamp oil to make it, when cold about the consistency of honey. Spread on writing paper, and place in a convenient spot. It will soon be filled with ants, flies, and other vermin.

How to Expel Insects.—All insects dread pennyroyal; the smell of it destroys some, and drives others away. At the time that fresh pennyroyal cannot be gathered, get oil of pennyroyal; pour some into a saucer, and steep in it small pieces of wadding or raw cotton, and place them in corners, closet-shelves, bureau drawers, boxes, etc., and the cockroaches, ants, or other insects will soon disappear. It is also well to place some between the mattresses, and around the bed. It is also a splendid thing for brushing off that terrible little insect, the seed tick.

How to Destroy Mice.—1. Use tartar emetic mingled with some favorite food. The mice will leave the premises.

2. Take one part calomel, five parts of wheat flour, one part sugar, and one-tenth of a part of ultramarine. Mix together in a fine powder and place it in a dish. This is a most efficient poison for mice.

3. Any one desirous of keeping seeds from the depredations of mice can do so by mixing pieces of camphor gum in with the seeds. Camphor placed in drawers or trunks will prevent mice from doing them injury. The little animal objects to the odor and keeps a good distance from it. He will seek food elsewhere.

4. Gather all kinds of mint and scatter about your shelves, and they will forsake the premises.

How to Drive Away Mosquitoes.—1. A camphor bag hung up in an open casement will prove an effectual barrier to their entrance. Camphorated spirits applied as perfume to the face and hands will prove an effectual preventive; but when bitten by them, aromatic vinegar is the best antidote.

2. A small amount of oil of pennyroyal sprinkled around the room will drive away the mosquitoes. This is an excellent recipe.

3. Take of gum camphor a piece about half the size of an egg, and evaporate it by placing it in a tin vessel and holding it over a lamp or candle, taking care that it does not ignite. The smoke will soon fill the room and expel the mosquitoes.

How to Preserve Clothing from Moths.—1. Procure shavings of cedar wood and enclose in muslin bags, which should be distributed freely among clothes. 2. Procure shavings of camphor wood, and enclose in bags. 3. Sprinkle pimento (allspice) berries among the clothes. 4. Sprinkle the clothes with the seeds of the musk plant. 5. An ounce of gum camphor and one of the powdered shell of red pepper are macerated in eight ounces of strong alcohol for several days, then strained. With this tincture the furs or cloths are sprinkled over, and rolled up in sheets. 6. Carefully shake and brush woolens early in the spring, so as to be certain that no eggs are in them; then sew them up in cotton or linen wrappers, putting a piece of camphor gum, tied up in a bit of muslin, into each bundle, or into the chests and closets where the articles are to lie. No moth will approach while the smell of the camphor continues. When the gum is evaporated, it must be renewed. Enclose them in a moth-proof box with camphor, no matter whether made of white paper or white pine, before any eggs are laid on them by early spring moths. The notion of having a trunk made of some particular kind of wood for this purpose, is nonsense. Furs or woolens, put away in spring time, before moth eggs are laid, into boxes, trunks, drawers, or closets even, where moths cannot enter, will be safe from the ravages of moth-worms, provided none were in them that were laid late in the autumn, for they are not of spontaneous production.

How to Kill Moths in Carpets.—Wring a coarse crash towel out of clear water, spread it smoothly on the carpet, iron it dry with a good hot iron, repeating the operation on all parts of the carpet suspected of being infected with moths. No need to press hard, and neither the pile nor color of the carpet will be injured, and the moths will be destroyed by the heat and steam.

How to Destroy Rats.—1. When a house is invested with rats which refuse to be caught by cheese and other baits, a few drops of the highly-scented oil of rhodium poured on the bottom of the cage will be an attraction which they cannot refuse. 2. Place on the floor near where their holes are supposed to be a thin layer of moist caustic potash. When the rats travel on this, it will cause their feet to become sore, which they lick, and their tongues become likewise sore. The consequence is, that they shun this locality, and seem to inform all the neighboring rats about it, and the result is that they soon abandon a house that has such mean floors. 3. Cut some corks as thin as wafers, and fry, roast, or stew them in grease, and place the same in their track; or a dried sponge fried or dipped in molasses or honey, with a small quantity of bird lime or oil of rhodium, will fasten to their fur and cause them to depart. 4. If a live rat can be caught and smeared over with tar or train oil, and afterwards allowed to escape in the holes of other rats, he will cause all soon to take their departure. 5. If a live rat be caught, and a small bell be fastened around his neck, and allowed to escape, all of his brother rats as well as himself will very soon go to some other neighbor's house. 6. Take a pan, about twelve inches deep, and half fill it with water; then sprinkle some bran on the water and set the pan in a place where the rats most frequent. In the morning you will find several rats in the pan. 7. Flour, three parts; sugar, one-half part; sulphur, two parts, and phosphorus, two parts. Smear on meat, and place near where the rats are most troublesome. 8. Squills are an excellent poison for rats. The powder should be mixed with some fatty substance, and spread upon slices of bread. The pulp of onions is also very good. Rats are very fond of either. 9. Take two ounces of carbonate of barytes, and mix with one pound of suet or tallow, place a portion of this within their holes and about their haunts. It is greedily eaten, produces great thirst, and death ensues after drinking. This is a very effectual poison, because it is both tasteless and odorless. 10. Take one ounce of finely powdered arsenic, one ounce of lard; mix these into a paste with meal, put it about the haunts of rats. They will eat of it greedily. 11. Make a paste of one ounce of flour, one-half gill of water, one drachm of phosphorus, and one ounce of flour. Or, one ounce of flour, two ounces of powdered cheese crumbs, and one-half drachm of phosphorus; add to each of these mixtures a few drops of the oil of rhodium, and spread this on thin pieces of bread like butter; the rats will eat of this greedily, and it is a sure poison. 12. Mix some ground plaster of paris with some sugar and Indian meal. Set it about on plates, and leave beside each plate a saucer of water. When the rats have eaten the mixture they will drink the water and die. To attract them toward it, you may sprinkle on the edges of the plates a little of the oil of rhodium. Another method of getting rid of rats is, to strew pounded potash on their holes. The potash gets into their coats and irritates the skin, and the rats desert the place. 13. The Dutch method: this is said to be used successfully in Holland; we have, however, never tried it. A number of rats are left together to themselves in a very large trap or cage, with no food whatever; their craving hunger will, at last, cause them to fight and the weakest will be eaten by the others; after a short time the fight is renewed, and the next weakest is the victim, aud so it goes on till one strong rat is left. When this one has eaten the last remains of any of the others, it is set loose; the animal has now acquired such a taste for rat-flesh that he is the terror of rat-dom, going round seeking what rat he may devour. In an incredibly short time the premises are abandomed by all other rats, which will not come back before the cannibal rat has left or has died. 14. Catch a rat and smear him over with a mixture of phosphorus and lard, and then let him loose. The house will soon be emptied of these pests.

Vermin, in Water.—Go to the river or pond, and with a small net (a piece of old mosquito bar will do) collect a dozen or more of the small fishes known as minnows, and put them in your cistern, and in a short time you will have clear water, the wiggle-tails and reddish-colored bugs or lice being gobbled up by the fishes.

ACCIDENTS AND INJURIES
..AND HOW TO MEET THEM..

As accidents are constantly liable to occur, the importance of knowing how best to meet the various emergencies that may arise can hardly be over-estimated. In all cases, and under all circumstances, the best help to assist a party in this trying moment is *presence of mind*.

Harvest Bug Bites.—The best remedy is the use of benzine, which immediately kills the insect. A small drop of tincture of iodine has the same effect.

Bites and Stings of Insects.—Such as bees, wasps, hornets, etc., although generally painful, and ofttimes causing much disturbance, yet are rarely attended with fatal results. The pain and swelling may generally be promptly arrested by bathing freely with a strong solution of equal parts of common salt and baking soda, in warm water; or by the application of spirits of hartshorn; or of volatile liniment (one part of spirits of hartshorn and two of olive oil). In the absence of the other articles, warm oil may be used; or, if this is not at hand, apply a paste made from fresh clay-earth. If the sting of the insect is left in the wound, as is frequently the case, it should always be extracted. If there is faintness, give some stimulant; as, a tablespoonful or two of brandy and water, or brandy and ammonia.

Mad Dog Bites.—1. Take immediately warm vinegar or tepid water; wash the wound clean therewith and then dry it; pour upon the wound, then, ten or twelve drops of muriatic acid. Mineral acids destroy the poison of the saliva, by which means the evil effects of the latter are neutralized. 2. Many think that the only sure preventive of evil following the bite of a rabid dog is to suck the wound immediately, before the poison has had time to circulate with the blood. If the person bit cannot get to the wound to suck it, he must persuade or pay another to do it for him. There is no fear of any harm following this, for the poison entering by the stomach cannot hurt a person. A spoonful of the poison might be swallowed with impunity, but the person who sucks the place should have no wound on the lip or tongue, or it might be dangerous. The precaution alluded to is a most important one, and should never be omitted prior to an excision and the application of lunar caustic in every part, especially the interior and deep-seated portions. No injury need be anticipated if this treatment is adopted promptly and effectively. The poison of hydrophobia remains latent on an average six weeks; the part heals over, but there is a pimple or wound, more or less irritable; it then becomes painful; and the germ, whatever it is, ripe for dissemination into the system, and then all hope is gone. Nevertheless, between the time of the bite and the activity of the wound previous to dissemination, the caustic of nitrate of silver is a sure preventive; after that it is as useless as all the other means. The best mode of application of the nitrate of silver is by introducing it solidly into the wound.

Serpents Bites.—The poison inserted by the stings and bites of many venomous reptiles is so rapidly absorbed, and of so fatal a description, as frequently to occasion death before any remedy or antidote can be applied; and they are rendered yet more dangerous from the fact that these wounds are inflicted in parts of the country and world where precautionary measures are seldom thought of, and generally at times when people are least prepared to meet them. 1. In absence of any remedies, the first best plan to adopt on being bitten by any of the poisonous snakes is to do as recommended above in Mad Dog Bites—viz., to wash off the place immediately; if possible get the mouth to the spot, and forcibly suck out all the poison, first applying a ligature above the wound as tightly as can be borne. 2. A remedy promulgated by the Smithsonian Institute is to take 30 grs. iodide potassium, 30 grs. iodine, 1 oz. water, to be applied externally to the wound by saturating lint or batting—the same to be kept moist with the antidote until the cure be effected, which will be in one hour, and sometimes instantly. 3. An Australian physician has tried and recommends carbolic acid, diluted and administered internally every few minutes until recovery is certain. 4. Another Australian physician, Professor Halford, of Melbourne University, has discovered that if a proper amount of dilute ammonia be injected into the circulation of a patient suffering from snake-bite, the curative effect is usually sudden and startling, so that, in many cases, men have thus been brought back, as it were, by magic, from the very shadow of death.

Bleeding at the Nose.—1. Roll up a piece of paper, and press it under the upper lip. 2. In obstinate cases blow a little gum Arabic up the nostrils through a quill, which will immediately stop the discharge; powdered alum is also good. 3. Pressure by the finger over the small artery near the ala (wing) of the nose, on the side where the blood is flowing, is said to arrest the hemorrhage immediately.

Bleeding from the Lungs.—A New York physician has related a case in which inhalation of very dry persulphate of iron, reduced to a palpable powder, entirely arrested bleeding from the lungs, after all the usual remedies, lead, opium, etc., had failed. A small quantity was administered by drawing into the lungs every hour during part of the night and following day.

Bleeding from the Bowels.—The most common cause of this, when not a complication of some disease, is hemorrhoids or piles. Should serious hemorrhage occur, rest and quiet, and cold water poured slowly over the lower portion of the belly, or cloths wet with cold water, or better, with ice water applied over the belly and thighs, and to the lower end of the bowels, will ordinarily arrest it. In some cases it may be necessary to use injections of cold water, or even put small pieces of ice in the rectum.

Bleeding from the Mouth.—This is generally caused by some injury to the cheeks, gums or tongue, but it sometimes occurs without any direct cause of this kind, and no small alarm may be caused by mistaking it for bleeding from the lungs. Except when an artery of some size is injured, bleeding from the mouth can generally be controlled by gargling and washing the mouth with cold water, salt and water, or alum and water, or some persulphate of iron may be applied to the bleeding surface. Sometimes obstinate or even alarming bleeding may follow the pulling of a tooth. The best remedy for this is to plug the cavity with lint or cotton wet with the solution of persulphate of iron, and apply a compress which may be kept in place by closing the teeth on it.

Bleeding from the Stomach.—*Vomiting blood.*—Hemorrhage from the stomach is seldom so serious as to endanger life; but as it may be a symptom of some dangerous affection, it is always best to consult a physician concerning it. In the meantime, as in all other varieties of hemorrhage, perfect quiet should be preserved. A little salt, or vinegar, or lemon juice, should be taken at intervals, in a small glass of fresh cool water, or ice-water, as ice may be swallowed in small pieces, and cloths wet with ice-water, or pounded ice applied over the stomach.

Bleeding from Varicose Veins.—Serious and even fatal hemorrhage may occur from the bursting of a large varicose or "broken" vein. Should such an accident occur, the bleeding may be best controlled, until proper medical aid can be procured, by a tight bandage; or a "stick tourniquet," remembering that the blood comes toward the heart in the veins, and from it in the arteries.

The best thing to prevent the rupture of varicose or broken veins is to support the limb by wearing elastic stockings, or a carefully applied bandage.

Burns and Scalds.—There is no class of accidents that cause such an amount of agony, and none which are followed with more disastrous results.

1. By putting the burned part under cold water, milk, or other bland fluid, instantaneous and perfect relief from all pain will be experienced. On withdrawal, the burn should be perfectly covered with half an inch or more of common wheaten flour, put on with a dredging-box, or in any other way, and allowed to remain until a cure is effected, when the dry, caked flour will fall off, or can be softened with water, disclosing a beautiful, new and healthy skin, in all cases where the burns have been superficial. 2. Dissolve white lead in flaxseed oil to the consistency of milk, and apply over the entire burn or scald every five minutes. It can be applied with a soft feather. This is said to give relief sooner, and to be more permanent in its effects, than any other application. 3. Make a saturated solution of alum (four ounces to a quart of hot water). Dip a cotton cloth in this solution and apply immediately on the burn. As soon as it becomes hot or dry, replace it by another, and continue doing so as often as the cloth dries, which at first will be every few minutes. The pain will immediately cease, and after twenty-four hours of this treatment the burn will be healed; especially if commenced before blisters are formed. The astringent and drying qualities of the alum will entirely prevent their formation. 4. Glycerine, five ounces; white of egg, four ounces; tincture of arnica, three ounces. Mix the glycerine and white of egg thoroughly in a mortar, and gradually add the arnica. Apply freely on linen rags night and morning, washing previously with warm castile soap-suds. 5. Take one drachm of finely powdered alum, and mix thoroughly with the white of two eggs and one teacup of fresh lard; spread on a cloth, and apply to the parts burnt. It gives almost instant relief from pain, and, by excluding the air, prevents excessive inflammatory action. The application should be changed at least once a day. 6. M. Joel, of the Children's Hospital, Lausanne, finds that a tepid bath, containing a couple of pinches of sulphate of iron, gives immediate relief to young children who have been extensively burned. In a case of a child four years old, a bath repeated twice a day—twenty minutes each bath—the suppuration decreased, lost its odor, and the little sufferer was soon convalescent. 7. For severe scalding, carbolic acid has recently been used with marked benefit. It is to be mixed with thirty parts of the ordinary oil of lime water to one part of the acid. Linen rags satured in the carbolic emulsion are to be spread on the scalded parts, and kept moist by frequently smearing with the feather dipped in the liquid. Two advantages of this mode of treatment are, the exclusion of air, and the rapid healing by a natural restorative action without the formation of pus, thus preserving unmarred and personal appearance of the patient—a matter of no small importance to some people.

Choking.—In case of Choking, a violent slap with the open hand between the shoulders of the sufferer will often effect a dislodgment. In case the accident occurs with a child, and the slapping process does not afford instant relief, it should be grasped by the feet, and placed head downwards, and the slapping between the shoulders renewed; but in case this induced violent suffocative paroxysms it must not be repeated. If the substance, whatever it may be, has entered the windpipe, and the coughing and inverting the body fails to dislodge it, it is probable that nothing but cutting open the windpipe will be of any avail ; and for this the services of a surgeon should always be procured. If food has stuck in the throat or gullet, the forefinger should be immediately introduced ; and if lodged at the entrance of the gullet, the substance may be reached and extracted, possibly, with the forefinger alone, or may be seized with a pair of pincers, if at hand, or a curling tongs, or anything of the kind. This procedure may be facilitated by directing the person to put the tongue well out, in which position it may be retained by the individual himself, or a bystander by grasping it, covered with a handkerchief or towel. Should this fail, an effort should be made to excite retching or vomiting by passing the finger to the root of the tongue, in hopes that the offending substance may in this way be dislodged ; or it may possibly be effected by suddenly and unexpectedly dashing in the face a basin of cold water, the shock suddenly relaxing the muscular spasm present, and the involuntary gasp at the same time may move it up or down. If this cannot be done, as each instant's delay is of vital importance to a choking man, sieze a fork, a spoon, a penholder, pencil, quill, or anything suitable at hand, and endeavor to push the article down the throat. If it be low down the gullet, and other means fail, its dislodgment may sometimes be effected by dashing cold water on the spine, or vomiting may be induced by an emetic of sulphate of zinc (twenty grains in a couple of tablespoonfuls of warm water), or of common salt and mustard in like manner, or it may be pushed into the stomach by extemporizing a probang, by fastening a small sponge to the end of a stiff slrip of whalebone. If this cannot be done, a surgical operation will be necessary. Fish bones or other sharp substances, when they cannot be removed by the finger or forceps, may sometimes be dislodged by swallowing some pulpy mass, as masticated bread, etc. Irregularly shaped substances, a plate with artificial teeth for instance, can ordinarily be removed only by surgical interference.

Colic.—Use a hot fomentation over the abdomen, and a small quantity of ginger, pepermint or common tea. If not relieved in a few minutes, then give an injection of a quart of warm water with twenty or thirty drops of laudanum, and repeat it if necessary. A half teaspoonful of chloroform, in a tablespoonful of sweetened water, with or without a few drops of spirits of lavender or essence of peppermint, will often give prompt relief.

Convulsions.—In small children convulsions frequently happen from teething, sometimes from worms or from some irritating substance within the stomach or bowels, and sometimes from some affection of the brain.

When a child has convulsions, place it immediately in a warm of hot bath, and sponge its head with cold water. Then apply a hot mustard plaster to the wrists, ankles and soles of the feet, or, in case a plaster cannot be obtained, apply a cloth wrung out of hot mustard water. Allow these to remain until the skin reddens, and use care that the same do not blister. After the fit has subsided, use great care against its return by attention to the cause which gave rise to it.

Convulsions in adults must be treated in accordance with the manner which gave rise to them. During the attack great care should be taken that the party does not injure himself, and the best preventive is a cork or a soft piece of wood, or other suitable substance, placed between the teeth to prevent biting the tongue and cheeks: tight clothing must be removed or loosened ; mustard poultices should be applied to the extremities and over the abdomen ; abundance of fresh air should be secured by opening windows and doors, and preventing unnecessary crowding of persons around ; cold water may be dashed on the face and chest ; and if there be plethora, with full bounding pulse, with evidence of cerebral or other internal congestion, the abstraction of a few ounces of blood may be beneficial.

Cramp.—Spasmodic or involuntary contractions of the muscles generally of the extremities, accompained with great pain. The muscles of the legs and feet are the most commonly affected with cramp, especially after great exertion. The best treatment is immediately to stand upright, and to well rub the part with the hand. The application of strong stimulants, as spirits of ammonia, or of anodines, as opiate liniments, has been recommended. When cramp occurs in the stomach, a teaspoonful of sal volatile in water, or a dram glassful of good brandy, should be swallowed immediately. When cramp comes on during cold bathing, the limb should be thrown out as suddenly and violently as possible, which will generally remove it, care being also taken not to become flurried nor frightened, as presence of mind is very essential to personal safety on such an occasion. A common cause of cramp is indigestion, and the use of acescent liquors; these should be avoided.

Cuts.—In case the flow of blood is trifling, stop the bleeding by bringing the edges of the wound together. If the flow of blood is great, of a bright vermillion color, and flows in spurts or with a jerk, an artery is severed, and at once should pressure be made on the parts by the finger (between the cut and the heart), until a compress is arranged by a tight ligature above the wounded part. Then the finger may be taken off, and if the blood still flows, tighten the handkerchief or other article that forms the ligature, until it ceases. If at this point the attendance of a physician or surgeon cannot be secured, take strong silk thread, or wax together three or four threads, and cut them into lengths of about a foot long. Wash the parts with warm water, and then with a sharp hook or small pair of pincers in your hand, fix your eye steadfastly upon the wound, and directing the ligature to be slightly released, you will see the mouth of the artery from which the blood springs. At once seize it, draw it out a little, while an assistant passes a ligature round it, and ties it up tight with a double knot. In this way take up in succession every bleeding vessel you can see or get hold of. If the wound is too high up in a limb to apply the ligature, do not lose your presence of mind. If it is the thigh, press firmly on the groin; if in the arm, with the hand-end or ring of a common door-key make pressure above the collarbone, and about its middle, against its first rib, which lies under it. The pressure should be continued until assistance is procured and the vessel tied up. If the wound is on the face, or other place where pressure cannot effectually be made, place a piece of ice directly over the wound, allowing it to remain there until the blood coagulates, when it may be removed, and a compress and bandage be applied.

After the bleeding is arrested the surrounding blood should be cleared away, as well as any extraneous matter; then bring the sides of the wound into contact throughout the whole depth, in order that they may grow together as quickly as possible, retaining them in their position by strips of adhesive plaster. If the wound be deep and extensive, the wound itself and the adjacent parts must be supported by proper bandages. The position of the patient should be such as will relax the skin and muscles of the wounded part. Rest, low and unstimulating diet, will complete the requirements necessary to a speedy recovery.

How to Distinguish Death.—As many instances occur of parties being buried alive, they being to all appearance dead, the great importance of knowing how to distinguish real from imaginary death need not be explained. The appearances which mostly accompany death, are an entire stoppage of breathing, of the heart's action; the eyelids are partly closed, the eyes glassy, and the pupils usually dilated; the jaws are clenched, the fingers partially contracted, and the lips and nostrils more or less covered with frothy mucus, with increasing pallor and coldness of surface, and the muscles soon become rigid and the limbs fixed in their position. But as these same conditions may also exist in certain other cases of suspended animation, great care should be observed, whenever there is the least doubt concerning it, to prevent the unnecessary crowding of the room in which the corpse is, or of parties crowding around the body; nor should the body be allowed to remain lying on the back without the tongue being so secured as to prevent the glottis or orifice of the windpipe being closed by it; nor should the face be closely covered; nor rough usage of any kind be allowed. In case there is great doubt, the body should not be allowed to be inclosed in the coffin, and under no circumstances should burial be allowed until there are unmistakable signs of decomposition.

Of the numerous methods proposed as signs for real death, we select the following: 1. So long as breathing continues, the surface of a mirror held to the mouth and nostrils will become dimmed with moisture. 2. If a strong thread or small cord be tied tightly round the finger of a living person, the portion beyond the cord or thread will become red and swollen—if dead, no change is produced. 3. If the hand of a living person is held before a strong light a portion of the margin or edges of the fingers is translucent—if dead, every part of it is opaque. 4. A coal of fire, a piece of hot iron, or the flame of a candle, applied to the skin, if life remains, will blister—if dead it will merely sear. 5. A bright steel needle introduced and allowed to remain for half an hour in living flesh will be still bright—if dead, it will be tarnished by oxydation. 6. A few drops of a solution of atropia (two grains to one-half ounce of water) introduced into the eye, if the person is alive, will cause the pupils to dilate—if dead, no effect will be produced. 7. If the pupil is already dilated, and the person is alive, a few drops of tincture of the calabar bean will cause it to contract—if dead, no effect will be produced.

Dislocations.—These injuries can mostly be easily recognized; 1. By the deformity that the dislocation gives rise to by comparing the alteration in shape with the other side of the body. 2. Loss of some of the regular movements of the joints. 3. In case of dislocation, surgical aid should be procured at once. While waiting the arrival of a physician, the injured portion should be placed in the position most comfortable to the patient, and frequent cold bathing or cloths wrung out of cold water, applied to the parts affected, so as to relieve suffering and prevent inflammation.

Foreign Bodies in Ears.—Great care should be taken in removing foreign bodies from the ear, as serious injury may be inflicted. Most foreign bodies, especially those of small size, can be easily removed by the use of a syringe with warm water, and in most cases no other means should be used. Should the first efforts fail, repeat the operation. A syringe throwing a moderately small and continuous stream is the best adapted for the purpose, and the removal may generally be facilitated by inclining the ear downward while using the syringe. Severe inflammation may be excited, and serious injury done, by rash attempts to seize a foreign body in the ear, with a forceps or tweezers, or trying to pick it out with a pin or needle, or with an ear scoop. Should it be necessary from any cause to use instruments, great care should be observed, and but very little force exerted. It has lately been recommended, when foreign bodies cannot be removed by syringing the ear, to introduce a small brush or swab of frayed linen or muslin cloth, or a bit of sponge, moistened with a solution of glue,

and keep it in contact with the foreign body until the glue adheres, when the body may be easily removed.

Insects in the Ear.—Insects in the ear may be easily killed by pouring oil in the ear, after which remove by syringing. (See foreign bodies in ear.)

To Remove Hardened Ear Wax.—Hardened ear wax may be softened by dropping into the ear some oil or glycerine, and then syringing. (See foreign bodies in ear.)

Foreign Bodies in Eye.—To remove small particles from the eye, unless they have penetrated the globe, or become fixed in the conjunctiva, do as follows:

Grasp the upper lid between the thumb and forefinger, lift it from the eyeball, and having drawn it down as far as possible outside the lower lid, let it slide slowly back to its place, resting upon the lower lid as it goes back; and then wipe the edges of the lids with a soft handkerchief to remove the foreign substance. This may be repeated a number of times, if necessary, without injury. Should this means fail, evert the lids and remove the foreign substance by touching it lightly with the fold of a handkerchief, or with the point of a roll of paper made like a candle-lighter; or, if necessary, with a small pair of forceps. A drop of sweet oil instilled in the eye, while perfectly harmless, provokes a flow of tears that will frequently wash away any light substance.

Bits of metal, sharp pieces of sand, etc., sometimes penetrate the globe of the eye, and, unless removed, may excite so much inflammation as to destroy the eye. They should be removed by a competent surgeon.

Fainting.—Lay the person who has fainted in a current of air, or in such a position that the air from an open window or door will have full play upon the face. Do not allow parties to crowd closely around, but give the sufferer plenty of room. Recovery will take place in a few minutes. The clothes also may be opened, and cold water sprinkled upon the face, hands and chest; and some pungent substance, as smelling salts, camphor, aromatic vinegar, etc., may be applied to the nostrils; and as soon as able to swallow, a little fresh water, or spirits and water, may be given. Persons who faint easily should avoid crowded rooms and places where the air is close.

Fits.—See Convulsions.

Clothing on Fire.—If a woman's clothes catch on fire, let her instantly roll herself over and over on the ground. In case any one be present, let them throw her down and do the like, and then wrap her up in a table-cloth, rug, coat, or the first woolen article that can be found.

Fractures.—As we can only give general rules for treating the various fractures, we would advise any one suffering from such to immediately apply to the nearest surgeon, and not rely upon an inexperienced party.

Frost-Bite.—Place the party suffering in a room without fire, and rub the frozen or frosted parts with snow, or pour ice-water over them until sensation begins to return. As soon as a stinging pain is felt, and a change of color appears, then cease the rubbing, and apply clothes wet with ice-water, and subsequently, if active inflammation follow and suppuration results, a solution of carbolic acid in water, one part to thirty, should be applied. If mortification set in, amputation is generally necessary. Where persons suffer from the constitutional effects of cold, hot stimulants should be given internally, and the body rubbed briskly with the hands and warm flannel.

Poisons, Their Symptoms and Antidotes.—When a person has taken poison, the first thing to do is to compel the patient to vomit, and for that purpose give any emetic that can be most readily and quickly obtained, and which is prompt and energetic, but safe in its action.

For this purpose there is, perhaps, nothing better than a large teaspoonful of ground mustard in a tumblerful of warm water, and it has the advantage of being almost always at hand. If the dry mustard is not to be had, use mixed mustard from the mustard pot. Its operation may generally be facilitated by the addition of a like quantity of common table salt. If the mustard is not at hand, give two or three teaspoonfuls of powdered alum in syrup or molasses, and give freely of warm water to drink; or give ten to twenty grains of sulphate of zinc (white vitriol), or twenty to thirty grains of ipecac, with one or two grains of tartar emetic, in a large cup of warm water, and repeat every ten minutes until three or four doses are given, unless free vomiting is sooner produced. After vomiting has taken place, large draughts of warm water should be given the patient, so that the vomiting will continue until the poisonous substances have been thoroughly evacuated, and then suitable antidotes should be given. If vomiting cannot be produced, the stomach-pump should be used. When it is known what particular kind of poison has been swallowed, then the proper antidote for that poison should be given, but when this cannot be ascertained, as is often the case, give freely of equal parts of calcined magnesia, pulverized charcoal, and sesquioxide of iron, in sufficient quantity of water. This is a very harmless mixture, and is likely to be of great benefit, as the ingredients, though very simple, are antidotes for the most common and active poisons. In case this mixture cannot be obtained, the stomach should be soothed and protected by the free administration of demulcent, mucilaginous or oleaginous drinks, such as the whites of eggs, milk, mucilage of gum arabic, or slippery elm bark, flaxseed tea, starch, wheat, flour, or arrow-root mixed in water, linseed or olive oil, or melted butter or lard. Subsequently the bowels should be moved by some gentle laxative, as a tablespoonful or two of castor oil, or a teaspoonful of calcined magnesia; and pain or other evidence of inflammation must be relieved by the administration of a few drops of laudanum, and the repeated application of hot poultices, fomentations and mustard plasters. The following are the names of the articles that may give rise to poisoning, most commonly used, and their antidote:

Mineral Acids—Sulphuric Acid (Oil of Vitriol), Nitric Acid (Aqua Fortis), Muriatic Acid (Spirits of Salts).—Symptoms: Acid, burning taste in the mouth, acute pain in the throat, stomach and bowels; frequent vomiting, generally bloody, mouth and lips excoriated, shriveled, white or yellow; hiccough, copious stools, more or less bloody, with great tenderness in the abdomen; difficult breathing, irregular pulse, excessive thirst, while drink increases the pain and rarely remains in the stomach; frequent but vain efforts to urinate; cold sweats, altered countenance; convulsions generally preceding death; nitric acid causes yellow stains; sulphuric acid, black ones. Treatment: Mix calcined magnesia in milk or water to the consistence of cream, and give freely to drink a glassful every couple of minutes, if it can be swallowed. Common soap (hard or soft), chalk, whiting, or even mortar from the wall mixed in water, may be given, until magnesia can be obtained. Promote vomiting by tickling the throat, if necessary, and when the poison is got rid of, flaxseed or elm tea, gruel, or other mild drinks. The inflammation which always follows wants good treatment to save the patient's life.

Vegetable Acids—Acetic, Citric, Oxalic, Tartaric.—Symptoms: Intense burning pain of mouth, throat and stomach; vomiting blood which is highly acid, violent purging, collapse, stupor, death.

Oxalic Acid is frequently taken in mistake for Epsom salts, to which in shops it often bears a strong resemblance. Treatment: Give chalk or magnesia in a large quantity of water, or large draughts of lime water. If these are not at hand, scrape the wall or ceiling, and give the scrapings, mixed with water.

Prussic or Hydrocyanic Acid—Laurel Water, Cyanide of Potassium, Bitter Almond Oil, etc.—Symptoms: In large doses almost invariably instantaneously fatal, when not immediately fatal, sudden loss of sense and control of the voluntary muscles; the odor of the poison generally susceptible on the breath. Treatment: Chlorine, in the form of chlorine water, in doses of from one to four fluid drachms, diluted. Weak solution of chloride lime or soda; water of ammonia (spirits of hartshorn) largely diluted may be given, and the vapor of it cautiously inhaled. Cold affusion, and chloroform in half to teaspoonful doses in glycerine or mucilage, repeated every few minutes, until the symptoms are ameliorated. Artificial respiration.

Aconite — Monkshood, Wolfsbane. — Symptoms: Numbness and tingling in the mouth and throat, and afterwards in other portions of the body, with sore throat, pain over the stomach, and vomiting; dimness of vision, dizziness, great prostration, loss of sensibility and delirium. Treatment: An emetic and then brandy in tablespoonful doses, in ice-water, every half hour; spirits of ammonia in half teaspoonful doses in like manner; the cold douche over the head and chest, warmth to the extremities, etc.

Alkalies and their Salts—Concentrated Lye, Woodash Lye, Caustic Potash, Ammonia, Hartshorn.—Symptoms: Caustic, acrid taste, excessive heat in the throat, stomach and intenstines; vomiting of bloody matter, cold sweats, hiccough, purging of bloody stools.—Treatment: The common vegetable acids. Common vinegar being always at hand, is most frequently used. The fixed oils, as castor, flaxseed, almond and olive oils form soaps with the alkalies and thus also destroy their caustic effect. They should be given in large quantity.

Alcohol, Brandy, and other Spirituous Liquors.—Symptoms: Confusion of thought, inability to walk or stand, dizziness, stupor, highly flushed or pale face, noisy breathing.—Treatment: After emptying the stomach, pour cold water on the head and back of the neck, rub or slap the wrists and palms, and the ankles and soles of the feet, and give strong, hot coffee, or aromatic spirits of hartshorn, in teaspoonful doses in water. The warmth of the body must be sustained.

Antimony, and its Preparations. Tartar Emetic, Antimonial Wine, Kerme's Mineral.—Symptoms: Faintness and nausea, soon followed by painful and continued vomiting, severe diarrhœa, constriction and burning sensation in the throat, cramps, or spasmodic twitchings, with symptoms of nervous derangement, and great prostration of strength, often terminating in death.—Treatment: If vomiting has not been produced, it should be effected by tickling the fauces, and administering copious draughts of warm water. Astringment infusions, such as of gall, oak bark, Peruvian bark, act as antidotes, and should be given promptly. Powdered yellow bark may be used until the infusion is prepared, or very strong green tea should be given. To stop the vomiting, should it continue, blister over the stomach by applying a cloth wet with strong spirits of hartshorn, and then sprinkle on the one-eighth to one-fourth of a grain of morphia.

Arsenic and its Preparations—Ratsbane, Fowler's Solution, etc.—Symptoms: Generally within an hour pain and heat are felt in the stomach, soon followed by vomiting, with a burning dryness of the throat and great thirst; the matters vomited are generally colored, either green yellow, or brownish, and sometimes bloody. Diarrhœa or dysentery ensues, while the pulse becomes small and rapid, yet irregular. Breathing much oppressed; difficulty invomiting may occur, while cramps, convulsions, or even paralysis often precede death, which sometimes takes place within five or six hours after arsenic has been taken.—Treatment: Give a prompt emetic, and then hydrate of peroxide of iron (recently prepared) in table-spoonful doses every ten or fifteen minutes until the urgent symptoms are relieved. In the absence of this, or while it is being prepared, give large draughts of new milk and raw eggs, limewater and oil, melted butter, magnesia in a large quantity of water, or even if nothing else is at hand, flour and water, always, however, giving an emetic the first thing, or causing vomiting by tickling the throat with a feather, etc. The inflammation of the stomach which follows must be treated by blisters, hot fomentations, mucilaginous drinks, etc., etc.

Belladonna or Deadly Night Shade.—Symptoms: Dryness of the mouth and throat, great thirst, difficulty of swallowing, nausea, dimness, confusion or loss of vision, great enlargement of the pupils, dizziness, delirium and coma.—Treatment: There is no known antidote. Give a prompt emetic and then reliance must be placed on continual stimulation with brandy, whisky, etc., and to necessary artificial respiration. Opium and its preparations, as morphia, laudanum, etc., are thought by some to counteract the effect of belladonna, and may be given in small and repeated doses, as also strong black coffee and green tea.

Blue Vitriol, or Blue Stone.—See Copperas.

Cantharides (Spanish or Blistering Fly) and Modern Potato Bug.—Symptoms: Sickening odor of the breath, sour taste, with burning heat in the throat, stomach, and bowels; frequent vomiting, often bloody; copious bloody stools, great pain in the stomach, with burning sensation in the bladder and difficulty to urinate, followed with terrible convulsions, delirium and death.—Treatment: Excite vomiting by drinking plentifully of sweet oil or other wholesome oils, sugar and water, milk, or slippery elm tea; give injections of castor oil and starch, or warm milk. The inflammatory symptoms which generally follow must be treated by a medical man. Camphorated oil or camphorated spirits should be rubbed over the bowels, stomach and thighs.

Caustic Potash.—See Alkalies.

Cobalt, or Fly-Powder.—Symptoms: Heat and pain in the throat and stomach, violent retching and vomiting, cold and clammy skin, small and feeble pulse, hurried and difficult breathing, diarrhœa, etc.—Treatment: An emetic, followed by the free administration of milk, eggs, wheat flour and water, and mucilaginous drinks.

Copper—Blue Vitriol, Verdigris or Pickles or Food Cooked in Soul Copper Vessels.—Symptoms: General inflammation of the alimentary canal, suppression of urine; hiccough, a disagreeable metallic taste, vomiting, violent colic, excessive thirst, sense of tightness of the throat, anxiety; faintness, giddiness, and cramps and convulsions generally precede death.—Treatment: Large doses of simple syrup as warm as can be swallowed, until the stomach rejects the amount it contains. The whites of eggs and large quantities of milk. Hydrated peroxide of iron.

Copperas.—See Iron.

Creosote.—Carbolic Acid.—Symptoms: Burning pain, acrid, pungent taste, thirst, vomiting, purging, etc.—Treatment: An emetic, and the free administration of albumen, as the whites of eggs, or in the absence of these, milk, or flour and water.

Corrosive Sublimate.—See Mercury.

Deadly Night-Shade.—See Belladonna.

Fox-Glove, or Digitalis.—Symptoms: Loss of strength, feeble, fluttering pulse, faintness, nausea, and vomiting and stupor; cold perspiration, dilated pupils, sighing, irregular breathing, and sometimes convulsions.—Treatment: After vomiting, give brandy and ammonia in frequently repeated doses, apply warmth to the extremities, and if necessary resort to artificial respiration.

Gases—Carbonic Acid, Chlorine, Cyanogen, Hydrosulphuric Acid, etc.—Symptoms: Great drowsiness, difficult respiration, features swollen, face blue as in strangulation.—Treatment: Artificial respirations, cold douche, frictions with stimulating substances to the surface of the body. Inhalation of steam containing preparations of ammonia. Cupping from nape of neck. Internal use of chloroform.

Green Vitriol.—See Iron.

Hellebore, or Indian Poke.—Symptoms: Violent vomiting and purging, bloody stools, great anxiety, tremors, vertigo, fainting, sinking of the pulse, cold sweets and convulsions.—Treatment: Excite speedy vomiting by large draughts of warm water, molasses and water, tickling the throat with the finger or a feather, and emetics; give oily and mucilaginous drinks, oily purgatives, and clysters, acids, strong coffee, camphor and opium.

Hemlock (Conium).—Symptoms: Dryness of the throat, tremors, dizziness, difficulty of swallowing, prostration and faintness, limbs powerless or paralyzed, pupils dilated, pulse rapid and feeble; insensibility and convulsions sometimes precede death.—Treatment: Empty the stomach and give brandy in tablespoonful doses, with half teaspoonful of spirits of Ammonia, frequently repeated, and if much pain and vomiting, give bromide of ammonium in five-grain doses every half hour. Artificial respiration may be required.

Henbane or Hyoscyamus.—Symptoms: Muscular twitching, inability to articulate plainly, dimness of vision and stupor; later, vomiting and purging, small, intermittent pulse, convulsive movement of the extremities and coma. Treatment: Similar to Opium Poisoning, which see.

Iodine.—Symptoms: Burning pain in throat, lacerating pain in the stomach, fruitless effort to vomit, excessive tenderness of the epigastrium. Treatment: Free emesis, prompt administration of starch, wheat flour, or arrow-root, beat up in water.

Lead.—Acetate of Lead, Sugar of Lead, Dry White Lead, Red Lead, Litharge, or Pickles, Wine, or Vinegar, Sweetened by Lead.—Symptoms: When taken in large doses, a sweet but astringent metallic taste exists, with constriction in the throat, pain in the region of the stomach, painful, obstinate, and frequently bloody vomitings, hiccough, convulsions or spasms, and death. When taken in small but long-continued doses, it produces colic, called painter's colic; great pain, obstinate constipation, and in extreme cases paralytic symptoms, especially wrist-drop, with a blue line along the edge of the gums. Treatment: To counteract the poison, give alum in water, one and a half ounce to a quart; or, better still, Epsom salts or Glauber salts, an ounce of either in a quart of water; or dilute sulphuric acid, a teaspoonful to a quart of water. If a large quantity of sugar of lead has been recently taken, empty the stomach by an emetic of sulphate of zinc (one drachm in a quart of water), giving one-fourth to commence, and repeating smaller doses until free vomiting is produced; castor oil should be given to clear the bowels, and injections of oil and starch freely administered. If the body is cold, use the warm bath.

Meadow Saffron.—See Belladonna.

Laudanum.—See Opium.

Lunar Caustic.—See Silver.

Lobelia.—Indian Poke.—Symptoms: Excessive vomiting and purging, pains in the bowels, contraction of the pupils, delirium, coma, and convulsions. Treatment: Mustard over the stomach, and brandy and ammonia.

Mercury.—Corrosive Sublimate (bug poisons frequently contain this poison), **Red Precipitate, Chinese or English Vermillion.**—Symptoms: Acrid, metallic taste in the mouth, immediate constriction and burning in the throat, with anxiety and tearing pains in both stomach and bowels, sickness, and vomiting of various colored fluids, and sometimes bloody and profuse diarrhœa, with difficulty and pain in urinating; pulse quick, small and hard; faint sensations, great debility, difficult breathing, cramps, cold sweats, syncope and convulsions. Treatment: If vomiting does not already exist, emetics must be given immediately—albumen of eggs in continuous large doses, and infusion of catechu afterwards, sweet milk, mixtures of flour and water in successive cupfuls, and to check excessive salivation put a half ounce of chlorate of potash in a tumbler of water, and use freely as a gargle, and swallow a tablespoonful every hour or two.

Monkshood.—See Arnica.

Morphine.—See Opium.

Nitrate of Silver (Lunar Caustic.)—Symptoms: Intense pain and vomiting and purging of blood; mucus and shreds of mucus membranes; and if these stand they become dark. Treatment: Give freely of a solution of common salt in water, which decomposes the poison, and afterwards flax-seed or elm bark tea, and after a while a dose of castor oil.

Nux Vomica.—See Strychnine.

Opium and all its Preparations—Morphine, Laudanum, Paregoric, etc.—Symptoms: Giddiness, drowsiness, increasing to stupor, and insensibility; pulse usually, at first, quick and irregular, and breathing hurried, and afterwards pulse slow and feeble, and respiration slow and noisy; the pupils are contracted and the eyes and face congested, and later, as death approaches, the extremities become cold, the surface is covered with cold, clammy perspiration, and the sphincters relax. The effects of opium and its preparations, in poisonous doses, appear in from a half to two hours from its administration. Treatment: Empty the stomach immediately with an emetic or with the stomach pump. Then give very strong coffee without milk; put mustard plasters on the wrist and ankles; use the cold douche to the head and chest, and if the patient is cold and sinking give brandy, or whisky and ammonia. Belladonna is thought by many to counteract the poisonous effects of opium, and may be given in doses of half to a teaspoonful of the tincture, or two graius of the extract, every twenty minutes, until some effect is observed in causing the pupils to expand. Use warmth and friction, and if possible prevent sleep for some hours, for which purpose the patient should be walked about between two persons, and if necessary a bunch of switches may be freely used. Finally, as a last resort, use artificial respiration, and a persistance in it will sometimes be rewarded with success in apparently hopeless cases. Galvanism should also be tried.

Oxalic Acid.—See Acids.

Phosphorus—Found in Lucifer Matches and some Rat Poisons.—Symptoms: Symptoms of irritant poisoning; pain in the stomach and bowels; vomiting; diarrhœa; tenderness and tension of the abdomen. Treatment: An emetic is to be promptly given; copious draughts containing magnesia in suspension; mucilaginous drinks. General treatment for inflammatory symptoms.

Poisonous Fish.—Symptoms: In an hour or two—often in much shorter time—after the fish has been eaten, a weight at the stomach comes on, with slight vertigo and headache; sense of heat about the head and eyes; considerable thirst, and often an eruption of the skin. Treatment: After full vomiting, an active purgative should be given to remove any of the noxious matter from the intestines. Vinegar and water may be drunk after the above remedies have operated, and the body may be sponged with the same. Water made very sweet with sugar, with aromatic spirits of ammonia added, may be drunk freely as a corrective. A solution of chlorate of potash, or of alkali, the latter weak, may be given to obviate the effect of the poison. If spasms ensue after evacuation, laudanum in considerable doses is necessary. If inflammation should occur, combat in the usual way.

Poisonous Mushrooms.—Symptoms: Nausea, heat and pains in the stomach and bowels; vomiting and purging, thirst, convulsions and faintings, pulse small and frequent, dilated pupil and stupor, cold sweats and death.

Treatment: The stomach and bowels are to be cleared by an emetic of ground mustard or sulphate of zinc, followed by frequent doses of Glauber of Epsom salts, and large stimulating clysters. After the poison is evacuated, either may be given with small quantities of brandy and water. But if inflammatory symptoms manifest themselves, such stimuli should be avoided, and these symptoms appropriately treated.

Potash.—See Alkali.

Prussic Acid, Hydrocyanic.—See Acids.

Poison Ivy.—Symptoms. Contact with, and with many persons the near approach to the vine, gives rise to violent erysipelatous inflammation, especially of the face and hands, attended with itching, redness, burning and swelling, with watery blisters.

Treatment: Give saline laxatives, and apply weak lead and laudanum, or limewater and sweet oil, or bathe the parts freely with spirits of nitre. Anointing with oil will prevent poisoning from it.

Saltpetre, Nitrate of Potash.—Symptoms. Only poisonous in large quantities, and then causes nausea, painful vomiting, purging, convulsions, faintness, feeble pulse, cold feet and hands, with tearing pains in stomach and bowels.

Treatment: Treat just as is directed for arsenic, for there is no antidote known, and emptying the stomach and bowels with mild drinks must be relied on.

Savine.—Symptoms: Sharp pains in the bowels, hot skin, rapid pulse, violent vomiting and sometimes purging, with great prostration. Treatment: Mustard and hot fomentations over the stomach and bowels, and ice only allowed in the stomach until the inflammation ceases. If prostration comes on, food and stimulants must be given by injection.

Stramonium, Thorn-apple or Jamestown Weed.—Symptoms: Vertigo, headache, perversion of vision, slight delirium, sense of suffocation, disposition to sleep, bowels relaxed and all secretions augmented. Treatment: Same as Belladonna.

Strychnine and Nux Vomica.—Symptoms: Muscular twitching, constriction of the throat, difficult breathing and oppression of the chest; violent muscular spasms then occur, continuous in character like lock-jaw, with the body bent backwards, sometimes like a bow. Treatment: Give, if obtainable, one ounce or more of bone charcoal mixed with water, and follow with an active emetic; then give chloroform in teaspoonful doses, in flour and water or glycerine, every few minutes while the spasms last, and afterwards brandy and stimulants, and warmth of the extremities if necessary. Recoveries have followed the free and prompt administration of oils or melted butter or lard. In all cases empty the stomach if possible.

Sulphate of Zinc, White Vitriol.—See Zinc.

Tin—Chloride of Tin, Solution of Tin (Used by Dyers), Oxide of Tin or Putty Powder.—Symptoms: Vomiting, pains in the stomach, anxiety, restlessness, frequent pulse, delirium, etc. Treatment: Empty the stomach, and give whites of eggs in water, milk in large quantities, or flour beaten up in water, with magnesia or chalk.

Tartar Emetic.—See Antimony.

Tobacco. — Symptoms: Vertigo, stupor, fainting, nausea, vomiting, sudden nervous debility, cold sweat, tremors, and at times fatal prostration. Treatment: After the stomach is empty apply mustard to the abdomen and to the extremities, and give strong coffee, with brandy and other stimulants, with warmth to the extremities.

Zinc—Oxide of Zinc, Sulphate of Zinc, White Vitriol, Acetate of Zinc.—Symptoms: Violent vomiting, astringent taste, burning pain in the stomach, pale countenance, cold extremities, dull eyes, fluttering pulse. Death seldom ensues, in consequence of the emetic effect. Treatment: The vomiting may be relieved by copious draughts of warm water. Carbonate of soda, administered in solution, will decompose the sulphate of zinc. Milk and albumen will also act as antidotes. General principles to be observed in the subsequent treatment.

Woorara.—Symptoms: When taken into the stomach it is inert; when absorbed through a wound it causes sudden stupor and insensibility, frothing at the mouth and speedy death. Treatment: Suck the wound immediately, or cut it out and tie a cord around the limb between the wound and the heart. Apply iodine, or iodide of potassium, and give it internally, and try artificial respiration.

Scalds.—See Burns and Scalds.

Sprains.—The portions most frequently implicated are the wrist and ankle; no matter which portion it may be,
however, rest and quietness is a very important part of the treatment, and, when possible, in an elevated position. If the wrist is sprained it should be carried in a sling; if the ankle, it should be supported on a couch or stool. Cold lotions (see Bruises) should be freely applied, and irrigation by pouring water from a pitcher or tea-kettle resorted to several times a day to prevent inflammation. Later, frictions with opodeldoc, or with some stimulating liniment, and supporting the parts by pressure made with a flannel roller, or laced stocking when the ankle is involved, will be useful to restore tone; or strips of adhesive plaster properly applied will be useful for the same purpose. Recovery from severe sprains is always tedious. It is an old saying "that a bad sprain is worse than a broken bone."

Stings of Bees and Wasps.—See Bites and Stings.

Suffocation from Noxious Gases, Foul Air, Fire Damp, Etc.—Remove to fresh air and dash cold water over the head, neck and chest; carefully apply hartshorn, or smelling salts to the nostrils, and when the breathing is feeble or has ceased, resort immediately to artificial respiration (see Asphyxia and Drowning). Keep up the warmth of the body, and as soon as the patient can swallow give stimulants in small quantities.

Sunstroke.—This is caused by long exposure in great heat, especially when accompanied with great fatigue and exhaustion. Though generally happening from exposure to the sun's rays, yet precisely similar effects may be and are produced from any undue exposure to great and exhaustive heat, such as workmen are exposed to in foundries, gas factories, bakeries, and other similar employments. Its first symptom is pain in the head and dizziness, quickly followed by loss of consciousness, and resulting in complete prostration; sometimes, however, the attack is sudden, as in apoplexy. The head is generally burning hot, the face dark and swollen, the breathing labored and snoring, and the feet and hands cold. Remove the patient at once to a cool and shady place, and lay him down with his head a little raised; apply ice or iced water to the head and face; loosen all cloths around the neck or waist; bathe the chest with cold water, apply mustard plasters, or cloths wetted with turpentine, to the calves and soles of the feet, and as soon as the patient can swallow, give weak brandy or whisky and water.

THERE is no easy road to success:—I thank God for it. * * * * A trained man will make his life tell. Without training, you are left on a sea of luck, where thousands go down, while one meets with success.

JAMES A. GARFIELD.

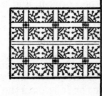

Family Physician

. . . . . .

The following receipts written by DR. J. H. GUNN will be found of great value, especially in emergencies :

Asthma.—Take hyssop water and poppy water, of each ten ounces; oxymel of squills, six ounces; syrup of maiden hair, two ounces. Take one spoonful when you find any difficulty in breathing.

Ague in the Breast.—Take one part of gum camphor, two parts yellow bees-wax, three parts clean lard; let all melt slowly, in any vessel [earthen best], on stove. Use either cold or warm; spread very thinly on cotton or linen cloths, covering those with flannel. No matter if the breast is broken, it will cure if persevered in. Do not, no matter how painful, cease from drawing milk from the breast that is affected.

Ague, Mixture.—Mix twenty grains quinine with one pint diluted gin or port wine, and add ten grains subcarbonate of iron. Dose, a wine-glass each hour until the ague is broken, and then two or three times a day until the whole has been used.

2. Take Peruvian bark, two ounces; wild cherry tree bark, 1 ounce; cinnamon, one drachm; powdered capsicum, one teaspoonful; sulphur, one ounce; port wine, two quarts. Let it stand a day or two. Dose, a wine-glassful every two or three hours until the disease is broken, and then two or three times a day until all is taken.

Sprained Ankle.—Wash the ankle frequently with cold salt and water, which is far better than warm vinegar or decoctions of herbs. Keep your foot as cold as possible to prevent inflammation, and sit with it elevated on a cushion. Live on very low diet, and take every day some cooling medicine. By obeying these directions only, a sprained ankle has been cured in a few days.

Apoplexy.—Occurs only in the corpulent or obese, and the gross or high livers. To treat, raise the head to a nearly upright position; unloose all tight clothes, strings, etc., and apply cold water to the head and warm water and warm cloths to the feet. Have the apartment cool and well ventilated. Give nothing by the mouth until the breathing is relieved, and then only draughts of cold water.

Preparation for the Cure of Baldness.—Rum, one pint; alcohol, one ounce; distilled water, one ounce, tincture of cantharides, a half drachm; carbonate of potash, a half drachm; carbonate of ammonia, one drachm. Mix the liquids after having dissolved the salts, and filter. After the skin of the head has been wetted with this preparation for several minutes, it should be washed with water.

Bilious Colic.—Mix two tablespoonfuls of Indian meal in half a pint of cold water; drink it at two draughts.

Bilious Complaints.—Take the root and branch of dandelion, and steep it in soft water a sufficient length of time to extract all the essence; then strain the liquor and simmer until it becomes quite thick. Dose: From one to three glasses a day may be taken with good effect.

Blackberry Cordial.—To one quart blackberry juice add one pound white sugar, one tablespoonful each cloves, allspice, cinnamon and nutmeg. Boil together fifteen minutes, and add a wine-glass of whisky, brandy or rum. Bottle while hot, cork tight and seal. Used in diarrhœa and dysentery. Dose, a wine-glassful for an adult, half that quantity for a child. It can be taken three or four times a day if the case is severe.

Blisters. — On the feet, occasioned by walking, are cured by drawing a needleful of worsted thread through them; clip it off at both ends and leave it till the skin peals off.

Raising Blood.—Make a tea of white oak bark, and drink freely during the day; or take half a pound of yellow dock root, boil in new milk, say one quart; drink one gill three times a day, and take one pill of white pine pitch every day.

How to Stop Blood.—Take the fine dust of tea, or the scrapings of the inside of tanned leather. Bind it upon the wound closely, and blood will soon cease to flow.

Boils.—Make a poultice of ginger and flour, and lay it on the boil. This will soon draw it to a head.

Swelled Bowels in Children.—Bathe the stomach of the child with catnip steeped, mixed with fresh butter and sugar.

Chilblains.—Dr. Fergus recommends sulphurous acid in this affection. It should be applied with a camel's hair brush, or by means of a spray producer. One application of this effects a cure. The acid should be used pure. A good wash for hands or feet affected with chilblains is sulphurous acid, three parts; glycerine, one part, and water one part. The acid will be found particularly useful in the irritating, tormenting stage of chilblains.

Chilblains and Chapped Hands.—When chilblains manifest themselves, the best remedy not only for preventing their ulcerating, but overcoming the tingling, itching pain, and stimulating the irculation of the part to healthy action, is the liniment of belladona, two drachms; the liniment of aconite, one drachm; carbolic acid, ten drops; collodion flexile, one ounce; painted with a camel's hair pencil over their surface. When the chilblains vesicate, ulcerate or slough, it is better to omit the aconite and apply the other components of the liniment without it. The collodion flexile forms a coating or protecting film, which excludes the air, while the sedative liniments allay the irritation, generally of no trivial nature. For chapped hands we advise the free use of glycerine and good oil, in the proportion of two parts of the former to four of the latter; after this has been well rubbed into the hands and allowed to remain for a little time, and the hands subsequently washed with Castile soap and water, we recommend the belladonna and collodion flexile to be painted on, and the protective film allowed to remain permanently. These complaints not unfrequently invade persons of languid circulation and relaxed habit, who should be put on a generous regimen, and treated with ferruginous tonics. Obstinate cases are occasionally met with which no local application will remedy, unless some disordered state of the system is removed, or the general condition of the patient's health improved. Chapped lips are also benefited by the stimulating form of application we advocate, but the aconite must not be allowed to get on the lips, or a disagreeable tingling results.

Chilblain Balm.—Boil together ten fluid ounces olive oil, two fluid ounces Venice turpentine, and one ounce yellow wax; strain, and while still warm add, constantly stirring, two and a half drachms balsam of Peru and ten grains camphor.

Cure for Chilblain.—Make a strong lye by boiling wood ashes in water. Put your feet in a small tub and cover them with the lye as hot as you can bear it. Gradually add more lye, hotter and hotter. Keep them in half an hour, bathing and rubbing them continually, and being very careful to keep the lye hot.

Chilblain Lotion.—Dissolve one ounce muriate of ammonia in one-half pint cider vinegar, and apply frequently. One-half pint of alcohol may be added to this lotion with good effects.

Chilblain Ointment.—Take mutton tallow and lard, of each three-fourths of a pound avoirdupois; melt in an iron vessel, and add hydrated oxide of iron, two ounces, stirring continually with an iron spoon until the mass is of a uniform black color; when nearly cool add Venice turpentine, two ounces; Armenian bole, one ounce; oil of bergamot, one drachm; rub up the bole with a little olive oil before putting it in. Apply several times daily by putting it upon lint or linen. It heals the worst cases in a few days.

Russian Remedy for Chilblains.—Slices of the rind of fully ripe cucumbers, dried with the soft parts attached. Previous to use they are softened by soaking them in warm water, and are then bound on the sore parts with the inner side next them, and left on all night. This treatment is said to be adopted for both broken and unbroken chilblains.

How to Cure Itching Chilblains.—Take hydrochloric acid, one part, and water, eight parts; mix. Apply on going to bed. This must not be used if the skin is broken.

Sal ammoniac, two ounces; rum, one pint; camphor, two drachms. The affected part is wetted night and morning, and when dry is touched with a little simple ointment of any kind — cold cream or pomatum.

Oil of turpentine, four ounces; camphor, six drachms; oil of cajeput, two drachms. Apply with friction.

How to Cure Broken Chilblains.—Mix together four fluid ounces collodion, one and a half fluid ounces Venice turpentine, and one fluid ounce castor oil.

How to Cure Corns.—Take equal parts of mercurial and galbanum ointments; mix them well together, spread on a piece of soft leather, and apply it to the corns morning and evening. In a few days benefit will be derived. Take two ounces of gum ammoniac, two ounces of yellow wax, and six ounces of verdigris; melt them together, and

spread the composition on soft leather; cut away as much of the corn as you can, then apply the plaster, and renew it every fortnight till the corn is away. Get four ounces of white diachylon plaster, four ounces of shoemaker's wax, and sixty drops of muriatic acid or spirits of salt. Boil them for a few minutes in an earthen pipkin, and when cold roll the mass between the hands, and apply it on a piece of white leather. Soak the feet well in warm water, then with a sharp instrument pare off as much of the corn as can be done without pain, and bind up the part with a piece of linen or muslin thoroughly saturated with sperm oil, or, which is better, the oil which floats upon the surface of the herring or mackerel. After three or four days the dressing may be removed by scraping, when the new skin will be found of a soft and healthy texture, and less liable to the formation of a new corn than before. Corns may be prevented by wearing easy shoes. Bathe the feet frequently in lukewarm water, with a little salt or potashes dissolved in it. The corn itself will be completely destroyed by rubbing it often with a little caustic solution of potash till the soft skin is formed. Scrape to a pulp sufficient Spanish garlic and bind on the corn over night, after first soaking it well in warm water, and scrape off as much as possible of the hardened portion in the morning. Repeat the application as required.

How to Cure Soft Corns.—Scrape a piece of common chalk, and put a pinch to the soft corn, and bind a piece of linen rag upon it.

How to Cure Tender Corns.—A strong solution of tannic acid is said to be an excellent application to tender feet as well as a preventive of the offensive odor attendant upon their profuse perspiration. To those of our readers who live far away in the country, we would suggest a strong decoction of oak bark as a substitute.

Caustic for Corns.—Tincture of iodine, four drachms; iodide of iron, twelve grains; chloride of antimony, four drachms; mix, and apply with a camel's hair brush, after paring the corn. It is said to cure in three times.

How to Relieve Corns.—Bind them up at night with a cloth wet with tincture of arnica, to relieve the pain, and during the day occasionally moisten the stocking over the corn with arnica if the shoe is not large enough to allow the corn being bound up with a piece of linen rag.

Remedy for Corns.—1. The pain occasioned by corns may be greatly alleviated by the following preparation: Into a one-ounce vial put two drachms of muriatic acid and six drachms of rose-water. With this mixture wet the corns night and morning for three days. Soak the feet every evening in warm water without soap. Put one-third of the acid into the water, and with a little picking the corn will be dissolved. 2. Take a lemon, cut off a small piece, then nick it so as to let in the toe with the corn, tie this on at night so that it cannot move, and in the morning you will find that, with a blunt knife, you may remove a considerable portion of the corn. Make two or three applications, and great relief will be the result.

How to Cure Solvent Corns.—Expose salt of tartar (pearlash) in a wide-mouth vial in a damp place until it forms an oil-like liquid, and apply to the corn.

How to Cure Cholera.—Take laudanum, tincture cayenne, compound tincture rhubarb, peppermint and camphor, of each equal parts. Dose, ten to thirty drops. In plain terms, take equal parts tincture of opium, red pepper, rhubarb, peppermint and camphor, and mix them for use. In case of diarrhœa, take a dose of ten to twenty drops in three or four teaspoonfuls of water. No one who has this by him, and takes it in time, will ever have the cholera.

Signs of Disease in Children.—In the case of a baby not yet able to talk, it must cry when it is ill. The colic makes a baby cry loud, long, and passionately, and shed tears—stopping for a moment and beginning again.

If the chest is affected, it gives one sharp cry, breaking off immediately, as if crying hurt it.

If the head is affected, it cries in sharp, piercing shrieks, with low moans and wails between. Or there may be quiet dozing, and startings between.

It is easy enough to perceive, where a child is attacked by disease, that there has some change taken place; for either its skin will be dry and hot, its appetite gone; it is stupidly sleepy, or fretful or crying; it is thirsty, or pale and languid, or in some way betrays that something is wrong. When a child vomits, or has a diarrhœa, or is costive and feverish, st is owing to some derangement, and needs attention. But these various symptoms may continue for a day or two before the nature of the disease can be determined. A warm bath, warm drinks, etc., can do no harm, and may help to determine the case. On coming out of the bath, and being well rubbed with the hand, the skin will show symptoms of rash, if it is a skin disease which has commenced. By the appearance of the rash, the nature of the disease can be learned. Measles are in patches, dark red, and come out first about the face. If scarlet fever is impending, the skin will look a deep pink all over the body, though most so about the neck and face. Chicken-pox shows fever, but not so much running at the nose, and appearances of cold, as in measles, nor is there as much of a cough. Besides, the spots are smaller, and do not run much together, and are more diffused over the whole surface of the skin; and enlarge into blisters in a day or two.

How to Cure Consumption.—Take one tablespoonful of tar, and the yolks of three hen's eggs, beat them well together. Dose, one tablespoonful morning, noon and night.

Croup, Remedy for in One Minute.—This remedy is simply alum. Take a knife or grater, and shave or grate off in small particles about a teaspoonful of alum; mix it with about twice its quantity of sugar, to make it palatable, and administer as quickly as possible. Its effects will be truly magical, as almost instantaneous relief will be afforded.

Cholera Remedy, Hartshorne's.—Take of chloroform, tincture of opium, spirits of camphor, and spirits of aromatic ammonia, each one and one-half fluid drachms; creosote, three drops; oil of cinnamon, eight drops; brandy, two fluid drachms. Dilute a teaspoonful with a wine-glass of water, and give two teaspoonfuls every five minutes, followed by a lump of ice.

Cure for Dandruff.—Good mild soap is one of the safest remedies, and is sufficient in ordinary cases; carbonate of potash or soda is too alkaline for the skin. Every application removes a portion of the cuticle, as you may observe by the smoothness of the skin of your hands after washing them with it. Borax is recommended; but this is also soda combined with a weak acid, boracic acid, and may by protracted use also injuriously act on the scalp. Soap is also soda or potash combined with the weak, fatty acids; and when the soap contains an excess of the alkalies or is sharp, it is as injurious as the carbonate of potash. All that injures the scalp injures the growth of the hair. One of the best applications from the vegetable kingdom is the mucilaginous decoction of the root of the burdock, called bardane in French (botanical name, *Lappa Minor*). In the mineral kingdom the best remedy is a solution of flowers of sulphur in water, which may be made by the addition of a very small portion of sulphide of potassium, say ten or twenty grains to the pint. This solution is shaken up with the sulphur, and the clear liquid remaining on the top is used. This recipe is founded on the fact that sulphur is a poison for inferior vegetable or animal growth, like dandruff, itch, etc., and is not at all a poison for the superior animal like man.

How to Cure Diphtheria.—A French physician expresses his preference for lemon juice, as a local application in diphtheria, to chlorate of potash, nitrate of silver, perchloride of lime water. He uses it by dipping a little plug of cottonwood, twisted around a wire, in the juice, and pressing it against the diseased surface four or five times daily.

How to Cure Bad Breath.—Bad or foul breath will be removed by taking a teaspoonful of the following mixture after each meal: One ounce liquor of potassa, one ounce chloride of soda, one and one-half ounces phosphate of soda, and three ounces of water.

2. Chlorate of potash, three drachms; rose-water, four ounces. Dose, a tablespoonful four or five times daily.

How to Cure Bunions.—A bunion is a swelling on the ball of the great toe, and is the result of pressure and irritation by friction. The treatment for corns applies also to bunions; but in consequence of the greater extension of the disease, the cure is more tedious. When a bunion is forming it may be stopped by poulticing and carefully opening it with a lancet.

How to Cure Burns and Scalds.—Take half a pound of powdered alum, dissolve it in a quart of water; bathe the burn or scald with a linen rag, wetted with this mixture, then bind the wet rag on it with a strip of linen, and moisten the bandage with the alum water frequently, without removing it during two or three days.

Tea Leaves for Burns.—Dr. Searles, of Warsaw, Wis., reports the immediate relief from pain in severe burns and scalds by the application of a poultice of tea leaves.

How to Cure Cancer.—Boil down the inner bark of red and white oak to the consistency of molasses; apply as a plaster, shifting it once a week; or, burn red-oak bark to ashes; sprinkle it on the sore till it is eaten out; then apply a plaster of tar; or, take garget berries and leaves of stramonium; simmer them together in equal parts of neatsfoot oil and the tops of hemlock; mix well together, and apply it to the parts affected; at the same time make a tea of winter-green (root and branch); put a handful into two quarts of water; add two ounces of sulphur and drink of this tea freely during the day.

Castor Oil Mixture.—Castor oil, one dessert spoonful; magnesia, one dessert spoonful. Rub together into a paste. By this combination, the taste of the oil is almost entirely concealed, and children take it without opposition.

How to Disguise Castor Oil.—Rub up two drops oil of cinnamon with an ounce of glycerine and add an ounce of castor oil. Children will take it as a luxury and ask for more.

Castor Oil Emulsions.—Take castor oil and syrup, each one ounce; the yolk of an egg, and orange flower water, one-half ounce. Mix. This makes a very pleasant emulsion, which is readily taken by adults as well as children.

How to Cure Catarrh.—Take the bark of sassafras root, dry and pound it, use it as a snuff, taking two or three pinches a day.

How to Cure Chilblains.—Wash the parts in strong alum water, apply as hot as can be borne.

How to Cure Cold.—Take three cents' worth of liquorice, three of rock candy, three of gum arabic, and put them into a quart of water; simmer them till thoroughly dissolved, then add three cents' worth paregoric, and a like quantity of antimonial wine.

How to Cure Corns.—Boil tobacco down to an extract, then mix with it a quantity of white pine pitch, and apply it to the corn; renew it once a week until the corn disappears.

Good Cough Mixture.—Two ounces ammonia mixture; five ounces camphor mixture; one drachm tincture of digitalis (foxglove); one-half ounce each of sweet spirits of nitre and syrup of poppies; two drachms solution of sulphate of morphia. A tablespoonful of this mixture is to be taken four times a day.

2. Tincture of blood-root, one ounce; sulphate of morphia, one and a half grains; tincture of digitalis, one-half ounce; wine of antimony, one-half ounce; oil of wintergreen, ten drops. Mix. Dose from twenty to forty drops twice or three times a day. Excellent for a hard, dry cough.

3. Common sweet cider, boiled down to one-half, makes a most excellent syrup for colds or coughs for children, is pleasant to the taste, and will keep for a year in a cool cellar. In recovering from an illness, the system has a craving for some pleasant drink. This is found in cider which is placed on the fire as soon as made, and allowed to come to a boil, then cooled, put in casks, and kept in a cool cellar.

4. Roast a large lemon very carefully without burning; when it is thoroughly hot, cut and squeeze into a cup upon three ounces of sugar candy, finely powdered; take a spoonful whenever your cough troubles you. It is as good as it is pleasant.

Cure for Deafness.—Take ant's eggs and union juice. Mix and drop them into the ear. Drop into the ear, at night, six or eight drops of hot sweet oil.

Remedies for Diarrhœa.—1. Take one teaspoonful of salt, the same of good vinegar, and a tablespoonful of water; mix and drink. It acts like a charm on the system, and even one dose will generally cure obstinate cases of diarrhœa, or the first stages of cholera. If the first does not bring complete relief, repeate the dose, as it is quite harmless. 2. The best rhubarb root, pulverized, 1 ounce; peppermint leaf, 1 ounce, capsicum, ⅛ ounce; cover with boiling water and steep thoroughly, strain, and add bicarbonate of potash and essence of cinnamon, of each ½ ounce; with brandy (or good whisky); equal in amount to the whole, and loaf sugar, four ounces. Dose—for an adult, 1 or 2 tablespoons; for a child, 1 to 2 teaspoons, from 3 to 6 times per day, until relief is obtained. 3. To half a bushel of blackberries; well mashed, add a quarter of a pound of allspice, 2 ounces of cinnamon, 2 ounces of cloves; pulverize well, mix and boil slowly until properly done; then strain or squeeze the juice through home-spun or flannel, and add to each pint of the juice 1 pound of loaf sugar, boil again for some time, take it off, and while cooling, add half a gallon of the best Cognac brandy.

Cure for Chronic Diarrhœa.—Rayer recommends the association of cinchona, charcoal and bismuth in the treatment of chronic diarrhœa, in the following proportions: Subnitrate of bismuth, one drachm; cinchona, yellow, powdered, one-half drachm; charcoal, vegetable, one drachm. Make twenty powders and take two or three a day during the intervals between meals.

Cures for Dysentery.—Tincture rhubarb, tincture of capsicum, tincture of camphor, essence of ginger and laudanum, equal parts. Mix; shake well and take from ten to twenty drops every thirty minutes until relief is obtained. This is a dose for an adult. Half the amount for a child under twelve years of age. 2. Take some butter off the churn, immediately after being churned, just as it is, without being salted or washed; clarify it over the fire like honey. Skim off all the milky particles when melted over a clear fire. Let the patient (if an adult) take two tablespoonfuls of the clarified remainder, twice or thrice within the day. This has never failed to effect a cure, and in many cases it has been almost instantaneous. 3. In diseases of this kind the Indians use the roots and leaves of the blackberry bush—a decoction of which, in hot water, well boiled down, is taken in doses of a gill before each meal, and before retiring to bed. It is an almost infallible cure. 4. Beat one egg in a teacup; add one tablespoonful of loaf sugar and half a teaspoonful of ground spice; fill the cup with sweet milk. Give the patient one tablespoonful once in ten minutes until relieved. 5. Take one tablespoonful of common salt, and mix it with two tablespoonfuls of vinegar and pour upon it a half pint of water, either hot or cold (only let it be taken cool.) A wine-glass full of this mixture in the above proportions, taken every half hour, will be found quite efficacious in curing dysentery. If the stomach be nauseated, a wine-glass full taken every hour will suffice. For a child, the quantity should be a teaspoonful of salt and one of vinegar in a teacupful of water.

Dropsy.—Take the leaves of a currant bush and make into tea, drink it.

Cure for Drunkenness.—The following singular means of curing habitual drunkenness is employed by a Russian physician, Dr. Schreiber, of Brzese Litewski: It consists in confining the drunkard in a room, and in furnishing him at discretion with his favorite spirit diluted with two-thirds of water; as much wine, beer and coffee as he desires, but containing one-third of spirit; all the food —the bread, meat, and the legumes are steeped in spirit and water. The poor devil is continually drunk and dort. On the fifth day of this regime he has an extreme disgust for spirit; he earnestly requests other diet; but his desire must not be yielded to, until the poor wretch no longer desires to eat or drink; he is then certainly cured of his penchant for drunkenness. He acquires such a disgust for brandy or other spirits that he is ready to vomit at the very sight of it.

Cure for Dyspepsia.—1. Take bark of white poplar root, boil it thick, and add a little spirit, and then lay it on the stomach.

2. Take wintergreen and black cherry-tree bark and yellow dock: put into two quarts of water; boil down to three pints; take two or three glasses a day.

Here are two remedies for dyspepsia, said by those who "have tried them" to be infallible. 1. Eat onions, 2. Take two parts of well-dried and pounded pods of red pepper, mixed with one part of ground mustard, and sift it over everything you eat or drink.

How to Cure Earache.—Take a small piece of cotton batting or cotton wool, make a depression in the center with the finger, and then fill it up with as much ground pepper as will rest on a five-cent piece; gather it into a ball and tie it up; dip the ball into sweet oil and insert it in the ear, covering the latter with cotton wool, and use a bandage or cap to retain it in its place. Almost instant relief will be experienced; and the application is so gentle that an infant will not get injured by it, but experience relief as well as adults. Roast a piece of lean mutton, squeeze out the juice and drop it into the ear as hot as it can be borne. Roast an onion and put into the ear as hot as it can be borne.

How to Cure Erysipelas.—Dissolve five ounces of salt in one pint of good brandy and take two tablespoonfuls three times per day.

Cure for Inflamed Eyes.—Pour boiling water on alder flowers, and steep them like tea; when cold, put three or four drops of laudanum into a small glass of the alder-tea, and let the mixture run into the eyes two or three times a day, and the eyes will become perfectly strong in the course of a week.

Cure for Weeping Eyes.—Wash the eyes in chamomile tea night and morning.

Eyes, Granular Inflammation.—A prominent oculist says that the contagious Egyptian or granular inflammation of the eyes is spreading throughout the country, and that he has been able in many, and indeed in a majority of cases, to trace the disease to what are commonly called rolling towels. Towels of this kind are generally found in country hotels and the dwellings of the working classes, and, being thus used by nearly every one, are made the carriers of one of the most troublesome diseases of the eye. This being the case, it is urgently recommended that the use of these rolling towels be discarded, and thus one of the special vehicles for the spread of a most dangerous disorder of the eyes—one by which thousands of working-men are annually deprived of their means of support—will no longer exist.

Cure for Sty in Eye.—Bathe frequently with warm water. When the sty bursts, use an ointment composed of one part of citron ointment and four of spermaceti, well rubbed together, and smear along the edge of the eye-lid.

Cure for Felons.—1. Stir one-half teaspoonful of water into an ounce of Venice turpentine until the mixture appears like granulated honey. Wrap a good coating of it around the finger with a cloth. If the felon is only recent, the pain will be removed in six hours.

2. As soon as the part begins to swell, wrap it with a cloth saturated thoroughly with the tincture of lobelia. An old physician says, that he has known this to cure scores of cases, and that it never fails if applied in season.

Cure for Fever and Ague.—Take of cloves and cream of tartar each one-half ounce, and one ounce of Peruvian bark. Mix in a small quantity of tea, and take it on well days, in such quantities as the stomach will bear.

Cure for Fever Sores.—Take of hoarhound, balm, sarsaparilla, loaf sugar, aloes, gum camphor, honey, spikenard, spirits of turpentine, each two ounces. Dose, one tablespoonful, three mornings, missing three; and for a wash, make a strong tea of sumach, washing the affected parts frequently, and keeping the bandage well wet.

Cure for Fits.—Take of tincture of fox-glove, ten drops at each time twice a day, and increase one drop at each time as long as the stomach will bear it, or it causes a nauseous feeling.

Glycerine Cream.—Receipt for chapped lips: Take of spermaceti, four drachms; white wax, one drachm; oil of almonds, two troy ounces; glycerine, one troy ounce. Melt the spermaceti, wax and oil together, and when cooling stir in glycerine and perfume.

Glycerine Lotion.—For softening the skin of the face and hands, especially during the commencement of cold weather, and also for allaying the irritation caused by the razor: Triturate, four and a half grains of cochineal with one and a half fluid ounces of boiling water, adding gradually; then add two and a half fluid ounces of alcohol. Also make an emulsion of eight drops of ottar of roses with thirty grains of gum arabic and eight fluid ounces of water; then add three fluid ounces of glycerine, and ten fluid drachms of quince mucilage. Mix the two liquids.

Fleshworms.—These specks, when they exist in any number, are a cause of much unsightliness. They are minute corks, if we may use the term, of coagulated lymp, which close the orifices of some of the pores or exhalent vessels of the skin. On the skin immediately adjacent to them being pressed with the finger nails, these bits of coagulated lymph will come from it in a vermicular form. They are vulgarly called "flesh worms," many persons fancying them to be living creatures. These may be got rid of and prevented from returning, by washing with tepid water, by proper friction with a towel, and by the application of a little cold cream. The longer these little piles are permitted to remain in the skin the more firmly they become fixed; and after a time, when they lose their moisture they are converted into long bony spines as dense as bristles, and having much of that character. They are known by the name of spotted achne. With regard to local treatment, the following lotions are calculated to be serviceable: 1. Distilled rose water, 1 pint; sulphate of zinc, 20 to 60 grains. Mix. 2. Sulphate of copper, 20 grains; rose-water, 4 ounces; water, 12 ounces. Mix. 3. Oil of sweet almonds, 1 ounce; fluid potash, 1 drachm. Shake well together and then add rose-water, 1 ounce; pure water, 6 ounces. Mix. The mode of using these remedies is to rub the pimples for some minutes with a rough towel, and then dab them with the lotion. 4. Wash the face twice a day with warm water, and rub dry with a coarse towel. Then with a soft towel rub in a lotion made of two ounces of white brandy, one ounce of cologne, and one-half ounce of liquor potassa.

How to Remove Freckles.—Freckles; so persistently regular in their annual return, have annoyed the fair sex from time immemorial, and various means have been devised to eradicate them, although thus far with no decidedly satisfactory results. The innumerable remedies in use for the removal of these vexatious intruders, are either simple and harmless washes, such as parsley or horseradish water, solutions of borax, etc., or injurious nostrums, consisting principally of lead and mercury salts.

If the exact cause of freckles were known, a remedy for them might be found. A chemist in Moravia, observing the bleaching effect of mercurial preparations, inferred that the growth of a local parasitical fungus was the cause of the discoloration of the skin, which extended and ripened its spores in the warmer season. Knowing that sulpho-carbolate of zinc is a deadly enemy to all parasitic vegetation (itself not being otherwise injurious), he applied this salt for the purpose of removing the freckles. The compound consists of two parts of sulpho-carbolate of zinc, twenty-five parts of distilled glycerine, twenty-five parts of rose-water, and five parts of scented alcohol, and is to be applied twice daily for from half an hour to an hour, then washed off with cold water. Protection against the sun by veiling and other means is recommended, and in addition, for persons of pale complexion, some mild preparation of iron.

Gravel.—1. Make a strong tea of the low herb called heart's ease, and drink freely. 2. Make of Jacob's ladder a strong tea, and drink freely. 3. Make of bean leaves a strong tea, and drink freely.

Wash for the Hair.—Castile soap, finely shaved, one teaspoonful; spirits of hartshorn, one drachm; alcohol, five ounces; cologne water and bay rum, in equal quantities enough to make eight ounces. This should be poured on the head, followed by warm water (soft water); the result will be, on washing, a copious lather and a smarting sensation to the person operated on. Rub this well into the hair. Finally, rinse with warm water, and afterwards with cold water. If the head is very much clogged with dirt, the hair will come out plentifully, but the scalp will become white and perfectly clean.

Hair Restorative.—Take of castor oil, six fluid ounces; alcohol, twenty-six fluid ounces. Dissolve. Then add tincture of cantharides (made with strong alcohol), one fluid ounce; essence of jessamine (or other perfume), one and a half fluid ounces.

Cure for Heartburn.—Sal volatile combined with camphor is a splendid remedy.

Sick Headache.—Take a teaspoonful of powdered charcoal in molasses every morning, and wash it down with a little tea, or drink half a glass of raw rum or gin, and drink freely of mayweed tea.

Headache.—Dr. Silvers, of Ohio, in the Philadelphia *Medical and Surgical Reporter*, recommends ergot in headache, especially the nervous or sick headache. He says it will cure a larger proportion of cases than any other remedy. His theory of its action is that it lessens the quantity of blood in the brain by contracting the muscular fibres of the arterial walls. He gives ten to twenty drops of the fluid extract, repeated every half hour till relief is obtained, or four or five doses used. In other forms of disease, where opium alone is contra-indicated, its bad effects are moderated, he says, by combining it with ergot.

Headache Drops.—For the cure of nervous, sun, and sick headache, take two quarts of alcohol, three ounces of Castile soap, one ounce camphor, and two ounces ammonia. Bathe forehead and temples.

Hive Syrup.—Put one ounce each of squills and seneca snake-root into one pint of water; boil down to one-half and strain. Then add one-half pound of clarified honey containing twelve grains tartrate of antimony. Dose for a child, ten drops to one teaspoonful, according to age. An excellent remedy for croup.

How to Clean the Hair.—From the too frequent use of oils in the hair, many ladies destroy the tone and color of their tresses. The Hindoos have a way of remedying this. They take a hand basin filled with cold water, and have ready a small quantity of pea flour. The hair is in the first place submitted to the operation of being washed in cold water, a handful of the pea flour is then applied to the head and rubbed into the hair for ten minutes at least, the servant adding fresh water at short intervals, until it becomes a perfect lather. The whole head is then washed quite clean with copious supplies of the aqueous fluid, combed, and afterwards rubbed dry by means of coarse towels. The hard and soft brush is then resorted to, when the hair will be found to be wholly free from all encumbering oils and other impurities, and assume a glossy softness, equal to the most delicate silk. This process tends to preserve the tone and natural color of the hair, which is so frequently destroyed by the too constant use of caustic cosmetics.

How to Soften Hands.—After cleansing the hands with soap, rub them well with oatmeal while wet.

How to Remove Stains from Hands.—Damp the hands first in water, then rub them with tartaric acid, or salt of lemons, as you would with soap; rinse them and rub them dry. Tartaric acid, or salt of lemons, will quickly remove stains from white muslin or linen. Put less than half a teaspoonful of salt or acid into a tablespoonful of water; wet the stain with it, and lay it in the sun for an hour; wet it once or twice with cold water during the time; if this does not quite remove it, repeat the acid water, and lay it in the sun.

How to Whiten Hands.—1. Stir ¼ of a pound of Castile soap, and place it in a jar near the fire, pour over it ½ pint of alcohol; when the soap is dissolved and mixed with the spirit, add 1 ounce of glycerine, the same of oil of almonds, with a few drops of essence of violets, or ottar of roses, then pour it into moulds to cool for use. 2. A wineglassful of eau-de-cologne, and one of lemon-juice, two

cakes of broken Windsor soap, mixed well together, when hard, will form an excellent substance.

How to Cure Scurf in the Head.—A simple and effectual remedy. Into a pint of water drop a lump of fresh quick lime, the size of a walnut; let it stand all night, then pour the water off clear from the sediment or deposit, add ¼ of a pint of the best vinegar, and wash the head with the mixture. Perfectly harmless; only wet the roots of the hair.

How to Cure Chapped Lips.—Take 2 ounces of white wax, 1 ounce of spermaceti, 4 ounces of oil of almonds, 2 ounces of honey, ¼ of an ounce of essence of bergamot, or any other scent. Melt the wax and spermaceti; then add the honey, and melt all together, and when hot add the almond oil by degrees, stirring till cold. 2. Take oil of almonds 3 ounces; spermaceti, ½ ounce; virgin rice, ½ ounce. Melt these together over a slow fire, mixing with them a little powder of alkane root to color it. Keep stirring till cold, and then add a few drops of the oil of rhodium. 3. Take oil of almonds, spermaceti, white wax, and white sugar candy, equal parts. These form a good, white lip salve.

How to Remove Moth Patches.—Wash the patches with solution of common bicarbonate of soda and water several times during the day for two days, or until the patches are removed, which will usually be in forty-eight hours. After the process wash with some nice toilet soap, and the skin will be left nice, smooth and clear of patches.

How to Take Care of the Nails.—The nails should be kept clean by the daily use of the nail brush and soap and water. After wiping the hands, but while they are still soft from the action of the water, gently push back the skin which is apt to grow over the nails, which will not only preserve them neatly rounded, but will prevent the skin from cracking around their roots (nail springs), and becoming sore. The points of the nail should be pared at least once a week; biting them should be avoided.

How to Cure Hiccough.—A convulsive motion of the diaphragm and parts adjacent. The common causes are flatuency, indigestion, acidity and worms. It may usually be removed by the exhibition of warm carminatives, cordials, cold water, weak spirits, camphor julep, or spirits of sal volatile. A sudden fright or surprise will often produce the like effect. An instance is recorded of a delicate young lady that was troubled with hiccough for some months, and who was reduced to a state of extreme debility from the loss of sleep occasioned thereby, who was cured by a fright, after medicines and topical applications had failed. A pinch of snuff, a glass of cold soda-water, or an ice-cream, will also frequently remove this complaint.

How to Cure Hoarseness.—Make a strong tea of horse-radish and yellow dock root, sweetened with honey and drink freely.

Remedies for Hoarseness.—Take one drachm of freshly scraped horse-radish root, to be infused with four ounces of water in a close vessel for three hours, and made into a syrup, with double its quantity of vinegar. A teaspoonful has often proved effectual.

How to Cure Humors.—Take equal parts of saffron and seneca snake root, make a strong tea, drink one half-pint a day, and this will drive out all humors from the system.

How to Cure Hysterics.—Take the leaves of motherwort and thoroughwort, and the bark of poplar root; equal parts. Mix them in molasses, and take four of them when the first symptoms of disorder are felt, and they will effectually check it.

How to Cure Barber's Itch.—Moisten the parts affected with saliva (spittle) and rub it over thoroughly three times a day with the ashes of a good Havana cigar. This is a simple remedy, yet it has cured the most obstinate cases.

Itch Ointment.—1. Take lard, one pound; suet, one pound; sugar of lead, eight ounces; vermillion, two ounces. Mix. Scent with a little bergamot. 2. Take bichloride of mercury, one ounce; lard, one pound; suet, one pound; hydrochloride acid, one and a half ounces. Melt and well mix, and when perfectly cold, stir in essence of lemon, four drachms; essence of bergamot, one drachm. 3. Take powdered chloride of lime, one ounce; lard, one pound. Mix well, then add essence of lemon, two drachms. 4. Take bichloride of mercury, one part; lard, fifteen parts. Mix well together. 5. Take white precipitate, one part; lard, twelve parts. Mix. A portion of either of these ointments must be well rubbed on the parts affected, night and morning.

How to Cure Seven-Year Itch.—1. Use plenty of castile soap and water, and then apply freely iodide of sulphur ointment; or take any given quantity of simple sulphur ointment and color it to a light brown or chocolate color with the subcarbonate of iron, and then perfume it. Apply this freely, and if the case should be a severe one, administer mild alteratives in conjunction with the outward application. 2. The sulphur bath is a good remedy for itch or any other kind of skin diseases. Leprosy (the most obstinate of all) has been completely cured by it, and the common itch only requires two or three applications to completely eradicate it from the system. 3. Benzine, it is said, will effect a complete cure for scabies in the course of half to three-quarters of an hour, after which the patient should take a warm bath from twenty to thirty minutes.

How to Cure Jaundice.—1. Take the whites of two hen's eggs, beat them up well in a gill of water; take of this a little every morning; it will soon do good. It also creates an appetite, and strengthens the stomach. 2. Take of black cherry-tree bark, two ounces; blood root and gold thread, each half an ounce; put in a pint of brandy. Dose, from a teaspoonful to a tablespoonful morning and night.

How to Cure Stiffened Joints.—Take of the bark of white oak and sweet apple trees, equal parts; boil them down to a thick substance, and then add the same quantity of goose-grease or oil, simmer all together, and then rub it on the parts warm.

How to Cure Kidney Disease.—Equal parts of the oil of red cedar and the oil of spearmint.

How to Cure Lame Back.—Take the berries of red cedar and allow them to simmer in neatsfoot oil, and use as an ointment.

How to Kill Lice.—All kinds of lice and their nits may be got rid of by washing with a simple decoction of stavesacre (*Delphinium staphisagria*), or with a lotion made with the bruised seed in vinegar, or with the tincture, or by rubbing in a salve made with the seeds and four times their weight of lard very carefully beaten together. The acetic solution and the tincture are the cleanliest and most agreeable preparations, but all are equally efficacious in destroying both the creatures and their eggs, and even in relieving the intolerable itching which their casual presence leaves behind on many sensitive skins. The alkaloid delphinia may also be employed, but possesses no advantage except in the preparation of an ointment, when from any reason that form of application should be preferred.

Rheumatic Liniment.—Olive oil, spirits of camphor and chloroform, of each two ounces; sassafras oil, 1 drachm. Add the oil of sassafras to the olive oil, then the spirits of camphor, and shake well before putting in the

chloroform; shake when used, and keep it corked, as the chloroform evaporates very fast if it is left open. Apply three or four times daily, rubbing in well, and always toward the body.

Sore Throat Liniment.—Gum camphor, two ounces; castile soap, shaved fine, one drachm; oil of turpentine and oil of origanum, each one-half ounce; opium, one-fourth of an ounce; alcohol, one pint. In a week or ten days they will be fit for use. Bathe the parts freely two or three times daily until relief is obtained.

A Wonderful Liniment.—Two ounces oil of spike, two ounces origanum, two ounces hemlock, two ounces wormwood, four ounces sweet oil, two ounces spirit of ammonia, two ounces gum camphor, two ounces spirits turpentine. Add one quart strong alcohol. Mix well together, and bottle tight. This is an unequaled horse liniment, and of the best ever made for human ailments such as rheumatism, sprains, etc.

How to Cure Sore Lips.—Wash the lips with a strong tea, made from the bark of the white oak.

Liver Complaint.—Make a strong tea of syrup of burdock, wormwood and dandelion, equal parts, and drink freely.

Lock Jaw.—It is said that the application of warm lye, made of ashes as strong as possible, to a wounded part, will prevent a locked jaw; if a foot or hand, immerse in it; if another part of the body, bathe with flannels wrung out of the warm lye.

Mumps.—This disease, most common among children, begins with soreness and stiffness in the side of the neck. Soon a swelling of the parotid gland takes place, which is painful, and continues to increase for four or five days, sometimes making it difficult to swallow, or open the mouth. The swelling sometimes comes on one side at a time, but commonly upon both. There is often heat, and sometimes fever, with a dry skin, quick pulse, furred tongue, constipated bowls, and scanty and high-colored urine. The disease is contagious. The treatment is very simple—a mild diet, gentle laxative, occasional hot fomentations, and wearing a piece of flannel round the throat.

How to Prevent Ingrowing Nails.—If the nail of your toe be hard, and apt to grow round, and into the corners of your toe, take a piece of broken glass and scrape the top very thin; do this whenever you cut your nails, and by constant use it makes the corners fly up and grow flat, so that it is impossible they should give you any pain.

How to Whiten Nails.—The best wash for whitening the nails is two drachms of diluted sulphuric acid, one drachm of tincture of myrrh, added to four ounces of spring water; first cleanse the hands, and then apply the wash.

Sure Cure for Neuralgia.—1. Fill a tight-top thimble with cotton wool, and drop on it a few drops of strong spirits of hartshorn. The open mouth of the thimble is then applied over the seat of pain for a minute or two, until the skin is blistered. The skin is then rubbed off, and upon the denuded surface a small quantity of morphia (one-fourth grain) is applied. This affords almost instant relief. A second application of the morphia, if required, is to be preceded by first rubbing off the new formation that has sprung up over the former blistered surface.

2. Dr. J. Knox Hodge recommends the following as an application which will relieve facial or any other neuralgia almost instantaneously: Albumen of egg, one drachm; rhigolene, four ounces; oil of peppermint, two ounces; colodion and chloroform, each one ounce. Mix. Agitate occasionally for twenty-four hours, and by gelatinization a beautiful and semi-solidified, opodeldoc-looking compound

results, which will retain its consistency and hold the ingredients intimately blended for months. Apply by smart friction with the hand, or gently with a soft brush or mop along the course of the nerve involved.

3. Mix one and one-half drachms iodide of potash, fifteen grains of quinine and one ounce ginger syrup, and two and a half ounces water. Dose, a tablespoonful every three hours.

4. **Of the Stomach.**—Take of distilled water of cherry laurel, five parts; muriate of morphia, one-tenth part. Mix and dissolve. One drop on a lump of sugar immediately before meals.

Ointment for Sore Nipples.—Glycerine, rose water and tannin, equal weights, rubbed together into an ointment, is very highly recommended for sore or cracked nipples.

Glycerine Ointment.—Melt together spermaceti, two drachms; white wax, one-half drachm; oil of sweet almonds, two ounces, and then add glycerine, one ounce, and stir briskly until cool. An admirable application for chapped hands, etc.

Ointment for Itch.—White precipitate, fifteen grains; saltpetre, one-half drachm; flour of sulphur, one drachm; Mix well with lard, two ounces. Long celebrated for the cure of itch.

Sulphur Ointment.—Flour of sulphur, eight ounces; oil of bergamot, two drachms; lard, one pound. Rub freely three times a day, for itch.

Ointment for Piles.—Tannin, two drachms; water, two fluid drachms; triturate together, and add lard, one and a half drachms. An excellent application for piles.

Ointment for Hemorrhoids.—Sulphate of morphia, three grains; extract of stramonia, thirty grains; olive oil, one drachm; carbonate of lead, sixty grains; lard, three drachms.

Pains.—1. Steep marigold in good cider vinegar and frequently wash the affected parts. This will afford speedy relief.

2. Take half a pound of tar and the same quantity of tobacco, and boil them down separately to a thick substance; then simmer them together. Spread a plaster and apply it to the affected parts, and it will afford immediate relief.

Painters' Colic.—Make of tartaric acid a syrup similar to that of lemon syrup; add a sufficient quantity of water, and drink two or three glasses a day.

Instantaneous Pain-Killer.—Another and even more instant cure of pain is made as follows: Take aqua-ammonia, sulphuric ether and alcohol, equal parts, and apply over the pain.

How to Cure Pimples.—Take a teaspoonful of the tincture of gum guaiacum and one teaspoonful of vinegar; mix well and apply to the affected parts.

Poor Man's Plaster.—Melt together beeswax, one ounce; tar, three ounces; resin, three ounces, and spread on paper or muslin.

Rheumatic Plaster.—One-fourth pound of resin and one-fourth pound of sulphur; melt by a slow fire, and add one ounce of Cayenne pepper and one-fourth of an ounce of camphor gum; stir well till mixed, and temper with neatsfoot oil.

Strengthening Plaster.—Litharge plasters, twenty-four parts; white resin, six parts; yellow wax and olive oil, of each three parts, and red oxide of iron, eight parts. Let the oxide be rubbed with the oil, and the other ingredients added melted, and mix the whole well together. The plaster, after being spread over the leather, should be cut into strips two inches wide and strapped firmly around the joint.

Mustard Plasters.—It is stated that in making a mustard plaster, no water whatever should be used, but the mustard mixed with the white of an egg; the result will be a plaster that will "draw" perfectly, but will not produce a blister even upon the skin of an infant, no matter how long it is allowed to remain upon the part.

Bread and Milk Poultice.—Take stale bread in crumbs, pour boiling sweet milk, or milk and water over it, and simmer till soft, stirring it well; then take it from the fire, and gradually stir in a little glycerine or sweet oil, so as to render the poultice pliable when applied.

Linseed Poultice.—Take of linseed, powdered, four ounces; hot water sufficient, mix and stir well with a spoon, until of suitable consistence. A little oil should be added, and some smeared over the surface as well, to prevent its getting hard. A very excellent poultice, suitable for many purposes.

Spice Poultice.—Powdered cinnamon, cloves and Cayenne pepper, of each two ounces; rye meal, or flour, spirits and honey, of each sufficient to make of suitable consistence.

Quinsy.—This is an inflammation of the tonsils, or common inflammatory sore throat; commences with a slight feverish attack, with considerable pain and swelling of the tonsils, causing some difficulty in swallowing; as the attack advances these symptoms become more intense, there is headache, thirst, a painful sense of tension, and acute darting pains in the ears. The attack is generally brought on by exposure to cold, and lasts from five to seven days, when it subsides naturally, or an abscess may form in tonsils and burst, or the tonsil may remain enlarged, the inflammation subsiding.

TREATMENT.—The patient should remain in a warm room, the diet chiefly milk and good broths, some cooling laxative and diaphoretic medicine may be given; but the greatest relief will be found in the frequent inhalation of the steam of hot water through an inhaler, or in the old-fashioned way, through the spout of a teapot.

Other Remedies for Rheumatism.—1. Bathe the parts affected with water in which potatoes have been boiled, as hot as can be borne, just before going to bed; by morning it will be much relieved, if not removed. One application of this simple remedy has cured the most obstinate of rheumatic pains. 2. Half an ounce of pulverized saltpetre put in half a pint of sweet oil; bathe the parts affected, and a sound cure will be speedily effected. 3. Rheumatism has frequently been cured by a persistent use of lemon juice, either undiluted or in the form of lemonade. Suck half a lemon every morning before breakfast, and occasionally during the day, and partake of lemonade when thirsty in preference to any other drink. If severely afflicted a physician should be consulted, but, in all cases, lemon juice will hasten the cure. 4. By the valerian bath, made simply by taking one pound of valerian root, boiling it gently for about a quarter of an hour in one gallon of water, straining and adding the strained liquid to about twenty gallons of water in an ordinary bath. The temperature should be about ninety-eight degrees, and the time of immersion from twenty minutes to half an hour. Pains must be taken to dry the patient perfectly upon getting out of the bath. If the inflammation remain refractory in any of the joints, linseed meal poultices should be made with a strong decoction of valerian root and applied.

How to Cure Ring-Worm.—To one part sulphuric acid, add sixteen to twenty parts water. Use a brush and feather, and apply it to the parts night and morning. A few dressings will generally cure. If the solution is too strong and causes pain, dilute it with water, and if the irritation is excessive, rub on a little oil or other softening application, but always avoid the use of soap.

Or, wash the head with soft soap every morning, and apply the following lotion every night: One-half drachm of sub-carbonate of soda dissolved in one gill of vinegar.

Healing Salve.—Sweet oil, three quarts; resin, three ounces; beeswax, three ounces. Melt together; then add powdered red lead, two pounds; heat all these together and when nearly cold add a piece of camphor as large as a nutmeg. Good for burns, etc.

Salt Rheum.—1. Make a strong tea of elm root bark; drink the tea freely, and wash the affected part in the same. 2. Take one ounce of blue flag root, steep it in half a pint of gin; take a teaspoonful three times a day, morning, noon and night, and wash with the same. 3. Take one ounce of oil of tar, one drachm of oil of checker berry; mix. Take from five to twenty drops morning and night as the stomach will bear.

Bleeding of the Stomach.—Take a teaspoonful of camomile tea every ten minutes until the bleeding stops.

Sickness of Stomach.—Drink three or four times a day of the steep made from the bark of white poplar roots.

Sunburn and Tan.—1. Take two drachms of borax, one drachm of Roman alum, one drachm of camphor, half an ounce of sugar candy, and a pound of ox-gall. Mix, and stir well for ten minutes or so, and repeat this stirring three or four times a day for a fortnight, till it appears clear and transparent. Strain through blotting paper, and bottle up for use. 2. Milk of almonds made thus: Take of blanched bitter almonds half an ounce, soft water half a pint; make an emulsion by beating the almonds and water together, strain through a muslin cloth, and it is made. 3. A preparation composed of equal parts of olive oil and lime water is also an excellent remedy for sunburn.

To Produce Sweat.—Take of nitre, one-half drachm; snake's head (herb), saffron, camphor, snake-root, seneca, bark of sassafras root, each one ounce; ipecac, and opium, each one half ounce; put the above in three quarts of Holland gin, and take a tablespoonful in catnip tea every few minutes, till a sweat is produced.

Teething.—Young children whilst cutting their first set of teeth often suffer severe constitutional disturbance. At first there is restlessness and peevishness, with slight fever, but not unfrequently these are followed by convulsive fits, as they are commonly called, which depends on the brain becoming irritated; and sometimes under this condition the child is either cut off suddenly, or the foundation of serious mischief to the brain is laid. The remedy, or rather the safeguard, against these frightful consequences is trifling, safe, and almost certain, and consists merely in lancing the gum covering the tooth which is making its making its way through. When teething is about it may be known by the spittle constantly driveling from the mouth and wetting the frock. The child has its fingers in its mouth, and bites hard any substance it can get hold of. If the gums be carefully looked at, the part where the tooth is pressing up is swollen and redder than usual; and if the finger be pressed on it the child shrinks and cries, showing that the gum is tender. When these symptoms occur, the gum should be lanced, and sometimes the tooth comes through the next day, if near the surface; but if not so far advanced the cut heals and a scar forms, which is thought by some objectionable, as rendering the passage of the tooth more difficult. This, however, is untrue, for the scar will give way much more easily than the uncut gum. If the tooth does not come through after two or three days, the lancing may be repeated; and this is more especially needed if the child be very fractious, and seems in much

pain. Lancing the gums is further advantageous, because it empties the inflamed part of its blood, and so relieves the pain and inflammation. The relief children experience in the course of two or three hours from the operation is often very remarkable, as they almost immediately become lively and cheerful.

Wash for Teeth and Gums.—The teeth should be washed night and morning, a moderately small and soft brush being used; after the morning ablution, pour on a second tooth-brush, slightly dampened, a little of the following lotion: Carbolic acid, 20 drops; spirits of wine, 2 drachms; distilled water, 6 ounces. After using this lotion a short time the gums become firmer and less tender, and impurity of the breath (which is most commonly caused by bad teeth), will be removed. It is a great mistake to use hard tooth-brushes, or to brush the teeth until the gums bleed.

Tetter.—After a slight feverish attack, lasting two or three days, clusters of small, transparent pimples, filled sometimes with a colorless, sometimes with a brownish lymph, appear on the cheeks or forehead, or on the extremities, and at times on the body. The pimples are about the size of a pea, and break after a few days, when a brown or yellow crust is formed over them, which falls off about the tenth day, leaving the skin red and irritable. The eruption is attended with heat; itching, tingling, fever, and restlessness, especially at night. Ringworm is a curious form of tetter, in which the inflamed patches assume the form of a ring.

TREATMENT—Should consist of light diet, and gentle laxatives. If the patient be advanced in life, and feeble, a tonic will be desirable. For a wash, white vitriol, 1 drachm; rose-water, 3 ounces, mixed; or an ointment made of alder-flower ointment, 1 ounce; oxide of zinc, 1 drachm.

To Remove Tan.—Tan may be removed from the face by mixing magnesia in soft water to the consistency of paste, which should then be spread on the face and allowed to remain a minute or two. Then wash off with Castile soap suds, and rinse with soft water.

Care of the Teeth.—The mouth has a temperature of 98 degrees, warmer than is ever experienced in the shade in the latitude of New England. It is well known that if beef, for example, be exposed in the shade during the warmest of our summer days, it will very soon decompose. If we eat beef for dinner, the particles invariably find their way into the spaces between the teeth. Now, if these particles of beef are not removed, they will frequently remain till they are softened by decomposition. In most mouths this process of decomposition is in constant progress. Ought we to be surprised that the gums and teeth against which these decomposing or putrefying masses lie should become subjects of disease?

How shall our teeth be preserved? The answer is very simple—keep them very clean. How shall they be kept clean? Answer—By a toothpick, rinsing with water, and the daily use of a brush.

The toothpick should be a quill, not because the metalic picks injure the enamel, but because the quill pick is so flexible it fits into all the irregularities between the teeth.

Always after using the toothpick the mouth should be thoroughly rinsed. If warm water be not at hand, cold may be used, although warm is much better. Closing the lips, with a motion familiar to all, everything may be thoroughly rinsed from the mouth.

Every morning (on rising), and every evening (on going to bed), the tooth-brush should be used, and the teeth, both outside and inside, thoroughly brushed.

Much has been said *pro* and *con.*, upon the use of soap with the tooth-brush. My own experience and the experience of members of my family is highly favorable to the regular morning and evening use of soap. Castile or other good soap will answer this purpose. (Whatever is good for the hands and face is good for the teeth.) The slightly unpleasant taste which soap has when we begin to use it will soon be unnoticed.

Tooth Powders.—Many persons, while laudably attentive to the preservation of their teeth, do them harm by too much officiousness. They daily apply to them some dentifrice powder, which they rub so hard as not only to injure the enamel by excessive friction, but to hurt the gums even more than by the abuse of the toothpick. The quality of some of the dentifrice powders advertised in newspapers is extremely suspicious, and there is reason to think that they are not altogether free from a corrosive ingredient. One of the safest and best compositions for the purpose is a mixture of two parts of prepared chalk, one of Peruvian bark, and one of hard soap, all finely powdered, which is calculated not only to clean the teeth without hurting them, but to preserve the firmness of the gums.

Besides the advantage of sound teeth for their use in mastication, a proper attention to their treatment conduces not a little to the sweetness of the breath. This is, indeed, often affected by other causes existing in the lungs, the stomach, and sometimes even in the bowels, but a rotten state of the teeth, both from the putrid smell emitted by carious bones and the impurities lodged in their cavities, never fails of aggravating an unpleasant breath wherever there is a tendency of that kind.

Remedies for Toothache.—1. One drachm of alum reduced to an impalpable powder, three drachms of nitrous spirits of ether—mix, and apply them to the tooth on cotton. 2. Mix a little salt and alum, equal portions, grind it fine, wet a little lock of cotton, fill it with the powder and put it in your tooth. One or two applications seldom fail to cure. 3. To one drachm of collodion add two drachms of Calvert's carbolic acid. A gelatinous mass is precipitated, a small portion of which, inserted in the cavity of an aching tooth, invariably gives immediate relief. 4. Saturate a small bit of clean cotton wool with a strong solution of ammonia, and apply it immediately to the affected tooth. The pleasing contrast immediately produced in some cases causes fits of laughter, although a moment previous extreme suffering and anguish prevailed. 5. Sometimes a sound tooth aches from sympathy of the nerves of the face with other nerves. But when toothache proceeds from a decayed tooth either have it taken out, or put hot fomentations upon the face, and hot drinks into the mouth, such as tincture of cayenne.

To Cure Warts.—Warts are formed by the small arteries, veins, and nerves united together, taking on a disposition to grow by extending themselves upward, carrying the scarf-skin along with them, which, thickening, forms a wart. Corns are a similar growth, brought about by the friction of tight boots and shoes. 1. Take a piece of diachylon plaster, cut a hole in the centre the size of the wart, and stick it on, the wart protruding through. Then touch it daily with aquafortis, or nitrate of silver. They may be removed by tying a string tightly around them. 2. Take a blacksmith's punch, heat it red hot and burn the warts with the end of it. When the burn gets well the warts will be gone forever. 3. Scrape down enough dry cobwebs to make a ball large enough to, or a little more than, cover the wart and not touch the flesh around the same; lay it on top of the wart, ignite it and let it be until it is all burnt up. The wart will turn white, and in a few days come out. 4. Pass a pin through the wart; apply one end of the pin to the flame of a lamp; hold it there until the wart fries under the action of the heat. A wart so treated will leave. 5. Dissolve as much common washing soda as the water

will take up; wash the warts with this for a minute or two, and let them dry without wiping. Keep the water in a bottle and repeat the washing often, and it will take away the largest warts. 6. They may be cured surely by paring them down until the blood comes slightly and then rubbing them with lunar caustic. It is needless to say this hurts a little, but it is a sure cure. The hydrochlorate of lime applied in the same way will cure after several applications and some patience; so will strong good vinegar, and so it is said will milk weed. The cures founded upon superstitious practices, such as muttering some phrases over the excrescence, stealing a piece of beef, rubbing the wart therewith and then burying it under the leaves to await its decay, etc., etc., are all the remnants of a past state of ignorance and are of no use whatever. Warts are generally only temporary and disappear as their possessors grow up.

How to Cure White Swelling.—Draw a blister on the inside of the leg below the knee; keep it running with ointment made of hen manure, by simmering it in hog's lard with onions; rub the knee with the following kind of ointment: Bits of peppermint, oil of sassafras, checkerberry, juniper, one drachm each; simmer in one-half pint neatsfoot oil, and rub on the knee three times a day.

How to Cure Wounds.—Catnip steeped, mixed with fresh butter and sugar.

How to Cure Whooping-Cough.—Take a quart of spring water, put in it a large handful of chin-cups that grow upon moss, a large handful of unset hyssop; boil it to a pint, strain it off, and sweeten it with sugar-candy. Let the child, as often as it coughs, take two spoonfuls at a time.

How to Cure Worms in Children.—1. Take one ounce of powdered snake-head (herb), and one drachm each of aloes and prickly ash bark; powder these, and to one-half teaspoonful of this powder add a teaspoonful of boiling water and a teaspoonful of molasses. Take this as a dose, night or morning, more or less, as the symptoms may require. 2. Take tobacco leaves, pound them up with honey, and lay them on the belly of the child or grown person, at the same time administering a dose of some good physic. 3. Take garden parsley, make it into a tea and let the patient drink freely of it. 4. Take the scales that will fall around the blacksmith's anvil, powder them fine, and put them in sweetened rum. Shake when you take them, and give a teaspoonful three times a day.

Scalding of the Urine.—Equal parts of the oil of red cedar, and the oil of spearmint.

Urinary Obstructions.—Steep pumpkin seeds in gin, and drink about three glasses a day; or, administer half a drachm uva ursi every morning, and a dose of spearmint.

Free Passage of Urine.—The leaves of the currant bush made into a tea, and taken as a common drink.

Venereal Complaints.—Equal parts of the oil of red cedar, combined with sarsaparilla, yellow dock and burdock made into a syrup; add to a pint of this syrup an ounce of gum guaiacum. Dose, from a tablespoonful to a wine-glass, as best you can bear.

How to Cure Sore Throat.—"One who has tried it" communicates the following sensible item about curing sore throat: Let each one of your half million readers buy at any drug store one ounce of camphorated oil and five cents' worth of chloride of potash. Whenever any soreness appears in the throat, put the potash in half a tumbler of water, and with it gargle the throat thoroughly; then rub the neck thoroughly with the camphorated oil at night before going to bed, and also pin around the throat a small strip of woolen flannel. This is a simple, cheap and sure remedy.

.. LANGUAGE OF FLOWERS ..

Acacia—Concealed love.
Adonis Vernalis — Sorrowful remembrances.
Almond—Hope.
Aloe—Religious superstition.
Alyssum, Sweet—Worth beyond beauty.
Ambrosia—Love returned.
Apple Blossom—Preference.
Arbor Vitæ—Unchanging friendship.

Bachelor's button—Hope in love.
Balsam—Impatience.
Begonia—Deformity.
Bellflower—Gratitude.
Belvidere, Wild (Licorice)—I declare against you.
Blue Bell—I will be constant.
Box—Stoical indifference.
Briers—Envy.
Burdock—Touch me not.

Cactus—Thou leavest not.
Camellia—Pity.
Candytuft—Indifference.
Canterbury Bell—Gratitude.
Cape Jessamine—Ecstasy; transport.
Calla Lily—Feminine beauty.
Carnation (Yellow)—Disdain.
Cedar—I live for thee.
China Aster—I will see about it.
Chrysanthemum Rose—I love.
Cowslip—Pensiveness.
Cypress—Mourning.
Crocus—Cheerfulness.
Cypress and Marigold—Despair.

Daffodil—Chivalry.
Dahlia—Forever thine.
Daisy (Garden)—I partake your sentiment.
Daisy (Wild)—I will think of it.
Dandelion—Coquetry.
Dead Leaves—Sadness.
Dock—Patience.
Dodder—Meanness.
Dogwood—Am I indifferent to you?

Ebony—Hypocrisy.
Eglantine—I wound to heal.
Elder—Compassion.
Endive—Frugality.
Evening Primrose—Inconstancy.
Evergreen—Poverty.
Everlasting—Perpetual remembrance.
Fennel—Strength.
Filbert—Reconciliation.
Fir-tree—Elevation.
Flax—I feel your kindness.
Forget-me-not — True love; remembrance.
Fox-glove—Insincerity.
Furze—Anger.
Fuchsia—Taste.

Gentian—Intrinsic worth.
Geranium, Ivy—Your hand for the next dance.
Geranium, Nutmeg—I expect a meeting.

Geranium, Oak—Lady, deign to smile.
Geranium, Rose—Preference.
Geranium, Silver leaf—Recall.
Gilliflower—Lasting beauty.
Gladiolus—Ready; armed.
Golden Rod—Encouragement.
Gorse—Endearing affection.
Gass—Utility.

Harebell—Grief.
Hawthorn—Hope.
Hazel—Recollection.
Hartsease—Think of me.
Heliotrope—Devotion.
Henbane—Blemish.
Holly—Foresight.
Hollyhock—Fruitfulness.
Hollyhock, White—Female ambition.
Honeysuckle—Bond of Love.
Honeysuckle, Coral—The color of my fate.
Hyacinth—Jealousy.
Hyacinth, Blue—Constancy.
Hyacinth, Purple—Sorrow.
Hydrangea—Heartlessness.

Ice plant—Your looks freeze me.
Iris—Message.
Ivy—Friendship; matrimony.

Jessamine, Cape—Transient joy; ecstasy.
Jessamine, White—Amiability.
Jessamine, Yellow—Grace; elegance.
Jonquil—I desire a return of affection.
Juniper—Asylum; shelter.
Justicia—Perfection of loveliness.

Kalmia (Mountain Laurel)—Treachery.
Kannedia—Mental beauty.
Laburnum—Pensive beauty.
Lady's Slipper—Capricious beauty.
Larch—Boldness.
Larkspur—Fickleness.
Laurel—Glory.
Lavender—Distrust.
Lettuce—Cold-hearted.
Lilac—First emotion of love.
Lily—Purity; modesty.
Lily of the Valley—Return of happiness.
Lily, Day—Coquetry,
Lily, Water—Eloquence.
Lily, Yellow—Falsehood.
Locust—Affection beyond the grave.
Love in a Mist—You puzzle me.
Love Lies Bleeding — Hopeless, not heartless.
Lupine—Imagination.
Mallow—Sweetness; mildness.
Maple—Reserve.
Marigold—Cruelty.
Marjoram—Blushes.
Marvel of Peru (Four O'clocks)—Timidity.
Mint—Virtue.
Mignonette—Your qualities surpass your charms.

Mistletoe—I surmount all difficulties.
Mock Orange (Syringa)—Counterfeit.
Morning Glory—Coquetry.
Maiden's Hair—Discretion.
Magnolia, Grandiflora—Peerless and proud.
Magnolia, Swamp—Perseverance.
Moss—Maternal love.
Motherwort—Secret love.
Mourning Bride—Unfortunate attachment.
Mulberry, Black—I will not survive you.
Mulberry, White—Wisdom.
Mushroom—Suspicion.
Musk-plant—Weakness.
Myrtle—Love faithful in absence.
Narcissus—Egotism.
Nasturtium—Patriotism.
Nettle—Cruelty; slander.
Night Blooming Cereus — Transient beauty.
Nightshade—Bitter truth.
Oak—Hospitality.
Oats—Music.
Oleander—Beware.
Olive-branch—Peace.
Orange-flower—Chastity.
Orchis—Beauty.
Osier—Frankness.
Osmunda—Dreams.

Pansy—Think of me.
Parsley—Entertainment; feasting.
Passion-flower—Religious fervor; susceptibility.
Pea, Sweet—Departure.
Peach Blossom—This heart is thine.
Peony—Anger.
Pennyroyal—Flee away.
Periwinkle—Sweet remembrances.
Petunia—Less proud than they deem thee.
Phlox—Our souls are united.
Pimpernel—Change.
Pink—Pure affection.
Pink, Double Red—Pure, ardent love.
Pink, Indian—Aversion.
Pink, Variegated—Refusal.
Pink, White—You are fair.
Pomegranite—Folly.
Poppy—Consolation.
Primrose—Inconstancy.

Rhododendron—Agitation.
Rose, Austrian—Thou art all that's lovely.
Rose, Bridal—Happy love.
Rose, Cabbage—Ambassador of love.
Rose, China—Grace.
Rose, Damask—Freshness.
Rose, Jacqueminot—Mellow love.
Rose, Maiden's Blush—If you *do* love me, you will find me out.
Rose, Moss—Superior merit.
Rose, Moss Rosebud—Confession of love.

Rose, Sweet-briar—Sympathy.
Rose, Tea—Always lovely.
Rose, White—I am worthy of you.
Rose, York and Lancaster—War.
Rose, Wild—Simplicity.
Rue—Disdain.

Saffron—Excess is dangerous.
Sardonia—Irony.
Sensitive Plant—Timidity.
Snap-Dragon—Presumption.
Snowball—Thoughts of Heaven.
Snowdrop—Consolation.
Sorrel—Wit ill-timed.
Spearment—Warm feelings.
Star of Bethlehem—Reconciliation.

Strawberry—Perfect excellence.
Sumac—Splendor.
Sunflower, Dwarf—Your devout admirer.
Sunflower, Tall—Pride.
Sweet William—Finesse.
Syringa—Memory.

Tansy—I declare against you.
Teazel—Misanthropy.
Thistle—Austerity.
Thorn Apple—Deceitful charms.
Touch-me-not—Impatience.
Trumpet-flower—Separation.
Tuberose—Dangerous pleasures.
Tulip—Declaration of love.

Tulip, Variegated—Beautiful eyes.
Tulip, Yellow—Hopeless love.

Venus' Flytrap—Have I caught you at last.
Venus' Looking-glass—Flattery.
Verbena—Sensibility.
Violet, Blue—Love.
Violet, White—Modesty.

Wallflower—Fidelity.
Weeping Willow—Forsaken.
Woodbine—Fraternal love.

Yew—Sorrow.

Zennæ—Absent friends.

MASTERPIECES OF ELOQUENCE

The following masterpieces of elegiac eloquence are unsurpassed in the repertory of the English classics, for lofty and noble sentiment, exquisite pathos, vivid imagery, tenderness of feeling, glowing power of description, brilliant command of language, and that immortal and seldom attained faculty of painting in the soul of the listener or reader a realistic picture whose sublimity of conception impresses the understanding with awe and admiration, and impels the mind to rise involuntarily for the time to an elevation out of and above the inconsequent contemplation of the common and sordid things of life.

AT HIS BROTHER'S GRAVE.

The following grand oration was delivered by Hon. Robert G. Ingersoll on the occasion of the funeral of his brother, Hon. Eben C. Ingersoll, in Washington, June 2:

"My friends, I am going to do that which the dead oft promised he would do for me. The loved and loving brother, husband, father, friend, died where manhood's morning almost touches noon, and while the shadows were still falling towards the west. He had not passed on life's highway the stone that marks the highest point, but being weary for a moment he lay down by the wayside, and using his burden for a pillow fell into that dreamless sleep that kisses down the eyelids. Still, while yet in love with life and raptured with the world, he passed to silence and pathetic dust. Yet, after all, it may be best, just in the happiest, sunniest hour of all the voyage, while eager winds are kissing every sail, to dash against the unseen rock and in an instant to hear the billows roar, 'A sunken ship;' for whether in mid sea or among the breakers of the farther shore, a wreck must mark at last the end of each and all, and every life, no matter if its every hour is rich with love, and every moment jeweled with a joy, will at its close become a tragedy as sad and deep and dark as can be woven of the warp and woof of mystery and death. This brave and tender man in every storm of life was oak and rock, but in the sunshine he was vine and flower. He was the friend of all heroic souls. He climbed the heights and left all superstitions far below, while on his forehead fell the golden dawning of a grander day. He loved the beautiful, and was with color, form and music touched to tears. He sided with the weak, and with a willing hand gave alms. With loyal heart, and with the purest hand he faithfully discharged all public trusts. He was a worshiper of liberty and a friend of the oppressed. A thousand times I have heard him quote the words, ' For Justice all place temple, and

all seasons summer.' He believed that happiness was the only good, reason the only torch, justice the only worshiper, humanity the only religion, and love the priest. He added to the sum of human joy, and were everyone for whom he did some loving service to bring a blossom to his grave, he would sleep to-night beneath a wilderness of flowers. Life is a narrow vale between the cold and barren peaks of two eternities. We strive in vain to look beyond the heights. We cry aloud, and the only answer is the echo of our wailing cry. From the voiceless lips of the unreplying dead there comes no word, but the light of death. Hope sees a star, and listening love can hear the rustle of a wing. He who sleeps here when dying, mistaking the approach of death for the return of health, whispered with his latest breath, "I am better now." Let us believe, in spite of doubts and dogmas, and tears and fears, that these dear words are true of all the countless dead. And now, to you who have been chosen from among the many men he loved to do the last sad office for the dead, we give his sacred dust. Speech cannot contain our love. There was, there is, no gentler, stronger, manlier man."

AT THE GRAVE OF A CHILD.

Colonel Ingersoll upon one occasion was one of a little party of sympathizing friends who had gathered in a drizzling rain to assist the sorrowing friends of a young boy—a bright and stainless flower, cut off in the bloom of its beauty and virgin purity by the ruthless north winds from the Plutonian shades—in the last sad office of committing the poor clay to the bosom of its mother earth. Inspired by that true sympathy of the great heart of a great man, Colonel Ingersoll stepped to the side of the grave and spoke as follows:

"My friends, I know how vain it is to gild grief with words, and yet I wish to take from every grave its fear. Here in this world, where life and death are equal kings, all should be brave enough to meet what all the dead have met. The future has been filled with fear, stained and polluted by the heartless past. From the wondrous tree of life the buds and blossoms fall with ripened fruit, and in the common bed of earth the patriarchs and babes sleep side by side. Why should we fear that which will come to all that is? We cannot tell; we do not know which is the greater blessing—life or death. We cannot say that death is not a good; we do not know whether the grave is the end of this life or the door of another, or whether the night here is not somewhere else a dawn. Neither can we tell which is the more fortunate, the child dying in its mother's arms, before its lips have learned to form a word, or he who journeys all the length of life's uneven road, taking the last slow steps painfully with staff and crutch. Every cradle asks us 'whence,' and every coffin 'whither?' The poor barbarian, weeping above his dead, can answer these questions as intelligently and satisfactorily as the robed priest of the most authentic creed. The tearful ignorance of the one is just as good as the learned and unmeaning words of the other. No man, standing where the horizon of life has touched a grave, has any right to prophesy a future filled with pain and tears. It may be that death gives all there is of worth to live. If those we press and strain against our hearts could never die, perhaps that love would wither from the earth. May be this common fate treads from out the paths between our hearts the weeds of selfishness and hate, and I had rather live and love where death is king, than have eternal life where love is not. Another life is naught, unless we know and love again the ones who love us here. They who stand with breaking hearts around this little grave need have no fear. The larger and the nobler faith in all that is and is to be, tells us that death, even at its worst, is only perfect rest. We know that through the common wants of life, the needs and duties of each hour, their grief will lessen day by day, until at last these graves will be to them a place of rest and peace, almost of joy. There is for them this consolation, the dead do not suffer. If they live again, their lives will surely be as good as ours. We have no fear; we are all the children of the same mother, and the same fate awaits us all. We, too, have our religion, and it is this: 'Help for the living; hope for the dead.'"

SUNDRY BRIEF ITEMS OF INTEREST.

In 1492 America was discovered.

In 1848 gold was found in California.

Invention of telescopes, 1590.

Elias Howe, Jr., invented sewing machines in 1846.

In 1839 envelopes came into use.

Steel pens first made in 1830.

The first watch was constructed in 1476.

First manufacture of sulphur matches in 1829.

Glass windows introduced into England in the eighth century.

First coaches introduced into England in 1569.

In 1545 needles of the modern style first came into use.

In 1527 Albert Durer first engraved on wood.

1559 saw knives introduced into England.

In the same year wheeled carriages were first used in France.

In 1588 the first newspaper appeared in England.

In 1629 the first printing press was brought to America.

The first newspaper advertisement appeared in 1652.

England sent the first steam engine to this continent in 1703.

The first steamboat in the United States ascended the Hudson in 1807.

Locomotive first used in the United States in 1830.

First horse railroad constructed in 1827.

In 1830 the first iron steamship was built.

Coal oil first used for illuminating purposes in 1836.

Looms introduced as a substitute for spinning wheels in 1776.

The velocity of a severe storm is 36 miles an hour; that of a hurricane, 80 miles an hour.

National ensign of the United States formally adopted by Congress in 1777.

A square acre is a trifle less than 209 feet each way.

Six hundred and forty acres make a square mile.

A "hand" (employed in measuring horses' height) is four inches.

A span is $10\frac{7}{8}$ inches.

Six hundred pounds make a barrel of rice.

One hundred and ninety-six pounds make a barrel of flour.

Two hundred pounds make a barrel of pork.

Fifty-six pounds make a firkin of butter.

The number of languages is 2,750.

The average duration of human life is 31 years.

PHYSICIANS' DIGESTION TABLE.

SHOWING THE TIME REQUIRED FOR THE DIGESTION OF THE ORDINARY ARTICLES OF FOOD.

Soups.—Chicken, 3 hours; mutton, $3\frac{1}{2}$ hours; oyster, $3\frac{1}{2}$ hours; vegetable, 4 hours.

Fish.—Bass, broiled, 3 hours; codfish, boiled, 2 hours; oysters, raw, 3 hours; oysters, roasted, $3\frac{1}{4}$ hours; oysters, stewed, $3\frac{1}{2}$ hours; salmon (fresh), boiled, $1\frac{3}{4}$ hours; trout, fried, $1\frac{1}{2}$ hours.

Meats.—Beef, roasted, 3 hours; beefsteak, broiled, 3 hours; beef (corned), boiled, $4\frac{1}{4}$ hours; lamb, roast, $2\frac{1}{2}$ hours; lamb, boiled, 3 hours; meat, hashed, $2\frac{1}{2}$ hours; mutton, broiled, 3 hours; mutton, roast, $3\frac{1}{4}$ hours; pig's feet, soused, 1 hour; pork, roast, $5\frac{1}{4}$ hours; pork, boiled, $4\frac{1}{2}$ hours; pork, fried, $4\frac{1}{4}$ hours; pork, broiled, $3\frac{1}{4}$ hours; sausage, fried, 4 hours; veal, broiled, 4 hours; veal, roast. $4\frac{1}{4}$ hours.

Poultry and game.—Chicken, fricasseed, $3\frac{3}{4}$ hours; duck (tame), roasted, 4 hours; duck (wild), roasted, $4\frac{3}{4}$ hours; fowls (domestic), roasted or boiled, 4 hours; goose (wild), roasted, $2\frac{1}{2}$ hours; goose (tame), roasted, $2\frac{1}{4}$ hours; turkey, boiled or roasted, $2\frac{1}{2}$ hours; venison, broiled or roasted, $1\frac{1}{2}$ hours.

Vegetables.—Asparagus, boiled, $2\frac{1}{2}$ hours; beans (Lima), boiled, $2\frac{1}{2}$ hours, beans (string), boiled, 3 hours; beans, baked (with pork), $4\frac{1}{2}$ hours; beets (young), boiled, $3\frac{3}{4}$ hours; beets (old) boiled, 4 hours; cabbage, raw, 2 hours; cabbage, boiled, $4\frac{1}{2}$ hours; cauliflower, boiled, $2\frac{1}{2}$ hours; corn (green), boiled, 4 hours; onions, boiled, 3 hours; parsnips, boiled, 3 hours; potatoes, boiled or baked, $3\frac{1}{2}$ hours; rice, boiled, 1 hour; spinach, boiled, $2\frac{1}{2}$ hours; tomatoes, raw or stewed, $2\frac{1}{2}$ hours; turnips, boiled, $3\frac{1}{2}$ hours.

Bread, Eggs, Milk, etc.—Bread, corn, $3\frac{1}{4}$ hours; bread, wheat, $3\frac{1}{2}$ hours; eggs, raw, 2 hours; cheese, $3\frac{1}{4}$ hours; custard, $2\frac{3}{4}$ hours; eggs, soft-boiled, 3 hours; eggs, hard-boiled or fried, $3\frac{1}{2}$ hours; gelatine, $2\frac{1}{2}$ hours; tapioca, 2 hours.

THEMES FOR DEBATE.

Following are one hundred and fifty topics for debate. The more usual form in their presentation is that of a direct proposition or statement, rather than that of a question. The opponents then debate the "affirmative" and "negative" of the proposition. It is well to be very careful, in adopting a subject for a debate, to so state or explain it that misunderstandings may be mutually avoided, and quibbles on the meaning of words prevented.

THEMES FOR DEBATE.

Which is the better for this nation, high or low import tariffs?

Is assassination ever justifiable?

Was England justifiable in interfering between Egypt and the Soudan rebels?

Is the production of great works of literature favored by the conditions of modern civilized life?

Is it politic to place restrictions upon the immigration of the Chinese to the United States?

Will coal always constitute the main source of artificial heat?

Has the experiment of universal suffrage proven a success?

Was Grant or Lee the greater general?

Is an income-tax commendable?

Ought the national banking system to be abolished?

Should the government lease to stockgrowers any portion of the public domain?

Is it advisable longer to attempt to maintain both a gold and silver standard of coinage?

Which is the more important to the student, physical science or mathematics?

Is the study of current politics a duty?

Which was the more influential congressman, Blaine or Garfield?

Which gives rise to more objectionable idioms and localisms of language, New England or the West?

Was the purchase of Alaska by this government wise?

Which is the more important as a continent, Africa or South America?

Should the government interfere to stop the spread of contagious diseases among cattle?

Was Cæsar or Hannibal the more able general?

Is the study of ancient or modern history the more important to the student?

Should aliens be allowed to acquire property in this country?

Should aliens be allowed to own real estate in this country?

Do the benefits of the signal service justify its costs?

Should usury laws be abolished?

Should all laws for the collection of debt be abolished?

Is labor entitled to more remuneration than it receives?

Should the continuance of militia organizations by the several States be encouraged?

Is an untarnished reputation of more importance to a woman than to a man?

Does home life promote the growth of selfishness?

Are mineral veins aqueous or igneous in origin?

Is the theory of evolution tenable?

Was Rome justifiable in annihilating Carthage as a nation?

Which has left the more permanent impress upon mankind, Greece or Rome?

Which was the greater thinker, Emerson or Bacon?

Which is the more important as a branch of education, mineralogy or astronomy?

Is there any improvement in the quality of the literature of to-day over that of last century?

Should the "Spoils System" be continued in American politics?

Should the co-education of the sexes be encouraged?

Which should be the more encouraged, novelists or dramatists?

Will the African and Caucasian races ever be amalgamated in the United States?

Should the military or the interior department have charge over the Indians in the United States?

Which is of more benefit to his race, the inventor or the explorer?

Is history or philosophy the better exercise for the mind?

Can any effectual provision be made by the State against "hard times?"

Which is of the more benefit to society, journalism or the law?

Which was the greater general, Napoleon or Wellington?

Should the volume of greenback money be increased?

Should the volume of national bank ciculation be increased?

Should the railroads be under the direct control of the government?

Is the doctrine of "State rights" to be commeded?

Is the "Monroe doctrine" to be commended and upheld?

Is the pursuit of politics an honorable avocation?

Which is of the greater importance, the college or the university?

Does the study of physical science militate against religious belief?

Should "landlordism" in Ireland be supplanted by home rule?

Is life more desirable now than in ancient Rome?

Should men and women receive the same amount of wages for the same kind of work?

Is the prohibitory liquor law preferable to a system of high license?

Has any State a right to secede?

Should any limit be placed by the constitution of a State upon its ability to contract indebtedness?

Should the contract labor system in public prisons be forbidden?

Should there be a censor for the public press?

Should Arctic expeditions be encouraged?

Is it the duty of the State to encourage art and literature as much as science?

Is suicide cowardice?

Has our Government a right to disfranchise the polygamists of Utah?

Should capital punishment be abolished?

Should the law place a limit upon the hours of daily labor for workingmen?

Is "socialism" treason?

Should the education of the young be compulsory?

In a hundred years will republics be as numerous as monarchies?

Should book-keeping be taught in the public schools?

Should Latin be taught in the public schools?

Do our methods of government promote centralization?

Is life worth living?

Should Ireland and Scotland be independent nations?

Should internal revenue taxation be abolished?

Which is of greater benefit at the present day, books or newspapers?

Is honesty always the best policy?

Which has been of greater benefit to mankind, geology or chemistry?

Which could mankind dispense with at least inconvenience, wood or coal?

Which is the greater nation, Germany or France?

Which can support the greater population in proportion to area, our Northern or Southern States?

Would mankind be the loser if the earth should cease to produce gold and silver?

Is the occasional destruction of large numbers of people, by war and disaster, a benefit to the world?

Which could man best do without, steam or horse power?

Should women be given the right of suffrage in the United States?

Should cremation be substituted for burial?

Should the government establish a national system of telegraph?

Will the population of Chicago ever exceed that of New York?

Should the electoral college be continued?

Will the population of St. Louis ever exceed that of Chicago?

Should restrictions be placed upon the amount of property inheritable?

Which is more desirable as the chief business of a city—commerce or manufactures?

Which is more desirable as the chief business of a city—transportation by water or by rail?

Should the rate of taxation be graduated to a ratio with the amount of property taxed?

Will a time ever come when the population of the earth will be limited by the earth's capacity of food production?

Is it probable that any language will ever become universal?

Is it probable that any planet, except the earth, is inhabited?

Should the State prohibit the manufacture and sale of alcoholic liquors?

Should the government prohibit the manufacture and sale of alcoholic liquors?

Should the guillotine be substituted for the gallows?

Was Bryant or Longfellow the greater poet?

Should the jury system be continued?

Should the languages of alien nations be taught in the public schools?

Should a right to vote in any part of the United States depend upon a property qualification?

Can a horse trot faster in harness, or under saddle?

Should the pooling system among American railroads be abolished by law?

Is dancing, as usually conducted, compatible with a high standard of morality?

Should the grand jury system of making indictments be continued?

Which should be the more highly remunerated, skilled labor or the work of professional men?

Which is the more desirable as an occupation, medicine or law?

Should the formation of trade unions be encouraged?

Which has been the greater curse to man, war or drunkenness?

Which can man the more easily do without, electricity or petroleum?

Should the law interfere against the growth of class distinctions in society?

Which was the greater genius, Mohammed or Buddha?

Which was the more able leader, Pizarro or Cortez?

Which can to-day wield the greater influence, the orator or the writer?

Is genius hereditary?

Is Saxon blood deteriorating?

Which will predominate in five hundred years, the Saxon or Latin races?

Should American railroad companies be allowed to sell their bonds in other countries?

Should Sumner's civil rights bill be made constitutional by an amendment?

Does civilization promote the happiness of the world?

Should land subsidies be granted to railroads by the government?

Which is the stronger military power, England or the United States?

Would a rebellion in Russia be justifiable?

Should the theater be encouraged?

Which has the greater resources, Pennsylvania or Texas?

Is agriculture the noblest occupation?

Can democratic forms of government be made universal?

Is legal punishment for crime as severe as it should be?

Should the formation of monopolies be prevented by the State?

Has Spanish influence been helpful or harmful to Mexico as a people?

Which is of more importance, the primary or the high school?

Will the tide of emigration ever turn eastward instead of westward?

Should the art of war be taught more widely than at present in the United States?

Was slavery the cause of the American civil war?

Is life insurance a benefit?

How to Make 32 Kinds of Solder.—1. Plumbers' solder.—Lead 2 parts, tin 1 part. 2. Tinmen's solder.—Lead 1 part, tin 1 part. 3. Zinc solder.—Tin 1 part, lead 1 to parts. 4. Pewter solder. Lead 1 part, bismuth 1 to 2 parts. 5. Spelter solder.—Equal parts copper and zinc. 6. Pewterers' soft solder.—Bismuth 2, lead 4, tin 3 parts. 7. Another.—Bismuth 1, lead 1, tin 2 parts. 8. Another pewter solder.—Tin 2 parts, lead 1 part. 9. Glaziers' solder.—Tin 3 parts, lead 1 part. 10. Solder for copper.—Copper 10 parts, zinc 9 parts. 11. Yellow solder for brass or copper.—Copper 32 lbs., zinc 29 lbs., tin 1 lb. 12. Brass solder.—Copper 61.25 parts, zinc 38.75 parts. 13. Brass solder, yellow and easily fusible.—Copper 45, zinc 55 parts. 14. Brass solder, white.—Copper 57.41 parts, tin 14.60 parts, zinc 27.99 parts. 15. Another solder for copper.—Tin 2 parts, lead 1 part. When the copper is thick heat it by a naked fire, if thin use a tinned copper tool. Use muriate or chloride of zinc as a flux. The same solder will do for iron, cast iron, or steel; if the pieces are thick, heat by a naked fire or immerse in the solder. 16. Black solder.—Copper 2, zinc 3, tin 2 parts. 17. Another.—Sheet brass 20 lbs., tin 6 lbs., zinc 1 lb. 18. Cold brazing without fire or lamp.—Fluoric acid 1 oz., oxy muriatic acid 1 oz., mix in a lead bottle. Put a chalk mark each side where you want to braze. This mixture will keep about 6 months in one bottle. 19. Cold soldering without fire or lamp.—Bismuth $\frac{1}{4}$ oz., quicksilver $\frac{1}{4}$ oz., block tin filings 1 oz., spirits salts 1 oz., all mixed together. 20. To solder iron to steel or either to brass.—Tin 3 parts, copper $39\frac{1}{2}$ parts, zinc $7\frac{1}{2}$ parts. When applied in a molten state it will firmly unite metals first named to each other. 21. Plumbers' solder.—Bismuth 1, lead 5, tin 3 parts, is a first-class composition. 22. White solder for raised Britannia ware.—Tin 100 lbs., hardening 8 lbs., antimony 8 lbs. 23. Hardening for Britannia.—(To be mixed separately from the other ingredients.) Copper 2 lbs., tin 1 lb. 24. Best soft solder for cast Britannia ware.—Tin 8 lbs., lead 5 lbs. 25. Bismuth solder.—Tin 1, lead 3, bismuth 3 parts. 26. Solder for brass that will stand hammering.—Brass 78.26 parts, zinc 17.41 parts, silver 4.33 parts, add a little chloride of potassium to your borax for a flux. 27. Solder for steel joints.—Silver 19 parts, copper 1 part, brass 2 parts. Melt all together. 28. Hard solder.—Copper 2 parts, zinc 1 part. Melt together. 29. Solder for brass.—Copper 3 parts, zinc 1 part, with borax. 30. Solder for copper.—Brass 6 parts, zinc 1 part, tin 1 part, melt all together well and pour out to cool. 31. Solder for platina.—Gold with borax. 32. Solder for iron.—The best solder for iron is good tough brass with a little borax.

N. B.—In soldering, the surfaces to be joined are made perfectly clean and smooth, and then covered with sal. ammoniac, resin or other flux, the solder is then applied, being melted on and smoothed over by a tinned soldering iron.

COOKERY RECIPES

Ale to Mull.—Take a pint of good strong ale, and pour it into a saucepan with three cloves and a little nutmeg; sugar to your taste. Set it over the fire, and when it boils take it off to cool. Beat up the yolks of four eggs exceedingly well; mix them first with a little cold ale, then add them to the warm ale, and pour it in and out of the pan several times. Set it over a slow fire, beat it a little, take it off again; do this three times until it is hot, then serve it with dry toast.

Ale, Spiced.—Is made hot, sweetened with sugar and spiced with grated nutmeg, and a hot toast is served in it. This is the wassail drink.

Beef Tea.—Cut a pound of fleshy beef in thin slices; simmer with a quart of water twenty minutes, after it has once boiled and been skimmed. Season if approved.

Beef Tea.—To one pound of lean beef add one and one-half tumblers of cold water; cut the beef in small pieces, cover, and let it boil slowly for ten minutes, and add a little salt after it is boiled. Excellent.

Beef Tea.—Cut lean, tender beef into small pieces, put them into a bottle, cork and set in a pot of cold water, then put on the stove and boil for one hour. Season to taste.

Black Currant Cordial.—To every four quarts of black currants, picked from the stems and lightly bruised, add one gallon of the best whisky; let it remain four months, shaking the jar occasionally, then drain off the liquor and strain. Add three pounds of loaf sugar and a quarter of a pound of best cloves, slightly bruised; bottle well and seal.

Boston Cream (a Summer Drink).—Make a syrup of four pounds of white sugar with four quarts of water; boil; when cold add four ounces of tartaric acid, one and a half ounces of essence of lemon, and the whites of six eggs beaten to a stiff froth; bottle. A wine-glass of the cream to a tumbler of water, with sufficient carbonate of soda to make it effervesce.

Champagne Cup.—One quart bottle of champagne, two bottles of soda-water, one liqueur-glass of brandy, two tablespoons of powdered sugar, a few thin strips of cucumber rind; make this just in time for use, and add a large piece of ice.

Chocolate.—Scrape Cadbury's chocolate fine, mix with a little cold water and the yolks of eggs well beaten; add this to equal parts of milk and water, and boil well, being careful that it does not burn. Sweeten to the taste, and serve hot.

Coffee—Is a tonic and stimulating beverage, of a wholesome nature. Use the best. For eight cups use nearly eight cups of water; put in coffee as much as you like, boil a minute and take off, and throw in a cup of cold water to throw the grounds to the bottom; in five minutes it will be very clear.

Or, beat one or two eggs, which mix with ground coffee to form a ball; nearly fill the pot with cold water, simmer gently for half an hour, having introduced the ball; *do not boil*, or you will destroy the aroma.

Coffee.—The following is a delicious dish either for summer breakfast or dessert : Make a strong infusion of Mocha coffee; put it in a porcelain bowl, sugar it properly and add to it an equal portion of boiled milk, or one-third the quantity of rich cream. Surround the bowl with pounded ice.

Currant Wine.—One quart currant juice, three pounds of sugar, sufficient water to make a gallon.

Egg Gruel.—Boil eggs from one to three hours until hard enough to grate; then boil new milk and thicken with the egg, and add a little salt. Excellent in case of nausea.

Lemon Syrup.—Pare off the yellow rind of the lemon, slice the lemon and put a layer of lemon and a thick layer of sugar in a deep plate; cover close with a saucer, and set in a warm place. This is an excellent remedy for a cold.

Lemonade.—Tak a quart of boiling water, and add to it five ounces of lump-sugar, the yellow rind of the lemon rubbed off with a bit of sugar, and the juice of three lemons. Stir all together and let it stand till cool. Two ounces of cream of tartar may be used instead of the lemons, water being poured upon it.

Raspberry Vinegar.—Fill a jar with red raspberries picked from the stalks. Pour in as much vinegar as it will hold. Let it stand ten days, then strain it through a sieve. Don't press the berries, just let the juice run through. To every pint add one pound loaf sugar. Boil it like other syrup; skim, and bottle when cold.

Summer Drink.—Boil together for five minutes two ounces of tartaric acid, two pounds white sugar, three lemons sliced, two quarts of water; when nearly cold add the whites of four eggs beaten to a froth, one tablespoonful of flour and half an ounce of wintergreen. Two tablespoonfuls in a glass of water make a pleasant drink; for those who like effervescence add as much soda as a ten-cent piece will hold, stirring it briskly before drinking.

Blackberry Syrup.—To one pint of juice put one pound of white sugar, one-half ounce of powdered cinnamon, one-fourth ounce mace, and two teaspoons cloves; boil all together for a qarter of an hour, then strain the syrup, and add to each pint a glass of French brandy.

Tea.—When the water in the teakettle begins to boil, have ready a tin tea-steeper; pour into the tea-steeper just a very little of the boiling water, and then put in tea, allowing one teaspoon of tea to each person. Pour over this boiling water until the steeper is a little more than half full; cover tightly and let it stand where it will keep hot, but not to boil. Let the tea infuse for ten or fifteen minutes, and then pour into the tea-urn, adding more boiling water, in the proportion of one cup of water for every teaspoon of dry tea which has been infused. Have boiling water in a water-pot, and weaken each cup of tea as desired. Do not use water for tea that has been boiled long. Spring water is best for tea, and filtered water next best.

Iced Tea a la Russe .—To each glass of tea add the juice of half a lemon, fill up the glass with pounded ice, and sweeten.

General Directions for Making Bread.—In the composition of good bread, there are three important requisites: Good flour, good yeast, [and here let us recommend Gillett's Magic Yeast Cakes. They keep good for one year in any climate, and once used you will not do without it. All grocers keep it] and strength to knead it well. Flour should be white and dry, crumbling easily again after it is pressed in the hand.

A very good method of ascertaining the quality of yeast will be to add a little flour to a very small quantity, setting it in a warm place. If in the course of ten or fifteen minutes it raises, it will do to use.

When you make bread, first set the sponge with warm milk or water, keeping it in a warm place until quite light. Then mold this sponge, by adding flour, into one large loaf, kneading it well. Set this to rise again, and then when sufficiently light mold it into smaller loaves, let it rise again, then bake. Care should be taken not to get the dough too stiff with flour; it should be as soft as it can be to knead well. To make bread or biscuits a nice color, wet the dough over top with water just before putting it into the oven. Flour should always be sifted.

Brown Bread, for those who can eat corn-meal: Two cups Indian meal to one cup flour; one-half teacup syrup, 2½ cups milk; 1 teaspoon salt; 3 teaspoons of Gillett's baking powder. Steam an hour and a half. To be eaten hot. It goes very nicely with a corn-beef dinner.

Brown Bread.—Stir together wheat meal and cold water (nothing else, not even salt) to the consistency of a thick batter. Bake in small circular pans, from three to three and a half inches in diameter, (ordinary tin patty-pans do very well) in a quick, hot oven. It is quite essential that it be baked in this sized cake, as it is upon this that the raising depends. [In this article there are none of the injurious qualities of either fermented or superfine flour bread; and it is so palpably wholesome food, that it appeals at once to the common sense of all who are interested in the subject.]

Brown Bread—Take part of the sponge that has been prepared for your white bread, warm water can be added, mix it with graham flour (not too stiff).

Boston Brown Bread.—To make one loaf:—Rye meal unsifted, half a pint; Indian meal sifted, one pint; sour milk, one pint; molasses, half a gill. Add a teaspoonful of salt, one teaspoonful of soda dissolved in a little hot water; stir well, put in a greased pan, let it rise one hour, and steam four hours.

Boston Brown Bread.—One and one-half cups of graham flour, two cups of corn meal, one-half cup of molasses, one pint of sweet milk, and one-half a teaspoon of soda; steam three hours.

Corn Bread.—One-half pint of buttermilk, one-half pint of sweet milk; sweeten the sour milk with one-half teaspoon of soda; beat two eggs, whites and yolks together; pour the milk into the eggs, then thicken with about nine tablespoons of sifted corn meal. Put the pan on the stove with a piece of lard the size of an egg; when melted pour it in the batter; this lard by stirring it will grease the pan to bake in; add a teaspoon of salt.

Excellent Bread.—Four potatoes mashed fine, four teaspoons of salt, two quarts of lukewarm milk, one-half cake Gillett's magic yeast dissolved in one-half cup of warm water, flour enough to make a pliable dough; mold with hands well greased with lard; place in pans, and when sufficiently light, it is ready for baking.

French Bread.—With a quarter of a peck of fine flour mix the yolks of three and whites of two eggs, beaten and strained, a little salt, half a pint of good yeast that is not bitter, and as much milk, made a little warm, as will work into a thin light dough. Stir it about, but don't knead it. Have ready three quart wooden dishes, divide the dough among them, set to rise, then turn them out into the oven, which must be quick. Rasp when done.

Graham Bread.—For one loaf, take two cups of white bread sponge, to which add two tablespoons of brown sugar, and graham flour to make a stiff batter; let it rise, after which add graham flour sufficient to knead, but not very stiff; then put it in the pan to rise and bake.

Italian Bread.—Make a stiff dough, with two pounds of fine flour, six of white powdered sugar, three or four eggs, a lemon-peel grated, and two ounces of fresh butter. If the dough is not firm enough, add more flour and sugar. Then turn it out, and work it well with the hand, cut it into round long biscuits, and glaze them with white of egg.

Rice and Wheat Bread.—Simmer a pound of rice in two quarts of water till soft; when it is of a proper warmth, mix it well with four pounds of flour, and yeast, and salt as for other bread; of yeast about four large spoonfuls; knead it well; then set to rise before the fire. Some of the flour should be reserved to make up the loaves. If the rice should require more water, it must be added, as some rice swells more than others.

Sago Bread.—Boil two lbs. of sago in three pints of water until reduced to a quart, then mix with it half a pint of yeast, and pour the mixture into fourteen lbs. of flour. Make into bread in the usual way.

Steamed Bread.—Two cups corn meal; 1 cup graham flour; ½ cup N. O. molasses; salt and teaspoonful of soda. Mix soft with sour milk, or make with sweet milk and Gillett's baking powder. Put in tight mold in kettle of water; steam three hours or more. This is as nice as Boston brown bread.

Use this receipt with flour instead of graham; add a cup of beef suet, and it makes a nice pudding in the winter. Eat with syrup or cream.

Biscuits.—Mix a quart of sweet milk with half a cup of melted butter; stir in a pinch of salt, two teaspoonfuls of baking powder and flour enough for a stiff batter. Have the oven at a brisk heat. Drop the batter, a spoonful in a place, on buttered pans. They will bake in fifteen minutes.

Cream Biscuits.—Three heaping tablespoons of sour cream; put in a bowl or vessel containing a quart and fill two-thirds full of sweet milk, two teaspoons cream tartar, one teaspoon of soda, a little salt; pour the cream in the flour, mix soft and bake in a quick oven.

French Biscuits.—Two cups of butter, two cups of sugar, one egg (or the whites of two), half a cup of sour milk, half a teaspoon of soda; flour to roll; sprinkle with sugar.

Rye Biscuits.—Two cups of rye meal, one and a half cups flour, one-third cup molasses, one egg, a little salt, two cups sour milk, two even teaspoons saleratus.

Soda Biscuits.—To each quart of flour add one tablespoon of shortening, one-half teaspoon of salt, and three and a half heaping teaspoons of Gillett's baking powder; mix baking powder thoroughly through the flour, then add other ingredients. Do not knead, and bake quickly. To use cream tartar and soda, take the same proportions without the baking powder, using instead two heaping teaspoons cream tartar and one of soda. If good they will bake in five minutes.

Tea Biscuits.—One cup of hot water, two of milk, three tablespoons of yeast; mix thoroughly; after it is risen, take two-thirds of a cup of butter and a little sugar and mold it; then let it rise, and mold it into small cakes.

Bannocks.—One pint corn meal, pour on it boiling water to thoroughly wet it. Let it stand a few minutes; add salt and one egg and a little sweet cream, or a tablespoon melted butter. Make into balls and fry in hot lard.

Breakfast Cakes.—One cup milk, one pint flour, three eggs, piece butter size of an egg, two teaspoons cream tartar, one teaspoon soda, one tablespoon butter.

Buckwheat Cakes.—One quart buckwheat flour, four tablespoons yeast, one tablespoon salt, one handful Indian meal, two tablespoons molasses, not syrup. Warm water enough to make a thin batter; beat very well and set in a warm place. If the batter is the least sour in the morning, add a little soda.

Quick Buckwheat Cakes.—One quart of buckwheat flour, one-half a teacup of corn meal or wheat flour, a little salt, and two tablespoons of syrup. Wet these with cold or warm water to a thin batter, and add, lastly, four good-tablespoons of Gillett's baking powder.

Spanish Buns.—Five eggs well beaten; cut up in a cup of warm new milk half a pound of good butter, one pound of sifted flour, and a wineglassful of good yeast; stir these well together; set it to rise for an hour, in rather a warm place; when risen, sift in half a pound of white sugar, and half a grated nutmeg; add one wineglass of wine and brandy, mixed, one wineglass of rose-water, and one cupful of currants, which have been cleaned thoroughly. Mix these well, pour it into pans, and set it to rise again for half an hour. Then bake one hour. Icing is a great improvement to their appearance.

Bath Buns.—Take 1 lb. of flour, put it in a dish, and make a hole in the middle, and pour in a dessert spoonful of good yeast; pour upon the yeast half a cupful of warm milk, mix in one-third of the flour, and let it rise an hour. When it has risen, put in 6 ozs. of cold butter, 4 eggs, and a few caraway seeds; mix all together with the rest of the flour. Put it in a warm place to rise. Flatten it with the hand on a pasteboard. Sift 6 ozs. of loaf sugar, half the size of a pea; sprinkle the particles over the dough; roll together to mix the sugar; let it rise in a warm place about 20 minutes. Make into buns, and lay on buttered tins; put sugar and 9 or 10 comfits on the tops, sprinkle them with water; bake in a pretty hot oven.

Graham Gems.—One quart of sweet milk, one cup syrup, one teaspoon soda, two teaspoons cream tartar, little salt; mix cream tartar in graham flour, soda in milk, and make it as stiff with the flour as will make it drop easily from the spoon into muffin rings.

Brown Griddle Cakes.—Take stale bread, soak in water till soft, drain off water through colander, beat up fine with fork, to one quart of the crumb batter, add one quart each milk and flour, and four eggs well beaten. Mix, bake in a griddle.

Wheat Gems.—One pint milk, two eggs, flour enough to make a batter not very stiff, two large spoons melted butter, yeast to raise them, a little soda and salt. Bake in gem irons.

Johnnie Cake.—One pint of corn meal, one teacup of flour, two eggs, one pint of sweet milk, one tablespoon of molasses, one tablespoon of melted butter, a little salt, one

teaspoon of soda, one teaspoon of cream of tartar; bake in square tins.

Mush.—Indian or oatmeal mush is best made in the following manner: Put fresh water in a kettle over the fire to boil, and put in some salt; when the water boils, stir in handful by handful corn or oatmeal until thick enough for use. In order to have excellent mush, the meal should be allowed to cook well, and long as possible while thin, and before the final handful is added.

Fried Mush.—When desired to be fried for breakfast, turn into an earthen dish and set away to cool. Then cut in slices when you wish to fry; dip each piece in beaten eggs and fry on a hot griddle.

Muffins.—One tablespoonful of butter, two tablespoons sugar, two eggs—stir altogether; add one cup of sweet milk, three teaspoons of baking powder, flour to make a stiff batter. Bake twenty minutes in a quick oven.

English Pancakes.—Make a batter of two teacups of flour, four eggs, and one quart of milk. Add, as a great improvement, one tablespoonful of brandy with a little nutmeg scraped in. Make the sixe of frying pan. Sprinkle a little granulated sugar over the pancake, roll it up, and send to the table hot.

Pop Overs.—Three cups of milk and three cups flour, three eggs, a little salt, one tablespoon melted butter put in the last thing; two tablespoons to a puff.

Rolls.—To the quantity of light bread-dough that you would take for twelve persons, add the white of one egg well beaten, two tablespoons of white sugar, and two tablespoons of butter; work these thoroughly together; roll out about half an inch thick; cut the size desired, and spread one with melted butter and lay another upon the top of it. Bake delicately when they have risen.

French Rolls.—One quart flour, add two eggs, one half-pint milk, tablespoon of yeast, kneed it well; let rise till morning. Work in one ounce of butter, and mold in small rolls. Bake immediately.

Rusks.—Milk enough with one-half cup of yeast to make a pint; make a sponge and rise, then add one and a half cups of white sugar, three eggs, one-half cup of butter; spice to your taste; mold, then put in pan to rise. When baked, cover the tops with sugar dissolved in milk.

Waffles.—One quart of sweet or sour milk, four eggs, two-thirds of a cup of butter, half a teaspoonful of salt, three teaspoonfuls of baking-powder; flour enough to make a nice batter. If you use sour milk leave out the baking-powder, and use two teaspoons soda. Splendid.

Yeast.—In reference to yeast, we advise the use of Magic Yeast Cakes; it keeps good a year, and works quicker and better than other yeasts.

Suggestions in Making Cake.—It is very desirable that the materials be of the finest quality. Sweet, fresh butter, eggs, and good flour are the first essentials. The process of putting together is also quite an important feature, and where other methods are not given in this work by contributors, it would be well for the young housekeeper to observe the following directions:

Never allow the butter to oil, but soften it by putting in a moderately warm place before you commence other preparations for your cake; then put it into an earthen dish—tin, if not new, will discolor your cake as you stir it—and add your sugar; beat the butter and sugar to a cream, add the yolks of the eggs, then the milk, and lastly the beaten whites of the eggs and flour. Spices and liquors may be added after the yolks of the eggs are put in, and fruit should be put in with the flour.

The oven should be pretty hot for small cakes, and moderate for larger. To ascertain if a large cake is sufficiently baked, pierce it with a broom-straw through the center; if done, the straw will come out free from dough; if not done, dough will adhere to the straw. Take it out of the tin about fifteen minutes after it is taken from the oven (not sooner), and do not turn it over on the top to cool.

Frosting.—One pint granulated sugar, moisten thoroughly with water sufficient to dissolve it when heated; let it boil until it threads from the spoon, stirring often; while the sugar is boiling, beat the whites of two eggs till they are firm; then when thoroughly beaten, turn them into a deep dish, and when the sugar is boiled, turn it over the whites, beating all rapidly together until of the right consistency to spread over the cake. Flavor with lemon, if preferred. This is sufficient for two loaves.

Frosting, for Cake.—One cup frosting-sugar, two tablespoons of water boiled together; take it off the stove, and stir in the white of one egg beaten to a stiff froth; stir all together well, then frost your cake with it, and you will never want a nicer frosting than this.

Chocolate Frosting.—Whites of two eggs, one and one-half cups of fine sugar, six great spoons of grated chocolate, two teaspoons of vanilla; spread rather thickly between layers and on top of cake. Best when freshly made. It should be made like any frosting.

Icing.—The following rules should be observed where boiled icing is not used:

Put the whites of your eggs in a shallow earthern dish, and allow at least a quarter of a pound or sixteen tablespoons of the finest white sugar for each egg. Take part of the sugar at first and sprinkle over the eggs; beat them for about half an hour, stirring in gradually the rest of the sugar; then add the flavor. If you use the juice of a lemon, allow more sugar. Tartaric and lemon-juice whitens icing. It may be shaded a pretty pink with strawberry-juice or cranberry syrup, or colored yellow by putting the juice and rind of a lemon in a thick muslin bag, and squeezing it hard into the egg and sugar.

If cake is well dredged with flour after baking, and then carefully wiped before the icing is put on, it will not run, and can be spread more smoothly. Put frosting on to the cake in large spoonfuls, commencing over the center; then spread it over the cake, using a large knife, dipping it occasionally in cold water. Dry the frosting on the cake in a cool, dry place.

Ice-Cream Icing, for White Cake.—Two cups pulverized white sugar, boiled to a thick syrup; add three teaspoons vanilla; when cold, add the whites of two eggs well beaten, and flavored with two teaspoons of citric acid.

Icing, for Cakes.—Take ten whites of eggs whipped to a stiff froth, with twenty large spoonfuls of orange-flower water. This is to be laid smoothly on the cakes after they are baked. Then return them to the oven for fifteen minutes to harden the icing.

Icing.—One pound pulverized sugar, pour over one tablespoon cold water, beat whites of three eggs a little, not to a stiff froth; add to the sugar and water, put in a deep bowl, place in a vessel of boiling water, and heat. It will become thin and clear, afterward begin to thicken. When it becomes quite thick, remove from the fire and stir while it becomes cool till thick enough to spread with a knife. This will frost several ordinary-sized cakes.

Almond Cake.—Take ten eggs, beaten separately, the yolks from the whites; beat the yolks with half a pound of white sugar; blanch a quarter of a pound of almonds by pouring hot water on them, and remove the skins; pound them in a mortar smooth; add three drops of oil of bitter almonds; and rose-water to prevent the oiling of the almonds. Stir this also into the eggs. Half a pound of sifted flour stirred very slowly into the eggs; lastly, stir in the whites, which must have been whipped to a stiff froth. Pour this into the pans, and bake immediately three-quarters of an hour.

Cocoanut Cake.—Whip the whites of ten eggs, grate two nice cocoanuts, and add them; sift one pound of white sugar into half a pound of sifted flour; stir this well; add a little rose-water to flavor; pour into pans, and bake three-fourths of an hour.

Cocoanut Drops.—One pound each grated cocoanut and sugar; four well beaten eggs; four tablespoonfuls of flour, mix well, drop on pan, and bake.

Cocoanut Jumbles.—Take one cup butter, two cups sugar, three eggs well whipped, one grated cocoanut, stirred in lightly with the flour, which must be sufficient to stiffen to the required consistency. Bake one to know when enough flour is added.

Coffee Cake.—Take three eggs, two cups brown sugar, one cup strong coffee, quarter of a cup of butter, three cups flour, one teaspoonful cream tartar, half teaspoonful each soda and ground cinnamon and cloves, half a nutmeg grated, one cup of raisins, stoned; beat butter and sugar to a cream, then add eggs beaten, coffee, flour sifted, and cream tartar, well mixed with it. Spices and raisins, then soda dissolved in sufficient warm water to absorb it. Thoroughly mix, and bake in round tins.

Cookies.—Two cups bright brown sugar, one cup butter, half cup sweet milk, two eggs, one teaspoonful soda, flour enough to roll out.

Composition Cake.—Five eggs, three cups sugar, two cups butter, five cups flour, one wine-glass brandy, one nutmeg grated, half pound each raisins and currants, three teaspoonfuls Gillett's baking powder.

Corn Starch Cake.—Two cups pulverized sugar, one cup butter, cup corn starch, two cups sifted flour, seven eggs (whites beaten very light), one teaspoon soda, two teaspoons cream tartar (or two teaspoons baking powder instead of soda and cream tartar), flavor with lemon. In putting this together, beat butter and sugar to a light cream, dissolve corn starch in a cup of sweet milk, leaving enough of the milk to dissolve the soda if it is used, put cream of tartar or baking powder in the flour, beat the whites of the eggs separate when the butter and sugar are ready, put all the ingredients together first, leaving the eggs and flour to the last.

Cream Cake.—Half pint cream, one tablespoon butter rubbed into one tablespoon flour. Put the cream on the fire. When it boils stir in the butter and flour mixed, add half a tea cup sugar, two eggs very light, flavor with vanilla. Spread between cakes, and frost or sugar top of cake to please fancy.

Cinnamon Cake.—Take two cups of brown sugar, one cup of butter, three-quarters cup of milk, half cup of vinegar, four eggs, large tablespoon of cinnamon, four cups of flour, one teaspoon of soda, two teaspoons cream tartar, mix all but vinegar and soda, then add vinegar, then soda, bake in large tin or patty pans.

Currant Cake.—Take two pounds of flour, half a pound of butter rubbed in the flour, half a pound of moist sugar, a few caraway seeds, three or four tablespoonfuls of yeast, and a pint of milk made a little warm. Mix all together, and let it stand an hour or two at the fire to rise; then beat it up with three eggs and a half pound of currants.   Put it into a tin, and bake two hours in a moderate oven.

Cup Cake.—Cream half a cup of butter, and four cups of sugar by beating; stir in five well-beaten eggs; dissolve one teaspoonful of soda in a cup of good milk or cream, and six cups of sifted flour; stir all well together, and bake in tins.

Delicate Cake.—Mix two cups of sugar, four of flour, half cup butter, half cup sweet milk, the whites of seven eggs, two teaspoons cream tartar, one teaspoon soda, rub the cream tartar in the flour and other ingredients, and flavor to suit the taste.

Delicious Swiss Cake.—Beat the yolks of five eggs and one pound of sifted loaf sugar well together; then sift in one pound of best flour, and a large spoonful of anise seed; beat these together for twenty minutes; then whip to a stiff froth the five whites, and add them; beat all well; then roll out the paste an inch thick, and cut them with a molded cutter rather small; set them aside till the next morning to bake.   Rub the tins on which they are baked with yellow wax; it is necessary to warm the tins to receive the wax; then let them become cool, wipe them, and lay on the cakes.   Bake a light brown.

Doughnuts.—One and a half cup of sugar; half cup sour milk, two teaspoons soda, little nutmeg, four eggs, flour enough to roll out.

Drop Cake.—To one pint cream, three eggs, one pinch of salt, thicken with rye till a spoon will stand upright in it, then drop on a well buttered iron pan which must be hot in the oven.

Drop Cookies.—Whites of two eggs, one large cup of milk, one cup of sugar, one-half cup of butter, two teaspoonfuls baking-powder, flavor with vanilla, rose, or nutmeg; flour enough for thick batter, beat thoroughly, drop in buttered pans, dust granulated sugar on top, and bake with dispatch.

Fruit Cake.—Take one pint each of sour milk and sugar, two eggs, half pint melted butter, two teaspoons even full of soda, dissolve in milk flour enough to roll out into shape, and fry in hot lard.

Fried Cakes.—Three eggs, one cup of sugar, one pint of new milk, salt, nutmeg, and flour enough to permit the spoon to stand upright in the mixture; add two teaspoonfuls of Gillett's baking powder and beat until very light. Drop by the dessert-spoonful into boiling lard.   These will not absorb a bit of fat, and are the least pernicious of the doughnut family.

Fruit Cake.—Take four pounds of brown sugar, four pounds of good butter, beaten to cream; put four pounds of sifted flour into a pan; whip thirty-two eggs to a fine froth, and add to the creamed butter and sugar; then take six pounds of cleaned currants, four pounds of stoned rasins, two pounds of cut citron, one pound of blanched almonds, crushed, but not pounded, to a paste—a large cup of molasses, two large spoonfuls of ground ginger, half an ounce of pounded mace, half an ounce of grated nutmeg, half an ounce of pounded and sifted cloves, and one of cinnamon.   Mix these well together, then add four large wineglasses of good French brandy, and lastly, stir in the flour; beat this well, put it all into a stone jar, cover very closely, for twelve hours; then make into six loaves, and bake in iron pans.   These cakes will keep a year, if attention is paid to their being put in a tin case, and covered lightly in an airy place.   They improve by keeping.

Ginger Drop Cake.—Cup each sugar, molasses, lard and boiling water, one teaspoon soda, half teaspoon cream

tartar, stir in flour until it is as thick as cake, add sugar and salt.

Ginger Snaps.—Take one cup each of sugar, molasses, butter, half cup sour milk, two teaspoons cream tartar, one teaspoon soda, flour enough to roll out, cut into size desired and bake.

Ginger Snaps.—Two cups of New Orleans molasses, one cup of sugar, one of butter, one teaspoonful of soda, one of cloves, one of black pepper, and two tablespoons of ginger.   These will keep good a month if you wish to keep them.

Graham Cakes.—Half a cup of butter, one-half cup sugar, one egg, one teacup sour milk, one-half teaspoon soda.   Make a stiff batter by adding graham flour.

Good Graham Cakes.—Two cups sweet milk, one cup sweet cream, the white of one egg beaten to froth, half a spoonful of salt, dessert spoonful baking powder, stir in stiffened graham flour until quite thick, bake in muffin-rings or gem-tins, until well browned on top.

Indian Breakfast Patties.—To one pint of Indian meal add one egg, and a little salt, pour boiling water upon it, and fry brown immediately in pork fat.   Cut open and put butter between, and send to the table hot.

Jumbles.—Stir together till of a light brown color, one pound sugar, one-half pound butter, then add eight eggs beaten to a froth, add flour enough to make them stiff enough to roll out, flavor with lemon, cut in rings half an inch thick, bake in quick oven.

Kisses.—Beat the whites of four eggs to a froth, stir into them half pound powdered white sugar; flavor with lemon, continue to beat it until it will be in a heap; lay the mixture on letter-paper, in the size and shape of half an egg, an inch apart, then lay the paper on hard wood and place in the oven without closing it, when they begin to look yellowish take them out and let them cool three or four minutes, then slip a thin knife carefully under and turn them into your left hand, take another and join the two by the sides next the paper, then lay them in a dish handling them gently.   They may be batted a little harder, the soft inside taken out and jelly substituted.

Light Fruit Cake.—Take one cup butter, two cups sugar, four of flour, four eggs, one teaspoon cream tartar, half teaspoon soda, one cup sweet milk, one pound currants, half pound citron.

Marble Cake, Light Part.—One and a half cups white sugar, half cup butter, half cup sweet milk, one teaspoon cream tartar, half teaspoon soda, whites of four eggs, two and half cups flour.

Dark Part.—One cup brown sugar, half cup each molasses, butter and sour milk, one teaspoon cream tartar, one teaspoon soda, two and a half cups flour, yolks four eggs, half teaspoon cloves, allspice and cinnamon.

Molasses Cookies.—Three cups New Orleans molasses, one cup butter, one-half cup lard, one heaped teaspoon soda, one tablespoon ginger, one cup hot water. Roll thick.   Better after standing.

Muffins.—Take two cups flour, one cup milk, half cup sugar, four eggs, one-half teaspoon each of soda and cream tartar, one tablespoon butter.   Bake in rings.

Graham Muffins.—Mix one pint sweet milk, sift your flour, then take half pound each Graham and wheat flour, five or six spoonfuls melted butter, two half spoons baking powder.   Bake in rings in very quick oven.

Nut Cake.—Mix each two tablespoons of butter and sugar, two eggs, one cup milk, three cups flour, one teaspoon cream tartar, half teaspoon soda, pint of nuts or almonds.   Nuts may be sliced or not as suits taste.

Oat Cakes.—Mix fine and coarse oatmeal in equal proportions; add sugar, caraway-seeds, a dust of salt to three pounds of meal, a heaping teaspoonful of carbonate of soda; mix all thoroughly together, then add enough boiling water to make the whole a stiff paste; roll out this paste quite thin, and sprinkle meal on a griddle. Lay the cakes on to bake, or toast them quite dry in a Dutch oven in front of the fire; they should not scorch, but gradually dry through.

Orange Cake, the Most Delicate and Delicious Cake there is.—Grated rind of one orange; two cups sugar; whites of four eggs and yolks of five; one cup sweet milk; one cup butter; two large teaspoonfuls baking powder, to be sifted through with the flour; bake quick in jelly tins. Filling: Take white of the one egg that was left; beat to a froth, add a little sugar and the juice of the orange, beat together, and spread between the layers. If oranges are not to be had, lemons will do instead.

Plain Fruit Cake.—One pound each butter beaten to a cream, sifted sugar, sifted flour, twelve eggs, whites and yolks, beaten separately. Two pounds currants, three pounds of stoned raisins chopped, one nutmeg, a little cinnamon and other spices, half pint wine and brandy mixed, one pound citron cut in slices and stuck in the batter after it is in the tin. Bake slowly two to three hours.

Plain Cake.—Flour, three-quarters of a pound; sugar, the same quantity; butter, four ounces; one egg and two tablespoonfuls of milk. Mix all together and bake.

Puffs.—Two eggs beaten very light; one cup of milk, one cup of flour, and a pinch of salt. The gems should be heated while making the puffs, which are then placed in a quick oven.

Plum Cake.—Six eggs well beaten, one pound of sugar, the same of flour, butter and currants, four ounces of candied peel, two tablespoonfuls of mixed spice. When it is all mixed, add one teaspoonful of carbonate of soda, and one of tartaric acid. Beat it all up quickly and bake directly.

Pound Cake.—Take four and a half cups flour, 3 cups each butter and sugar. Ten eggs, yolks and whites beaten separately. Mix.

Pork Cake.—Take one pound salt pork chopped fine, boil a few minutes in half pint water, one cup molasses, two cups sugar, three eggs, two teaspoons soda, cinnamon, cloves, nutmeg to taste, one pound raisins chopped fine, flour to make a stiff batter.

Rich Shortbread.—Two pounds of flour, one pound butter, and quarter pound each of the following ingredients:—Candied orange and lemon peel, sifted loaf sugar, blanched sweet almonds and caraway comfits. Cut the peel and almonds into thin slices, and mix them with one pound and a half of flour and the sugar. Melt the butter, and when cool, pour it into the flour, mixing it quickly with a spoon. Then with the hands mix it, working in the remainder of the flour; give it one roll out till it is an inch thick, cut it into the size you wish, and pinch round the edges. Prick the top with a fork, and stick in some caraway comfits; put it on white paper, and bake on tins in a slow oven.

Seed Cake.—Take half a pound of butter and three-fourths of a pound of sugar, creamed; three eggs, beaten lightly, and two tablespoonfuls of picked and bruised caraway seed; dissolve half a teaspoonful of soda in a cup of new milk; mix these well together until they are about the consistency of cream; then sift in two pounds of flour, mix well with a knife, and roll them out into thin cakes, about an inch in thickness. Bake in a quick oven.

Sponge Cake.—Take sixteen eggs; separate the whites from the yolks; beat them very lightly; sift into the yolks one pound of flour, adding a few drops of essence of almond or lemon, to flavor with; then add one pound and a quarter of pulverized loaf sugar; beat this well with a knife; then add the whites whipped to a stiff froth. Have ready the pans, and bake.

Sponge Cake, white.—One and one-third coffee cups of sugar; one coffee cup flour; whites of ten eggs; beat eggs and sugar as if for frosting; add flour by degrees and bake.

Snow Cake.—Take one pound arrow-root, half pound white sugar, half pound butter, the whites of six eggs, flavor with lemon, beat the butter to a cream, stir in the sugar and arrow-root, whisk the whites of the eggs to a stiff froth, beat for twenty minutes. Bake one hour.

Washington Cake.—One cup of sugar; $\frac{1}{2}$ cup of butter; $\frac{1}{2}$ cup sweet milk; 2 eggs; 2 cups flour; 2 teaspoons baking powder. Bake in layers as jelly cake. Jelly part: One pint of grated apples; 1 egg; 1 cup of sugar; grated rind and juice of one lemon; put in a vessel of some kind, and boil; put it on the cakes hot.

Waffles.—Take one quart milk, two eggs; beat the whites and yolks separately; four tablespoons melted butter, two teaspoons Gillett's baking powder, flour to make a stiff batter. Bake in waffle irons.

Alpine Snow.—Wash cup of rice, cook till tender in a covered dish to keep it white, when nearly done add cup rich milk, salt to taste, stir in the beaten yolks of two eggs, allow it to simmer for a moment, then place in a dish, beat the whites in two tablespoons fine sugar. Put the rice in little heaps upon the tin, intermingling with pieces of red jelly, eat with fine sugar and cream.

Apple Charlotte.—Take two pounds of apples, pare and core and slice them into a pan and add one pound loaf sugar, juice of three lemons and the grated rind of one, let these boil until they become a thick mass. Turn into a mould and serve it cold with thick custard or cream.

Apple Cream.—One cup thick cream, one cup sugar, beat till very smooth; then beat the whites of two eggs and add; stew apples in water till soft; take them from the water with a fork; steam them if you prefer. Pour the cream over the apples when cold.

Apple Custard.—Pare tart apples, core them, put them into a deep dish with a small piece of butter, and one teaspoon of sugar and a little nutmeg, in the opening of each apple, pour in water enough to cook them, when soft cool them and pour over an unbaked custard so as to cover them and bake until the custard is done.

Apple Fancy.—Pare and core apples, stew with sugar and lemon peels, beat four eggs to a froth, add a cupful of grated bread crumbs, a little sugar and nutmeg, lay the apples in the bottom of a dish and cover with the bread crumbs, laying a few pieces of butter over the top, bake in a quick oven, when done turn out upside down on a flat dish, scatter fine sugar over the top of apples, boil potatoes and beat fine with cream, large piece butter and salt, drop on tin, make smooth on top, score with knife, lay a thin slice of butter on top, then put in oven till brown.

Apple Fritters.—One pint milk, three eggs, salt to taste, as much flour as will make a batter, beat yolks and whites of eggs separately, add yolks to milk, stir in the whites when mixing the batter, have tender apples, pare, core, and cut in large thin slices, around the apple, to be fried in hot lard, ladle batter into spider, lay slice of apple in centre of each quantity of batter, fry light brown.

Apple Snow Balls.—Pare six apples, cut them into quarters, remove the cores, reconstruct the position of the apples, introduce into the cavities one clove and a slice of lemon peel, have six small pudding cloths at hand and cover the apples severally in an upright position with rice, tying them up tight, then place them in a large saucepan of scalding water and boil one hour, on taking them up open the top and add a little grated nutmeg with butter and sugar.

Arrow-Root Blanc-Mange.—Put two tablespoonfuls of arrow-root to a quart of milk, and a pinch of salt. Scald the milk, sweeten it, and stir in the arrow-root, which must first be wet up with some of the milk. Boil up once. Orange-water, rose-water or lemon-peel may be used to flavor it. Pour into molds to cool.

Arrow-Root Custard.—Arrow-root, one tablespoonful; milk, 1 pint; sugar, 1 tablespoonful, and 1 egg. Mix the arrow-root with a little of the milk, cold; when the milk boils, stir in the arrow-root, egg and sugar, previously well beaten together. Let it scald, and pour into cups to cool. To flavor it, boil a little ground cinnamon in the milk.

Arrow-Root Jelly.—To a dessert-spoonful of the powder, add as much cold water as will make it into a paste, then pour on half a pint of boiling water, stir briskly and boil it a few minutes, when it will become a clear smooth jelly; a little sugar and sherry wine may be added for debilitated adults; but for infants, a drop or two of essence of caraway seeds or cinnamon is preferable, wine being very liable to become acid in the stomachs of infants, and to disorder the bowels. Fresh milk, either alone or diluted with water, may be substituted for the water.

Baked Apples.—Take a dozen tart apples, pare and core them, place sugar and small lump of butter in centre of each, put them in a pan with half pint of water, bake until tender, basting occasionally with syrup while baking, when done, serve with cream.

Chocolate Cream Custard.—Scrape quarter pound chocolate, pour on it one teacup boiling water, and stand it by fire until dissolved, beat eight eggs light, omitting the whites of two, and stir them by degrees into a quart of milk alternately with the chocolate and three tablespoons of white sugar, put the mixture into cups and bake 10 minutes.

Charlotte Russe.—Whip one quart rich cream to a stiff froth, and drain well on a nice sieve. To one scant pint of milk add six eggs beaten very light; make very sweet; flavor high with vanilla. Cook over hot water till it is a thick custard. Soak one full ounce Coxe's gelatine in a very little water, and warm over hot water. When the custard is very cold, beat in lightly the gelatine and the whipped cream. Line the bottom of your mold with buttered paper, and the sides with sponge cake or ladyfingers fastened together with the white of an egg. Fill with the cream, put in a cold place or in summer on ice. To turn out dip the mold for a moment in hot water. In draining the whipped cream, all that drips through can be re-whipped.

Cocoa Snow.—Grate the white part of a cocoanut and mix it with white sugar, serve with whipped cream, or not, as desired.

Cream and Snow.—Make a rich boiled custard, and put it in the bottom of a dish; take the whites of eight eggs, beat with rose-water, and a spoonful of fine sugar, till it be a strong froth; put some milk and water into a stew-pan; when it boils take the froth off the eggs, and lay it on the milk and water; boil up once; take off carefully and lay it on the custard.

Baked Custards.—Boil a pint of cream with some mace and cinnamon; and when it is cold, take four yolks and two whites of eggs, a little rose and orange-flower water, sack, nutmeg, and sugar to your palate. Mix them well, and bake it in cups.

Or, pour into a deep dish, with or without lining or rim of paste; grate nutmeg and lemon peel over the top, and bake in a slow oven about thirty minutes.

Gooseberry Cream.—Boil them in milk till soft; beat them, and strain the pulp through a coarse sieve. Sweeten cream with sugar to your taste; mix with the pulp; when cold, place in glasses for use.

Imperial Cream.—Boil a quart of cream with the thin rind of a lemon; stir till nearly cold; have ready in a dish to serve in, the juice of three lemons strained with as much sugar as will sweeten the cream; pour it into the dish from a large tea-pot, holding it high, and moving it about to mix with the juice. It should be made from 6 to 12 hours before it is served.

Jumballs.—Flour, 1 lb.; sugar, 1 lb.; make into a light paste with whites of eggs beaten fine; add ½ pint of cream; ½ lb. of butter, melted; and 1 lb. of blanched almonds, well beaten; knead all together, with a little rose-water; cut into any form; bake in a slow oven. A little butter may be melted with a spoonful of white wine and throw fine sugar over the dish.

Lemon Puffs.—Beat and sift 1 pound of refined sugar; put into a bowl, with the juice of two lemons, and mix them together; beat the white of an egg to a high froth; put it into the bowl; put in 3 eggs with two rinds of lemon grated; mix it well up, and throw sugar on the buttered papers; drop on the puffs in small drops, and bake them in a moderately heated oven.

Lemon Tarts.—Pare the rinds of four lemons, and boil tender in two waters, and beat fine. Add to it 4 ounces of blanched almonds, cut thin, 4 ozs. of lump sugar, the juice of the lemons, and a little grated peel. Simmer to a syrup. When cold, turn into a shallow tin tart dish, lined with a rich thin puff paste, and lay bars of the same over, and bake carefully.

Macaroons.—Blanch 4 ozs. of almonds, and pound with 4 spoonfuls of orange-flower water; whisk the whites of four eggs to a froth, then mix it, and 1 lb. of sugar, sifted with the almonds to a paste; and laying a sheet of wafer-paper on a tin, put it on in different little cakes, the shape of macaroons.

Oatmeal Custard.—Take two teaspoons of the finest Scotch oatmeal, beat it up into a sufficiency of cold water in a basin to allow it to run freely. Add to it the yoke of a fresh egg, well worked up; have a pint of scalding new milk on the fire, and pour the oatmeal mixture into it, stirring it round with a spoon so as to incorporate the whole. Add sugar to your taste, and throw in a glass of sherry to the mixture, with a little grated nutmeg. Pour it into a basin, and take it warm in bed. It will be found very grateful and soothing in cases of colds or chills. Some persons scald a little cinnamon in the milk they use for the occasion.

Orange Crumpets.—Cream, 1 pint; new milk, 1 pint; warm it, and put in it a little rennet or citric acid; when broken, stir it gently; lay it on a cloth to drain all night, and then take the rinds of three oranges, boiled, as for preserving, in three different waters; pound them very fine, and mix them with the curd, and eight eggs in a mortar, a little nutmeg, the juice of a lemon or orange, and sugar to your taste; bake them in buttered tin pans. When baked put a little wine and sugar over them.

Orange Custards.—Boil the rind of half a Seville orange very tender; beat it very fine in a mortar; add a spoonful of the best brandy, the juice of a Seville orange, 4 ozs. loaf sugar, and the yolks of four eggs; beat all together ten minutes; then pour in gradually a pint of boiling cream; keep beating them until they are cold; put them into custard cups, and set them in an earthen dish of hot water; let them stand until they are set, take out, and stick preserved oranges on the top, and serve them hot or cold.

Pommes Au Riz.—Peel a number of apples of a good sort, take out the cores, and let them simmer in a syrup of clarified sugar, with a little lemon peel. Wash and pick some rice, and cook it in milk, moistening it therewith little by little, so that the grains may remain whole. Sweeten it to taste; add a little salt and a taste of lemon-peel. Spread the rice upon a dish, mixing some apple preserve with it, and place the apples upon it, and fill up the vacancies between the apples with some of the rice. Place the dish in the oven until the surface gets brown, and garnish with spoonfuls of bright colored preserve or jelly.

Raspberry Cream.—Mash the fruit gently, and let it drain; then sprinkle a little sugar over, and that will produce more juice; put it through a hair sieve to take out the seeds; then put the juice to some cream, and sweeten it; after which, if you choose to lower it with some milk, it will not curdle; which it would if put to the milk before the cream; but it is best made of raspberry jelly, instead of jam, when the fresh fruit cannot be obtained.

Rice Fritters.—One pint of cooked rice, half cup of sweet milk, two eggs, a tablespoon of flour, and a little salt. Have the lard hot in the skillet, allow a tablespoon to each fritter, fry brown on each side, then turn same as griddle cakes. If you find the rice spatters in the fat, add a very little more flour. You can judge after frying one.

Rice Croquettes.—Make little balls or oblong rolls of cooked rice; season with salt, and pepper if you like; dip in egg; fry in hot lard.

Rice Custards.—Boil 3 pints of new milk with a bit of lemon-peel, cinnamon, and three bay leaves; sweeten; then mix a large spoonful of rice flour into a cup of cold milk, very smooth; mix it with the yolks of four eggs well beaten. Take a basin of the boiling milk, and mix with the cold that has the rice in it; add the remainder of the boiling milk; stir it one way till it boils; pour immediately into a pan; stir till cool, and add a spoonful of brandy, or orange-flower water.

Rice Flummery.—Boil with a pint of new milk, a bit of lemon-peel, and cinnamon; mix with a little cold milk, as much rice flour as will make the whole of a good consistence, sweeten and add a spoonful of peach-water, or a bitter almond beaten; boil it, observing it does not burn; pour it into a shape or a pint basin, taken out the spice. When cold, turn the flummery into a dish, and serve with cream, milk, or custard round; or put a teacupful of cream into half a pint of new milk, a glass of white wine, half a lemon squeezed, and sugar.

Rock Cream.—Boil a teacupful of rice till quite soft in new milk and then sweeten it with sugar, and pile it on a dish, lay on it current jelly or preserved fruit, beat up the whites of five eggs with a little powdered sugar and flour, add to this when beaten very stiff about a tablespoon of rich cream and drop it over the rice.

Strawberry and Apple Souffle.—Stew the apple with a little lemon-peel; sweeten them, then lay them pretty high round the inside of a dish. Make a custard of the yolks of two eggs, a little cinnamon, sugar and milk. Let it thicken over a slow fire, but not boil; when ready, pour it in the inside of the apple. Beat the whites of the eggs to a strong froth, and cover the whole. Throw over it a good deal of pounded sugar, and brown it to a fine brown. Any fruit made of a proper consistence does for the walls, strawberries, when ripe, are delicious.

Strawberry Short-Cake.—First prepare the berries by picking; after they have been well washed—the best way to wash them is to hold the boxes under the faucet and let a gentle stream of water run over and through them, then drain, and pick them into an earthen bowl; now take the potato-masher and bruise them and cover with a thick layer of white sugar; now set them aside till the cake is made. Take a quart of sifted flour; half a cup of sweet butter; one egg, well beaten; three teaspoonfuls of baking-powder, and milk enough to make a rather stiff dough; knead well, and roll with a rolling-pin till about one inch thick; bake till a nice brown, and when done, remove it to the table; turn it out of the pan; with a light, sharp knife, cut it down lengthwise and crossways; now run the knife through it, and lay it open for a few moments, just to let the steam escape (the steam ruins the color of the berries); then set the bottom crust on the platter; cover thickly with the berries, an inch and a half deep; lay the top crust on the fruit; dust thickly with powdered sugar, and if any berry juice is left in the bowl, pour it round the cake, not over it, and you will have a delicious short-cake.

Snow Cream.—To a quart of cream add the whites of three eggs, cut to a stiff froth, add four spoonfuls of sweet wine, sugar to taste, flavor with essence of lemon. Whip all to a froth, and as soon as it forms take it off and serve in glasses.

Stewed Figs.—Take four ounces of fine sugar, the thin rind of a large lemon, and a pint of cold water, when the sugar is dissolved, add one pound turkey figs, and place the stew-pan over a moderate fire where they may heat and swell slowly and stew gently for two hours, when they are quite tender, add the juice of one lemon, arrange them in a glass dish and serve cold.

Spanish Cream.—Dissolve in $\frac{1}{2}$ pint of rose-water, 1 oz. of isinglass cut small; run it through a hair sieve; add the yolks of three or four eggs, beaten and mixed with half a pint of cream, and two sorrel leaves. Pour it into a deep dish, sweeten with loaf sugar powdered. Stir it till cold, and put it into molds. Lay rings round in different colored sweetmeats. Add, if you like, a little sherry, and a lump or two of sugar, rubbed well upon the rind of a lemon to extract the flavor.

Whipped Cream.—To one quart of good cream, put a few drops of bergamot water, a little orange-flower water, and $\frac{1}{2}$ lb. of sugar. When it is dissolved, whip the cream to a froth, and take it up with a skimmer; drain on a sieve, and if for icing, let it settle half an hour before you put it into cups or glasses. Use that which drops into the dish under the sieve, to make it froth the better, adding two whites of eggs. Colored powdered sugar may, if you like, be sprinkled on the top of each.

Asparagus Omelet.—Boil a dozen of the largest and finest asparagus heads you can pick; cut off all the green portion, and chop it in thin slices; season with a small teaspoonful of salt, and about one-fourth of that quantity of soluble cayenne. Then beat up six eggs in a sufficient quantity of new milk to make a stiffish batter. Melt in the frying-pan a quarter of a pound of good, clean dripping, and just before you pour on the batter place a small piece of butter in the center of the pan. When the dripping is quite hot, pour on half your batter, and as it begins to set, place on it the asparagus tops, and cover over with the remainder. This omelet is generally served on a round of buttered toast, with the crusts removed. The batter is richer if made of cream.

Buttered Eggs.—Beat four or five eggs, yolks and whites together, put a quarter of a pound of butter in a basin, and then put that in boiling water, stir it till melted, then pour the butter and the eggs into a saucepan ; keep a basin in your hand, just hold the sauce-pan in the other over a slow part of the fire, shaking it one way, as it begins to warm; pour it into a basin, and back, then hold it again over the fire, stirring it constantly in the saucepan, and pouring it into the basin, more perfectly to mix the egg and butter until they shall be hot without boiling.

Serve on toasted bread ; or in a basin, to eat with salt fish, or red herrings.

Corn-Oysters.—Take a half dozen ears of sweet corn (those which are not too old); with a sharp knife split each row of the corn in the center of the kernel lengthwise ; scrape out all the pulp ; add one egg, well beaten, a little salt, one tablespoonful of sweet milk; flour enough to make a pretty stiff batter. Drop in hot lard, and fry a delicate brown. If the corn is quite young, omit the milk, using as little flour as possible.

Cheese Omelet.—Mix to a smooth batter three table-spoonfuls of fine flour, with half a pint of milk. Beat up well the yolks and whites of four eggs, a little salt, and a quarter of a pound of grated old English cheese. Add these to the flour and milk, and whisk all the ingredients together for half an hour. Put three ounces of butter into a frying-pan, and when it is boiling pour in the above mixture, fry it for a few minutes, and then turn it carefully ; when it is sufficiently cooked on the other side, turn it on to a hot dish and serve.

Irish Stew.—Take a loin of mutton, cut it into chops, season it with a very little pepper and salt, put it into a saucepan, just cover it with water, and let it cook half an hour. Boil two dozen of potatoes, peel and mash them, and stir in a cup of cream while they are hot ; then line a deep dish with the potatoes, and lay in the cooked mutton chops, and cover them over with the rest of the potatoes ; then set it in the oven to bake. Make some gravy of the broth in which the chops were cooked. This is a very nice dish.

Irish Stew.—Cut off the fat of part of a loin of mutton, and cut it into chops. Pare, wash, and slice very thin some potatoes, two onions, and two small carrots ; season with pepper and salt. Cover with water in a stew-pan, and stew gently till the meat is tender, and the potatoes are dissolved in the gravy. It may be made of beef-steaks, or mutton and beef mixed.

Macaroni, Dressed Sweet.—Boil 2 ozs. in a pint of milk, with a bit of lemon peel, and a good bit of cinnamon, till the pipes are swelled to their utmost size without breaking. Lay them on a custard-dish, and pour a custard over them hot. Serve cold.

Macaroni, as Usually Served.—Boil it in milk, or a weak veal broth, flavored with salt. When tender, put it into a dish without the liquor, with bits of butter and grated cheese, and over the top grate more, and put a little more butter. Put the dish into a Dutch oven, a quarter of an hour, and do not let the top become hard.

Omelet.—Six eggs beaten separately, beaten hard, two teaspoons of corn starch, two tablespoons milk, whites of eggs, put in slow at last. Fry in butter.

Rumbled Eggs.—This is very convenient for invalids, or a light dish for supper. Beat up three eggs with two ounces of fresh butter, or well-washed salt butter ; add a teaspoonful of cream or new milk. Put all in a saucepan and keep stirring it over the fire for nearly five minutes, until it rises up like scuffle, when it should be immediately dished on buttered toast.

Poached Eggs.—Break an egg into a cup, and put it gently into boiling water ; and when the white looks quite set, which will be in about three or four minutes, take it up with an egg slice, and lay it on toast and butter, or spinach. Serve them hot ; if fresh laid, they will poach well, without breaking.

Savory Potato-Cakes.—Quarter of a pound of grated ham, one pound of mashed potatoes, and a little suet, mixed with the yolks of two eggs, pepper, salt and nutmeg. Roll it into little balls, or cakes, and fry it a light brown. Sweet herbs may be used in place of ham. Plain potato cakes are made with potatoes and eggs only.

Tomato Toast.—Remove the stem and all the seeds from the tomatoes ; they must be ripe, mind, not *over ripe*; stew them to a pulp, season with butter, pepper and salt ; toast some bread (not new bread), butter it, and then spread the tomato on each side, and send it up to table, two slices on each dish, the slices cut in two ; and the person who helps it must serve with two half-slices, not attempt to lift the top slice, otherwise the appearance of the under slice will be destroyed.

HOW TO COOK FISH . .

OF DIFFERENT KINDS

How to Choose Anchovies.—They are preserved in barrels, with bay-salt ; no other fish has the fine flavor of the anchovy. The best look red and mellow, and the bones moist and oily ; the flesh should be high flavored, the liquor reddish, and have a fine smell.

Baked Black Bass.—Eight good-sized onions chopped fine ; half that quantity of bread crumbs ; butter size of hen's egg ; plenty of pepper and salt ; mix thoroughly with anchovy sauce until quite red. Stuff your fish with this compound and pour the rest over it, previously sprinkling it with a little red pepper. Shad, pickerel and trout are good the same way. Tomatoes can be used instead of anchovies, and are more economical. If using them, take pork in place of butter, and chop fine.

Boiled White Fish.—Lay the fish open ; put it in a dripping pan with the back down ; nearly cover with water ; to one fish put two tablespoons salt, cover tightly and simmer (not boil) one-half hour ; dress with gravy, butter and pepper ; garnish with sliced eggs.

For sauce use a piece of butter the size of an egg, one tablespoon of flour, one half pint boiling water ; boil a few minutes, and add three hard boiled eggs, sliced.

Fresh Broiled White Fish.—Wash and drain the fish: sprinkle with pepper and lay with the inside down upon the gridiron, and broil over fresh bright coals, When a nice brown, turn for a moment on the other side. then take up and spread with butter. This is a very nice way of broiling all kinds of fish, fresh or salted. A little smoke under the fish adds to its flavor. This may be made by putting two or three cobs under the gridiron.

To Boil Codfish.—If boiled fresh, it is watery; but it is excellent if salted, and hung for a day, to give it firmness. Wash and clean the fish well, and rub salt inside of it; tie it up, and put it on the fire in cold water; throw a handful of salt into the fish-kettle. Boil a small fish 15 minutes; a large one 30 minutes. Serve it without the smallest speck and scum; drain. Garnish it with lemon, horseradish, the milt, roe, and liver. Oyster or shrimp sauce may be used.

Chowder.—Five pounds of codfish cut in squares; fry plenty of salt pork cut in thin slices; put a layer of pork in your kettle, then one of fish; one of potatoes in thick slices, and one of onions in slices; plenty of pepper and salt; repeat as long as your materials last, and finish with a layer of Boston crackers or crusts of bread. Water sufficient to cook with, or milk if you prefer. Cook one-half hour and turn over on your platter, disturbing as little as possible. Clams and eels the same way.

Clam Fritters.—Twelve clams chopped or not, one pint milk, three eggs, add liquor from clams; salt and pepper, and flour enough for thin batter. Fry in hot lard.

Clam Stew.—Lay the clams on a gridiron over hot coals, taking them out of the shell as soon as open, saving the juice; add a little hot water, pepper, a very little salt and butter rolled in flour sufficient for seasoning; cook for five minutes and pour over toast.

Eels, to Stew.—Of the above fish, that of the "silver" kind is preferable to its congener, and, therefore, ought to be procured for all cuisine purposes. Take from three to four pounds of these eels, and let the same be thoroughly cleansed, inside and out, rescinding the heads and tails from the bodies. Cut them into pieces three inches in length each, and lay them down in a stew pan, covering them with a sufficiency of sweet mutton gravy to keep them seething over a slow fire, when introduced into the pan, for twenty minutes. Add to the liquor, before you place your eels into it, a quarter of an ounce of whole black pepper, quarter of an ounce of allspice, with one or two pieces of white ginger. Thicken with a light admixture of flour and butter, stirring it carfully round, adding thereto, at the same time, one gill of good portwine, and half a gill of sweet ketchup. Lemon-peel and salt may be added in accordance with your taste.

How to Keep Fish Sound.—To prevent meat, fish, etc., going bad, put a few pieces of charcoal into the sauce-pan wherein the fish or flesh is to be boiled.

How to Render Boiled Fish Firm.—Add a little saltpetre to the salt in the water in which the fish is to be boiled; a quarter of an ounce to one gallon.

Fish Balls.—Bone, cooked fresh, or salt fish, add double the quantity of mashed potatoes, one beaten egg, a little butter, pepper and salt to taste. Make in cakes or balls; dredge with flour and fry in hot lard.

Potted Fish.—Take out the back-bone of the fish; for one weighing two pounds take a tablespoon of allspice and cloves mixed; these spices should be put into bags of not too thick muslin; put sufficient salt directly upon each fish; then roll in cloth, over which sprinkle a little cayenne pepper; put alternate layers of fish, spice and sago in an earthen jar; cover with the best cider vinegar; cover the jar closely with a plate and over this put a covering of dough, rolled out to twice the thickness of pie crust. Make the edges of paste, to adhere closely to the sides of the jar, so as to make it air-tight. Put the jar into a pot of cold water and let it boil from three to five hours, according to quantity. Ready when cold.

How to Broil or Roast Fresh Herrings.—Scale, gut and wash; cut off the heads; steep them in salt and vinegar ten minutes; dust them with flour, and broil them over or before the fire, or in the oven. Serve with melted butter and parsley.

Herrings are nice *jarred*, and done in the oven, with pepper, cloves, salt, a little vinegar, a few bay-leaves, and a little butter.

How to Fry Fresh Herrings.—Slice small onions, and lay in the pan with the herrings; add a little butter, and fry them. Perhaps it is better to fry the onions separately with a little parsley, and butter or drip.

How to Pot Herrings.—Clean, cut off the heads, and lay them close in an earthen pot. Strew a little salt between every layer; put in cloves, mace, whole pepper,

cayenne and nutmeg; fill up the jar with vinegar, water, and a quarter of a pint of sherry, cover, tie down; bake in an oven, and when cold pot it for use. A few anchovies and bay leaves intermixed will improve the flavor much.

Buttered Lobsters.—Pick the meat out, cut it, and warm with a little brown gravy, nutmeg, salt, pepper and butter, with a little flour. If done white, a little white gravy and cream.

Curry of Lobster.—Take them from the shells, and lay into a pan, with a small piece of mace, three or four spoonfuls of veal gravy, and four of cream; rub smooth one or two teaspoonfuls of curry-powder, a teaspoonful of flour, and an ounce of butter, simmer an hour; squeeze half a lemon in, and add salt.

Lobster Chowder.—Four or five pounds of lobster, chopped fine; take the green part and add to it four pounded crackers; stir this into one quart of boiling milk; then add the lobster, a piece of butter one-half the size of an egg, a little pepper and salt, and bring it to a boil.

How to Boil Mackerel.—Rub them with vinegar; when the water boils, put them in with a little salt, and boil gently 15 minutes. Serve with fennel and parsley chopped, boil, and put into melted butter, and gooseberry sauce.

Salt Mackerel.—Soak the fish for a few hours in lukewarm water, changing the water several times; then put into cold water loosely tied in cloths, and let the fish come to a boil, turning off the water once, and pouring over the fish hot water from the tea-kettle; let this just come to a boil, then take them out and drain them, lay them on a platter, butter and pepper them, and place them for a few moments in the oven. Serve with sliced lemons, or with any fish sauce.

How to Fry Oysters.—Use the largest and best oysters; lay them in rows upon a clean cloth and press another upon them, to absorb the moisture; have ready several beaten eggs; and in another dish some finely crushed crackers: in the frying pan heat enough butter to entirely cover the oysters; dip the oysters first into the eggs, then into the crackers, rolling it or them over, that they may become well incrusted; drop into the frying pan and fry quickly to a light brown. Serve dry and let the dish be warm. A chafing dish is best.

Oyster Patties.—Make some rich puff paste and bake it in very small tin patty pans; when cool, turn them out upon a large dish; stew some large fresh oysters with a few cloves, and a little mace and nutmeg; then add the yolk of one egg, boiled hard and grated; add a little butter, and as much of the oyster liquor as will cover them. When they have stewed a little while, take them off the pan and set them to cool. When quite cold, lay two or three oysters in each shell of puff paste.

Oysters, Stewed.—In all cases, unless shell oysters, wash and drain; mix half a cup of butter and a tablespoon of corn starch; put with the oysters in a porcelain kettle; stir until they boil; add two cups of cream or milk; salt to taste; do not use the liquor of the oysters in either stewing or escaloping.

Oysters Stewed.—Scald the oysters in their own liquor, then take them out, beard them, and strain the liquor carefully from the grit. Put into a stewpan an ounce of butter, with sufficient flour dredged in to dry it up; add the oyster liquor, and a blade of pounded mace, a little cayenne, and a very little salt to taste; stir it well over a brisk fire with a wooden spoon, and when it comes to the boil, throw in your oysters, say a dozen and a half or a score, and a good tablespoonful of cream, or more, if you have it at hand. Shake the pan over the fire, and let it simmer for one or two minutes, but not any longer, and do not let it boil, or the fish will harden. Serve in a hot dish, garnished with sippets of toasted bread. Some persons think that the flavor is improved by boiling a small piece of lemon-peel with the oyster liquor, taking it out, however, before the cream is added.

Oysters Scolloped.—Beard and trim your oysters, and strain the liquor. Melt in a stewpan, with a dredging of flour sufficient to dry it up, an ounce of butter, and two tablespoonfuls of white stock, and the same of cream; the strained liquor and pepper, and salt to taste. Put in the oysters and gradually heat them through, but be sure not to let them boil. Have your scallop-shells buttered, lay in the oysters, and as much liquid as they will hold; cover them well over with bread-crumbs, over which spread, or drop, some tiny bits of butter. Brown them in the oven, or before the fire, and serve while very hot.

Oysters, To Pickle.—Take two hundred of the plumpest, nicest oysters to be had, open them, saving the liquor, remove the beards, put them, with the liquor, into a stewpan, and let them simmer for twenty minutes over a very gentle fire, taking care to skim them well. Take the stewpan off the fire, take out the oysters, and strain the liquor through a fine cloth, returning the oysters to the stewpan. Add to a pint of the hot liquor half an ounce of mace, and half an ounce of cloves; give it a boil, and put it in with the oysters, stirring the spice well in amongst them. Then put in about a spoonful of salt, three-quarters of a pint of white-wine vinegar, and one ounce of whole pepper, and let the oysters stand until they are quite cold. They will be ready for use in about twelve or twenty-four hours; if to be kept longer they should be put in wide-mouthed botttles, or stone jars, and well drawn down with bladder. It is very important that they should be quite cold before they are put into the bottles, or jars.

Salmon, To Boil.—Clean it carefully, boil it gently with salt and a little horse radish; take it out of the water as soon as done. Let the water be warm if the fish be split. If underdone it is very unwholesome. Serve with shrimp, lobster, or anchovy sauce, and fennel and butter.

Salmon, To Marinate.—Cut the salmon in slices; take off the skin and take out the middle bone; cut each slice asunder; put into a saucepan and season with salt, pepper, 6 cloves, a sliced onion, some whole chives, a little sweet basil, parsley, and a bay leaf; then squeeze in the juice of three lemons, or use vinegar. Let the salmon lie in the marinate for two hours; take it out; dry with a cloth; dredge with flour, and fry brown in clarified butter; then lay a clean napkin in a dish; lay the slices upon it; garnish with fried parsley.

Salt Cod, To Dress.—Soak the cod all night in 2 parts water, and one part vinegar. Boil; and break into flakes on the dish; pour over it boiled parsnips, beaten in a mortar, and then boil up with cream, and a large piece of butter rolled in a bit of flour. It may be served with egg-sauce instead of parsnip, or boiled and served without flaking with the usual sauce.

All *Salt Fish* may be done in a similar way. Pour egg-sauce over it, or parsnips, boiled and beaten fine with butter and cream.

How to Boil Sturgeon—Water, 2 quarts; vinegar, 1 pint; a stick of horseradish; a little lemon-peel, salt, pepper, a bay leaf. In this boil the fish; when the fish is ready to leave the bones, take it up; melt ½ lb. of butter; add an anchovy, some mace, a few shrimps, good mushroom ketchup, and lemon juice; when it boils, put in the dish; serve with the sauce; garnish with fried oysters, horseradish and lemon.

How to Broil Sturgeon.—Cut slices, rub beaten eggs over them, and sprinkle them with crumbs of bread, parsley, pepper and salt; wrap them in white paper, and broil gently. Use for sauce, butter, anchovy and soy.

How to Dress Fresh Sturgeon.—Cut slices, rub egg over them, then sprinkle with crumbs of bread, parsley, pepper, salt; fold them in paper, and broil gently. Sauce; butter, anchovy and soy.

How to Roast Sturgeon.—Put a piece of butter, rolled in flour, into a stewpan with four cloves, a bunch of sweet herbs, two onions, some pepper and salt, half a pint of water and a glass of vinegar. Set it over the fire till hot; then let it become lukewarm, and steep the fish in it an hour or two. Butter a paper well, tie it round, and roast it without letting the spit run through. Serve with sorrel and anchovy sauce.

Trout, a-la-Genevoise—Clean the fish well; put it into the stewpan, adding half champagne and half sherry wine. Season it with pepper, salt, an onion, a few cloves stuck in it, and a small bunch of parsley and thyme; put in it a crust of French bread; set it on a quick fire. When done take the bread out, bruise it and thicken the sauce: add flour and a little butter, and boil it up. Lay the fish on the dish, and pour the sauce over it. Serve it with sliced lemon and fried bread.

How to Broil Trout—Wash, dry, tie it, to cause it to keep its shape; melt butter, add salt, and cover the trout with it. Broil it gradually in a Dutch oven, or in a common oven. Cut an anchovy small, and chop some capers. Melt some butter with a little flour, pepper, salt, nutmeg, and half a spoonful of vinegar. Pour it over the trout and serve it hot.

HOW TO CHOOSE ——
.. AND COOK GAME

How to Choose Ducks—A young duck should have supple feet, breast and belly hard and thick. A tame duck has dusky yellow feet. They should be picked dry, and ducklings scalded.

How to Roast Ducks.—Carefully pick, and clean the inside. Boil two or three onions in two waters; chop them very small. Mix the onions with about half the quantity of sage leaves, bread crumbs finely powdered, a spoonful of salt, and a little cayenne paper; beat up the yolk of an egg, and rub the stuffing well together. With a brisk fire roast about 35 minutes. Serve with gravy sauce.

How to Stew Ducks.—Lard two young ducks down each side the breast; dust with flour; brown before the fire; put into a stewpan with a quart of water, a pint of port wine, a spoonful of walnut ketchup, the same of browning, one anchovy, a clove of garlick, sweet herbs and cayenne pepper. Stew till they are tender, about half an hour; skim and strain, and pour over the duck.

How to Hash Partridge.—Cut up the partridges as for eating; slice an onion into rings; roll a little butter in flour; put them into the tossing pan, and shake it over the fire till it boils; put in the partridge with a little port wine and vinegar; and when it is thoroughly hot, lay it on the dish with sippets round it; strain the sauce over the partridge, and lay on the onion in rings.

How to Pot Partridge.—Clean them nicely; and season with mace, allspice, white pepper and salt, in fine powder. Rub every part well; then lay the breast downward in a pan, and pack the birds as closely as you possibly can. Put a good deal of butter on them; then cover he pan with a coarse flour paste and a paper over, tie it close, and bake. When cold, put the birds into pots, and cover with butter.

How to Roast Partridge.—Roast them like a turkey, and when a little under roasted, dredge them with flour, and baste them with butter; let them go to table with a fine froth; put gravy sauce in the dish, and bread sauce on the table.

How to Stew Partridge.—Truss as for roasting; stuff the craws, and lard them down each side of the breast; roll a lump of butter in pepper, salt and beaten mace, and put them inside; sew up the vents; dredge them well and fry a light brown; put them into a stewpan with a quart of good gravy, a spoonful of sherry wine, the same of mushroom ketchup, a teaspoonful of lemon pickle, and a little mushroom powder, one anchovy, half a lemon, a sprig of sweet marjoram; cover the pan close, and stew half an hour; take out, and thicken the gravy; boil a little, and pour it over the partridge, and lay round them artichoke buttons, boiled, and cut in quarters, and the yolks of four hard eggs, if agreeable.

How to Roast Pheasant.—Roast them as turkey; and serve with a fine gravy (into which put a very small bit of garlic) and bread sauce. When cold, they may be made into excellent patties, but their flavor should not be overpowered by lemon.

How to Roast Plovers.—Roast the *green* ones in the same way as woodcocks and quails, without drawing, and serve on a toast. *Grey* plovers may be either roasted or stewed with gravy, herbs and spice.

How to Fricassee Quails.—Having tossed them up in a sauce-pan with a little melted butter and mushrooms, put in a slice of ham, well beaten, with salt, pepper, cloves and savory herbs; add good gravy, and a glass of sherry; simmer over a slow fire; when almost done, thicken the ragout with a good cullis, (i. e. a good broth, strained, gelatined, etc.) or with two or three eggs, well beaten up in a little gravy.

How to Roast Quails.—Roast them without drawing and serve on toast. Butter only should be eaten with them, as gravy takes off the fine flavor. The thigh and the back are the most esteemed.

How to Roast Rabbits.—Baste them with butter, and dredge them with flour; half an hour will do them at a brisk fire; and if small, twenty minutes. Take the livers with a bunch of parsley, boil them, and chop them very fine together; melt some butter, and put half the liver and parsley into the butter; pour it into the dish, and garnish the dish with the other half; roast them to a fine light brown.

How to Make Rabbit Taste Like a Hare.—Choose one that is young, but full grown; hang it in the skin three or four days; then skin it, and lay it, without washing, in a seasoning of black pepper and allspice in a very fine powder, a glass of port wine, and the same quantity of vinegar. Baste it occasionally for 40 hours, then stuff it and roast it as a hare, and with the same sauce. Do not wash off the liquor that it was soaked in.

How to Roast Snipes—Do not draw them. Split them; flour them, and baste with butter. Toast a slice of bread brown; place it in the dish under the birds for the trail to drop on. When they are done enough, take up, and lay them on the toast; put good gravy in the dish. Serve with butter, and garnish with orange or lemon.

Snipe Pie—Bone 4 snipes, and truss them. Put in their insides finely chopped bacon, or other forcemeat; put them in the dish with the breast downwards, and put forcemeat balls around them. Add gravy made of butter, and chopped veal and ham, parsley, pepper and shalots. Cover with nice puff paste; close it well to keep in the gravy. When nearly done, pour in more gravy, and a little sherry wine. Bake two or three hours.

How to Fry Venison—Cut the meat into slices, and make a gravy of the bones; fry it of a light brown, and keep it hot before the fire; put butter rolled in flour into the pan, and stir it till thick and brown; add ½ lb. of loaf sugar powdered, with the gravy made from the bones, and some port wine. Let it be as thick as cream; squeeze in a lemon; warm the venison in it; put it in the dish, and pour the sauce over it.

HOW TO MAKE ICE CREAMS
WATER-ICE AND JELLIES

To Mold Ices—Fill your mold as quicly as possible with the frozen cream, wrap it up in paper, and bury it in ice and salt, and let it remain for an hour or more to harden. For dishing, have the dish ready, dip the mold in hot water for an instant, wipe it, take off the top and bottom covers, and turn it into the dish. This must be done expeditiously. In molding ices, it is advisable not to have the cream too stifly frozen before putting it into the mold.

Ice Cream—Take two quarts milk, one pint cream, three eggs beaten very light, and two teaspoons of arrowroot; boil in one-half pint milk, strain eggs, arrow-root, and flavor to suit, then freeze.

Ginger Ice Cream—Bruise six ounces of the best preserved ginger in a mortar; add the juice of one lemon, half a pound of sugar, one pint of cream. Mix well; strain through a hair sieve; freeze. One quart.

Italian Ice Cream—Rasp two lemons on some sugar, which, with their juice, add to one pint of cream, one glass of brandy, half a pound of sugar; freeze. One quart.

Lemon Ice Cream—Take one pint of cream, rasp two lemons on sugar; squeeze them, and add the juice with half a pound of sugar. Mix; freeze. One quart.

Pine-Apple Ice Cream—Take one pound of pineapple, when peeled, bruise it in a marble mortar, pass it through a hair sieve, add three-quarters of a pound of powdered sugar, and one pint of cream. Freeze.

Raspberry and Currant Ice Cream—Take one pound of raspberries, half a pound of red currants, three-quarters of a pound of sugar, and one pint of cream. Strain, color and freeze. One quart.

Strawberry Ice Cream—Take two pounds of fresh strawberries, carefully picked, and, with a wooden spoon, rub them through a hair seive, and about half a pound of powdered sugar, and the juice of one lemon; color with a few drops of prepared cochineal; cream, one pint; then freeze. This will make a reputed quart. When fresh strawberries are not in season take strawberry jam, the juice of two lemons, cream, to one quart. Color, strain, and freeze. Milk may be substituted for cream, and makes good ices. If too much sugar is used, the ices will prove watery, or, perhaps not freeze at all.

Vanilla Ice Cream—Pound one stick of vanilla, or sufficient to flavor it to palate, in a mortar, with half a pound of sugar; strain through a sieve upon the yolks of two eggs, put it into a stewpan, with half a pint of milk; simmer over a slow fire, stirring all the time, the same as custard; when cool add one pint of cream and the juice of one lemon; freeze. One quart.

Cherry Water-Ice—One lb. cherries, bruised in a mortar with the stones; add the juice of two lemons, half a pint of water, one pint of clarified sugar, one glass of noyeau, and a little color; strain; freeze. One quart.

Lemon Water-Ice.—Take two lemons, and rasp them on sugar, the juice of six lemons, the juice of one orange, one pint of clarified sugar, and half a pint of water. Mix; strain through a hair sieve; freeze. One quart.

Melon Water-Ice.—Half a lb. of ripe melon pounded in a mortar, two ounces of orange-flower water, the juice of two lemons, half a pint of water and one pint of clarified sugar; strain; freeze. One quart.

Strawberry or Raspberry Water-Ice.—One pound of scarlet strawberries or raspberries, half a pound currants, half a pint of water, one pint of clarified sugar, and a little color; strain and freeze. One quart.

Apple Jelly.—Cut the apples and boil in water to cover, boil down, then strain, and take a pound of sugar to a pint of juice, then boil fifteen minutes hard.

Apple Jelly.—Cut off all spots and decayed places on the apples; quarter them, but do not pare or core them; put in the peel of as many lemons as you like, about two to six or eight dozen of the apples; fill the preserving-pan, and cover the fruit with spring water; boil them till they are in pulp, then pour them into a jelly-bag; let them strain all night, do not squeeze them. To every pint of juice put one pound of white sugar; put in the juice of the lemons you had before pared, but strain it through muslin. You may also put in about a teaspoonful of essense of lemon; let it boil for at least twenty minutes; it will look redder than at first; skim it well at the time. Put it either in shapes or pots, and cover it the next day. It ought to be quite stiff and very clear.

Apple Jelly.—Prepare twenty golden pippins; boil them in a pint and a half of water from the spring till quite tender; then strain the liquor through a colander. To every pint put a pound of fine sugar; add cinnamon, grated orange or lemon; then boil to a jelly.

Another.—Prepare apples as before, by boiling and straining; have ready half an ounce of isinglass boiled in half a pint of water to a jelly; put this to the apple-water and apple, as strained through a coarse sieve; add sugar, a little lemon-juice and peel; boil all together, and put into a dish. Take out the peel.

Calf's Foot Lemon Jelly—Boil four quarts of water with three calf's feet, or two cow heels, till half wasted; take the jelly from the fat and sediment, mix with it the juice of a Seville orange and twelve lemons, the peels of three ditto. the whites and shells of twelve eggs, sugar to taste, a pint of raisin wine, 1 oz. of coriander seeds, ¼ oz. of allspice, a bit of cinnamon, and six cloves, all bruised, after having mixed them cold. The jelly should boil fifteen minutes without stirring; then clear it through a flannel bag.

Cherry Jelly.—Cherries, 5 lbs.; stone them; red currants, 2 lbs.; strain them, that the liquor may be clear; add 2 lbs. of sifted loaf sugar, and 2 ozs. of isinglass.

Chocolate Caramel—One pint milk, half pound butter, half pound Cadburry's chocolate, three pounds sugar, two spoons vanilla. Boil slowly until brittle.

Currant Jelly, Red or Black—Strip the fruit, and in a stone jar stew them in a saucepan of water or on the fire; strain off the liquor, and to every pint weigh 1 lb. of loaf sugar; put the latter in large lumps into it, in a stone or China vessel, till nearly dissolved; then put it into a preserving-pan; simmer and skim. When it will jelly on a plate put it in small jars or glasses.

Green Gooseberry Jelly—Place the berries in hot water on a slow fire till they rise to the surface; take off;

cool with a little water, add also a little vinegar and salt to green them. In two hours drain, and put them in cold water a minute; drain, and mix with an equal weight of sugar; boil slowly 20 minutes; sieve, and put into glasses.

Iceland Moss Jelly—Moss, ½ to 1 oz.; water, 1 quart. Simmer down to ½ pint. Add fine sugar and a little lemon juice. It may be improved with ¼ ounce of isinglass. The moss should first be steeped in cold water an hour or two.

Isinglass Jelly—Boil one ounce of isinglass in a quart of water, with ¼ ounce of Jamaica pepper-corns or cloves, and a crust of bread, till reduced to a pint. Add sugar. It keeps well, and may be taken in wine and water, milk, tea, soup, etc.

Lemon Jelly Cake—Take four eggs, one cup sugar, butter the size of an egg, one and a half cups flour, half cup sweet milk, two teaspoons of baking powder. Jelly.—One grated lemon, one grated apple, one egg, one cup sugar, beat all together, put in a tin and stir till boils.

Lemon Jelly—Take one and a half packages of gelatine, one pint cold water, soak two hours, then add two teacups sugar, one pint boiling water; stir all together, add the juice of two lemons or one wineglass wine, strain through a cloth, and put in a mold.

Orange Jelly—It may be made the same as lemon jelly, which see. Grate the rind of two Seville and of two China oranges, and two lemons; squeeze the juice of three of each, and strain, and add to the juice a quarter of a pound of lump sugar, a quarter of a pint of water, and boil till it almost candies. Have ready a quart of isinglass jelly made with two ounces; put to it the syrup, boil it once up; strain off the jelly, and let it stand to settle as above, before it is put into the mold.

Quince Jelly—Cut in pieces a sufficient quantity of quinces; draw off the juice by boiling them in water, in which they ought only to swim, no more. When fully done drain, and have ready clarified sugar, of which put one spoonful to two of the juice; bring the sugar to the *souffle;* add the juice, and finish. When it drops from the skimmer it is enough; take it off, and pot it.

Jelly of Siberian Crabs—Take off the stalks, weigh and wash the crabs. To each one and a half pounds, add one pint of water. Boil them gently until broken, but do not allow them to fall to a pulp. Pour the whole through a jelly-bag, and when the juice is quite transparent weigh it; put it into a clean preserving-pan, boil it quickly for ten minutes, then add ten ounces of fine sugar to each pound of juice; boil it from twelve to fifteen minutes, skim it very clean, and pour into molds

Siberian Crab-Apple Jelly—Mash the crab apples, take off stems and heads, put in pot, cover with water, let them boil to a pulp, then turn them in a flannel bag, and leave all night to strain, then add one pound of sugar to a pint of juice, boil ten to fifteen minutes, skim and put in jelly glasses.

Siberian Crab Jelly—Fill a large flannel bag with crabs. Put the bag in a preserving-pan of spring water, and boil for about seven hours; then take out the bag, and fill it so that all the syrup can run through, and the water that remains in the pan; and to each pint of syrup add one pound of loaf sugar, and boil for about an hour, and it will be a clear, bright red jelly.

TELEGRAPH wires have to be renewed every five or seven years. The Western Union Telegraph Company exchange about one thousand tons of old wire for new every year. The new wire costs from seven to eight cents per pound, and for the old about one-eighth of a cent a pound is allowed.

HOW TO SELECT ..
.. AND COOK MEATS

How to Dress Bacon and Beans—When you dress beans and bacon, boil the bacon by itself, and the beans by themselves, for the bacon will spoil the color of the beans. Always throw some salt into the water and some parsley nicely picked. When the beans are done enough, which you will know by their being tender, throw them into a colander to drain. Take up the bacon and skin it; throw some raspings of the bread over the top, and if you have a salamander, make it red hot, and hold it over it to brown the top of the bacon; if you have not one, set it before the fire to brown. Lay the beans in the dish, and the bacon in the middle on the top, and send them to table, with butter in a tureen.

Corned Beef—Make the following pickle: Water, 2 gallons; salt, 2½ lbs.; molasses, ¼ lb.; sugar, 1 lb.; saltpetre, 1½ ozs.; pearlash, ¼ oz. Boil all together; skim, and pour the pickle on about 25 lbs. of beef. Let it stay in a few days. Boil in plenty of water when cooked to remove the salt, and eat with it plenty of vegetables. It is nice to eat cold, and makes excellent sandwiches.

Rolled Beef—Hang three ribs three or four days ; take out the bones from the whole length, sprinkle it with salt, roll the meat tight and roast it. Nothing can look nicer. The above done with spices, etc., and baked as hunters' beef is excellent.

Beef, Rolled to equal Hare—Take the inside of a large sirloin, soak it in a glass of port wine and a glass of vinegar mixed, for forty-eight hours; have ready a very fine stuffing, and bind it up tight. Roast it on a hanging spit ; and baste it with a glass of port wine, the same quantity of vinegar, and a teaspoonful of pounded allspice. Larding it improves the look and flavor; serve with a rich gravy in the dish ; currant-jelly and melted butter in tureens.

Round of Beef—Should be carefully salted and wet with the pickle for eight or ten days. The bone should be cut out first, and the beef skewered and tied up to make it quite round. It may be stuffed with parsley, if approved, in which case the holes to admit the parsley must be made with a sharp pointed knife, and the parsley coarsely cut and stuffed in tight. As soon as it boils, it should be skimmed: and afterwards kept boiling very gently.

Beef Steak, Stewed—Peel and chop two Spanish onions, cut into small parts four pickled walnuts, and put them at the bottom of a stewpan ; add a teacupful of mushroom ketchup, two teaspoonfuls of walnut ditto, one of shalot, one of Chile vinegar, and a lump of butter. Let the rump-steak be cut about three-quarters of an inch thick, and beat it flat with a rolling-pin, place the meat on the top of the onions, etc., let it stew for one hour and a half, turning it every twenty minutes. Ten minutes before serving up, throw a dozen oysters with the liquor strained.

Beef Steak and Oyster Sauce—Select a good, tender rump-steak, about an inch thick, and broil it carefully. Nothing but experience and attention will serve in broiling a steaks; one thing, however, is always to be remembered, never malt or season broiled meat until cooked. Have the gridiron clean and hot, grease it with either butter, or good lard, before laying on the meat, to prevent its sticking or marking the meat ; have clear, bright coals, and turn it frequently. When cooked, cover tightly, and have ready nicely stewed oysters; then lay the steak in a hot dish and pour over some of the oysters. Serve the rest in a tureen. Twenty-five oysters will make a nice sauce for a steak.

Fricassee of Cold Roast Beef—Cut the beef into very thin slices ; shred a handful of parsley very small, cut an onion into quarters, and put all together into a stewpan, with a piece of butter, and some strong broth ; season with salt and pepper, and simmer very gently a quarter of an hour ; then mix into it the yolks of two eggs, a glass of port wine, and a spoonful of vinegar; stir it quickly, rub the dish with shalot, and turn the fricassee into it.

Brawn—Clean a pig's head, and rub it over with salt and a little saltpetre, and let it lie two or three days ; then boil it until the bones will leave the meat; season with salt and pepper, and lay the meat hot in a mold, and press and weigh it down for a few hours. Boil another hour, covering. Be sure and cut the tongue, and lay the slices in the middle, as it much improves the flavor.

Calf's Liver and Bacon—Cut the liver into slices, and fry it first, then the bacon ; lay the liver in the dish, and the bacon upon it; serve it up with gravy, made in the pan with boiling water, thickened with flour and butter, and lemon juice ; and, if agreeable, a little parsley and onion may be chopped into it, or a little boiled parsley strewed over the liver. Garnish with slices of lemon.

Nice Form of Cold Meats—Remains of boiled ham, mutton, roast beef, etc., are good chopped fine with hard boiled eggs, two heads of lettuce, a bit of onion, and seasoned with mustard, oil, vinegar, and, if needed, more salt. Fix it smoothly in a salad dish, and adorn the edges with sprigs of parsley or leaves of curled lettuce. Keep by the ice or in a cool place until wanted.

Fried Ham and Eggs—Cut thin slices, place in the pan, and fry carefully. Do not burn. When done break the eggs into the fat; pepper slightly; keep them whole; do not turn them.

Ham Rashers may be served with spinach and poached eggs.

To Cook Ham—Scrape it clean. Do not put into cold nor boiling water. Let the water become warm; then put the ham in. Simmer or boil lightly for five or six hours; take out, and shave the rind off. Rub granulated sugar into the whole surface of the ham, so long as it can be made to receive it. Place the ham in a baking-dish with a bottle of champagne or prime cider. Baste occasionally with the juice, and let it bake an hour in a gentle heat.

A slice from a nicely cured ham thus cooked is enough to animate the ribs of death.

Or, having taken off the rind, strew bread crumbs or raspings over it, so as to cover it; set it before the fire, or in the oven till the bread is crisp and brown. Garnish with carrots, parsley, etc. The water should simmer all the time, and never boil fast.

Ham and Chicken, in Jelly—This is a nice dish for supper or luncheon. Make with a small knuckle of veal some good white stock. When cold, skim and strain it. Melt it, and put a quart of it into a saucepan with the well beaten whites of three eggs; a dessert-spoonful of Chili, or a tablespoonful of tarragon vinegar, and a little salt. Beat the mixture well with a fork till it boils; let it simmer till it is reduced to a little more than a pint; strain it; put half of it into a mold; let it nearly set. Cut the meat of a roast chicken into small thin pieces; arrange it in the jelly with some neat little slices of cold boiled ham, and sprinkle chopped parsley between the slices. When it has got quite cold, pour in the remainder of the jelly, and stand the mold in cold water, or in a cool place, so that it sets speedily. Dip the mold in boiling water to turn it out. Do not let it remain in the water more than a minute, or it will spoil the appearance of the dish. Garnish with a wreath of parsley.

Leg of Lamb—Should be boiled in a cloth to look as white as possible. The loin fried in steaks and served round, garnished with dried or fried parsley; spinach to eat with it; or dressed separately or roasted.

Loin of Mutton—Take off the skin, separate the joints with the chopper; if a large size, cut the chine-bone with a saw, so as to allow it to be carved in smaller pieces; run a small spit from one extremity to the other, and affix it to a larger spit, and roast it like the haunch. A loin weighing six pounds will take one hour to roast.

Observations on Meat—In all kinds of provisions, the best of the kind goes the farthest; it cuts out with most advantage, and affords most nourishment. Round of beef, fillet of veal, and leg of mutton, are joints of higher price; but as they have more solid meat, they deserve the preference. But those joints which are inferior may be dressed as palatably.

In loins of meat, the long pipe that runs by the bone should be taken out, as it is apt to taint; as also the kernels of beef. Do not purchase joints bruised by the blows of drovers.

Save shank bones of mutton to enrich gravies or soups.

When sirloins of beef, or loins of veal or mutton, come in, part of the suet may be cut off for puddings, or to clarify.

Dripping will baste anything as well as butter; except fowls and game; and for kitchen pies, nothing else should be used.

The fat of a neck or loin of mutton makes a far lighter pudding than suet.

Frosted meat and vegetables should be soaked in *cold water* two or three hours before using.

If the weather permit, meat eats much better for hanging two or three days before it is salted.

Roast-beef bones, or shank bones of ham, make fine peas-soup; and should be boiled with the peas the day before eaten, that the fat may be taken off.

Boiled Leg of Mutton—Soak well for an hour or two in salt and water; do not use much salt. Wipe well and boil in a floured cloth. Boil from two hours to two hours and a half. Serve with caper sauce, potatoes, mashed turnips, greens, oyster sauce, etc.

☞ To preserve the gravy in the leg, do not put it in the water till it boils; for the sudden contact with water causes a slight film over the surface, which prevents the escape of the gravy, which is abundant when carved.

How to Hash Mutton.—Cut thin slices of dressed mutton, fat and lean; flour them; have ready a little onion boiled in two or three spoonfuls of water; add to it a little gravy and the meat seasoned, and make it hot, but not to boil. Serve in a covered dish. Instead of onion, a clove, a spoonful of current jelly, and half a glass of port wine will give an agreeable flavor of venison, if the meat be fine.

Pickled cucumber, or walnut cut small, warm in it for change.

How to Prepare Pig's Cheek for Boiling.—Cut off the snout, and clean the head; divide it, and take out the eyes and the brains; sprinkle the head with salt, and let it drain 24 hours. Salt it with common salt and saltpetre; let it lie nine days if to be dressed without stewing with peas, but less if to be dressed with peas, and it must be washed first, and then simmer till all is tender.

Pig's Feet and Ears.—Clean carefully, and soak some hours, and boil them tender; then take them out; boil some vinegar and a little salt with some of the water, and when cold put it over them. When they are to be dressed, dry them, cut the feet in two, and slice the ears; fry, and serve with butter, mustard and vinegar. They may be either done in batter, or only floured.

Pork, Loin of.—Score it, and joint it, that the chops may separate easily; and then roast it as a loin of mutton. Or, put it into sufficient water to cover it; simmer till almost enough; then peel off the skin, and coat it with yolk of egg and bread crumbs, and roast for 15 or 20 minutes, till it is done enough.

How to Pickle Pork.—Cut the pork in such pieces as will lie in the pickling tub; rub each piece with saltpetre; then take one part bay salt, and two parts common salt, and rub each piece well; lay them close in the tub, and throw salt over them.

Some use a little sal prunnella, and a little sugar.

Pork Pie, to Eat Cold.—Raise a common boiled crust into either a round or oval form, which you choose, have ready the trimmings and small bits of pork cut off a sweet bone, when the hog is killed, beat it with a rolling-pin, season with pepper and salt, and keep the fat and lean separate, put it in layers quite close to the top, lay on the lid, cut the edge smooth, round, and pinch it; bake in a slow-soaking oven, as the meat is very solid. Observe, put no bone or water in the pork pie; the outside pieces will be hard if they are not cut small and pressed close.

How to Roast a Leg of Pork.—Choose a small leg of fine young pork; cut a slit in the knuckle with a sharp knife; and fill the space with sage and onion chopped, and a little pepper and salt. When half done, score the skin in slices, but don't cut deeper than the outer rind.

Apple sauce and potatoes should be served to eat with it.

Pork Rolled Neck of.—Bone it; put a forcemeat of chopped sage, a very few crumbs of bread, salt, pepper and two or three berries of allspice over the inside; then roll the meat as tight as you can, and roast it slowly, and at a good distance at first.

Chine of Pork.—Salt three days before cooking Wash it well; score the skin, and roast with sage and onions finely shred. Serve with apple sauce.—The chine is often sent to the table boiled.

How to Collar Pork.—Bone a breast or spring of pork; season it with plenty of thyme, parsley and sage; roll it hard; put in a cloth, tie both ends, and boil it; then press it; when cold, take it out of the cloth, and keep it in its own liquor.

Pork as Lamb.—Kill a young pig of four or five months old: cut up the forequarter for roasting as you do lamb, and truss the shank close. The other parts will make delicate pickled pork; or steaks, pies, etc.

Pork Sausages.—Take 6 lbs. of young pork, free from gristle, or fat; cut small and beat fine in a mortar. Chop 6 lbs. of beef suet very fine; pick off the leaves of a handfull of sage, and shred it fine; spread the meat on a clean dresser, and shake the sage over the meat; shred the rind of a lemon very fine, and throw it, with sweet herbs, on the meat; grate two nutmegs, to which put a spoonful of pepper, and a large spoonful of salt; throw the suet over, and mix all well together. Put it down close in the pot; and when you use it, roll it up with as much egg as will make it roll smooth.

Sausage Rolls.—One pound of flour, half a pound of the best lard, quarter of a pound of butter, and the yolks of three eggs well beaten. Put the flour into a dish, make a whole in the middle of it, and rub in about one ounce of the lard, then the yolks of the eggs, and enough water to mix the whole into a smooth paste. Roll it out about an inch thick; flour your paste and board. Put the butter and lard in a lump into the paste, sprinkle it with flour, and turn the paste over it; beat it with a rolling-pin until you have got it flat enough to roll; roll it lightly until very thin; then divide your meat and put it into two layers of paste, and pinch the ends. Sausage rolls are now usually made small. Two pounds of sausage meat will be required for this quantity of paste, and it will make about two and a half dozen of rolls. Whites of the eggs should be beaten a little, and brushed over the rolls to glaze them. They will require from twenty minutes to half an hour to bake, and should be served on a dish covered with a neatly-fold napkin.

Spiced Beef.—Take a round of an ox; or young heifer, from 20 to 40 lbs. Cut it neatly, so that the thin flank end can wrap nearly round. Take from 2 to 4 ounces salpetre, and 1 ounce of coarse sugar, and two handfuls of common salt. Mix them well together and rub it all over. The next day salt it well as for boiling. Let it lie from two to three weeks, turning it every two or three days. Take out of the pickle, and wipe it dry. Then take cloves, mace, well powdered, a spoonful of gravy, and rub it well into the beef. Roll it up as tightly as possible; skewer it, and tie it up tight. Pour in the liquor till the meat is quite saturated, in which state it must be kept.

Stewed Beef.—Take five pounds of buttock, place it in a deep dish; half a pint of white wine vinegar, three bay leaves, two or three cloves, salt and pepper; turn it over twice the first day, and every morning after for a week or ten days. Boil half a pound or a quarter of a pound of butter, and throw in two onions, chopped very small, four cloves, and some pepper-corns; stew five hours till tender and a nice light brown.

How to Boil Tongue.—If the the tongue be a dry one, steep in water all night. Boil it three hours. If you prefer it hot, stick it with cloves. Clear off the scum, and add savory herbs when it has boiled two hours; but this is optional. Rub it over with the yolk of an egg; strew over it bread crumbs; baste it with butter; set it before the fire till it is of a light brown. When you dish it up, pour a little brown gravy, or port wine sauce mixed the same way as for venison. Lay slices of currant jelly around it.

How to Fricassee Tripe.—Cut into small square pieces. Put them into the stewpan with as much sherry as will cover them, with pepper, ginger, a blade of mace, sweet herbs and an onion. Stew 15 minutes. Take out the herbs and onion, and put in a little shred of parsley, the juice of a small lemon, half an anchovy cut small, a gill of cream and a little butter, or yolk of an egg. Garnish with lemon.

How to Fry Tripe.—Cut the tripe into small square pieces; dip them in yolks of eggs, and fry them in good dripping, till nicely brown; take out and drain, and serve with plain melted butter.

Veal Cutlets, Maintenon.—Cut slices about three quarters of an inch thick, beat them with a rolling-pin, and wet them on both sides with egg; dip them into a seasoning of bread-crumbs, parsley, thyme, knotted marjoram, pepper, salt and a little nutmeg grated; then put them in papers folded over, and broil them; and serve with a boat of melted butter, with a little mushroom ketchup.

Veal Cutlets.—Another way.—Prepare as above, and fry them; lay into a dish, and keep them hot; dredge a little flour, and put a bit of butter into the pan; brown it, then pour some boiling water into it and boil quickly; season with pepper, salt and ketchup and pour over them.

Another Way.—Prepare as before, and dress the cutlets in a dutch oven; pour over them melted butter and mushrooms.

Fillet of Veal.—Veal requires a good, bright fire for roasting. Before cooking, stuff with a force-meat, composed of 2 ozs. of finely-powdered bread crumbs, half a lemon-peel chopped fine, half a teaspoonful of salt, and the same quantity of mixed mace and cayenne pepper, powdered parsley, and some sweet herbs; break an egg, and mix all well together. Baste your joint with fresh butter, and send it to table well browned. A nice bit of bacon should be served with the fillet of veal, unless ham is provided.

Veal Patties.—Mince some veal that is not quite done with a little parsley, lemon-peel, a scrape of nutmeg, and a bit of salt; add a little cream and gravy just to moisten the meat; and add a little ham. Do not warm it till the patties are baked.

Veal Pie.—Take some of the middle, or scrag, of a small neck; season it; and either put to it, or not, a few slices of lean bacon or ham. If it is wanted of a high relish, add mace, cayenne, and nutmeg, to the salt and pepper; and also force-meat and eggs; and if you choose, add truffles, morels, mushrooms, sweet-bread, cut into small bits, and cocks'-combs blanched, if liked. Have a rich gravy ready, to pour in after baking.—It will be very good without any of the latter additions.

Common Veal Pie.—Cut a breast of veal into pieces; season with pepper and salt, and lay them in the dish. Boil hard six or eight yolks of eggs, and put them into different places in the pie; pour in as much water as will nearly fill the dish; put on the lid, and bake.—*Lamb Pie* may be done this way.

Stewed Veal.—Cut the veal as for small cutlets; put into the bottom of a pie-dish a layer of the veal, and sprinkle it with some finely-rubbed sweet basil and chopped parsley, the grated rind of one lemon with the juice, half a nut-meg, grated, a little salt and pepper; and cut into very small peices a large spoonful of butter; then another layer of slices of veal, with exactly the same seasoning as before; and over this pour one pint of Lisbon wine and half a pint of cold water; then cover it over very thickly with grated stale bread; put this in the oven and bake slowly for three-quarters of an hour, and brown it. Serve it in a pie-dish hot.

Breast of Veal Stuffed—Cut off the gristle of a breast of veal, and raise the meat off the bones, then lay a good force-meat, made of pounded veal, some sausage-meat, parsley, and a few shalots chopped very fine, and well seasoned with pepper, salt, and nutmeg; then roll the veal tightly, and sew it with fine twine to keep it in shape, and prevent the force-meat escaping; lay some slices of fat bacon in a stew-pan, and put the veal roll on it; add some stock, pepper, salt, and a bunch of sweet herbs; let it stew three hours, then cut carefully out the twine, strain the sauce after skimming it well, thicken it with brown flour; let it boil up once, and pour it over the veal garnish with slices of lemon, each cut in four. A fillet of veal first stuffed with force-meat can be dressed in the same manner, but is must first be roasted, so as to brown it a good color; and force-meat balls, highly seasoned, should be served round the veal.

.. HOW TO MAKE PIES
----OF VARIOUS KINDS

Beef-Steak Pie—Prepare the steaks as stated under *Beefsteaks,* and when seasoned and rolled with fat in each, put them in a dish with puff paste round the edges; put a little water in the dish, and cover it with a good crust.

Chicken Pie—Cut the chicken in pieces, and boil nearly tender. Make a rich crust with an egg or two to make it light and puffy. Season the chicken and slices of ham with pepper, salt, mace, nutmeg, and cayenne. Put them in layers, first the ham, chicken, force-meat balls, and hard eggs in layers. Make a gravy of knuckle of veal, mutton bones, seasoned with herbs, onions, pepper, etc. Pour it over the contents of the pie, and cover with paste. bake an hour.

Cocoanut Pie—Take a teacup of coaconut, put it into a coffee-cup, fill it up with sweet milk, and let it soak a few hours. When ready to bake the pie, take two tablespoonfuls of flour, mix with milk, and stir in three-fourths of a cup of milk (or water); place on the stove, and stir until it thickens. Add butter the size of a walnut, while warm. When cool, add a little salt, two eggs, saving out the white of one for the top. Sweeten to taste. Add the cocoanut, beating well. Fill the crust and bake. When done, have the extra white beaten ready to spread over the top. Return to the oven and brown lightly.

Cream Pie—Take eight eggs, eight ounces pounded sugar, eight ounces flour, put all together into a stew-pan with two glasses of milk, stir until it boils, then add quarter pound of butter, and quarter pound of almonds, chopped fine; mix well together, make paste, roll it out half an inch thich, cut out a piece the size of a teaplate, put in a baking tin, spread out on it the cream, and lay strips, of paste across each way and a plain broad piece around the edge, egg and sugar the top and bake in a quick oven.

Fish Pie—Pike, perch and carp may be made into very savory pies if cut into fillets, seasoned and baked in paste, sauce made of veal broth, or cream put in before baking.

Game Pie—Divide the birds, if large, into pieces or joints. They may be pheasants, partridges, etc. Add a little bacon or ham. Season well. Cover with puff paste, and bake carefully. Pour into the pie half a cupful of melted butter, the juice of a lemon, and a glass of sherry, when rather more than half baked.

Giblet Pie—Clean the giblets well; stew with a little water, onion, pepper, salt, sweet herbs, till nearly done. Cool, and add beef, veal or mutton steaks. Put the liquor of the stew to the giblets. Cover with paste, and when the pie is baked, pour into it a large teacupful of cream.

Lamb Pasty—Bone the lamb, cut it into square pieces; season with salt, pepper; cloves, mace, nutmeg, and minced thyme; lay in some beef suet, and the lamb upon it, making a high border about it; then turn over the paste close, and bake it. When it is enough, put in some claret, sugar, vinegar, and the yolks of eggs, beaten, together. To have the sauce only savory, and not sweet, let it be gravy only, or the baking of bones in claret.

Salmon Pie.—Grate the rind of one small lemon, or half a large one; beat the yolks of 2 eggs; 4 tablespoons of sugar; beat all together; add to this ½ pint of cold water, with 1½ tablespoons of flour in it; rub smooth so there will be no lumps; beat the whites of two eggs to a stiff froth; stir this in your pie-custard before you put it in the pan. Bake with one crust, and bake slowly.

Salmon Pie—Grate the rind of a lemon into the yolks of three fresh eggs; beat for five minutes, adding three heaping tablespoonfuls of granulated sugar; after squeezing in the juice of the lemon add half a teacupful of water; mix all thoroughly, and place in a crust the same as made for custard pie; place in oven and bake slowly. Take the whites of the three eggs, and beat to a stiff froth, adding two tablespoonfuls of pulverized sugar, and juice of half a lemon; after the pie bakes and is cool, place the frosting on top, and put into a hot oven to brown.

Mince-Meat—There are various opinons as to the result of adding meat to the sweet ingredients used in making this favorite dish. Many housewives think it an improvement, and use either the under-cut of a well-roasted surloin of beef or a boiled fresh ox-tongue for the purpose. Either of these meats may be chosen with advantage, and one pound, after it has been cooked, will be found sufficient; this should be freed from fat, and well mince. In making mince-meat, each ingredient should be minced separately and finely before it is added to the others. For a moderate quantity, take two pounds of raisins (stoned), the same quantity of currants, well washed and dried, ditto of beef suet, chopped fine, one pound of American apples, pared and cored, two pounds of moist sugar, half a pound of candied orange-peel, and a quarter of a pound of citron, the grated rinds of three lemons, one grated nutmeg, a little mace, half an ounce of salt, and one teaspoonful of ginger. After having minced the fruit separately, mix all well together with the hand; then add half a pint of French brandy and the same of sherry. Mix well with a spoon, press it down in jars, and cover it with a bladder.

Good Mince Pies.—Six pounds beef; 5 pounds suet; 5 pounds sugar; 2 ounces allspice; 2 ounces cloves; ¾ pound cinnamon; ½ pint molasses; 1¼ pounds seedless raisins; 2 pounds currants; ½ pound citron chopped fine; 1 pound almonds, chopped fine; 2 oranges; 1 lemon-skin, and all chopped fine; 2 parts chopped apples to one of meat; brandy and cider to taste.

Mock Mince Pies.—One teacup of bread; one of vinegar; one of water; one of raisins; one of sugar; one of molasses; one half-cup of butter; one teaspoon of cloves; one of nutmeg; one of cinnamon. The quantity is sufficient for three pies. They are equally as good as those made in the usual way,

Potato Pasty.—Boil and peel and mash potatoes as fine as possible; mix them with salt, pepper, and a good bit of butter. Make a paste; roll it out thin like a large puff, and put in the potato; fold over one half, pinching the edges. Bake in a moderate oven.

Potato Pie.—Skin some potatoes and cut them in slices; season them; and also some mutton, beef, pork or veal, and a lump of butter. Put layers of them and of the meat. A few eggs boiled and chopped fine improves it.

Veal and Ham Pie.—Cut about one pound and a half of veal into thin slices, as also a quarter of a pound of cooked ham; season the veal rather highly with white pepper and salt, with which cover the bottom of the dish; then lay over a few slices of ham, then the remainder of the veal, finishing with the remainder of the ham; add a wineglassful of water, and cover with a good paste, and bake; a bay-leaf will be an improvement.

Vinegar Pie.—Five tablespoons vinegar, five sugar, two flour, two water, a little nutmeg. Put in dish and bake.

HOW TO MAKE PRESERVES
OF VARIOUS KINDS

Apple Jam.—Fill a wide jar nearly half full of water; cut the apples unpeeled into quarters, take out the core, then fill the jar with the apples; tie a paper over it, and put it into a slow oven. When quite soft and cool, pulp them through a sieve. To each pound of pulp put three-quarters of a pound of crushed sugar, and boil it gently until it will jelly. Put it into large tart dishes or jars. It will keep for five or more years in a cool, dry place. If for present use, or a month hence, half a pound of sugar is enough.

Apple Marmalade.—Scald apples till they will pulp from the core; then take an equal weight of sugar in large lumps, just dip them in water, and boil it till it can be well skimmed, and is a thick syrup, put to it the pulp, and simmer it on a quick fire a quarter of an hour. Grate a little lemon-peel before boiled, but if too much it will be bitter.

Barberry Jam.—The barberries for this preserve should be quite ripe, though they should not be allowed to hang until they begin to decay. Strip them from the stalks; throw aside such as are spotted, and for one pound of fruit allow eighteen onnces well-refined sugar; boil this, with about a pint of water to every four pounds, until it becomes white, and falls in thick masses from the spoon; then throw in the fruit, and keep it stirred over a brisk fire for six minutes only; take off the scum, and pour it into jars or glasses. Sugar four and a half pounds; water a pint and a quarter, boil to candy height; barberries four pounds; six minutes.

How to Preserve Black Currants.—Get the currants when they are dry, and pick them; to every 1¼ lbs. of currants put 1 lb. of sugar into a preserving pan, with as much juice of currants as will dissolve it; when it boils skim it, and put in the currants, and boil them till they are clear; put them into a jar, lay brandy paper over them, tie them down, and keep in a dry place. A little raspberry juice is an improvement.

Cherry Jam.—Pick and stone 4 lbs. of May-duke cherries; press them through a sieve; then boil together half a pint of red currant or raspberry juice, and ¾ lb. of white sugar, put the cherries into them while boiling; add 1 lb. of fine white sugar. Boil quickly 35 minutes, jar, and cover well.

Cherry Marmalade.—Take some very ripe cherries; cut off the stalks and take out the stones; crush them and boil them well; put them into a hand sieve, and force them through with a spatula, till the whole is pressed through and nothing remains but the skins; put it again upon the fire to dry; when reduced to half weigh it, and add an equal weight of sugar; boil again; and when it threads between the fingers, it is finished.

How to Preserve Currants for Tarts.—Let the currants be ripe, dry and well picked. To every 1¼ lbs. of currants put 1 lb. of sugar into a preserving pan with as much juice of currants as will dissolve it; when it boils skim it, and put in the currans; boil till clear; jar, and put brandy-paper over; tie down; keep in a dry place.

How to Preserve Grapes.—Into an air-tight cask put a layer of bran dried in an oven; upon this place a layer of grapes, well dried, and not quite ripe, and so on alternately till the barrel is filled; end with bran, and close air-tight; they will keep 9 or 10 months. To restore them to their original freshness, cut the end off each bunch stalk, and put into wine, like flowers. Or,

Bunches of grapes may be preserved through winter by inserting the end of the stem into a potato. The bunches should be laid on dry straw, and turned occasionally.

How to Preserve Green Gages.—Choose the largest when they begin to soften; split them without paring; strew upon them part of the sugar. Blanch the kernels with a sharp knife. Next day pour the syrup from the fruit, and boil it with the other sugar six or eight minutes gently; skim and add the plums and kernels. Simmer

till clear, taking off the scum; put the fruit singly into small pots, and pour the syrup and kernels to it. To candy it, do not add the syrup, but observe the directions given for candying fruit; some may be done each way.

Green Gage Jam.—Peel and take out the stones. To 1 lb. of pulp put ¾ lb. loaf sugar; boil half an hour; add lemon juice.

Transparently Beautiful Marmalade.—Take 3 lbs. bitter oranges; pare them as you would potatoes; cut the skin into fine shreds, and put them into a muslin bag; quarter all the oranges; press out the juice. Boil the pulp and shreds in three quarts of water 2½ hours, down to three pints; strain through a hair sieve. Then put six pounds of sugar to the liquid, the juice and the shreds, the outside of two lemons grated, and the insides squeezed in; add three cents worth of isinglass. Simmer altogether slowly for 15 or 20 minutes.

Tomato Marmalade.—Take ripe tomatoes in the height of the season; weigh them, and to every pound of tomatoes add one pound of sugar. Put the tomatoes into a large pan or small tub, and scald them with boiling water, so as to make the skin peel off easily; When you have entirely removed the skin, put the tomatoes (without any water) into a preserving kettle, wash them, and add the sugar, with one ounce of powdered ginger to every three pounds of fruit, and the juice of two lemons, the grated rind of three always to every three pounds of fruit. Stir up the whole together, and set it over a moderate fire. Boil it gently for two or three hours; till the whole becomes a thick, smooth mass, skimming it well, and stirring it to the bottom after every skimming. When done, put it warm into jars, and cover tightly. This will be found a very fine sweetmeat.

How to Preserve Green Peas.—Shell, and put them into a kettle of water when it boils; give them two or three warms only, and pour them in a colander. Drain, and turn them out on a cloth, and then on another to dry perfectly. When dry bottle them in wide mouthed bottles; leaving only room to pour clarified mutton suet upon them an inch thick, and for the cork. Rosin it down; and keep in the cellar, or in the earth, as directed for gooseberries. When they are to be used, boil them till tender, with a bit of butter, a spoonful of sugar, and a bit of mint.

How to Preserve Green Peas for Winter Use.—Carefully shell the peas; then place them in the canister, not too large ones; put in a small piece of alum, about the size of a horse-bean to a pint of peas. When the canister is full of peas, fill up the interstices with water, and solder on the lid perfectly air-tight, and boil the canisters for about twenty minutes; then remove them to a cool place, and by the time of January they will be found but little inferior to fresh, new-gathered peas. Bottling is not so good; at least, we have not found it so; for the air gets in, the liquid turns sour, and the peas acquire a bad taste.

How to Keep Preserves.—Apply the white of an egg, with a brush, to a single thickness of white tissue paper, with which covers the jars, lapping over an inch or two. It will require no tying, as it will become, when dry, inconceivably tight and strong, and impervious to the air.

Quinces for the Tea-table.—Bake ripe quinces thoroughly; when cold, strip off the skins, place them in a glass dish, and sprinkle with white sugar, and serve them with cream. They make a fine looking dish for the tea-table, and a more luscious and inexpensive one than the same fruit made into sweetmeats. Those who once taste the fruit thus prepared, will probably desire to store away a few bushels in the fall to use in the above manner.

Pickled Pears.—Three pounds of sugar to a pint of vinegar, spice in a bag and boil, then cook the pears in the vinegar till done through.

Boiled Pears.—Boil pears in water till soft, then add one pound of sugar to three pounds of fruit.

Pickled Citron.—One quart vinegar, two pounds sugar, cloves and cinnamon each one tablespoon, boil the citron tender in water, take them out and drain, then put them in the syrup and cook till done.

How to Preserve Raspberries.—Take raspberries that are not too ripe, and put them to their weight in sugar, with a little water. Boil softly, and do not break them; when they are clear, take them up, and boil the syrup till it be thick enough; then put them in again, and when they are cold, put them in glasses or jars.

Raspberry Jam.—One pound sugar to four pounds fruit, with a few currants.

Spiced Currants.—Six pounds currants, four pounds sugar, two tablespoons cloves and two of cinnamon, and one pint of vinegar; boil two hours until quite thick.

Stewed Pears—Pare and halve or quarter a dozen pears, according to their size; carefully remove the cores, but leave the sloths on. Place them in a clean baking-jar, with a closely fitting lid; add to them the rind of one lemon, cut in strips, and the juice of half a lemon, six cloves, and whole allspice, according to discretion. Put in just enough water to cover the whole, and allow half a pound of loaf-sugar to every pint. Cover down close, and bake in a very cool oven for five hours, or stew them very gently in a lined saucepan from three to four hours. When done, lift them out on a glass dish without breaking them; boil up the syrup quickly for two or three minutes; let it cool a little, and pour it over the pears. A little cochineal greatly enhances the appearance of the fruit; you may add a few drops of prepared cochineal; and a little port wine is often used, and much improves the flavor.

How to Preserve Whole Strawberries—Take equal weights of the fruit and refined sugar, lay the former in a large dish, and sprinkle half the sugar in fine powder over, give a gentle shake to the dish that the sugar may touch the whole of the fruit; next day make a thin syrup with the remainder of the sugar, and instead of water allow one pint of red currant juice to every pound of strawberries; in this simmer them until sufficiently jellied. Choose the largest scarlets, or others when not dead ripe.

How to Preserve Strawberries in Wine—Put a quantity of the finest large strawberries into a gooseberry-bottle, and strew in three large spoonfuls of fine sugar; fill up with Madeira wine or fine sherry.

Preserved Tomatoes—One pound of sugar to one pound of ripe tomatoes boiled down; flavor with lemon.

. . . HOW TO BOIL, BAKE AND STEAM

——————— PUDDINGS . .

Amber Pudding—Put a pound of butter into a saucepan, with three quarters of a pound of loaf sugar finely powdered; melt the butter, and mix well with it; then add the yolks of fifteen eggs well beaten, and as much fresh candied orange as will add color and flavor to it, being first beaten to a fine paste. Line the dish with paste for turning out; and when filled with the above, lay a crust over, as you would a pie, and bake in a slow oven. It is as good cold as hot.

Baked Apple Pudding—Pare and quarter four large apples; boil them tender with the rind of a lemon, in so little water, that when done, none may remain; beat them quite fine in a mortar; add the crumbs of a small roll, four ounces of butter melted, the yolks of five, and whites of three eggs, juice of half a lemon, and sugar to taste; beat all together, and lay it in a dish with paste to turn out.

Boiled Apple Pudding—Suet, 5 ozs.; flour, 8 ozs.; chop the suet very fine, and roll it into the flour. Make it into a light paste with water. Roll out. Pare and core 8 good sized apples; slice them; put them on the paste, and scatter upon them ½ lb. of sugar; draw the paste round the apples, and boil two hours or more, in a well floured cloth. Serve with melted butter sweetened.

Swiss Apple Pudding—Butter a deep dish; put into it a layer of bread crumbs; then a layer of finely chopped suet; a thick layer of finely chopped apples, and a thick layer of sugar. Repeat from the first layer till the dish is full, the last layer to be finger biscuits soaked in milk. Cover it till nearly enough; then uncover, till the top is nicely browned. Flavor with cinnamon, nutmeg, etc., as you please. Bake from 30 to 40 minutes.

Apple and Sago Pudding—Boil a cup of sago in boiling water with a little cinnamon, a cup of sugar, lemon flavoring; cut apples in thin slices, mix them with the sago; after it is well boiled add a small piece of butter; pour into a pudding dish and bake half an hour.

Apple Pudding—Pare and stew three pints of apples, mash them, and add four eggs, a quarter of a pound of butter, sugar and nutmeg, or grated lemon. Bake it on a short crust.

Apple Potatoe Pudding.—Six potatoes boiled and mashed fine, add a little salt and piece of butter, size of an egg, roll this out with a little flour, enough to make a good pastry crust which is for the outside of the dumpling, into this put peeled and chopped apples, roll up like any apple dumpling, steam one hour, eat hot with liquid sauce.

Arrow-root Pudding.—Take 2 teacupfuls of arrow-root, and mix it with half a pint of cold milk; boil another half pint of milk, flavoring it with cinnamon, nutmeg or lemon peel, stir the arrowroot and milk into the boiling milk. When cold, add the yolks of 3 eggs beaten into 3 ozs. of sugar. Then add the whites beaten to a stiff broth, and bake in a buttered dish an hour. Ornament the tops with sweetmeats, or citron sliced.

Aunt Nelly's Pudding—Half a pound of flour half pound of treacle, six ounces of chopped suet, the juice and peel of one lemon, 4 tablespoonfuls of cream, two or three eggs. Mix and beat all together. Boil in a basin (previously well buttered) four hours.—For sauce, melted butter, a wine-glassful of sherry, and two or three tablespoonfuls of apricot jam.

Baked Indian Pudding.—Two quarts sweet milk; 1 pint New Orleans molasses; 1 pint Indian meal; 1 tablespoonful butter; nutmeg or cinnamon. Boil the milk; pour it over the meal and molasses; add salt and spice; bake three hours. This is a large family pudding.

Batter, to be used with all Sorts of Roasting Meat.—Melt good butter; put to it three eggs, with the whites well beaten up, and warm them together, stirring them continually. With this you may baste any roasting meat, and then sprinkle bread crumbs thereon; and so continue to make a crust as thick as you please.

Batter, for Frying Fruit, Vegetables, etc.—Cut four ounces of fresh butter into small pieces, pour on it half a pint of barley water, and when dissolved, add a pint of cold water; mix by degrees with a pound of fine dry flour, and a small pinch of salt. Just before it is used, stir into it the whites of two eggs beaten to a solid froth; use quickly, that the batter may be light.

Beef Steak Pudding.—Take some fine rump steaks; roll them with fat between; and if you approve a little shred onion. Lay a paste of suet in a basin, and put in the chopped steaks; cover the basin with a suet paste, and pinch the edges to keep the gravy in. Cover with a cloth tied close, let the pudding boil slowly for two hours.

Baked Beef Steak Pudding.—Make a batter of milk, two eggs and flour, or, which is much better, potatoes boiled and mashed through a colander; lay a little of it at the bottom of the dish; then put in the steaks very well seasoned; pour the remainder of the batter over them, and bake it.

Beef Steak Pudding.—Prepare a good suet crust, and line a cake-tin with it; put in layers of steak with onions, tomatoes, and mushrooms, chopped fine, a seasoning of pepper, salt and cayenne, and half a cup of water before you close it. Bake from an hour and a half to two hours, according to the size of the pudding and serve very hot.

Black Cap Pudding.—Make a batter with milk, flour and eggs; butter a basin; pour in the batter, and 5 or 6 ounces of well-cleaned currants. Cover it with a cloth well floured, and tie the cloth very tight. Boil nearly one hour. The currants will have settled to the bottom; therefore dish it bottom upwards. Serve with sweet sauce and a little rum.

Oswego Blanc Mange.—Four tablespoonfuls or three ounces of Oswego prepared corn to one quart of milk. Dissolve the corn to some of the milk. Put into the remainder of the milk four ounces of sugar, a little salt, a piece of lemon rind, or cinnamon stick, and heat to *near* boiling. Then add the mixed corn, and boil (stirring it briskly) four minutes; take out the rind, and pour into a mold or cup, and keep until cold. When turned out, pour round it any kind of stewed or preserved fruits, or a sauce of milk and sugar.

Nice Blanc-Mange.—Swell four ounces of rice in water; drain and boil it to a mash in good milk, with sugar, a bit of lemon peel, and a stick of cinnamon. Take care it does not burn, and when quite soft pour it into cups, or into a shape dipped into cold water. When cold turn it out, garnish with currant jelly, or any red preserved fruit. Serve with cream or plain custard.

Boiled Batter Pudding.—Three eggs, one ounce of butter, one pint of milk, three tablespoonfuls of flour, a little salt. Put the flour into a basin, and add sufficient milk to moisten it; carefully rub down all the lumps with a spoon, then pour in the remainder of the milk, and stir in the butter, which should be previously melted; keep beating the mixture, add the eggs and a pinch of salt, and when the batter is quite smooth, put into a well-buttered basin, tie it down very tightly, and put it into boiling water; move the basin about for a few minutes after it is put into the water, to prevent the flour settling in any part, and boil for one hour and a quarter. This pudding may also be boiled in a floured cloth that has been wetted in hot water; it will then take a few minutes less than when boiled in a basin. Send these puddings very quickly to table, and serve with sweet sauce, wine-sauce, stewed fruit, or jam of any kind; when the latter is used, a little of it may be placed round the dish in small quantities, as a garnish.

Bread and Butter Pudding.—Butter a dish well, lay in a few slices of bread and butter, boil one pint of milk, pour out over two eggs well beaten, and then over the bread and butter, bake over half hour.

Simple Bread Pudding.—Take the crumbs of a stale roll, pour over it one pint of boiling milk, and set it by to cool. When quite cold, beat it up very fine with two ounces of butter, sifted sugar sufficient to sweeten it; grate in half a nutmeg, and add a pound of well-washed currants, beat up four eggs separately, and then mix them up with the rest, adding, if desired, a few strips of candied orange peel. All the ingredients must be beaten up together for about half an hour, as the lightness of the pudding depends upon that. Tie it up in a cloth, and boil for an hour. When it is dished, pour a little white wine sauce over the top.

Christmas Plum Pudding.—Suet, chopped small, six ounces; raisins, stoned, etc., eight ounces; bread crumbs, six ounces; three eggs, a wine glass of brandy, a little nutmeg and cinnamon pounded as fine as possible, half a teaspoonful of salt, rather less than half pint milk, fine sugar, four ounces; candied lemon, one ounce; citron half an ounce. Beat the eggs and spice well together; mix the milk by degrees, then the rest of the ingredients. Dip a fine, close, linen cloth into boiling water, and put in a sieve (hair), flour it a little, and tie it up close. Put the pudding into a saucepan containing six quarts of boiling water; keep a kettle of boiling water alongside, and fill up as it wastes. Be sure to keep it boiling at least six hours. Serve with any sauce; or arrow-root with brandy.

Christmas Pudding.—Suet 1½ lbs., minced small; currants, 1½ lbs., raisins, stoned, ¼ lb.; sugar, 1 lb.; ten eggs, a grated nutmeg; 2 ozs. citron and lemon peel; 1 oz. of mixed spice, a teaspoonful of grated ginger, ½ lb. of bread crumbs, ½ lb. of flour, 1 pint of milk, and a wine glassful of brandy. Beat first the eggs, add half the milk, beat all together, and gradually stir in all the milk, then the suet, fruit, etc., and as much milk to mix it very thick. Boil in a cloth six or seven hours.

Cottage Pudding.—One pint sifted flour, three tablespoons melted butter, 2 eggs, one cup sweet milk, two teaspoonfuls cream tartar, one teaspoon soda, mix and bake.

Cream Pudding.—Cream, 1 pint; the yolks of seven eggs, seven tablespoonfuls of flour, 2 tablespoonfuls of sugar, salt, and a small bit of soda. Rub the cream with the eggs and flour; add the rest, the milk last, just before baking, and pour the whole into the pudding dish. Serve with sauce of wine, sugar, butter, flavored as you like.

Crumb Pudding.—The yolks and whites of three eggs, beaten separately, one ounce moist sugar, and sufficient bread crumbs to make it into a thick but not stiff mixture; a little powdered cinnamon. Beat all together for five minutes, and bake in a buttered tin. When baked, turn it out of the tin, pour two glasses of boiling wine over it, and serve. Cherries, either fresh or preserved, are very nice mixed in the pudding.

Damson Pudding.—Four or five tablespoonfuls of flour, three eggs beaten, a pint of milk, made into batter. Stone 1½ lbs., of damsons, put them and 6 ozs. of sugar into the batter, and boil in a buttered basin for one hour and a half.

Egg Pudding.—It is made chiefly of eggs. It is nice made thus:—Beat well seven eggs; mix well with 2 ozs. of flour, pint and a half of milk, a little salt; flavor with nutmeg, lemon juice, and orange-flour water. Boil 1¼ hours in a floured cloth. Serve with wine sauce sweetened.

Excellent Family Plum Pudding.—Grate three-quarters of a pound of a stale loaf, leaving out the crusts; chop very fine three-quarters of a pound of firm beef suet (if you wish your pudding less rich, half a pound will do); mix well together with a quarter of a pound of flour; then add a pound of currants, well washed and well dried; half a pound of raisins, stoned, and the peel of a lemon, very finely shred and cut; four ounces of candied peel, either lemon, orange or citron, or all mingled (do not cut your peel too small or its flavor is lost); six ounces of sugar, a small teaspoonful of salt, three eggs, well beaten; mix all thoroughly together with as much milk as suffices to bring the pudding to a proper consistency, grate in a small nutmeg, and again stir the mixture vigorously. If you choose, add a small glass of brandy. Butter your mold or basin, which you must be sure to fill quite full, or the water will get in and spoil your handiwork; have your pudding cloth scrupulously clean and sweet, and of a proper thickness; tie down securely, and boil for seven or even eight hours.

Extra Pudding.—Cut light bread into thin slices. Form into the shape of a pudding in a dish. Then add a layer of any preserve, then a slice of bread, and repeat till the dish is full. Beat four or five eggs, and mix well with a pint of milk; then pour it over the bread and preserve, having previously dusted the same with a coating of rice flour. Boil twenty-five minutes.

Fig Pudding.—Procure one pound of good figs, and chop them very fine, and also a quarter of a pound of suet, likewise chopped as fine as possible; dust them both with a little flour as you proceed—it helps to bind the pudding together; then take one pound of fine bread crumbs, and not quite a quarter of a pound of sugar; beat two eggs in a teacupful of milk, and mix all well together. Boil four hours. If you choose, serve it with wine or brandy sauce, and ornament your pudding with blanched almonds. Simply cooked, however, it is better where there are children, with whom it is generally a favorite. We forgot to say, flavor with a little allspice or nutmeg, as you like; but add the spice before the milk and eggs.

Gelatine Pudding.—Half box gelatine dissolved in a large half pint boiling water, when cold stir in two teacups sugar, the juice of three lemons, the whites of four eggs beaten to a froth, put this in a mold to get stiff, and with the yolks of these four eggs, and a quart of milk make boiled custard, flavor with vanilla, when cold pour the custard round the mold in same dish.

Gooseberry Pudding.—One quart of scalded gooseberries; when cold rub them smooth with the back of a spoon. Take six tablespoonfuls of the pulp, half a pound of sugar, quarter of a pound of melted butter, six eggs, the rind of two lemons, a handful of grated bread, two tablespoonfuls of brandy. Half an hour will bake it.

Ground Rice Pudding.—Boil one pint of milk with a little piece of lemon peel, mix quarter pound of rice, ground, with half pint milk, two ounces sugar, one ounce butter, add these to the boiling milk. Keep stirring, take it off the fire, break in two eggs, keep stirring, butter a pie dish, pour in the mixture and bake until set.

Ice Pudding.—Put one quart of milk in a stew pan with half pound of white sugar, and stick of vanilla, boil it ten minutes, mix the yolks of ten eggs with a gill of cream, pour in the milk, then put it back again into the stew pan, and stir till it thickens (do not let it boil), strain it into a basin and leave it to cool. Take twelve pounds of ice, add two pounds of salt, mix together, cover the bottom of a pail, place the ice pot in it and build it around with the ice and salt, this done pour the cream into the pot, put on the cover, and do not cease turning till the cream is thick, the mold should be cold, pour in the cream, 3 or 4 pieces of white paper, wetted with cold water, are placed on it before the cover is placed on. Cover with ice till wanted, dip in cold water and turn out, fruit may be put in when put in the mold.

Indian Pudding.—Indian meal, a cupful, a little salt, butter, 1 oz.; molasses 3 ozs., 2 teaspoonfuls of ginger, or cinnamon. Put into a quart of boiling milk. Mix a cup of cold water with it; bake in a buttered dish 50 minutes.

Kidney Pudding.—If kidney, split and soak it, and season that or the meat. Make a paste of suet, flour and milk; roll it, and line a basin with some; put the kidney or steak in, cover with paste, and pinch round the edge. Cover with a cloth and boil a considerable time.

Lemon Dumplings.—Two tablespoonfuls of flour; bread crumbs, ½ lb.; beef suet, 6 ozs.; the grated rind of a large lemon, sugar, pounded, 4 ozs.; 4 eggs well beaten, and strained, and the juice of three lemons strained. Make into dumplings, and boil in a cloth one hour.

Lemon Pudding.—Three tablespoons powdered crackers, eight tablespoons sugar, six eggs, one quart milk, butter size of an egg, the juice of one lemon and grated rind. Stir it first when put in oven.

Macaroni Pudding.—Take an equal quantity of ham and chicken, mince fine, half the quantity of macaroni which must be boiled tender in broth, two eggs beaten, one ounce butter, cayenne pepper and salt to taste, all these ingredients to be mixed thoroughly together, put in molds and boil two hours.

Marrow Pudding.—Pour a pint of cream boiling hot on the crumbs of a penny loaf, or French roll; cut 1 lb. of beef marrow very thin; beat 4 eggs well; add a glass of brandy, with sugar and nutmeg to taste, and mix all well together. It may be either boiled or baked 40 or 50 minutes; cut 2 ozs. of citron very thin, and stick them all over it when you dish it up.

Another way.—Blanch ½ lb. of almonds; put them in cold water all night; next day beat them in a mortar very fine, with orange or rose water. Take the crumbs of a penny loaf, and pour on the whole a pint of boiling cream; while it is cooling, beat the yolks of four eggs, and two whites, 15 minutes; a little sugar and grated nutmeg to your palate. Shred the marrow of the bones, and mix all well together, with a little candied orange cut small; bake, etc.

Meat and Potato Pudding.—Boil some mealy potatoes till ready to crumble to pieces; drain; mash them very smooth. Make them into a thickish batter with an egg or two, and milk, placing a layer of steaks or chops well-seasoned with salt and pepper at the bottom of the baking dish; cover with a layer of batter, and so alternately, till the dish is full, ending with batter at the top. Butter the dish to prevent sticking or burning. Bake of a fine brown color.

Nesselrode Pudding.—Prepare a custard of one pint of cream, half a pint of milk, the yolks of six eggs, half a stick of vanilla, one ounce of sweet almonds, pounded, and half a pound of sugar; put them in a stewpan over a slow fire, and stir until the proper consistence, being careful not to let it boil; when cold, add a wine-glass of brandy; partially freeze, and add two ounces of rasins and half a pound of preserved fruits, cut small. Mix well, and mold. (Basket shape generally used.)

Potato Pudding.—Take ½ lb. of boiled potatoes, 2 ozs. of butter, the yolks and whites of two eggs, a quarter of a pint of cream, one spoonful of white wine, a morsel of salt, the juice and rind of a lemon; beat all to a froth; sugar to taste. A crust or not, as you like. Bake it. If wanted richer, put 3 ozs. more butter, sweetmeats and almonds, and another egg.

Prince of Wales Pudding.—Chop four ounces of apples, the same quantity of bread crumbs, suet, and currants, well washed and picked; two ounces of candied lemon, orange, and citron, chopped fine; five ounces pounded loaf sugar; half a nutmeg, grated. Mix all together with four eggs. Butter well and flour a tin, put in the mixture, and place a buttered paper on the top, and a cloth over the paper. If you steam it the paper is sufficient. It will take two hours boiling. When you dish it, stick cut blanched almonds on it, and serve with wine sauce.

Pudding.—One cup sugar, half cup milk, one egg, two tablespoons melted butter, two cups flour, two teaspoons baking powder, a little nutmeg, bake in a dish and when sent to the table, put raspberry jam under same with wine sauce.

Baked Pudding.—Three tablespoonfuls of Oswego Prepared Corn to one quart of milk. Prepare, and cook the same as Blanc-Mange. After it is cool, stir up with it *thoroughly* two or three eggs well beaten, and bake half an hour. It is very good.

Boiled Pudding.—Three tablespoonfuls of Oswego Prepared Corn to one quart of milk. Dissolve the corn in some of the milk, and mix with it two or three eggs, well beaten, and a little salt. Heat the remainder of the milk to near boiling, add the above preparation, and boil four minutes, stirring it briskly. To be eaten warm with a sauce. It is delicious.

Queen Pudding.—One pint of bread crumbs, one quart milk, one cup sugar, yolks four eggs, a little butter, bake half an hour, then put over the top a layer of fruit, then white of eggs beaten to a froth with sugar; to be eaten cold with cream.

Plain Rice Pudding.—Wash and pick some rice; throw among it some pimento finely pounded, but not much; tie the rice in a cloth and leave plenty of room for it to swell. When done, eat it with butter and sugar, or milk. Put lemon peel if you please.

It is very good without spice, and eaten with salt and butter.

ANOTHER.—Put into a very deep pan half a pound of rice washed and picked; two ounces of butter, four ounces of sugar, a few allspice pounded, and two quarts of milk. Less butter will do, or some suet. Bake in a slow oven.

Rich Rice Pudding—Boil ½ lb. of rice in water, with a bit of salt, till quite tender; drain it dry; mix it with the yolks and whites of four eggs, a quarter of a pint of cream, with 2 ozs. of fresh butter melted in the latter; 4 ozs. of beef suet or marrow, or veal suet taken from a fillet of veal, finely shred, ¾ lb. of currants, two spoonfuls of brandy, one of peach-water, or ratafia, nutmeg, and a grated lemon peel. When well mixed, put a paste round the edge, and fill the dish. Slices of candied orange, lemon, and citron, if approved. Bake in a moderate oven.

Rice Pudding with Fruit—Swell the rice with a very little milk over the fire; then mix fruit of any kind with it (currants, gooseberries, scalded, pared, and quartered apples, raisins, or black currants); put one egg into the rice to bind it; boil it well, and serve with sugar.

Roman Pudding—Oil a plain tin mold, sprinkle it with vermicelli, line it with a thin paste; have some boiled macaroni ready cut in pieces an inch long; weigh it, and take the same weight of Parmesan cheese, grated; boil a rabbit, cut off all the white meat in slices, as thin as paper, season with pepper, salt, and shalot; add cream sufficient to moisten the whole, put it into the mold, and cover it with paste; bake in a moderate oven for an hour, turn the pudding out of the mold, and serve it with a rich brown gravy.

Sago Pudding—Boil 4 ozs. of sago in water a few minutes; strain, and add milk, and boil till tender. Boil lemon peel and cinnamon in a little milk, and strain it to the sago. Put the whole into a basin; break 8 eggs; mix

it well together, and sweeten with moist sugar; add a glass of brandy, and some nutmeg; put puff paste round the rim of the dish, and butter the bottom. Bake three quarters of an hour.

Spanish Pudding—To one pint of water, put two ounces of butter, and a little salt, when it boils add as much flour as will make it the consistency of hasty pudding. Keep it well stirred, after it is taken off the fire and has stood till quite cold, beat it up with three eggs, add a little grated lemon peel and nutmeg, drop the batter with a spoon into the frying pan with boiling lard, fry quickly, put sugar over them when sent to the table.

Suet Dumplings—Shred 1 lb. of suet; mix with 1¼ lbs. flour, 2 eggs beaten separately, a little salt, and as little milk as will make it. Make it into two small balls. Boil 20 minutes. The fat of loins or necks of mutton finely shred makes a more delicate dumpling than suet.

Suet Pudding—Take six spoonfuls of flour, 1 lb. of suet, shred small, 4 eggs, a spoonful of beaten ginger, a spoonful of salt, and a quart of milk. Mix the eggs and flour with a pint of milk very thick, and with the seasoning, mix in the rest of the milk with the suet. Boil two hours.

Tapioca Pudding.—Put ¼ lb. of tapioca into a sauce pan of cold water; when it boils, strain it to a pint of new milk; boil till it soaks up all the milk, and put it out to cool. Beat the yolks of four eggs, and the whites of two, a tablespoonful of brandy, sugar, nutmeg, and 2 ounces of butter. Mix all together; put a puff paste round the dish, and send it to the oven. It is very good boiled with melted butter, wine and sugar.

Vermicelli Pudding.—Boil 4 ounces of vermicelli in a pint of new milk till soft, with a stick or two of cinnamon. Then put in half a pint of thick cream, ¼ lb. of butter, the same of sugar, and the yolks of 4 eggs. Bake without paste in an earthen dish.

Another.—Simmer 2 ounces of vermicelli in a cupful of milk till tender; flavor it with a stick or two of cinnamon or other spice. Beat up three eggs, 1 ounce of sugar, half a pint of milk and a glass of wine. Add to the vermicelli. Bake in a slow oven.

HOW TO PUT UP PICKLES
AND MAKE CATSUPS

How to Pickle Beet Roots.—Beet roots are a very pretty garnish for made dishes, and are thus pickled. Boil the roots till they are tender, then take off the skins, cut them in slices, gimp them in the shape of wheels, or what form you please, and put them into a jar. Take as much vinegar as you think will cover them, and boil it with a a little mace, a race of ginger sliced, and a few slices of horseradish. Pour it hot upon your roots and tie them down.

Chow-Chow.—Two quarts of small white onions, two quarts of gherkins, two quarts of string beans, two small cauliflowers, half a dozen ripe, red peppers, one-half pound mustard seed, one-half pound whole pepper, one pound ground mustard, and, as there is nothing so adulterated as ground mustard, it's better to get it at the druggist's; twenty or thirty bay leaves (not bog leaves, as some one of the ladies facetiously remarked), and two quarts of good cider, or wine vinegar. Peel the onions, halve the cucumbers, string the beans, and cut in pieces the cauliflower. Put all in a wooden tray, and sprinkle well with salt. In the morning wash and drain thoroughly, and put all into the cold vinegar, except the red peppers. Let boil twenty minutes slowly, frequently turning over. Have wax melted in a deepish dish, and, as you fill and cork, dip into the wax. The peppers you can put in to show to the best advantage. If you have over six jars full, it's good to put the rest in a jar and eat from it for every dinner. Some add a little turmeric for the yellow color.

Corn, Green, Pickling.—When the corn is a little past the tenderest roasting ear state, pull it, take off one thickness of the husk, tie the rest of the husk down at the silk end loosely, place the ears in a clean cask compactly together, and put on a brine to cover them of about two-thirds the strength of meat pickle. When ready to use in winter, soak in cold water over night, and if this does not appear sufficient, change the water and freshen still more. Corn, prepared in this way, is excellent, very much resembling fresh corn from the stalk.

Indian Pickle.—One gallon of the best vinegar, quarter of a pound of bruised ginger, quarter of a pound of shalots, quarter of a pound of flour of mustard, quarter of a pound of salt, two ounces of mustard seed, two ounces of turmeric, one ounce of black pepper, ground fine, one ounce of cayenne. Mix all together, and put in cauliflower sprigs, radish pods, French beans, white cabbage, cucumber, onions, or any other vegetable; stir it well two or three days after any fresh vegetable is added, and wipe the vegetable with a dry cloth. The vinegar should not be boiled.

How to Pickle Mushrooms.—Buttons must be rubbed with a bit of flannel and salt; and from the larger take out the *red* inside, for when they are black they will not do, being too old. Throw a little salt over, and put them into a stewpan with some mace and pepper; as the liquor comes out, shake them well, and keep them over a gentle fire till all of it be dried into them again; then put as much vinegar into the pan as will cover them, give it one warm, and turn all into a glass or stone jar. They will keep two years, and are delicious.

Pickle Sauce.—Slice green tomatoes, onions, cabbage, cucumbers, and green peppers. Let all stand covered with salt over night. Wash, drain and chop fine. Be careful to keep as dry as possible. To two quarts of the hash, add four tablespoons of American mustard seed and two of English; two tablespoonfuls ground allspice, one of ground cloves, two teaspoonfuls of ground black pepper, one teaspoonful of celery seed. Cover with sharp vinegar, and boil slowly an hour. Put away in stone jar, and eat when wanted.

Pickled Eggs.—At the season of the year when eggs are plentiful, boil some four or six dozen in a capacious saucepan, until they become quite hard. Then, after carefully removing the shells, lay them in large-mouthed jars, and pour over them scalding vinegar, well seasoned with whole pepper, allspice, a few races of ginger, and a few cloves or garlic. When cold, bung down closely, and in a month they are fit for use. Where eggs are plentiful, the above pickle is by no means expensive, and is a relishing accompaniment to cold meat.

How to Pickle Red Cabbage.—Slice it into a colander, and sprinkle each layer with salt; let it drain two days, then put it into a jar, with boiling vinegar enough to cover it, and put in a few slices of beet-root. Observe to choose the purple red-cabbage. Those who like the flavor of spice will boil some pepper-corns, mustard-seed, or other spice, *whole*, with the vinegar. Califlower in branches, and thrown in after being salted, will color a beautiful red.

ANOTHER.—Choose a sound large cabbage; shred it finely, and sprinkle it with salt, and let it stand in a dish for a day and night. Then boil vinegar (from a pint) with ginger, cloves, and cayenne pepper. Put the cabbage into jars, and pour the liquor upon it when cold.

Spiced Tomatoes.—Eight pounds tomatoes, four pounds of sugar, one quart vinegar, one tablespoon each of cloves, cinnamon and allspice, make a syrup of the sugar and vinegar. Tie the spice in a bag and put in syrup, take the skins off the tomatoes, and put them in the syrup, when scalded through skim them out and cook away one-half, leave the spices in, then put in your tomatoes again and boil until the syrup is thick.

Tomato Lilly.—Prepare one peck of green tomatoes by slicing and laying them in a jar over night, with a little salt, than chop them and cook in water until you think them sufficiently tender then take them up in a colander and drain nicely, then take two large cabbages, chop and cook same as tomatoes, then chop six green peppers and add one quart vinegar, put all in kettle together and boil a short time; add fresh vinegar and spice with one ounce each cinnamon and cloves, one pound sugar and half pint molasses. Onions can be used instead of cabbage if preferred.

How to Pickle Walnuts.—When a pin will go into them, put a brine of salt and water boiled, and strong enough to bear an egg, being quite cold first. Let them soak six days; then change the brine, let them stand six more; then drain, and pour over them in a jar a pickle of the best vinegar, with plenty of pepper, pimento, ginger, mace, cloves, mustard-seed and horseradish; all boiled together, but cold. To every hundred of walnuts put six spoonfuls of mustard-seed, and two or three heads of garlic or shalot, but the latter is least strong. In this way they will be good for several years, if closely covered. They will not be fit to eat under six months. This pickle makes good ketchup.

A Good Ketchup.—Boil one bushel of tomatoes until soft enough to rub through a sieve. Then add to the liquid a half gallon of vinegar, 1½ pints salt, 2 ounces of cloves, ¼ pound allspice, 3 ounces good cayenne pepper, five heads of garlic, skinned and separated, 1 pound of sugar. Boil slowly until reduced to one-half. It takes about one day. Set away for a week, boil over once, and, if too thick, thin with vinegar; bottle and seal as for chow-chow.

How to Keep Ketchup Twenty Years.—Take a gallon of strong stale beer, 1 lb. of anchovies, washed from the pickle; 1 lb. of shalots, ½ oz. of mace, ½ oz. of cloves, ¼ oz. whole pepper, ½ oz. of ginger, 2 quarts of large mushroom flaps, rubbed to pieces; cover all close, and simmer till it is half wasted, strain, cool, then bottle. A spoonful of this ketchup is sufficient for a pint of melted butter.

Mushroom Ketchup.—Sprinkle mushroom flaps, gathered in September, with common salt, stir them occasionally for two or three days; then lightly squeeze out the juice, and add to each gallon bruised cloves and mustard seed, of each, half an ounce; bruised allspice, black pepper, and ginger, of each, one ounce; gently heat to the boiling point in a covered vessel, macerate for fourteen days, and strain; should it exhibit any indication of change in a few weeks, bring it again to the boiling point, with a little more spice.

Oyster Ketchup:—Beard the oysters; boil them up in their liquor; strain, and pound them in a mortar; boil the beards in spring water, and strain it to the first oyster liquor; boil the pounded oysters in the mixed liquors, with beaten mace and pepper. Some add a very little mushroom ketchup, vinegar, or lemon-juice; but the less the natural flavor is overpowered the better; only spice is necessary for its preservation. This oyster ketchup will keep perfectly good longer than oysters are ever out of season.

Tomato Ketchup.—Put them over the fire crushing each one as you drop it into the pot; let them boil five minutes; take them off, strain through a colander, and then through a sieve, get them over the fire again as soon as possible, and boil down two-thirds, when boiled down add to every gallon of this liquid one ounce of cayenne pepper, one ounce of black pepper, one pint vinegar, four ounces each of cinnamon and mace, two spoonfuls salt.

Very Fine Walnut Ketchup.—Boil a gallon of the expressed juice of green tender walnuts, and skim it well; then put in 2 lbs. of anchovies, bones and liquor, 2 lbs. shalots, 1 oz. each of cloves, mace, pepper, and one clove of garlic. Let all simmer till the shalots sink; then put the liquor into a pan till cold; bottle and divide the spice to each. Cork closely, and tie a bladder over. It will keep twenty years, but is not good the first. Be very careful to express the juice at home; for it is rarely unadulterated, if bought.

HOW TO ROAST, BOIL, OR BROIL.
POULTRY

How to Roast Chickens.—Pluck carefully, draw and truss them, and put them to a good fire; singe, dust, and baste them with butter. Cover the breast with a sheet of buttered paper; remove it ten minutes before it is enough; that it may brown. A chicken will take 15 to 20 minutes. Serve with butter and parsley.

How to Boil Chickens.—Fasten the wings and legs to the body by threads tied round. Steep them in skim milk two hours. Then put them in cold water, and boil over a slow fire. Skim clean. Serve with white sauce or melted butter sauce, or parsley and butter.—Or melt 1 oz. of butter in a cupful of milk; add to it the yolk of an egg beat up with a little flour and cream; heat over the fire, stirring well.

Geese (a la mode).—Skin and bone the goose; boil and peel a dried tongue, also a fowl; season with pepper, salt and mace, and then roll it round the tongue; season the goose in the same way, and lay the fowl and tongue on the goose, with slices of ham between them. Beef marrow rolled between the fowl and the goose, will greatly enrich it. Put it all together in a pan, with two quarts of beef gravy, the bones of the goose and fowl, sweet herbs and onion; cover close, and stew an hour slowly; take up the goose; skim off the fat, strain, and put in a glassful of good port wine, two tablespoonfuls of ketchup, a veal sweetbread cut small, some mushrooms, a piece of butter rolled in flour, pepper and salt; stew the goose half an hour longer; take up and pour the ragout over it. Garnish with lemon.

How to Roast Pigeons.—Take a little pepper and salt, a piece of butter, and parsley cut small; mix and put the mixture into the bellies of the pigeons, tying the necks tight; take another string; fasten one end of it to their legs and rumps, and the other to a hanging spit, basting them with butter; when done, lay them in a dish, and they will swim with gravy.

How to Boil Pigeons.—Wash clean; chop some parsley small; mix it with crumbs of bread, pepper, salt and a bit of butter; stuff the pigeons, and boil 15 minutes in some mutton broth or gravy. Boil some rice soft in milk; when it begins to thicken, beat the yolks of two or three eggs, with two or three spoonfuls of cream,

and a little nutmeg; mix well with a bit of butter rolled in flour.

How to Broil Pigeons.—After cleaning, split the backs, pepper and salt them, and broil them very nicely; pour over them either stewed or pickled mushrooms, in melted butter, and serve as hot as possible.

Scalloped Cold Chickens.—Mince the meat very small, and set it over the fire, with a scrape of nutmeg, a little pepper and salt, and a little cream, for a few minutes. put it into the scallop shells, and fill them with crumbs of bread, over which put some bits of butter, and brown them before the fire. Veal and ham eat well done the same way, and lightly covered with crumbs of bread, or they may be put on in little heaps.

How to Roast Turkey.—The sinews of the legs should be drawn whichever way it is dressed. The head should be twisted under the wing; and in drawing it, take care not to tear the liver, nor let the gall touch it.

Put a stuffing of sausage-meat; or, if sausages are to be served in a dish a bread stuffing. As this makes a large addition to the size of the bird, observe that the heat of the fire is constantly to that part; for the breast is often not done enough. A little strip of paper should be put on the bone to hinder it from scorching while the other parts roast. Baste well and froth it up. Serve with gravy in the dish, and plenty of bread-sauce in a sauce-tureen. Add a few crumbs, and a beaten egg to the stuffing of sausage-meat.

SAUCES FOR MEATS, FISH, ETC.

Anchovy Sauce.—Chop one or two anchovies, without washing, put to them some flour and butter, and a little water; stir it over the fire till it boils once or twice. If the anchovies are good, they will dissolve.

Essence of Anchovies.—Take two dozen of anchovies, chop them, and without the bone, but with some of their liquor strained, add to them sixteen large spoonfuls of water; boil gently till dissolved, which will be in a few minutes—when cold, strain and bottle it.

Apple Sauce.—Pare, core, and quarter half a dozen good sized apples, and throw them into cold water to preserve their whiteness. Boil them in a saucepan till they are soft enough to mash—it is impossible to specify any particular time, as some apples cook much more speedily than others. When done, bruise them to a pulp, put in a piece of butter as large as a nutmeg, and sweeten them to taste. Put into saucepan only sufficient water to prevent them burning. Some persons put the apples in a stone jar placed in boiling water; there is then no danger of their catching.

Apple Sauce for Goose or Roast Pork.—Pare, core, and slice some apples, and put them in a strong jar, into a pan of water. When sufficiently boiled, bruise to a pulp, adding a little butter, and a little brown sugar.

A Substitute for Cream.—Beat up the whole of a fresh egg in a basin, and then pour boiling tea over it gradually to prevent its curdling; it is difficult from the taste, to distinguish it from rich cream.

Bechamel Sauce.—Put a few slices of ham into a stew-pan, a few mushrooms, two or three shalots, two cloves, also a bay leaf and a bit of butter. Let them stand a few hours. Add a little water, flour and milk or cream; simmer forty minutes. Scalded parsley, very fine may be added.

Bread Sauce.—Break three-quarters of a pound of stale bread into small pieces, carefully excluding any crusty and outside bits, having previously simmered till quite tender, an onion, well peeled and quartered in a pint of milk. Put the crumbs into a very clean saucepan, and, if you like the flavor, a small teaspoonful of sliced onion, chopped, or rather minced, as finely as possible. Pour over the milk, taking away the onion simmered in it, cover it up, and let it stand for an hour to soak. Then, with a fork, beat it quite smooth, and seasoned with a very little powdered mace, cayenne and salt to taste, adding one ounce of butter; give the whole a boil, stirring all the time, and it is ready to serve. A small quantity of cream added at the last moment, makes the sauce richer and smoother. Common white pepper may take the place of cayenne, a few peppercorns may be simmered in the milk, but they should be extracted before sending to table.

Bread Sauce.—Grate some old bread into a basin; pour boiling new milk over it; add an onion with five cloves stuck in it, with pepper and salt to taste. Cover it and simmer in a slow oven. When enough, take out the onion and cloves; beat it well, and add a little melted butter. The addition of cream very much improves this sauce.

Caper Sauce.—Melt some butter, chop the capers fine, boil them with the butter. An ounce of capers will be sufficient for a moderate size sauce-boat. Add, if you like, a little chopped parsley, and a little vinegar. More vinegar, a little cayenne, and essence of anchovy, make it suitable for fish.

As a substitute for capers, some use chopped pickled gherkins.

Essence of Celery.—Soak the seeds in spirits of wine or brandy; or infuse the root in the same for 24 hours, then take out, squeezing out all the liquor, and infuse more root in the same liquor to make it stronger. A few drops will flvor broth, soup, etc.

Celery Sauce.—Wash well the inside leaves of three heads of celery; cut them into slices quarter inch thick, boil for six minutes, and drain; take a tablespoonful of flour, two ounces of butter, and a teacupful of cream; beat well, and when warm, put in the celery and stir well over the fire about twelve minutes. The sauce is very goood for boiled fowl, etc.

Cocoa Sauce.—Scrape a portion of the kernel of a Cocoa nut, adding the juice of three lemons, a teaspoonful of the tincture of cayenne pepper, a teaspoonful of shallot vinegar, and half a cupful of water. Gently simmer for a few hours.

Egg Sauce.—Boil two eggs hard, half chop the whites, put in the yolks, chop them together, but not very fine, put them with ¼ lb. of good melted butter.

Egg Sauce.—Four eggs boiled twelve minutes, then lay them in fresh water, cold, pull off the shells, chop whites and yolks separately, mix them lightly, half pint melted butter, made in proportion of quarter pound of butter, to a large tablespoon flour, four of milk and hot water, add powdered mace or nutmeg, to be eaten with pork, boiled, or poultry, use chicken gravy or the water the chicken were boiled in.

Horseradish Sauce.—Perhaps a good receipt for horseradish sauce, which is so excellent with both hot and cold beef, but which we do not always see served up with either. Two tablespoonfuls of mustard, the same of vinegar, three tablespoonfuls of cream or milk and one of pounded white sugar, well beaten up together with a small quantity of grated horseradish. This is, of course, to be served up cold.

Mint Sauce.—Pick, mash and chop fine green spearmint, to two tablespoons of the minced leaves, put eight of vinegar, adding a little sugar. Serve cold.

Mint Sauce.—Wash fresh gathered mint; pick the leaves from the stalks; mince them very fine, and put them into a sauce-boat with a teaspoonful of sugar and four tablespoonfuls of vinegar. It may also be made with dried mint or with mint vinegar.

Onion Sauce.—Peel the onions, and boil them tender; squeeze the water from them, then chop them, and add to them butter that has been melted, rich and smooth, as will be hereafter directed, but with a little good milk instead of water; boil it up once, and serve it for boiled rabbits, partridge, scrag, or knuckle of veal, or roast mutton. A turnip boiled with the onions makes them milder.

Quin's Fish Sauce.—Half a pint of mushroom pickle, the same of walnut, six long anchovies pounded, six cloves of garlic, three of them pounded; half a spoonful of cayenne pepper; put them into a bottle, and shake well before using. It is also good with beefsteaks.

Sauce for Cold Partridges, Moor-Game, Etc.—Pound four anchovies and two cloves of garlic in a mortar; add oil and vinegar to the taste. Mince the meat, and put the sauce to it as wanted.

Sauce for Ducks.—Serve a rich gravy in the dish; cut the breast into slices, but don't take them off; cut a lemon, and put pepper and salt on it, then squeeze it on the breast, and pour a spoonful of gravy over before you help.

Sauce for Fowl of any Sort.—Boil some veal gravy, pepper, salt, the juice of a Seville orange and a lemon, and a quarter as much of port wine as of gravy; pour it into the dish or a boat.

Sauce for Hot or Cold Roast Beef.—Grate, or scrape very fine, some horseradish, a little made mustard, some pounded white sugar and four large spoonfuls of vinegar. Serve in a saucer.

Sauce for Salmon.—Boil a bunch of fennel and parsley chop them small, and put into it some good melted butter. Gravy sauce should be served with it; put a little brown gravy into a saucepan, with one anchovy, a teaspoonful of lemon pickle, a tablespoonful of walnut pickle, two spoonfuls of water in which the fish was boiled, a stick of horseradish, a little browning, and salt; boil them four minutes; thicken with flour and a good lump of butter, and strain through a hair sieve.

Sauce for Savoury Pies.—Take some gravy, one anchovy, a sprig of sweet herbs, an onion, and a little mushroom liquor; boil it a little, and thicken it with burnt butter, or a bit of butter rolled in flour; add a little port wine, and open the pie, and put it in. It will serve for lamb, mutton, veal or beef pies.

Sauce for a Turkey.—Open some oysters into a basin, and wash them in their own liquor, and as soon as settled pour into a saucepan; add a little white gravy, a teaspoonful of lemon pickle; thicken with flour and butter; boil it three or four minutes; add a spoonful of thick cream, and then the oysters; shake them over the fire till they are hot, but do not let them boil.

Sauce for Wild Fowl.—Simmer a teacupful of port wine, the same quantity of good meat gravy, a little shalot, a little pepper, salt, a grate of nutmeg and a bit of mace, for ten minutes; put in a bit of butter and flour, give it all one boil, and pour it through the birds. In general they are not stuffed as tame, but may be done so if liked.

French Tomato Sauce.—Cut ten or a dozen tomatoes into quarters, and put them into a saucepan, with four onions, sliced, a little parsley, thyme, a clove, and a quarter of a pound of butter; then set the saucepan on the fire, stirring occasionally for three-quarters of an hour; strain the sauce through a horse-hair sieve, and serve with the directed articles.

Tomato Sauce.—Take 12 tomatoes, very red and ripe; take off the stalks, take out the seeds, and press out the water. Put the expressed tomatoes into a stewpan, with 1½ ozs. of butter, a bay leaf, and a little thyme; put it upon a moderate fire, stir it into a pulp; put into it a good cullis, or the top of broth, which will be better. Rub it through a search, and put it into a stewpan with two spoonfuls of cullis; put in a little salt and cayenne.

ANOTHER.—Proceed as above with the seeds and water. Put them into a stewpan, with salt and cayenne, and three tablespoonfuls of beef gravy. Set them on a slow stove for an hour, or till properly melted. Strain, and add a little good stock; and simmer a few minutes.

White Sauce.—One pound of knuckle of veal, or any veal trimmings, or cold white meat, from which all brown skin has been removed; if meat has been cooked, more will be required. It is best to have a little butcher's meat fresh, even if you have plenty of cold meat in the larder; any chicken bones greatly improve the stock. This should simmer for five hours, together with a little salt, a dozen white peppercorns, one or two small onions stuck with cloves, according to taste, a slice or two of lean ham, and a little shred of celery and a carrot (if in season) in a quart of water. Strain it, and skim off all the fat; then mix one dessert-spoonful of flour in a half pint of cream; or, for economy's sake, half milk and half cream, or even all good new milk; add this to the stock, and if not salt enough, cautiously add more seasoning. Boil all together very gently for ten minutes, stirring all the time, as the sauce easily burns and very quickly spoils. This stock, made in large quantities, makes white soup; for this an old fowl, stewed down, is excellent, and the liquor in which a young turkey has been boiled is as good a foundation as can be desired.

Economical White Sauce.—Cut up fine one carrot, two small onions, and put them into a stewpan with two ounces of butter, and simmer till the butter is nearly absorbed. Then mix a small teacupful of flour in a pint of new milk, boil the whole quietly till it thickens, strain it, season with salt and white pepper or cayenne, and it is ready to serve. Or mix well two ounces of flour with one ounce of butter; with a little nutmeg, pepper and salt; add a pint of milk, and throw in a strip of lemon peel; stir well over the fire till quite thick, and strain.

Wine Sauce.—One and ½ cups sugar, three quarters cup of wine, a large spoonful flour, and a large piece of butter.

HOW TO MAKE SOUPS
... AND BROTHS

Artichoke Soup.—Take Jerusalem artichokes according to the quantity of soup required to be made, cut them in slices, with a quarter of a pound of butter, two or three onions and turnips, sliced into a stewpan, and stew over a very slow fire till done enough, and thin it with good veal stock. Just before you serve, at the last boil, add a quarter of a pint of good cream. This is an excellent soup. Season to taste with a little salt and cayenne. As it is necessary to vary soups, we shall give you a few to choose from according to season and taste. All brown soups must be clear and thin, with the exception of mock turtle, which must be thickened with flour first browned with butter in a stewpan. If the flour is added without previous browning, it preserves a raw taste that by no means improves the flavor.

Asparagus Soup.—Three or four pounds of veal cut fine, a little salt pork, two or three bunches of asparagus and three quarts of water. Boil one-half of the asparagus with the meat, leaving the rest in water until about twenty minutes before serving; then add the rest of the asparagus and boil just before serving; add one pint of milk; thicken with a little flour, and season. The soup should boil about three hours before adding the last half of the asparagus.

Beef Broth.—Put two pounds of lean beef, one pound of scrag of veal, one pound of scrag of mutton, sweet herbs, and ten peppercorns, into a nice tin saucepan, with five quarts of water; simmer to three quarts, and clear from the fat when cold. Add one onion, if approved.

Soup and broth made of different meats are more supporting, as well as better flavored.

To remove the fat, take it off, when cold, as clean as possible; and if there be still any remaining, lay a bit of clean blotting or cap paper on the broth when in the basin, and it will take up every particle.

Beef Soup.—Cut all the lean off the shank, and with a little beef suet in the bottom of the kettle, fry it to a nice brown; put in the bones and cover with water; cover the kettle closely; let it cook slowly until the meat drops from the bones; strain through a colander and leave it in the dish during the night, which is the only way to get off all the fat. The day it is wanted for the table, fry as brown as possible a carrot, an onion, and a very small turnip sliced thin. Just before taking up, put in half a tablespoonful of sugar, a blade of mace, six cloves, a dozen kernels of allspice, a small tablespoonful of celery seed. With the vegetables this must cook slowly in the soup an hour; then strain again for the table. If you use vermicelli or pearl barley, soak in water.

Dr. Liebig's Beef Tea.—When one pound of lean beef, free from fat, and separated from the bones, in a finely-chopped state in which it is used for mince-meat, or beef-sausages, is uniformly mixed with its own weight of cold water, slowly heated till boiling, and the liquid, after boiling briskly for a minute or two, is strained through the towel from the coagulated albumen and the fibrine, now become hard and horny, we obtain an equal weight of the most aromatic soup, of such strength as cannot be obtained even by boiling for hours from a piece of flesh. When mixed with salt and the other additions by which soup is usually seasoned, and tinged somewhat darker by means of roasted onions, or burnt bread, it forms the very best soup which can, in any way, be prepared from one pound of flesh.

Brown Gravy Soup.—Shred a small plate of onions, put some dripping into a frying-pan and fry the onions till they are of a dark brown; then, having about three pounds of beef cut up in dice, without fat or bone, brown that in a frying-pan. Now get a sauce-pan to contain about a gallon, and put in the onions and meat, with a carrot and a turnip cut small, and a little celery, if you have it; if not, add two seeds of celery; put three quarts, or three and a half quarts of water to this, and stir all together with a little pepper and salt; simmer very slowly, and skim off what rises; in three or four hours the soup will be clear. When served, add a little vermicelli, which should have previously been boiled in water; the liquid should be carefully poured off through a sieve. A large quantity may be made in the same proportions. Of course, the meat and onions must be stirred whilst frying, and constantly turned; they should be of a fine brown, not black, and celery-seed will give a flavor, it is so strong.

Carrot Soup.—Put some beef bones, with four quarts of the liquor in which a leg of mutton or beef has been boiled, two large onions, a turnip, pepper and salt into a sauce-pan, and stew for three hours. Have ready six large carrots, scraped and cut thin, strain the soup on them, and stew them till soft enough to pulp through a hair sieve or coarse cloth, then boil the pulp with the soup, which is to be as thick as pea-soup. Use two wooden spoons to rub the carrots through. Make the soup the day before it is to be used. Add cayenne. Pulp only the red part of the carrot, and not the yellow.

Clam Soup.—Cut salt pork in very small squares and fry light brown; add one large or two small onions cut very fine, and cook about ten minutes; add two quarts water and one quart of raw potatoes, sliced; let it boil; then add one quart of clams. Mix one tablespoonful of flour with water, put it with one pint of milk, and pour into the soup, and let it boil about five minutes. Butter, pepper, salt. Worcestershire sauce to taste.

Groutons.—These are simply pieces of bread fried brown and crisp, to be used in soups.

Game Soups.—Cut in pieces a partridge, pheasant, or rabbit; add slices of veal, ham, onions, carrots, etc. Add a little water, heat a little on slow fire, as gravy is done; then add some good broth, boil the meat gently till it is done. Strain, and stew in the liquor what herbs you please.

Game Soup.—In the season for game, it is easy to have good game soup at very little expense, and very nice. Take the meat from off the bones of any cold game left, pound it in a mortar and break up the bones, and pour on them a quart of any good broth, and boil for an hour and a half. Boil and mash six turnips, and mix with the pounded meat, and then pass them through a sieve. Strain the broth, and stir in the mixture of meat and turnips which has been strained through the sieve; keep the soup-pot near the fire, but do not let it boil. When ready to dish the soup for table, beat the yolks of five eggs very lightly, and mix with them half a pint of good cream. Set the soup on to boil, and, as it boils, stir in the beaten eggs and cream, but be careful that it does not boil after they are stirred in, as the egg will curdle. Serve hot.

Julienne Soup.—Put a piece of butter the size of an egg into the soup-kettle; stir until melted. Cut three young onions small; fry them a nice brown; add three quarts of good clear beef-stock, a little mace, pepper and salt; let it boil an hour; add three young carrots and three turnips cut small, a stalk of celery cut fine, a pint of French beans, a pint of green peas; let this boil two hours; if not a bright, clear color, add a spoonful of soy. This is a nice summer soup.

Lobster Soup.—One large lobster or two small ones; pick all the meat from the shell and chop fine; scald one quart of milk and one pint of water, then add the lobster, one pound of butter, a teaspoonful of flour, and salt and red pepper to taste. Boil ten minutes and serve hot.

Mock Turtle Soup.—One soup-bone, one quart of turtle beans, one large spoonful of powdered cloves, salt and pepper. Soak the beans over night, put them on with the soup-bone in nearly six quarts of water, and cook five or six hours. When half done, add the cloves, salt and pepper; when done, strain through a colander, pressing the pulp of the beans through to make the soup the desired thickness, and serve with a few slices of hard-boiled egg and lemon sliced very thin. The turtle beans are black and can only be obtained from large groce.

Oyster Soup.—Take one quart of water, one teacup of butter, one pint of milk, two teaspoons of salt, four crackers rolled fine, and one teaspoon of pepper; bring to full boiling heat as soon as possible, then add one quart of oysters; let the whole come to boiling heat quickly and remove from the fire.

Oyster Soup.—Pour one quart of boiling water into a skillet; then one quart of good rich milk; stir in one teacup of rolled cracker crumbs; season with pepper and salt to taste. When all come to boil, add one quart of good fresh oysters; stir well, so as to keep from scorching; then add a piece of good sweet butter about the size of an egg; let it boil up once, then remove from the fire immediately; dish up and send to table.

Ox Tail Soup.—Take two ox tails and two whole onions, two carrots, a small turnip, two tablespoonfuls of flour, and a little white pepper; add a gallon of water, let all boil for two hours; then take out the tails and cut the meat into small pieces, return the bones to the pot for a short time, boil for another hour, then strain the soup, and rinse two spoonfuls of arrow-root to add to it with the meat cut from the bones, and let all boil for a quarter of an hour.

Scotch Broth.—Take one-half teacup barley, four quarts cold water; bring this to the boil and skim; now put in a neck of mutton and boil again for half an hour, skim well the sides of the pot also; have ready two carrots, one large onion, a small head of cabbage, one bunch parsley, one sprig of celery top; chop all these fine, add your chopped vegetables, pepper and salt to taste. This soup takes two hours to cook.

Soup and Bouille.—Stew a brisket of beef with some turnips, celery, leeks and onions, all finely cut. Put the pieces of beef into the pot first, then the roots, and half a pint of beef gravy, with a few cloves. Simmer for an hour. Add more beef gravy, and boil gently for half an hour.

Royal Soup.—Take a scrag or knuckle of veal, slices of undressed gammon of bacon, onions, mace, and a small quantity of water; simmer till very strong, and lower it with a good beef broth made the day before, and stewed till the meat is done to rags. Add cream, vermicelli, almonds and a roll.

Various Soups.—Good soups may be made from fried meats, where the fat and gravy are added to the boiled barley; and for that purpose, fat beef steaks, pork steaks, mutton chops, etc. should be preferred, as containing more of the nutritious principle. When nearly done frying, add a little water, which will produce a gravy to be added to the barley broth; a little wheat flour should be dredged in also; a quantity of onions, cut small, should also be fried with the fat, which gives the soup a fine flavor, assisted by seasoning, etc.

Soups may be made from broiled meats. While the fat beef steak is doing before the fire, or mutton chop, etc., save the drippings on a dish, in which a little flour, oatmeal, with cut onions, etc., are put.

Grand Consomme Soup.—Put into a pot two knuckles of veal, a piece of a leg of beef, a fowl, or an old cock, a rabbit, or two old partridges; add a ladleful of soup, and stir it well; when it comes to a jelly, put in a sufficient quantity of stock, and see that it is clear; let it boil, skimming and refreshing it with water; season it as the above; you may add, if you like, a clove of garlic; let it then boil slowly or simmer four or five hours; put it through a towel, and use it for mixing in sauces or clear soups.

Julienne Soup.—Take some carrots and turnips, and turn them riband-like; a few heads of celery, some leeks and onions, and cut them in lozenges, boil them till they are cooked, then put them into clear gravy soup. Brown thickening.—N. B. You may, in summer time, add green peas, asparagus tops, French beans, some lettuce or sorrel.

Soup and Soups.—It is not at all necessary to keep a special fire for five hours every day in order to have at dinner a first course of soup. Nor need a good, savory, nutritious soup for a family of five cost more than 10 cents. There is no use hurling any remarks about "swill-pails." Every housekeeper who knows anything of her kitchen and dining-room affairs, knows there are usually nice clean fragments of roasts and broils left over, and that broth in which lamb, mutton, beef, and fowls have been boiled is in existence, and that twice a week or so there is a bowl of drippings from roasted meats. All these when simmered with rice, macaroni, or well-chosen vegetables, and judiciously seasoned, make good soups, and can be had without a special fire, and without sending to the butcher's for special meats. We name a few of the soups we make, and beg leave to add that they are pretty well received. We make them in small quantities, for nobody with three additional courses before him wants to eat a *quart* of soup, you know!

1.—One pint of good gravy, three cups boiling water, a slice of turnip, and half an onion cut in small bits, two grated crackers. Simmer half an hour.

2.—On ironing day cut off the narrow ends from two or three sirloin steaks, chop them into morsels and put in a stewpan with a little salt, a tablespoonful of rice and a pint of cold water, and simmer slowly for three hours. Then add water enough to make a quart of soup, a tablespoonful of tomato catsup, and a little browned flour mixed with the yolk of an egg.

3.—Pare and slice very thin four good sized potatoes, pour over them two cups of boiling water, and simmer gently until the potatoes are dissolved. Add salt, a lump of nice butter, and a pint of sweet milk with a dust of pepper. Let it boil up once, and serve. You wouldn't think it, but it is real good, and children cry for it.

4.—One pint meat broth, one pint boiling water, slice in an onion, or a parsnip, or half a turnip—or all three if liked—boil until the vegetables are soft, add a little salt if needed, and a tablespoonful of Halford sauce.

5.—Let green corn, in the time of green corn, be grated, and to a pint of it put a pint of rich milk, a pint of water, a little butter, salt and pepper. Boil gently for fifteen or twenty minutes.

Split Pea Soup.—Take beef bones or any cold meats, and two pounds of corned pork; pour on them a gallon of hot water, and let them simmer three hours, removing all the scum. Boil one quart of split peas two hours, having been previously soaked, as they require much cooking: strain off the meat and mash the peas into the soup; season with black pepper, and let it simmer one hour; fry two or three slices of bread a nice brown, cut into slices and put into the bottom of the tureen, and on them pour the soup.

Tomato Soup.—Boil chicken or beef four hours; then strain; add to the soup one can of tomatoes and boil one hour. This will make four quarts of soup.

Tomato Soup without Meat.—One quart of tomatoes, one quart of water, one quart of milk. Butter, salt and pepper to taste. Cook the tomatoes thoroughly in the water, have the milk scalding (over water to prevent scorching). When the tomatoes are done add a large teaspoonful of saleratus, which will cause a violent effervescence. It is best to set the vessel in a pan before adding it to prevent waste. When the commotion has ceased add the milk and seasoning. When it is possible it is best to use more milk than water, and cream instead of butter. The soup is eaten with crackers and is by some preferred to oyster soup. This recipe is very valuable for those who keep abstinence days.

Turkey Soup.—Take the turkey bones and cook for one hour in water enough to cover them; then stir in a little dressing and a beaten egg. Take from the fire, and when the water has ceased boiling add a little butter with pepper and salt.

Veal Gravy.—Put in the stewpan bits of lard, then a few thin slices of ham, a few bits of butter, then slices of fillet of veal, sliced onions, carrots, parsnips, celery, a few cloves upon the meat, and two spoonfuls of broth; set it on the fire till the veal throws out its juices; then put it on a stronger fire till the meat catches to the bottom of the pan, and is brought to a proper color; then add a sufficient quantity of light broth, and simmer it upon a slow fire till the meat is well done. A little thyme and mushrooms may be added. Skim and sift it clear for use.

Veal Soup.—To a knuckle of veal of 6 pounds, put 7 or 9 quarts of water; boil down one-half; skim it well. This is better to do the day before you prepare the soup for the table. Thicken it by rubbing flour, butter, and water together. Season with salt and mace. When done and one pint new milk; let it just come to a boil; then pour into a soup dish, lined with macaroni well cooked.

Vegetable Soup.—Pare and slice five or six cucumbers; and add to these as many cos lettuces, a sprig or two of mint, two or three onions, some pepper and salt, a pint and a half of young peas and a little parsley. Put these, with half a pound of fresh butter, into a saucepan, to stew in their own liquor, near a gentle fire, half an hour. then pour two quarts of boiling water to the vegetables, and stew them two hours; rub down a little flour into a teacupful of water, boil it with the rest twenty minutes, and serve it.

Vermicelli Soup.—Boil tender ½ lb. of vermicelli in a quart of rich gravy; take half of it out, and add to it more gravy; boil till the vermicelli can be pulped through a sieve. To both put a pint of boiling cream, a little salt, and ¼ lb. of Parmesan cheese. Serve with rasped bread. Add two or three eggs, if you like.

Brown Vermicelli Soup.—Is made in the same manner, leaving out the eggs and cream, and adding one quart of strong beef gravy.

HOW TO COOK VEGETABLES

How to Boil Artichokes.—If the artichokes are very young, about an inch of the stalk can be left; but should they be full grown, the stalk must be cut quite close. Wash them well and put them into strong salt and water to soak for a couple of hours. Pull away a few of the lower leaves, and snip off the points of all. Fill a saucepan with water, throw some salt into it, let it boil up, and then remove the scum from the top; put the artichokes in, with the stalks upward, and let them boil until the leaves can be loosened easily; this will take from thirty to forty minutes, according to the age of the artichokes. The saucepan should not be covered during the time they are boiling. Rich melted butter is always sent to the table with them.

New Mode to Dress Asparagus.—Scrape the grass, tie it up in bundles, and cut the ends off an even length. Have ready a saucepan, with boiling water, and salt in proportion of a heaped saltspoonful to a quart of water. Put in the grass, standing it on the bottom with the green heads out of the water, so that they are not liable to be boiled off. If the water boils too fast, dash in a little cold water. When the grass has boiled a quarter of an hour it will be sufficiently done; remove it from the saucepan, cut off the ends down to the edible part, arrange it on a dish in a round pyramid, with the heads toward the middle of the dish, and boil some eggs hard; cut them in two, and place them round the dish quite hot. Serve melted butter in a sauce-tureen; and those who like it rub the yoke of a hard egg into the butter, which makes a delicious sauce to the asparagus.

How to Boil Asparagus.—Scrape the asparagus; tie them in small bunches; boil them in a large pan of water with salt in it; before you dish them up toast some slices of bread, and then dip them in the boiling water; lay the asparagus on the toasts; pour on them rich melted butter, and serve hot.

Ragout of Asparagus.—Cut small asparagus like green peas; the best method is to break them off first; then tie them in small bunches to cut, boil them till half done; then drain them, and finish with butter, a little broth, herbs, two cloves, and a sprig of savory. When done, take out the cloves, herbs, etc., mix two yolks of eggs, with a little flour, and broth, to garnish a first course dish. But if you intend to serve it in a second course mix cream, a little salt, and sugar.

French Beans, a la Creme.—Slice the beans and boil them in water with salt. When soft, drain. Put into a stewpan two ounces of fresh butter, the yolks of three eggs, beaten up into a gill of cream, and set over a slow fire. When hot, add a spoonful of vinegar, simmer for five minutes.

To Preserve French Beans for Winter.—Pick them young, and throw into a little wooden keg a layer of them three inches deep; then sprinkle them with salt, put another layer of beans, and do the same as high as you think proper, alternately with salt, but not too much of this. Lay over them a plate, or cover of wood, that will go into the keg, and put a heavy stone on it. A pickle will rise from the beans and salt. If they are too salt, the soaking and boiling will not be sufficient to make them pleasant to the taste.

Stewed Beans.—Boil them in water in which a lump of butter has been placed; preserve them as white as you can; chop a few sweet herbs with some parsley very fine; then stew them in a pint of the water in which the leaves have been boiled, and to which a quarter of a pint of cream has been added; stew until quite tender, then add the beans, and stew five minutes, thickening with butter and flour.

How to Boil Broccoli.—Peel the thick skin of the stalks, and boil for nearly a quarter of an hour, with a little bit of soda, then put in salt, and boil five minutes more. Broccoli and savoys taste better when a little bacon is boiled with them.

How to boil Cabbage.—Cut off the outside leaves, and cut it in quarters; pick it well, and wash it clean; boil it in a large quantity of water, with plenty of salt in it; when it is tender and a fine light green, lay it on a sieve to drain, but do not squeeze it, it will take off the flavor; have ready some very rich melted butter, or chop it with cold butter. Greens must be boiled the same way. Strong vegetables like turnips and cabbage, etc., require much water.

Cabbage Salad.—Three eggs well beaten, one cup of vinegar, two tablespoons of mustard, salt and pepper, one tablespoon of butter; let this mixture come to a boil, when cool add seven tablespoons of cream, half a head of cabbage shaved fine.

How to Boil Cauliflowers.—Strip the leaves which you do not intend to use, and put the cauliflowers into salt and water some time to force out snails, worms, etc. Boil them twelve minutes on a drainer in plenty of water,

then add salt, and boil five or six minutes longer. Skim well while boiling. Take out and drain. Serve with melted butter, or a sauce made of butter, cream, pepper and salt.

How to Fry Cauliflowers.—Wash as before. Boil twenty or thirty minutes; cut it into small portions, and cool. Dip the portions twice into a batter made of flour, milk and egg, and fry them in butter. Serve with gravy.

Cucumbers for Immediate Use.—Slice, sprinkle with salt; let them stand several hours, drain, and then put to them sliced onions, vinegar to cover them, and salt, pepper, etc. Cayenne pepper and ground mustard render them wholesome.

Stewed Celery.—Wash and clean six or eight heads of celery, let them be about three inches long; boil tender and pour off all the water; beat the yolks of four eggs, and mix with half a pint of cream, mace and salt; set it over the fire with the celery, and keep shaking until it thickens, then serve hot.

Cold Slaw.—Half a head of cabbage cut very fine, a stalk of celery cut fine—or teaspoon of celery seed—or, a tablespoon of celery essence, four hard-boiled eggs, whites chopped very fine, a teaspoon of mustard, a tablespoon of butter and the yolks of the boiled eggs, salt and pepper, mix well; take an egg well beaten and stir in a cup of boiling vinegar, pour over and cover for a few minutes.

Egg-Plant.—Slice the egg-plant an eighth of an inch in thickness, pare it, and sprinkle salt over it an hour before cooking; then drain off all the water, beat up the yolk of an egg, dip the slices first in the egg, and then in crumbs of bread; fry a nice brown. Serve hot, and free from fat.

How to Cook Egg-Plant.—Cut the egg-plant in slices half an inch thick, sprinkle a thin layer of salt between the slices, and lay them one over the other; and let them stand an hour. This draws out the bitter principal from the egg-plant, and also a part of the water. Then lay each slice in flour, put in hot fat and fry it brown on both sides. Or boil the egg-plant till tender, remove the skin, mash fine, mix with an equal quantity of bread or cracker crumbs, and salt, pepper and bake half an hour. This makes a delightful dish, and a very digestible one, as it has so little oily matter in it.

How to Broil Mushrooms.—Pare some large, open mushrooms, leaving the stalks on, paring them to a point; wash them well, and turn them on the back of a drying sieve to drain. Put into a stewpan two ounces of butter, some chopped parsley, and shalots, then fry them for a minute on the fire; when melted, place your mushroom stalks upward on a saucepan, then pour the butter and parsley over all the mushrooms; pepper and salt them well with black pepper put them in the oven to broil; when done, put a little good stock to them, give them a boil and dish them, pour the liquor over them, adding more gravy, but let it be put in hot.

How to Pickle Onions.—Take two quarts of the small white round onions. Scald them in very strong salt and water. Just let them boil. Strain, peel, place in jars; cover them with the best white wine vinegar. In two days pour all the vinegar off, and boil it half an hour, with a teaspoonful of cayenne pepper, 1 oz. of ginger, 16 cloves, $\frac{1}{2}$ oz. ground mustard, 2 ozs. mustard seed. When cold, pour upon the onions. Some persons prefer the vinegar boiling hot.

How to Fricassee Parsnips.—Boil in milk till they are soft, then cut them lengthwise in bits two or three inches long, and simmer in a white sauce, made of two spoonfuls of broth, and a bit of mace, half a cupful of cream, a bit of butter, and some flour, pepper and salt.

How to Mash Parsnips.—Boil them tender, scrape, then mash them in a stewpan with a little cream, a good piece of butter, and pepper and salt.

How to Stew Parsnips.—Boil them tender; scrape and cut into slices; put them into a saucepan with cream enough; for sauce, a piece of butter rolled in flour, and a little salt; shake the saucepan often, when the cream boils, pour them into a dish.

How to Boil Peas.—Peas should not be shelled long before they are wanted, nor boiled in much water; when the water boils, put them in with a little salt (some add a little loaf sugar, but if they are sweet of themselves, it is superfluous); when the peas begin to dent in the middle they are boiled enough. Strain, and put a piece of butter in the dish, and stir. A little mint should be boiled with the peas.

Puree of Potatoes.—This differs from mashed potatoes only in the employment of more milk and butter, and in the whole being carefully reduced to a perfectly smooth, thick, cream-like mixture. Where economy is a great object, and where rich dishes are not desired, the following is an admirable mode of mashing potatoes: Boil them till thoroughly done, having added a handful of salt to the water, then dry them well, and with two forks placed back to back beat the whole up until no lumps are left. If done rapidly, potatoes thus cooked are extremely light and digestible.

How to Boil Potatoes.—Boil in a saucepan without lid, with only sufficient water to cover them; more would spoil them, as the potatoes contain much water, and it requires to be expelled. When the water nearly boils pour it off, and add cold water, with a good portion of salt. The cold water sends the heat from the surface to the center of the potato, and makes it mealy. Boiling with a lid on often produces cracking.

New Potatoes.—Should be cooked soon after having been dug; wash well, and boil.

The Irish, who boil potatoes to perfection, say they should always be boiled in their *jackets;* as peeling them for boiling is only offering a premium for water to run through the potato, and rendering it sad and unpalatable; they should be well washed, and put into cold water.

New Potatoes.—Have them as freshly dug as may be convenient; the longer they have been out of the ground the less well-flavored they are. Well wash them, rub off the skins with a coarse cloth or brush, and put them into boiling water, to which has been added salt, at the rate of one heaped teaspoonful to two quarts. Let them boil till tender—try them with a fork; they will take from ten or fifteen minutes to half an hour, according to size. When done, pour away the water, and set by the side of the fire, with the lid aslant. When they are quite dry, have ready a hot vegetable dish, and in the middle of it put a piece of butter the size of a walnut—some people like more—heap the potatoes round it and over it, and serve immediately. We have seen very young potatoes, no larger than a marble, parboiled, and then fried in cream till they are of a fine auburn color; or else, when larger, boiled till nearly ready, then sliced and fried in cream, with pepper, salt, a very little nutmeg, and a flavoring of lemon juice. Both make pretty little supper dishes.

Potatoes Roasted under the Meat.—These are very good; they should be nicely browned. Half boil large mealy potatoes; put into a baking dish, under the meat roasting; ladle the gravy upon them occasionally. They are best done in an oven.

Potato Ribbons.—Cut the potatoes into slices, rather more than half an inch thick, and then pare round and round in very long ribbons. Place them in a pan of cold water, and a short time before wanted drain them from the water. Fry them in hot lard, or good dripping, until crisp and browned; dry them on a soft cloth, pile them on a hot dish, and season with salt and cayenne.

Potato Rolls.—Boil three lbs. of potatoes; crush and work them with two ozs. of butter and as much milk as will cause them to pass through a colander; take half a pint of yeast and half a pint of warm water; mix with the potatoes; pour the whole upon 5 lbs. of flour; add salt; knead it well; if too thick, put to it a little more milk and warm water; stand before the fire for an hour to rise; work it well and make it into rolls. Bake it half an hour.

Potato Rissoles.—Boil the potatoes floury; mash them, seasoning them with salt and a little cayenne; mince parsley very fine, and work up with the potatoes, adding eschalot, also chopped small. Bind with yolk of egg, roll into balls, and fry with fresh butter over a clear fire. Meat shred finely, bacon or ham may be added.

Potato Sautees.—These are even more agreeable with meat than fried potatoes. Cold boiled potatoes are sliced up, and tossed up in a saucepan with butter, mixed with a little chopped parsley, till they are lightly browned. Pure goose or other dripping is by many cooks preferred to butter for this purpose.

Potato Souffles.—The delicious blistered potatoes are prepared as follows: The potatoes, if small, are simply cut in halves; if large, cut in three or more slices; these are fried in the usual way, but are taken out before they are quite done, and set aside to get cold; when wanted they are fried a second time, but only till they are of a light golden color, not brown.

Tomatoes.—Cut ripe tomatoes into slices, put them in a buttered dish with some bread crumbs, butter, pepper and salt, and bake till slightly brown on top.

Forced Tomatoes.—Prepare the following forcemeat: Two ounces of mushrooms, minced small, a couple of shalots, likewise minced, a small quantity of parsley, a slice of lean ham, chopped fine, a few savory herbs, and a little cayenne and salt. Put all these ingredients into a saucepan with a lump of butter, and stew all together until quite tender, taking care that they do not burn. Put it by to cool, and then mix with them some bread crumbs and the well beaten yolks of two eggs. Choose large tomatoes, as nearly of the same size as possible, cut a slice from the stalk end of each, and take out carefully the seeds and juice; fill them with the mixture which has already been prepared, strew them over with bread and some melted butter, and bake them in a quick oven until they assume a rich color. They are a good accompaniment to veal or calf's head.

To Mash Turnips.—Boil them very tender. Strain till no water is left. Place in a saucepan over a gentle fire, and stir well a few minutes. Do not let them burn. Add a little cream, or milk, or both, salt butter and pepper. Add a tablespoonful of fine sugar. Stir and simmer five minutes longer.

To Boil or Stew Vegetable Marrow.—This excellent vegetable may be boiled as asparagus. When boiled, divide it lengthways into two, and serve it upon a toast accompanied by melted butter; or when nearly boiled, divide it as above, and stew gently in gravy like cucumbers. Care should be taken to choose young ones not exceeding six inches in length.

PRACTICAL RULES, SHORT METHODS, AND PROBLEMS USED IN BUSINESS COMPUTATIONS.

APIDITY and accuracy in making estimates and in figuring out the result of business transactions is of the greatest necessity to the man of business. A miscalculation may involve the loss of hundreds or thousands of dollars, in many cases, while a slow and tedious calculation involves loss of time and the advantage which should have been seized at the moment. It is proposed in the following pages to give a few brief methods and practical rules for performing calculations which occur in every-day transactions among men, presuming that a fair knowledge of the ordinary rules of arithmetic has previously been attained.

ADDITION.

To be able to add up long columns of figures rapidly and correctly is of great value to the merchant. This requires not only a knowledge of addition, but in order to have a correct result, one that can be relied upon, it requires concentration of the mind. Never allow other thoughts to be flitting through the mind, or any outside matter to disturb or draw it away from the figures, until the result is obtained. Write the tens to be carried each time in a smaller figure underneath the units, so that afterwards any column can be added over again without repeating the entire operation. By the practice of addition the eye and mind soon become accustomed to act rapidly, and this is the art of addition. Grouping figures together is a valuable aid in rapid addition, as we group letters into words in reading.

$$
\begin{array}{r}
862 \\
538 \\
674 \\
843 \\
\hline
2917
\end{array}
$$

Thus, in the above example. we do not say 3 and 4 are 7 and 8 are 15 and 2 are 17, but speak the sum of the couplet, thus 7 and 10 are 17, and in the second column, 12 and 9 are 21. This method of grouping the figures soon becomes easy and reduces the labor of addition about one-half, while those somewhat expert may group three or more figures, still more reducing the time and labor, and sometimes two or more columns may be added at once, by ready reckoners.

Another method is to group into tens when it can be conveniently done, and still another method in adding up long columns is to add from the bottom to the top, and whenever the numbers make even 10, 20, 30, 40 or 50, write with pencil a small figure opposite, 1, 2, 3, 4 or 5, and then proceed to add as units. The sum of these figures thus set out will be the number of tens to be carried to the next column.

$$
\begin{array}{r}
6^2\ 2\ 8 \\
3\ 5^2\ 4^1 \\
2\ 8\ 4 \\
9\ 6\ 2 \\
7^2\ 1\ 8^2 \\
8\ 3^2\ 5 \\
5\ 2\ 7 \\
1^1\ 3\ 2^1 \\
5\ 8\ 8 \\
\hline
5\ 0\ 2\ 8
\end{array}
$$

SHORT METHODS OF MULTIPLICATION.

For certain classes of examples in multiplication short methods may be employed and the labor of calculation reduced, but of course for the great bulk of multiplications no practical abbreviation remains. A person having much multiplying to do should learn the table up to twenty, which can be done without much labor.

To multiply any number by 10, 100, or 1000, simply annex one, two, or three ciphers, as the case may be. If it is desired to multiply by 20, 300, 5000, or a number greater than one with any number of ciphers annexed, multiply first by the number and then annex as many ciphers as the multiplier contains.

TABLE.

5	cents equal 1-20 of a dollar.	20	cents equal 1-5 of a dollar.
10	" " 1-10 " "	25	" " ¼ " "
12½	" " ⅛ " "	33⅓	" " ⅓ " "
16⅔	" " 1-6 " "	50	" " ½ " "

Articles of merchandise are often bought and sold by the pound, yard, or gallon, and whenever the price is an equal part of a dollar, as seen in the above table, the whole cost may be easily found by adding two ciphers to the number of pounds or yards and dividing by the equivalent in the table.

Example. What cost 18 dozen eggs at 16⅔c per dozen?

$$6)\overline{1800}$$
$$\$3.00$$

Example. What cost 10 pounds butter at 25c per pound?

$$4)\overline{1000}$$
$$\$2.50$$

Or, if the pounds are equal parts of one hundred and the price is not, then the same result may be obtained by dividing the price by the equivalent of the quantity as seen in the table; thus, in the above case, if the price were 10c and the number of pounds 25, it would be worked just the same.

Example. Find the cost of 50 yards of gingham at 14c a yard.

$$2)\overline{1400}$$
$$\$7.00$$

When the price is one dollar and twenty-five cents, fifty cents, or any number found in the table, the result may be quickly found by finding the price for the extra cents, as in the above examples, and then adding this to the number of pounds or yards and calling the result dollars.

Example. Find the cost of 20 bushels potatoes at $1.12½ per bushel.

$$8)\overline{2000}$$
$$\underline{250}$$
$$\$22.50$$

If the price is $2 or $3 instead of $1, then the number of bushels must first be multiplied by 2 or 3, as the case may be.

Example. Find the cost of 6 hats at $4.33⅓ apiece.

$$3)\overline{600}$$
$$\underline{4}$$
$$24.00$$
$$\underline{2.00}$$
$$\$26$$

When 125 or 250 are multipliers add three ciphers and divide by 8 and 4 respectively.

To multiply a number consisting of two figures by 11, write the sum of the two figures between them.

Example. Multiply 53 by 11. Ans. 583.

If the sum of the two numbers exceeds 10 then the units only must be placed between and the tens figure carried and added to the next figure to the left.

Example. Multiply 87 by 11. Ans. 957.

FRACTIONS.

Fractional parts of a cent should never be despised. They often make fortunes, and the counting of all the fractions may constitute the difference between the rich and the poor man. The business man readily understands the value of the fractional part of a bushel, yard, pound, or cent, and calculates them very sharply, for in them lies perhaps his entire profit.

TO REDUCE A FRACTION TO ITS SIMPLEST FORM.

Divide both the numerator and denominator by any number that will leave no remainder and repeat the operation until no number will divide them both.

Example. The simplest form of $\frac{36}{45}$ is found by dividing by $9 = \frac{4}{5}$.

To reduce a whole number and a fraction, as $4\frac{1}{2}$, to fractional form, multiply the whole number by the denominator, add the numerator and write the result over the denominator. Thus, $4 \times 2 = 8 + 1 = 9$ placed over 2 is $\frac{9}{2}$.

TO ADD FRACTIONS.

Reduce the fractions to like denominators, add their numerators and write the denominator under the result.

Example. Add $\frac{2}{3}$ to $\frac{3}{4}$.

$$\frac{2}{3} = \frac{8}{12}, \frac{3}{4} = \frac{9}{12}, \frac{8}{12} + \frac{9}{12} = \frac{17}{12} = 1\frac{5}{12} \text{ Ans.}$$

TO SUBTRACT FRACTIONS.

Reduce the fractions to like denominators, subtract the numerators and write the denominators under the result.

Example. Find the difference between ⅘ and ¾.

⅘ = 16⁄20, ¾ = 15⁄20, 16⁄20 − 15⁄20 = 1⁄20. Ans.

TO MULTIPLY FRACTIONS.

Multiply the numerators together for a new numerator and the denominators together for a new denominator.

Example. Multiply ⅞ by ⅚.

⅞ × ⅚ = 35⁄48. Ans.

TO DIVIDE FRACTIONS.

Multiply the dividend by the divisor inverted.

Example. Divide ⅞ by ⅚.

⅞ × 6⁄5 = 42⁄40. Reduced to simple form by dividing by 2 is 21⁄20 = 1 1. Ans.

TO MULTIPLY MIXED NUMBERS.

When two numbers are to be multiplied, one of which contains a fraction, first multiply the whole numbers together, then multiply the fraction by the other whole number, add the two results together for the correct answer.

Example. What cost 5⅓ yards at 18c a yard?

18c
5⅓
18 × 5 = 90
18 × ⅓ = 6
96c

When both numbers contain a fraction,

First, multiply the whole numbers together;

Second, multiply the lower whole number by the upper fraction;

Third, multiply the upper whole number by the lower fraction;

Fourth, multiply the fractions together;

Fifth, add all the results for the correct answer.

Example. What cost 12⅔ pounds of butter at 18¾c per pound?

18¾
12⅔
18 × 12 = 216
12 × ¾ = 9
18 × ⅔ = 12
¾ × ⅔ = 6⁄12 = ½
$2.37½

Common fractions may often be changed to decimals very readily, and the calculations thereby made much easier.

TO CHANGE COMMON FRACTIONS TO DECIMALS.

Annex one or more ciphers to the numerator and divide by the denominator.

Example. Change ¾ to a decimal. Ans. .75.

We add two ciphers to the 3, making it 300, and divide by 4, which gives us .75. In the same way ½ = .5, or ¾ = .75, and so on. When a quantity is in dollars and fractions of a dollar, the fractions should always be thus reduced to cents and mills.

TWENTY THOUSAND THINGS WORTH KNOWING.

RELATIVE HARDNESS OF WOODS.

Taking shell bark hickory as the highest standard of our forest trees, and calling that 100, other trees will compare with it for hardness as follows:

Shell Bark Hickory	100	Yellow Oak	60
Pignut Hickory	96	Hard Maple	56
White Oak	84	White Elm	58
White Ash	77	Red Cedar	56
Dogwood	75	Wild Cherry	55
Scrub Oak	73	Yellow Pine	54
White Hazel	72	Chesnut	52
Apple Tree	70	Yellow Poplar	51
Red Oak	69	Buternut	43
White Beech	65	White Birch	43
Black Walnut	65	White Pine	30
Black Birch	62		

Timber intended for posts is rendered almost proof against rot by thorough seasoning, charring and immersion in hot coal tar.

The slide of Alpnach, extending from Mount Pilatus to Lake Lucerne, a distance of 8 miles, is composed of 25,000 trees, stripped of their bark, and laid at an inclination of 10 to 18 degrees. Trees placed in the slide rush from the mountain into the lake in 6 minutes.

The Alps comprise about 180 mountains, from 4,000 to 15,732 feet high, the latter being the height of Mount Blanc, the highest spot in Europe. The summit is a sharp ridge, like the roof of a house, consisting of nearly vertical granite rocks. The ascent requires 2 days, 6 or 8 guides are required, and each guide is paid 100 francs ($20.00). It was ascended by two natives, Jacques Belmat and Dr. Packard, August 8, 1786, at 6 a. m. They staid up 30 minutes, with the thermometer at 14 degrees below the freezing point. The provisions froze in their pockets; their faces were frost-bitten, lips swollen, and their sight much weakened, but they soon recovered on their descent. De Saussure records in his ascent August 2, 1760, that the color of the sky was deep blue; the stars were visible in the shade; the barometer sunk to 16.08 inches (being 27.08 in Geneva) the thermometer was 26½ degrees, in the sun 29 degrees (being 87 degrees at Geneva). The thin air works the blood into a high fever, you feel as if you hardly touched the ground, and you scarcely make yourself heard. A French woman, Mademoiselle d'Angeville, ascended in September, 1840, being dragged up the last 1,200 feet by guides, and crying out: "If I die, carry me to the top." When there, she made them lift her up, that she might boast she had been higher than any man in Europe. The ascent of these awful solitudes is most perilous, owing to the narrow paths, tremendous ravines, icy barriers, precipices, etc. In many places every step has to be cut in the ice, the party being tied to each other by ropes, so that if one slips he may be held up by the rest, and silence is enforced, lest the noise of talking should dislodge the avalanches of the Aiguille du Midi. The view from the mountain is inexpressibly grand. On the Alps the limit of the vine is an elevation of 1,600 feet; below 1,000 feet, figs, oranges and olives are produced. The limit of the oak is 3,800 feet, of the chesnut 2,800 feet, of the pine 6,500 feet, of heaths and furze to 8,700 and 9,700 feet; and perpetual snow exists at an elevation of 8,200 feet.

On the Andes, in lat. 2 degrees, the limit of perpetual snow is 14,760 feet; in Mexico, lat. 19 degrees, the limit is 13,800 feet; on the peak of Teneriffe, 11,454 feet; on Mount Etna, 9,000 feet; on the Caucasus, 9,900 feet; in the Pyrenees, 8,400 feet; in Lapland, 3,100 feet; in Iceland, 2,890 feet. The walnut ceases to grow at an elevation of 3,600 feet; the yellow pine at 6,200 feet; the ash at 4,800 feet, and the fir at 6,700 feet. The loftiest inhabited spot on the globe is the Port House of Ancomarca, on the Andes, in Peru, 16,000 feet above the level of the sea. The 14th peak of the Himalayas, in Asia, 25,659 feet high, is the loftiest mountain in the world.

Lauterbrunnen is a deep part of an Alpine pass, where the sun hardly shines in winter. It abounds with falls, the most remarkable of which is the Staubbach, which falls over the Balm precipice in a drizzling spray from a height of 925 feet; best viewed in the morning sun or by moonlight. In general, it is like a gauze veil, with rainbows dancing up and down it, and when clouds hide the top of the mountain, it seems as poured out of the sky.

In Canada, the falls of Montmorenci are 250 feet high, the falls of Niagara (the Horse Shoe Falls) are 158 feet high and 2,000 feet wide, the American Falls are 164 feet high and 900 feet wide. The Yosemite Valley Falls are 2,600 feet high, and the Ribbon Falls of the Yosemite are 3,300 feet high. The waterfall of the Arve, in Bavaria, is 2,000 feet.

THE PERIODS OF GESTATION are the same in the horse and ass or eleven months each, camel 12 months, elephant 2 years, lion 5 months, buffalo 12 months, in the human female 9 months, cow 9 months, sheep 5 months, dog 9 weeks, cat 8 weeks, sow 16 weeks, she wolf from 90 to 95 days. The goose sits 30 days, swans 42, hens 21, ducks 30, peahens and turkeys 28, canaries 14, pigeons 14, parrots 40 days.

AGES OF ANIMALS, ETC.—Elephant 100 years and upward, Rhinoceros 20, Camel 100, Lion 25 to 70, Tigers, Leopards, Jaguars and Hyenas (in confinement) about 25 years, Beaver 50, deer 20, wolf 20, Fox 14 to 16, Llamas 15, Chamois 25, Monkeys and Baboons 16 to 18 years, Hare 8, Squirrel 7, Rabbit 7, Swine 25, Stag under 50, Horse 30, Ass 30, Sheep under 10, Cow 20, Ox 30, Swans, Parrots and Ravens 200, Eagle 100, Geese 80, Hens and Pigeons 10 to 16, Hawks 36 to 40, Cranes 24, Blackbird 10 to 12, Peacock 20, Pelican 40 to 50, Thrush 8 to 10, Wren 2 to 3, Nightingale 15, Blackcap 15, Linnet 14 to 23, Goldfinch 20 to 24, Redbreast 10 to 12, Skylark 10 to 30, Titlark 5 to 6, Chaffinch 20 to 24, Starling 10 to 12, Carp 70 to 150, Pike 30 to 40, Salmon 16, Codfish 14 to 17, Eel 10, Crocodile 100, Tortoise 100 to 200, Whale estimated 1,000, Queen Bees live 4 years, Drones 4 months, Working Bees 6 months.

The melody of singing birds ranks as follows : The nightingale first, then the linnet, titlark, sky lark and wood lark. The mocking bird has the greatest powers of imitation, the robin and goldfinch are superior in vigorous notes.

The condor of Peru has spread wings 40 feet, feathers 20 feet, quills 8 inches round.

In England, a quarter of wheat, comprising 8 bushels, yields 14 bushels 2½ pecks, divided into seven distinct kinds of flour, as follows: Fine flour, 5 bushels 3 pecks; bran, 3 bushels; twenty-penny, 3 bushels; seconds, 2 pecks; pollard, 2 bushels; fine middlings, 1 peck; coarse ditto, 1 peck.

The ancient Greek phalanx comprised 8,000 men, forming a square battalion, with spears crossing each other, and shields united.

The Roman legion was composed of 6,000 men, comprising 10 cohorts of 600 men each, with 300 horsemen.

The ancient battering ram was of massive timber, 60 to 100 feet long, fitted with an iron head. It was erected under shelter to protect the 60 or 100 men required to work it. The largest was equal in force to a 36-lb. shot from a cannon.

Pile Driving on Sandy Soils.—The greatest force will not effect a penetration exceeding 15 feet.

Various Sizes of Type.—It requires 205 lines of Diamond type to make 12 inches, of Pearl 178, of Ruby 166, of Nonpareil 143, of Minion 128, of Brevier 112½, of Bourgeois 102½, of Long Primer 89, of Small Pica 83, of Pica 71½, of English 64.

Wire ropes for the transmission of power vary in size from ⅜ to ¼ inch diam. for from 3 to 300 horse power; to promote flexibility, the rope, made of iron, steel, or copper wire, as may be preferred, is provided with a core of hemp, and the speed is 1 mile per minute, more or less, as desired. The rope should run on a well-balanced, grooved, cast iron wheel, of from 4 to 15 feet diam., according as the transmitted power ranges from 3 to 300 horse; the groove should be well cushioned with soft material, as leather or rubber, for the formation of a durable bed for the rope. With good care the rope will last from 3 to 5 years.

Cannon balls go furthest at an elevation of 30 degrees, and less as the balls are less; the range is furthest when fired from west to east in the direction of the earth's motion, which for the diurnal rotation on its axis, is at the rate of 1,037 miles per hour, and in its orbit, 66,092 miles.

The air's resistance is such that a cannon ball of 3 lbs. weight, diameter, 2.78 ins. moving with a velocity of 1,800 feet per second, is resisted by a force equal to 156 lbs.

Bricklayers ascend ladders with loads of 90 lbs., 1 foot per second. There are 484 bricks in a cubic yard, and 4,356 in a rod.

A power of 250 tons is necessary to start a vessel weighing 3,000 tons over greased slides on a marine railway, when in motion, 150 tons only is required.

A modern dredging machine, 123 ft. long, beam 26 ft., breadth over all, 11 ft., will raise 180 tons of mud and clay per hour, 11 feet from water-line.

In tanning, 4 lbs. of oak bark make 1 lb. of leather.

Flame is quenched in air containing 3 per cent. of carbonic acid; the same percentage is fatal to animal life.

100 parts of oak make nearly 23 of charcoal; beech 21, deal 19, apple 23.7, elm 23, ash 25, birch 24, maple 22.8, willow 18, poplar 20, red pine 22.10, white pine 23. The charcoal used in gunpowder is made from willow, alder, and a few other woods. The charred timber found in the ruins of Herculaneum has undergone no change in 1,800 years.

Four volumes of nitrogen and one of oxygen compose atmospheric air in all localities on the globe.

Air extracted from pure water, under an air pump, contains 34.8 per cent. of oxygen. Fish breathe this air, respiring about 35 times per minute. The oxhydrogen lime light may be seen from mountains at the distance of 200 miles round.

Lightning is reflected 150 to 200 miles.

1,000 cubic feet of 13 candle gas is equivalent to over 7 gals. of sperm oil, 52.9 lbs. of tallow candles, and over 44 lbs. of sperm candles.

The time occupied by gas in traveling from a gas well (in Pennsylvania) through 32 miles of pipe was 22 minutes, pressure at the well was 55 lbs. per inch, pressure at discharge 49 lbs.

At birth, the beats of the pulse are from 165 to 104, and the inspirations of breath from 70 to 23. From 15 to 20, the pulsations are from 90 to 57, the inspirations, from 24 to 16; from 29 to 50, the pulsations are 112 to 56, the inspirations 23 to 11. In usual states it is 4 to 1. The action of the heart distributes 2 ozs. of blood from 70 to 80 times in a minute.

The mean heat of the human body is 98 degs. and of the skin 90 degs. Tea and coffee are usually drank at 110 degs.

The deepest coal mine in England is at Killingworth, near Newcastle, and the mean annual temperature at 400 yards below the surface is 77 degrees, and at 300 yards 70 degrees, while at the surface it is but 48 degrees, being 1 degree of increase for every 15 yards. This explains the origin of hot springs, for at 3,300 yards the heat would be equal to boiling water, taking 20 yards to a degree. The heat of the Bath waters is 116 degrees, hence they would appear to rise 1,320 yards.

Peron relates that at the depth of 2,144 feet in the sea the thermometer falls to 45 degrees, when it is 86 degrees at the surface.

Swemberg and Fourier calculate the temperature of the celestial spaces at 50 degrees centigrade below freezing.

In Northern Siberia the ground is frozen permanently to the depth of 660 feet, and only thaws to the extent of 3 or 4 feet in summer. Below 660 feet internal heat begins.

River water contains about 30 grs. of solid matter in every cubic foot. Fresh water springs of great size abound under the sea. Perhaps the most remarkable springs exist in California, where they are noted for producing sulphuric acid, ink, and other remarkable products.

St. Winifred's Well, in England, evolves 120 tons of water per minute, furnishing abundant water power to drive 11 mills within little more than a mile.

The French removed a red granite column 95 feet high, weighing 210 tons, from Thebes, and carried it to Paris. The display of costly architectural ruins at Thebes is one of the most astonishing to be seen anywhere in the world. The ruins and costly buildings in old Eastern countries, are so vast in their proportions and so many in number that it would require volumes to describe them.

Babel, now called Birs Nimroud, built at Babylon by Belus, was used as an observatory and as a temple of the Sun. It was composed of 8 square towers, one over the other, in all 670 feet high, and the same dimensions on each side on the ground.

The Coliseum at Rome, built by Vespasian for 100,000 spectators, was in its longest diameter 615-5 feet, and in the shortest 510, embraced 5½ acres, and was 120 feet high.

Eight aqueducts supplied ancient Rome with water, delivering 40 millions of cubit daily. That of Claudia was 47 miles long and 100 feet high, so as to furnish the hills. Martia was 41 miles, of which 37 were on 7,000 acres 70 feet high. These vast erections would never have been built had the Romans known that water always rises to its own level.

The Temple of Diana, at Ephesus, was 425 feet long and 225 feet broad, with 127 columns, 60 feet high, to support the roof. It was 220 years in building.

Solomon's Temple, built B. C. 1014, was 60 cubits or 107 feet in length, the breadth 20 cubits or 36 feet, and the height 30 cubits or 54 feet. The porch was 36 feet long and 18 feet wide.

The largest one of the Egyptian pyramids is 543 feet high, 693 feet on the sides, and its base covers 11 acres. The layers of stones are 208 in number. Many stones are over 30 feet long, 4 broad and 3 thick.

The Temple of Ypsambul, in Nubia, is enormously massive and cut out of the solid rock. Belzoni found in it 4 immense figures, 65 feet high, 25 feet over the shoulders, with a face of 7 feet and the ears over 3 feet.

Sesostris erected in the temple in Memphis immense statues of himself and his wife, 50 feet high, and of his children, 28 feet.

In the Temple of the Sun, at Baalbec, are stones more than 60 feet long, 24 feet thick and 16 broad, each embracing 23,000 cubic feet, cut, squared, sculptured, and transported from neighboring quarries. Six enormous columns are each 72 feet high, composed of 3 stones 7 feet in diameter. Sesostris is credited with having transported from the mountains of Arabia a rock 32 feet wide and 240 feet long.

The engineering appliances used by the ancients in the movement of these immense masses are but imperfectly understood at the present day.

During modern times, a block of granite weighing 1,217 tons, now used as the pedestal of the equestrian statute of Peter the Great, at St. Petersburg, was transported 4 miles by land over a railway, and 13 miles in a vast caisson by water. The railway consisted of two lines of timber furnished with hard metal grooves; between these grooves were placed spheres of hard brass about 6 inches in diameter. On these spheres the frame with its massive load was easily moved by 60 men, working at capstans with treble purchase blocks.

In 1716 Swedenborg contrived to transport (on rolling machines of his own invention) over valleys and mountains, 2 galleys, 5 large boats and 1 sloop, from Stromstadt to Iderfjol (which divides Sweden from Norway on the South), a distance of 14 miles, by which means Charles XII. was able to carry on his plans, and under cover of the galleys and boats to transport on pontoons his heavy artillery to the very walls of Frederickshall.

Belzoni considered the tract between the first and second cataract of the Nile as the hottest on the globe, owing to there being no rain. The natives do not credit the phenomenon of water falling from above. Hence it is that all monuments are so nicely preserved. Buckingham found a building left unfinished about 4,000 years ago, and the chalk marks on the stones were still perfect.

Pompey's Pillar is 92 feet high, and 27½ round at the base.

Water is the absolute master, former and secondary agent of the power of motion in everything terrestrial. It is the irresistible power which elaborates everything, and the waters contain more organized beings than the land.

Rivers hold in suspension 100th of their volume (more or less) of mud, so that if 36 cubic miles of water (the estimated quantity) flow daily into the sea, 0.36 cubic miles of soil are daily displaced. The Rhine carries to the sea every day 145,980 cubic feet of mud. The Po carries out the land 228 feet per annum, consequently Adria which 2,500 years ago was on the sea, is now over 20 miles from it.

The enormous amount of alluvium deposited by the Mississippi is almost incalculable, and constantly renders necessary extensive engineering operations in order to remove the impediments to navigation.

As an exponent of the laws of friction, it may be stated that a square stone weighing 1,080 lbs. which required a force of 758 lbs. to drag it along the floor of a quarry, roughly chiseled, required only a force of 22 lbs. to move it when mounted on a platform and rollers over a plank floor.

The flight of wild ducks is estimated at 90 miles per hour, that of the swift at 200 miles, carrier pigeons 38 miles, swallows 60 miles, migratory birds have crossed the Mediterranean at a speed of 120 miles per hour.

The Nile has a fall of 6 ins. in 1,000 miles. The rise of the river commences in June, continuing until the middle of August, attaining an elevation of from 24 to 26 feet, and flowing the valley of Egypt 12 miles wide. In 1829 it rose to 26 cubits, by which 30,000 persons were drowned. It is a terrible climate to live in, owing to the festering heat and detestable exhalations from the mud, etc., left on the retiring of the Nile, which adds about 4 inches to the soil in a century, and encroaches on the sea 16 feet every year. Bricks have been found at the depth of 60 feet, showing the vast antiquity of the country. In productiveness of soil it is excelled by no other in the world.

How to Splice a Belt in Order to Make it Run Like an Endless Belt.—Use the toughest yellow glue prepared in the ordinary way, while hot, stirring in thoroughly about 20 per cent of its weight of tannic acid, or extract of tan bark. Apply to the splice and quickly clamp together. The splice should be made of scarfed edges extending 3 to 6 inches back, according to thickness of belt. The surface to be perfectly clean and free from oil.

How Many Pounds of Coal it Requires to Maintain Steam of One-Horse Power per Hour.—Anthracite $1\frac{1}{2}$ to 5 pounds, according to the economy of boiler and engine. Bituminous and anthracite coal are very nearly equal for equal qualities. They both vary from 7 to 10 pounds of water evaporated per pound of coal from a temperature of 212 degrees.

A Formula for Collodio-bromide Emulsion that is Rapid.—Ether s. g. 0.720, 4 fluid ounces; alcohol s. g. 0.820, $2\frac{1}{2}$ fluid ounces; pyroxyline, 40 grains; castile soap dissolved in alcohol, 30 grains; bromide of ammonium and cadmium, 56 grains.

How to Deaden the Noise of Steam While Blowing off Through a Wrought Iron Stand Pipe.—The sound may be much modified by enlarging the end of the pipe like a trumpet or cone; which should be long, 20 or 30 times the diameter of the pipe, opening to 4 or 5 times its initial size.

Why Fusible Plugs are Put in the Crown Sheet of Locomotive Boilers.—To save the crown sheet from burning in case of low water, when the plug melts and lets the steam and water into the fire chamber to dampen and put out the fire as well as to make an alarm. They may also be employed on other forms of boilers, and are much used in connection with whistles for low-water alarms only. Boilers should not be blown out for cleaning with fire under them or while the walls (if set in brick) are hot enough to do damage to the iron shell. Locomotive boilers may be blown out very soon after the fire is entirely removed. All brick-set boilers should be left several hours after the fire is drawn before blowing off for cleaning.

How to Lace a Quarter Turn Belt so as to Have an Equal Strain on Both Edges of the Belt.—Begin on the outside of the belt at the middle, pass one end of the lacing through one end of the belt and bring it out through the corresponding hole of the other end of the belt, laying it diagonally off to the left. Now pass the other end of the lacing through the hole last used, and carry it over the first strand of the lacing on the inside of the belt, passing it through the first hole used, and lay it diagonally off to the right. Now proceed to pass the lacing through the holes of the belt in a zigzag course, leaving all the strands inside the belt parallel with the belt, and all the strands outside the belt oblique. Pass the lace twice through the holes nearest the edge of the belt, then return the lace in the reverse order toward the center of the belt, so as to cross all the oblique strands, and make all the inside strands double. Finally pass the end of the lacing through the first hole used, then outward through an awl hole, then hammering it down to cause it to hold. The left side is to be laced in a similar way.

A Useful Hint to Draughtsmen.—To strain drawing paper on a board, cut the paper to the size required, lay it on the board face downwards and thoroughly wet the surface with a damp sponge or brush, then turn it over and wet the face in the same way; roll it up tightly and let it stay so for five or six minutes, unroll it, and turn up the edges about an inch all around. Take liquid glue (Jackson's is the best) and apply it carefully to the edges, then turn them down, and with a paper knife press them to the board all around. Put the board in an inclined position where it is not too dry or warm, or the paper will dry too fast and tear. If it is allowed to dry slowly the surface will be perfectly even and smooth, and a pleasure to draw upon.

Joints for Hot Water Pipes.—Sal-ammoniac, 2 oz.; sublimed sulphur, 1 oz.; cast-iron filings, 1 ℔. Mix in a mortar, and keep the powder dry. When it is to be used, mix it with twenty times its weight of clean iron filings, and grind the whole in a mortar. Wet with water until it becomes of convenient consistence. After a time it becomes as hard and strong as any part of the metal.

When the Process of Galvanizing Iron was First Known.—A. The process of coating iron with zinc, or zinc and tin, is a French invention, and was patented in England in 1837.

A Timber Test.—The soundness of timber may be ascertained by placing the ear close to one end of the log, while another person delivers a succession of smart blows with a hammer or mallet upon the opposite end, when a continuance of the vibrations will indicate to an experienced ear even the degree of soundness. If only a dull thud meets the ear, the listener may be certain that unsoundness exists.

Useful Hints and Recipes.—Following is a comparative statement of the toughness of various woods.—Ash, 100; beech, 85; cedar of Lebanon, 84; larch, 83; sycamore and common walnut, each, 68; occidental plane, 66; oak, hornbeam and Spanish mahogany, each, 62; teak and acacia, each, 58; elm and young chestnut, 52.

An ingenius device for stretching emery cloth for use in the workshop consists of a couple of strips of wood about 14 in. long, hinged longitudinally, and of round, half-round, triangular, or any other shape in cross section. On the inside faces of the wood strips are pointed studs, fitting into holes on the opposite side. The strip of emery cloth is laid on to one set of the studs, and the file, as it is called, closed, which fixes the strip on one side. It is then similarly fixed on the other side, and thus constitutes what is called an emery file and which is a handy and convenient arrangement for workshop use.

Method of making Artificial Whetstones.—Gelatine of good quality is dissolved in its own weight of water, the operation being conducted in a dark room. To the solution one and a half per cent. of bichromate of potash is added, which has previously been dissolved in a little water. A quantity of very fine emery, equal to nine times the weight of the gelatine, is itimately mixed with the gelatine solution. Pulverized flint may be substituted for emery. The mass is molded into any desired shape, and is then consolidated by heavy pressure. It is dried by exposure to strong sunlight for several hours.

How to Toughen Paper.—A plan for rendering paper as tough as wood or leather has been recently introduced; it consists in mixing chloride of zinc with the pulp in the course of manufacture. It has been found that the greater the degree of concentration of the zinc solution, the greater will be the toughness of the paper. It can be used for making boxes and for roofing.

How to Mend a Broken File.—There is no tool so easily broken as the file that the machinist has to work with, and is about the first thing that snaps when a kit of tools gets upset upon the cross-beam of a machine or a tool board from the bed of an engine lathe. It cannot even be passed from one workman to another without being broken, if the file is a new one or still good for anything, if an apprentice has got anything to do with it, and they are never worth mending, however great may be their first cost, unless the plaster of Paris and lime treatment can make a perfect weld without injuring the steel or disturbing the form of the teeth. Steel that is left as hard as a file is very brittle, and soft solder can hold as much on a steady pull if it has a new surface to work from. Take a file, as soon as it is broken, and wet the break with zinc dissolved in muriatic acid, and then tin over with the soldering iron, This must be done immediately as soon as the file is broken, as the break begins to oxydize when exposed to the air. and in an hour or two will gather sufficient to make it impossible for the parts to adhere. Heat the file as warm as it will bear without disturbing its temper as soon as well tinned, and press the two pieces firmly together, squeezing out nearly all the solder, and hold in place until the file cools. This can be done with very little to trim off, and every portion of the break fitting accurately in place. Bring both pieces in line with each other, and, for a file, it is as strong in one place as in another, and is all that could be asked for under the very best of welding treatment.

What will Fasten Pencil Markings, to Prevent Blurring.—Immerse paper containing the markings to be preserved in a bath of clear water, then flow or immerse in milk a moment; hang up to dry. Having often had recourse to this method, in preserving pencil and crayon drawings, I will warrant it a sure cure.

How to Transfer Newspaper Prints to Glass.—First coat the glass with dammar varnish, or else with Canada balsam, mixed with an equal volume of oil of turpentine, and let it dry until it is very sticky, which takes half a day or more. The printed paper to be transferred should be well soaked in soft water, and carefully laid upon the prepared glass, after removing surplus water with blotting paper, and pressed upon it, so that no air bubbles or drops of water are seen underneath. This should dry a whole day before it is touched; then with wetted fingers begin to rub off the paper at the back. If this be skillfully done, almost the whole of the paper can be removed, leaving simply the ink upon the varnish. When the paper has been removed, another coat of varnish will serve to make the whole more transparent. This recipe is sold at from $3 to $5 by itinerants.

A Liquid Cement for Cementing Leather, that Will Not be Affected by the Action of Water.—A good cement for splicing leather is gutta percha dissolved in carbon disulphide, until it is of the thickness of treacle; the parts to be cemented must first be well thinned down, then pour a small quantity of the cement on both ends, spreading it well so as to fill the pores of the leather; warm the parts over a fire for about half a minute, apply them quickly together, and hammer well. The bottle containing the cement should be tightly corked, and kept in a cool place.

The Quickest and Best Way to Drill Holes for Water Pipes in Rough Plate Glass.—Use a hardened (file temper) drill, with spirits of turpentine and camphor to make the drill bite. A broken file in a breast brace will do good work if a power drill is not obtainable.

A Recipe for Making Printers' Inks.—For black ink: Take of balsam of copaiba (pure), 9 ounces; lamp black, 3 ounces; indigo and Prussian blue, of each half an ounce; Indian red, ¼ ounce; yellow soap (dry), 3 ounces; grind the mixture to an impalpable smoothness by means of a stone and muller. Canada balsam may be substituted for balsam of copaiba where the smell of the latter is objectionable, but the ink then dries very quickly. The red inks are similarly made by using such pigments as carmine, lakes, vermilion, chrome yellow, red lead, orange red, Indian red and Venetian red.

A Cement to Stick White Metal Tops on Glass Bottles.—One of the best cap cements consists of resin, 5 ounces; beeswax, 1 ounce; red ocher or Venetian red in powder, 1 ounce. Dry the earth thoroughly on a stove at a temperature above 212° Fah. Melt the wax and resin together, and stir in the powder by degrees. Stir until cold, lest the earthy matter settle to the bottom.

The Correct Meaning of the Tonnage of a Vessel.—The law defines very carefully how the tonnage of different vessels shall be calculated. An approximate rule for finding the gross tonnage is to multiply the length of keel between perpendiculars by the breadth of vessel and depth of hold, all in feet, and dividing the product by 100. It is generally assumed that 40 cubic feet shall constitute a ton, and the tonnage of a vessel is considered to be the multiple of this ton, which most closely corresponds with the internal capacity of the vessel.

A Recipe for Re-inking Purple Type Ribbons.—Use: Aniline violet, ¼ ounce; pure alcohol, 15 ounces; concentrated glycerine, 15 ounces. Dissolve the aniline in the alcohol, and add the glycerine.

The Process of Giving a Tempered-Blue Color to the Steel Plate and Malleable Iron Castings of a Roller Skate.—In order to obtain an even blue, the work must have an even finish, and be made perfectly clean. Arrange a cast-iron pot in a fire so as to heat it to the temperature of melted lead, or just below a red heat. Make a flat bottom basket of wire or wire cloth to sit in the iron box, on which place the work to be blued, as many pieces as you may find you can manage, always putting in pieces of about the same thickness and size, so that they will heat evenly. Make a bail to the basket, so that it can be easily handled. When the desired color is obtained, dip quickly in hot water to stop the progress of the bluing, for an instant only, so that enough heat may be retained to dry the articles. A cover to the iron box may sometimes be used to advantage to hasten the heating. Another way, much used, is to varnish the work with ultramarine varnish, which may be obtained from the varnish makers.

Cement to Mend Iron Pots and Pans.—Take two parts of sulphur and one part, by weight, of fine black lead; put the sulphur in an old iron pan, holding it over the fire until it begins to melt, then add the lead; stir well until all is mixed and melted; then pour out on an iron plate or smooth stone. When cool, break into small pieces. A sufficient quantity of this compound being placed upon the crack of the iron pot to be mended, can be soldered by a hot iron in the same way a tinsmith solders his sheets. If there is a small hole in the pot, drive a copper rivet in it, and then solder over it with this cement.

The Best Method of Rendering Basement Walls Damp-Proof.—Construct on the outside an area wall so that the earth does not rest directly against the main wall of the house, but only against the outside wall or casing of the area. To form such an area, build a wall half or one brick thick parallel to and some 2 or 3 inches from the main wall, and form at the bottom a channel or gutter connected with the drains, so that any moisture or water finding its way in through the outer casing may be conducted away and will not therefore penetrate into the building. Thoroughly ventilate the areas by means of air bricks or other suitable connections with the outer air, and connect with one another by making through connections underneath the floor joists. Be very careful that the main wall is laid on a good and efficient damp course. The top of the space between the area and main walls may be covered in all around the building with bricks—ornamented or otherwise, as preferred—on a line just above the ground. Another plan of effecting the same object is to dispense with the area wall and in building the brick work to cover the whole of the work on the outside with a thick layer of bituminous asphalt. The plaster on the inside is in this case often rendered in nearly neat Portland cement.

How to Caseharden Large Pieces of Steel.—A box of cast or wrought iron should be provided large enough to hold one or two of the pieces, with sufficient room all around to pack well with the casehardening materials, which may be leather scrap, hoof shavings, or horn shavings, slightly burned and pulverized, which may be mixed with an equal quantity of pulverized charcoal. Pack the pieces to be casehardened in the iron box so as not to touch each other or the box. Put an iron cover on the box and lute with clay. Heat gradually in a furnace to a full red, keep at an even temperature for from 2 to 4 hours, raise the heat to a cherry red during the last hour, then remove the cover and take out the pieces and plunge endwise vertically in water at shop temperature; 2 per cent. of hydrochloric acid in the water improves its tempering qualities and gives the metal an even gray color.

A Good and Cheap Preparation to Put on Friction Matches.—The igniting composition varies with different makers. The following recipes may be taken as fairly representative, the first being the best: 1. Phosphorus by weight, ½ part; potassium chlorate, 4 parts; glue, 2 parts; whiting, 1 part; finely powdered glass, 4 parts; water, 11 parts. 2. Phosphorus by weight, 2 parts; potassium chlorate, 5 parts; glue, 3 parts; red lead, 1½ parts; water, 12 parts. 3. A German mixture for matches. Potassium chlorate, 7.8 parts; lead hyposulphite, 2·6 parts; gum arabic, 1 part.

To Find How Much Tin Vessels Will Hold.—For the contents of cylinders: Square the diameter, and multiply the product by 0.7854. Again, multiply by the height (all in inches). Divide the product by 231 for gallons. For the frustum of a cone: Add together the squares of the diameters of large and small ends; to this add the product of the diameter of the two ends. Multiply this sum by 0.7854. Multiply this product by the height (all in inches). Then divide by 231 for the number of gallons.

A Useful Recipe.—For stopping the joints between slates or shingles, etc., and chimneys, doors, windows, etc., a mixture of stiff white-lead paint, with sand enough to prevent it from running, is very good, especially if protected by a covering of strips of lead or copper, tin, etc., nailed to the mortar joints of the chimneys, after being bent so as to enter said joints, which should be scraped out for an inch in depth, and afterward refilled. Mortar protected in the same way, or even unprotected, is often used for the purpose, but it is not equal to the paint and sand. Mortar a few days old (to allow refractory particles of lime to slack), mixed with blacksmith's cinders and molasses, is much used for this purpose, and becomes very hard and effective.

Test for Hard or Soft Water.—Dissolve a small quantity of good soap in alcohol. Let a few drops fall into a glass of water. If it turns milky, it is hard; if not, it is soft.

Test for Earthy Matters or Alkali in Water.—Take litmus paper dipped in vinegar, and if, on immersion, the paper returns to its true shade, the water does not contain earthy matter or alkali. If a few drops of syrup be added to a water containing an earthy matter, it will turn green.

Test for Carbonic Acid in Water.—Take equal parts of water and clear lime water. If combined or free carbonic acid is present, a precipitate is seen, to which, if a few drops of muriatic acid be added, an effervescence commences.

Test for Magnesia in Water.—Boil the water to a twentieth part of its weight, and then drop a few grains of neutral carbonate of ammonia into a glass of it, and a few drops of phosphate of soda. If magnesia be present, it will fall to the bottom.

Test for Iron in Water.—1. Boil a little nutgall and add to the water. If it turns gray or slate, black iron is present. 2. Dissolve a little prussiate of potash, and, if iron is present, it will turn blue.

Test for Lime in Water.—Into a glass of water put two drops of oxalic acid and blow upon it. If it gets milky, lime is present.

Test for Acid in Water.—Take a piece of litmus paper. If it turns red, there must be acid. If it precipitates on adding lime water, it is carbonic acid. If a blue sugar paper is turned red, it is a mineral acid.

Value of Manufactured Steel.—A pound of very fine steel wire to make watch springs of, is worth about $4; this will make 17,000 springs, worth $7,000.

Horses in Norway have a very sensible way of taking their food, which perhaps might be beneficially followed here. They have a bucket of water put down beside their allowance of hay. It is interesting to see with what relish they take a sip of the one and a mouthful of the other alternately, sometimes only moistening their mouths, as a rational being would do while eating a dinner of such dry food. A broken-winded horse is scarcely ever seen in Norway, and the question is if the mode of feeding has not something to do with the preservation of the animal's respiratory organs.

The Process of Fastening Rubber Rolls on Clothes Wringer.—1. Clean shaft thoroughly between the shoulders or washers, where the rubber goes on. 2. Give the shaft a coat of copal varnish, between the shoulders, and let it dry. 3. Give shaft coat of varnish and wind shaft tightly as possible with five-ply jute twine at once, while varnish is green, and let it dry for about six hours. 4. Give shaft over the twine a coat of rubber cement, and let it dry for about six hours. 5. Give shaft over the twine a second coat of rubber cement, and let it dry for about six hours. 6. Remove washer on the short end of shaft, also the cogwheel if the shaft has cogs on both ends. 7. See that the rubber rolls are always longer than the space between the washers where the rubber goes on, as they shrink or take up a little in putting on the shaft. 8. Clean out the hole or inside of roll with benzine, using a small brush or swab. 9. Put the thimble or pointer on the end of shaft that the washer has been removed from, and give shaft over the twine and thimble another coat of cement, and stand same upright in a vise. 10. Give the inside or hole of roll a coat of cement with a small rod or stick. 11. Pull or force the roll on the shaft as quickly as possible with a jerk, then rivet the washer on with a cold chisel.

12. Let roll stand and get dry for two or three days before using same. Cement for use should be so thick that it will run freely; if it gets too thick, thin it with benzine or naphtha.

How to Make Effervescing Solution of Citrate of Magnesia.—Dissolve citric acid 400 grains in water 2,000 grains, add carbonate of magnesia 200 grains; stir until dissolved. Filter into a 12-ounce bottle containing syrup of citric acid 1,200 grains. Add boiled and filtered water to fill bottle, drop in bicarbonate of potash in crystals 30 grains and immediately cork. Shake until bicarbonate of potash is dissolved. The syrup of citric acid is made from citric acid 8 parts, water 8 parts, spirit of lemon 4 parts, syrup 980 parts.

A Receipt for Making the Black Cement that is Used for Filling Letters after They are Cut out in Brass.—Mix asphaltum, brown japan and lampblack into a putty-like mass, fill in the spaces, and finally clean the edges with turpentine.

Useful Workshop Hints.—Clean and oil leather belts without taking them off their pulleys. If taken off they will shrink. Then a piece must be put into them and removed again after the belt has run a few days. The decay of stone, either in buildings or monuments, may be arrested by heating and treating with paraffin mixed with a little creosote. A common "paint burner" may be used to heat the stone. Set an engine upon three or four movable points, as upon three cannon balls. Connect with steam, and exhaust by means of rubber hose. If the engine will run up to speed without moving itself back and forth, then that engine will run a long time with little repair. If it shakes itself around the room, then buy another engine. Safely moving a tall mill chimney has been accomplished several times. Chimneys which have been caused to lean slightly through settling of the foundation may be straightened up again by sawing out the mortar between courses of brick at the base. A chimney 100 ft. high and 12 ft. square at the base will be varied over 8 in. at the top by the removal of 1 in. at the base. When you begin to fix up the mill for cold weather, don't forget to put a steam trap in each and every steam pipe which can be opened into the atmosphere for heating purposes. For leading steam joints, mix the red lead or litharge with common commercial glycerine, instead of linseed oil. Put a little carbolic acid in your glue or paste pot. It will keep the contents sweet for a long time. Look well to the bearings of your shafting engine and machines. Sometimes 25, 30, 40 and even 50 per cent. of your power is consumed through lack of good oil. When you buy a water wheel, be sure to buy one small enough to run at full gate while the stream is low during the summer months. If you want more power than the small wheel will give, then put in two or more wheels of various sizes. When it becomes necessary to trim a piece of rubber, it will be found that the knife will cut much more readily if dipped in water. When forging a chisel or other cutting tool, never upset the end of the tool. If necessary cut it off, but don't try to force it back into a good cutting edge. In tubular boilers the handholes should be often opened, and all collections removed from over the fire. When boilers are fed in front, and are blown off through the same pipe, the collection of mud or sediment in the rear end should be often removed. Nearly all smoke may be consumed without special apparatus, by attending with a little common sense to a few simple rules. Suppose we have a battery of boilers, and "soft coal" is the fuel. Go to the first boiler, shut the damper nearly up, and fire up one-half of the furnace, close the door, open damper, and go to the next boiler and repeat the firing. By this method nearly, if not quite, all the smoke will be con-

sumed. A coiled spring inserted between engine and machinery is highly beneficial where extreme regularity of power is required. It is well known that a steam engine, in order to govern itself, must run too fast and too slow in order to close or open its valves; hence an irregularity of power is unavoidable.

A "Paste" Metal Polish for Cleaning and Polishing Brass.—Oxalic acid 1 part, iron peroxide 15 parts, powdered rottenstone 20 parts, palm oil 60 parts, petrolatum 4 parts. See that solids are thoroughly pulverized and sifted, then add and thoroughly incorporate oil and petrolatum.

Cough Candy or Troches.—Tincture of squills 2 ounces, camphorated tincture of opium and tincture of tolu of each $\frac{1}{4}$ ounce, wine of ipecac $\frac{1}{2}$ ounce, oil of gautheria 4 drops, sassafras 3 drops, and of anise seed oil 2 drops. The above mixture is to be put into 5 pounds of candy which is just ready to take from the fire; continue the boiling a little longer, so as to form into sticks.

How to Oxidize Silver.—For this purpose a pint of sulphide of potassium, made by intimately mixing and heating together 2 parts of thoroughly dried potash and 1 part of sulphur powder, is used. Dissolve 2 to 3 drachms of this compound in $1\frac{3}{4}$ pints of water, and bring the liquid to a temperature of from 155 degress to 175 degrees Fah., when it is ready for use. Silver objects, previously freed from dust and grease with soda lye and thorough rinsing in water, plunged into this bath are instantly covered with an iridescent film of silver sulphide, which in a few seconds more becomes blue black. The objects are then removed, rinsed off in plenty of fresh water, scratch brushed, and if necessary polished.

Useful Household Recipes.—To purify water in glass vessels and aquariums, it is recommended to add to every 100 grammes of water four drops of a solution of one gramme of salicylic acid in 300 grammes of water. The *Norsk Fiskeritidende*, published at Bergen, Norway, says that thereby the water may be kept fresh for three months without being renewed. A cement recommended as something which can hardly be picked to pieces is made as follows:—Mix equal parts of lime and brown sugar with water, and be sure the lime is thoroughly air-slacked. This mortar is equal to Portland cement, and is of extraordinary strength. For a few weeks' preservation of organic objects in their original form, dimensions and color, Professor Grawitz recommends a mixture composed of two and a half ounces of chloride of sodium, two and three-quarters drachms of saltpetre, and one pint of water, to which is to be added three per cent. of boric acid. To varnish chromos, take equal quantities of linseed oil and oil of turpentine; thicken by exposure to the sun and air until it becomes resinous and half evaporated; then add a portion of melted beeswax. Varnishing pictures should always be performed in fair weather, and out of any current of cold or damp air. A fireproof whitewash can be readily made by adding one part silicate of soda (or potash) to every five parts of whitewash. The addition of a solution of alum to whitewash is recommended as a means to prevent the rubbing off of the wash. A coating of a good glue size made by dissolving half a pound of glue in a gallon of water is employed when the wall is to be papered. The most nourishing steam bath that can be applied to a person who is unable to sweat and can take but little food in the stomach:—Produce the sweating by burning alcohol under a chair in which the person sits, with blanket covering to hold the heat. Use caution and but little alcohol. Fire it in a shallow iron pan or old saucer.

Own Your Own Homes.—Every man, whether he is a working man in the common acceptation of the word or not, feels a deep interest in the management of the affairs of the city, county and State in which he lives whenever he owns a home. He is more patriotic, and in many ways is a better citizen than the man who simply rents, and who has but little if any assurance of how long it will be before he can be ordered to move; to which may be added in many cases the saving of more money. Of course it requires some economy to lay up a sufficient amount of money to purchase and pay for a home; but this very fact, if properly carried out after the home is acquired, may be the instrument of furnishing the means to commence and prosecute a business upon your own responsibility. True, in some cases it will require more economy, perhaps, than we are now practicing. But the question with every man, and especially if he is the head of a family, is, Can he afford it? That is, can he afford to live up his wages as fast as he earns them, without laying up anything for the future? If he is the head of a family, he is obliged to pay rent, and it does not require very many years of rent paying to make up an amount sufficient to purchase and pay for a comfortable home. You have to pay the rent. This you say you cannot avoid and be honest. Well, you cannot be honest with your family unless you make a reasonable attempt to provide them a home of their own in case anything should happen to you. And the obligation to do this should be as strong as the one to pay rent or provide the other necessaries for the comfort of your family. When you own a home you feel a direct interest in public affairs that otherwise you might consider were of little interest.

A Formula for Nervous Headache.—Alcohol dilut., 4 ounces; Olei cinnamon, 4 minims; Potas. bromid., 5 drachms; Extr. hyoscyam., fl., 1½ drachms; Fiat lotio. One to two teaspoonfuls, if required.

How Beeswax is Refined and Made Nice and Yellow.— Pure white wax is obtained from the ordinary beeswax by exposure to the influence of the sun and weather. The wax is sliced into thin flakes and laid on sacking or coarse cloth, stretched on frames, resting on posts to raise them from the ground. The wax is turned over frequently and occasionally sprinkled with soft water if there be not dew and rain sufficient to moisten it. The wax should be bleached in about four weeks. If, on breaking the flakes, the wax still appears yellow inside, it is necessary to melt it again and flake and expose it a second time, or even oftener, before it becomes thoroughly bleached, the time required being mainly dependent upon the weather. There is a preliminary process by which, it is claimed, much time is saved in the subsequent bleaching; this consists in passing melted wax and steam through long pipes, so as to expose the wax as much as possible to the action of the steam; thence into a pan heated by a steam bath, where it is stirred thoroughly with water and then allowed to settle. The whole operation is repeated a second and third time, and the wax is then in condition to be more readily bleached.

How to Remove a Wart From the Hand.—Take of salicylic acid, 30 grains; ext. cannabis indic., 10 grains; collodion, ½ ounce. Mix and apply.

Recipe for Making Camphor Ice in Small Quantities for Home Use.—Melt together over a water bath white wax and spermaceti, each 1 ounce; camphor, 2 ounces, in sweet almond oil, 1 pound; then triturate until the mixture has become homogeneous, and allow one pound of rosewater to flow in slowly during the operation.

Recipe for Making Instantaneous Ink and Stain Extractor.—Take of chloride of lime 1 pound, thoroughly pulverized, and four quarts soft water. The foregoing must be thoroughly shaken when first put together. It is required to stand twenty-four hours to dissolve the chloride of lime; then strain through a cotton cloth, after which add a teaspoonful of acetic acid to every ounce of the chloride of lime water.

Removing Paint Spots From Wood.—To take spots of paint off wood, lay a thick coating of lime and soda mixed together over it, letting it stay twenty-four hours; then wash off with warm water, and the spot will have disappeared.

Polishing Plate Glass.—To polish plate glass and remove slight scratches, rub the surface gently, first with a clean pad of fine cotton wool, and afterwards with a similar pad covered over with cotton velvet which has been charged with fine rouge. The surface will acquire a polish of great brilliancy, quite free from any scratches.

Recipe for a Good Condition Powder.—Ground ginger 1 pound, antimony sulphide 1 pound, powdered sulphur 1 pound, saltpetre. Mix altogether and administer in a mash, in such quantities as may be required.

Recipe to Make Violet Ink.—Ordinary aniline violet soluble in water, with a little alcohol and glycerine, makes an excellent ink.

Recipe to Make Good Shaving Soap.—Either 66 pounds tallow and 34 pounds cocoanut oil, or 33 pounds of tallow and the same quantity of palm oil and 34 pounds cocoanut oil, treated by the cold process, with 120 pounds caustic soda lye of 27 deg. Baume, will make 214 pounds of shaving soap.

How to Make a Starch Enamel for Stiffening Collars, Cuffs, etc.—Use a little gum arabic thoroughly dissolved in the starch.

A Good Cough Syrup.—Put 1 quart hoarhound to 1 quart water, and boil it down to a pint; add two or three sticks of licorice and a tablespoonful of essence of lemon.

The Cause of the Disease Called "Hives," also Its Cure. —The trouble is caused by a perversion of the digestive functions, accompanied by a disturbance of the circulation. It is not attended with danger, and is of importance only from the annoyance which it causes. Relief may be obtained in most instances by the use of cream tartar daily to such extent as to move the bowels slightly. Make a strong solution, sweeten it pleasantly, and take a teaspoonful, say after each meal, until the effect above mentioned is produced, and continue the treatment until the hives cease to be troublesome.

A Bedbug Poison.—Set in the center of the room a dish containing 4 ounces of brimstone. Light it, and close the room as tight as possible, stopping the keyhole of the door with paper to keep the fumes of the brimstone in the room. Let it remain for three or four hours, then open the windows and air thoroughly. The brimstone will be found to have also bleached the paint, if it was a yellowish white. Mixtures such as equal parts of turpentine and kerosene oil are used; filling up the cracks with hard soap is an excellent remedy. Benzine and gasoline will kill bedbugs as fast as they can reach them. A weak solution of zinc chloride is also said to be an effectual banisher of these pests.

A Preparation by Which You can Take a Natural Flower and Dip It in, That Will Preserve It.—Dip the flowers in melted paraffine, withdrawing them quickly. The liquid should only be just hot enough to maintain its fluidity and the flowers should be dipped one at a time, held by the stalks, and moved about for an instant to get rid of air bubbles. Fresh cut specimens free from moisture make excellent specimens in this way.

What Causes Shaking Asp Leaves to be always in a Quiver?—The wind or vibration of the air only causes the quiver of the aspen leaf.

What "Sozodont" is Composed of.—Potassium carbonate, $\frac{1}{2}$ ounce; honey, 4 ounces; alcohol, 2 ounces; water, 10 ounces; oil of wintergreen and oil of rose, to flavor, sufficient.

What is Used to Measure Cold below 35 Degrees Fahrenheit?—Metallic thermometers are used to measure lowest temperatures, alcohol being quite irregular.

Is the Top Surface of Ice on a Pond, the Amount of Water let in and out being the Same Day by Day, on a Level with the Water Surface or above it?—Ice is slightly elastic, and when fast to the shore the central portion rises and falls with slight variations in water level, the proportion above and below water level being as is the weight of ice to the weight of water it displaces.

Of the Two Waters, Hard and Soft, Which Freezes the Quicker; and in ice Which Saves the Best in Like Packing?—Soft water freezes the quickest and keeps the best.

Does Water in Freezing Purify Itself?—It clears itself from chemicals; does not clear itself from mechanical mixtures as mud and clay.

A Receipt to Remove Freckles from the Face without Injury to the Skin.—A commonly used preparation for this purpose is: Sulpho-carbolate of zinc, 2 parts; distilled glycerine, 25 parts; rose water, 25 parts; scented alcohol, 5 parts. To be applied twice daily for from half an hour to an hour, and then washed off with cold water.

What will Remove Warts Painlessly?—Touch the wart with a little nitrate of silver, or with nitric acid, or with aromatic vinegar. The silver salt will produce a black, and the nitric acid a yellow stain, either of which will wear off in a short while. The vinegar scarcely discolors the skin.

A Good Receipt to Prevent Hair Coming Out.—Scald black tea, 2 ounces, with 1 gallon of boiling water, strain and add 3 ounces glycerine, tincture cantharides $\frac{1}{2}$ ounce, bay rum 1 quart. Mix well and perfume. This is a good preparation for frequent use in its effect both on the scalp and hair, but neither will be kept in good condition without care and attention to general health.

Deaths from Diphtheria per 100,000 Inhabitants in the Chief Cities of the World.—Amsterdam, 265; Berlin, 245; Madrid, 225; Dresden, 184; Warsaw, 167; Philadelphia, 163; Chicago, 146; Turin, 127; St. Petersburg, 121; Bucharest, 118; Berne, 115; Munich, 111; Stockholm, 107; Malines, 105; Antwerp, 104; New York, 91; Paris, 85; Hamburg, 76; Naples, 74; Lisbon, 74; Stuttgart, 61; Rome, 56; Edinburgh, 50; Buda-Pesth, 50; The Hague, 45; Vienna, 44; London, 44; Christiania, 43; Copenhagen, 42; Suburbs of Brussels, 36; City of Brussels, 35.

A Receipt for Marshmallows, as Made by Confectioners.—Dissolve one-half pound of gum arabic in one pint of water, strain, and add one-half pound of fine sugar, and place over the fire, stirring constantly until the syrup is dissolved, and all of the consistency of honey. Add gradually the whites of four eggs well beaten. Stir the mixture until it becomes somewhat thin and does not adhere to the finger. Flavor to taste, and pour into a tin slightly dusted with powdered starch, and when cool divide into small squares.

A Receipt for Making Compressed Yeast.—This yeast is obtained by straining the common yeast in breweries and distilleries until a moist mass is obtained, which is then placed in hair bags, and the rest of the water pressed out until the mass is nearly dry. It is then sewed up in strong linen bags for transportation.

How to Tell the Age of Eggs.—We recommend the following process (which has been known for some time, but has been forgotten) for finding out the age of eggs, and distinguishing those that are fresh from those that are not. This method is based upon the decrease in the density of eggs as they grow old. Dissolve two ounces of kitchen salt in a pint of water. When a fresh-laid egg is placed in this solution it will descend to the bottom of the vessel, while one that has been laid on the day previous will not quite reach the bottom. If the egg be three days old it will swim in the liquid, and if it is more than three days old it will float on the surface, and project above the latter more and more in proportion as it is older.

A Recipe for Making Court Plaster.—Isinglass 125 grains, alcohol 1$\frac{1}{4}$ fluid ounces, glycerine 12 minims, water and tincture of benzoin each sufficient quanity. Dissolve the isinglass in enough water to make the solution weigh four fluid ounces. Spread half of the latter with a brush upon successive layers of taffeta, waiting after each application until the layer is dry. Mix the second half of the isinglass solution with the alcohol and glycerine, and apply in the same manner. Then reverse the taffeta, coat it on the back with tincture of benzoin, and allow it to become perfectly dry. There are many other formulas, but this is official. The above quantities are sufficient to make a piece of court plaster fifteen inches square.

One of the Very Best Scouring Pastes Consists of—Oxalic acid, 1 part; Iron peroxide, 15 parts; Powdered rottenstone, 20 parts; Palm oil, 60 parts; Petrolatum, 4 parts. Pulverize the oxalic acid and add rouge and rottenstone, mixing thoroughly, and sift to remove all grit; then add gradually the palm oil and petrolatum, incorporating thoroughly. Add oil of myrbane, or oil of lavender to suit. By substituting your red ashes from stove coal, an inferior representative of the foregoing paste will be produced.

How to Manufacture Worcestershire Sauce.—A. Mix together 1$\frac{1}{2}$ gallons white wine vinegar, 1 gallon walnut catsup, 1 gallon mushroom catsup, $\frac{1}{2}$ gallon Madeira wine, $\frac{1}{2}$ gallon Canton soy, 2$\frac{1}{2}$ pounds moist sugar, 19 ounces salt, 3 ounces powdered capsicum, 1$\frac{1}{2}$ ounces each of pimento and coriander, 1$\frac{1}{2}$ ounces chutney, $\frac{3}{4}$ ounce each of cloves, mace and cinnamon, and 6$\frac{1}{2}$ drachms assafœtida dissolved in pint brandy 20 above proof. Boil 2 pounds hog's liver for twelve hours in 1 gallon of water, adding water as required to keep up the quantity, then mix the boiled liver thoroughly with the water, strain it through a coarse sieve. Add this to the sauce.

A Good Receipt for Making Honey, Without Using Honey as One of the Ingredients.—5 lbs. white sugar, 2 lbs. water, gradually bring to a boil, and skim well. When cool add 1 lb. bees' honey, and 4 drops peppermint, To make of better quality add less water and more real honey.

What the Chemical Composition of Honey is.—Principally of saccharine matter and water, about as follows: Levulose 33$\frac{1}{2}$ to 40 per cent., dextrose 31$\frac{1}{4}$ to 39 per cent., water 20 to 30 per cent., besides ash and other minor constituents.

How to Clean Carpets on the Floor to Make Them Look Bright.—To a pailful of water add three pints of oxgall, wash the carpet with this until a lather is produced, which is washed off with clean water.

How to Take Out Varnish Spots from Cloth.—Use chloroform or benzine, and as a last resource spirits of turpentine, followed after drying by benzine.

Flour Paste for all Purposes.—Mix 1 pound rye flour in lukewarm water, to which has been added one teaspoonful of pulverized alum; stir until free of lumps. Boil in the regular way, or slowly pour on boiling water, stirring all the time until the paste becomes stiff. When cold add a full quarter pound of common strained honey, mix well (regular bee honey, no patent mixture).

How to Make Liquid Glue.—Take a wide mouthed bottle, and dissolve in it 8 ounces best glue in ½ pint water, by setting it in a vessel of water, and heating until dissolved. Then add slowly 2½ ounces strong nitric acid 36 deg. Baume, stirring all the while. Effervescence takes place, with generation of fumes. When all the acid has been added, the liquid is allowed to cool. Keep it well corked, and it will be ready for use at any time.

How the World is Weighed and Its Density and Mass Computed.—The density, mass, or weight of the earth was found by the observed force of attraction of a known mass of lead or iron for another mass; or of a mountain by the deflection of a torsion thread or plumb line. In this manner the mean density of the earth has been found to be from 4.71 to 6.56 times the weight of water, 5.66 being accredited as the most reliable. The weight of a cubic foot of water being known, and the contents of the earth being computed in cubic feet, we have but to multiply the number of cubic feet by 5.66 times the weight of 1 cubic foot of water to obtain the weight of the earth in pounds, or units of gravity at its surface, which is the unit usually used. Another method of determining the mean density of the earth is founded on the change of the intensity of gravity in descending deep mines.

A Theory as to the Origin of Petroleum.—Professor Mendelejef has recently advanced the theory that petroleum is of purely mineral origin and that the formation of it is going on every day. He has, moreover, succeeded in producing artificial petroleum by a reaction that he describes, and he states that it is impossible to detect any difference between the natural product and the manufactured article. His theory is as follows: Infiltration of water, reaching a certain depth, come into contact with incandescent masses of carburets of metals, chiefly of iron, and are at once decomposed into oxygen and hydrogen. The oxygen unites with the iron, while the hydrogen seizes on the carbon and rises to an upper level, where the vapors are condensed in part into mineral oil, and the rest remains in a state of natural gas. The petroleum strata are generally met with in the vicinity of mountains, and it may be granted that geological upheavals have dislocated the ground in such a way as to permit of the admistoin of water to great depths. If the center of the earth contains great masses of metallic carburets, we may, in case this theory is verified, count upon an almost inexhaustible source of fuel for the day when our coal deposits shall fail us.

How Vaseline is Purified.—The residuum from which vaseline is made is placed in settling tanks heated by steam, in order to keep their contents in a liquid state. After the complete separation of the fine coke it is withdrawn from these tanks and passed through the bone black cylinders, during which process the color is nearly all removed, as well as its empyreumatic odor.

The Latest and Best Process Employed by Cutters and Others in Etching Names and Designs on Steel.—Take copper sulphate, sulphate of alum and sodium chloride, of each 2 drachms, and strong acetic acid 1½ ounces, mixed together. Smear the metal with yellow soap and write with a quill pen without a split.

The History of the Discovery of Circulation of the Blood recapitulated, divides itself naturally into a series of epoch-making periods: 1. The structure and functions of the valves of the heart, Erasistratus, B. C. 304. 2. The arteries carry blood during life, not air, Galen, A. D. 165. 3. The pulmonary circulation, Servetus, 1553. 4. The systemic circulation, Cæsalpinus, 1593. 5. The pulmonic and systemic circulations, Harvey, 1628. 6. The capillaries. Malpighi, 1661.

How to Make Hand Fire Grenades.—Make your hand grenades. Fill ordinary quart wine bottles with a saturated solution of common salt, and place them where they will do the most good in case of need. They will be found nearly as serviceable as the expensive hand grenades you buy. Should a fire break out, throw them with force sufficient to break them into the center of the fire. The salt will form a coating on whatever object the water touches, and make it nearly incombustible, and it will prove effectual in many cases, where a fire is just starting, when the delay in procuring water might be fatal.

How the Kind of White Metal is Made That is Used in the Manufacture of Cheap Table Ware.—How same can be hardened and still retain its color? The following are formulas for white metal. Melt together: (a) Tin 82, lead 18, antimony 5, zinc 1, copper 4 parts. (b) Brass 32, lead 2, tin 2, zinc 1 part. For a hard metal, not so white, melt together bismuth 6 parts, zinc 3 parts, lead 13 parts. Or use type metal—lead 3 to 7 parts, antimony 1 part.

What Metal Expands Most, for the Same Change in Temperature?—For one degree Centigrade the following are coefficients of linear expansion: aluminum, 0.0000222; silver, 0.0000191 to 0.0000212; nickel, 0.0000128; copper, 0.0000167 to 0.0000178; zinc, 0.0000220 to 0.0000292; brass, 0.0000178 to 0.0000193; platinum, 0.0000088.

Heavy Timbers.—There are sixteen species of trees in America, whose perfectly dry wood will sink in water. The heaviest of these is the black ironwood (confalia feriea) of Southern Florida, which is more than 30 per cent. heavier than water. Of the others, the best known are lignum vitæ (gualacum sanctum) and mangrove (cbizphora mangle). Another is a small oak (quercus gsisea) found in the mountains of Texas, Southern New Mexico and Arizona, and westward to the Colorado desert, at an elevation of 5,000 to 10,000 feet. All the species in which the wood is heavier than water belong to semi-tropical Florida or the arid interior Pacific region.

Highest Point Reached by Man was by balloon 27,000 feet. Travelers have rarely exceeded 20,000 feet, at which point the air from its rarity is very debilitating.

Has a Rate of Speed Equal to Ninety Miles an Hour, ever Been Attained by Railroad Locomotive?—It is extremely doubtful if any locomotive ever made so high a speed. A mile in 48 seconds is the shortest time we have heard of. A rate of 70 to 75 miles per hour has been made on a spurt, on good straight track. The Grant Locomotive Works could make such an engine. Sixty miles an hour for a train is considered a very high rate of speed, and is seldom attained in practice for more than a short run.

The Fastest Boat in the World.—Messrs. Thornycroft & Co., of Chiswick, in making preliminary trials of a torpedo boat built by them for the Spanish navy, have obtained a speed which is worthy of special record. The boat is twin-screw, and the principal dimensions are: Length 147 ft. 6 in., beam 14 ft. 6 in., by 4 ft. 9 in. draught. On a trial at Lower Hope, on April 27, the remarkable mean speed of 26.11 knots was attained, being equal to a speed of 30.06 miles an hour, which is the highest speed yet attained by any vessel afloat.

Staining and Polishing Mahogany.—Your best plan will be to scrape off all the old polish, and well glass paper; then oil with linseed oil both old and new parts. To stain the new pieces, get half an ounce of bichromate of potash, and pour a pint of boiling water over it; when cold bottle it. This, used with care, will stain the new or light parts as dark as you please, if done as follows:—wipe off the oil clean, and apply the solution with a piece of rag, held firmly in the hand, and just moistened with the stain. Great care is required to prevent the stain running over the old part, for any place touched with it will show the mark through the polish when finished. You can vary the color by giving two or more coats if required. Then repolish your job altogether in the usual way. Should you wish to brighten up the old mahogany, use polish dyed with Bismarck brown as follows:—Get three pennyworth of Bismarck brown, and put it into a bottle with enough naphtha or methylated spirits to dissolve it. Pour a few drops of this into your polish, and you will find that it gives a nice rich red color to the work, but don't dye the polish too much, just tint it.

Value of Eggs for Food and Other Purposes.—Every element that is necessary to the support of man is contained within the limits of an egg shell, in the best proportions and in the most palatable form. Plain boiled, they are wholesome. It is easy to dress them in more than 500 different ways, each method not only economical, but salutary in the highest degree. No honest appetite ever yet rejected an egg in some guise. It is nutriment in the most portable form, and in the most concentrated shape. Whole nations of mankind rarely touch any other animal food. Kings eat them plain as readily as do the humble tradesmen. After the victory of Muhldorf, when the Kaiser Ludwig sat at a meal with his burggrafs and great captains, he determined on a piece of luxury—"one egg to every man, and two to the excellently valiant Schwepperman." Far more than fish—for it is watery diet—eggs are the scholar's fare. They contain phosphorus, which is brain food, and sulphur, which performs a variety of functions in the economy. And they are the best of nutriment for children, for, in a compact form, they contain everything that is necessary for the growth of the youthful frame. Eggs are, however, not only food—they are medicine also. The white is the most efficacious of remedies for burns, and the oil extractable from the yolk is regarded by the Russians as an almost miraculous salve for cuts, bruises and scratches. A raw egg, if swallowed in time, will effectually detach a fish bone fastened in the throat, and the white of two eggs will render the deadly corrosive sublimate as harmless as a dose of calomel. They strengthen the consumptive, invigorate the feeble, and render the most susceptible all but proof against jaundice in its more malignant phase. They can also be drunk in the shape of that "egg flip" which sustains the oratorical efforts of modern statesmen. The merits of eggs do not even end here. In France alone the wine clarifiers use more than 80,000,000 a year, and the Alsatians consume fully 38,000,000 in calico printing and for dressing the leather used in making the finest of French kid gloves. Finally, not to mention various other employments for eggs in the arts, they may, of course, almost without trouble on the farmer's part, be converted in fowls, which, in any shape, are profitable to the seller and welcome to the buyer. Even egg shells are valuable, for allopath and homeopath alike agree in regarding them as the purest of carbonate of lime.

History of Big Ships.—In the history of mankind several vessels of extraordinary magnitude have been constructed, all distinctively styled great, and all unfortunately disastrous, with the honorable exception of Noah's Ark. Setting aside this antediluvian craft, concerning the authenticity of whose dimensions authorities differ, and which, if Biblical measures are correct, was inferior in size to the vessel of most importance to modern shipowners, the great galley, constructed by the great engineer Archimedes for the great King Hiero II., of Syracuse, is the first illustration. This ship without a name (for history does not record one) transcended all wonders of ancient maritime construction. It abounded in statues and painting, marble and mosaic work. It

contained a gymnasium, baths, a garden, and arbored walks. Its artillery discharged stones of 3 cwt., and arrows 18 ft. in length. An Athenian advertising poet, who wrote a six-line puff of its glories, received the royal reward of six thousand bushels of corn. Literary merit was at a higher premium in the year 240 B.C., than it is to-day. The great ship of antiquity was found to be too large for the accommodation of the Syracusan port, and famine reigning in Egypt, Hiero, the charitably disposed, embarked a cargo of ten thousand huge jars of salted fish, two million pounds of salted meat, twenty thousand bundles of different clothes, filled the hold with corn, and consigned her to the seven mouths of the Nile, and since she weighed anchor nothing more has been heard of her fate. The next great ship worthy of mention is the mythical Saracen encountered in the Mediterranean Sea by the crusading fleet of Richard Cœur de Lion, Duke of Guienne and King of England, which, after much slaughter and damage incident to its infidel habit of vomiting Greek fire upon its adversaries, was captured and sunk. Next in rotation appears the Great Harry, built by Henry VIII., of England, and which careened in harbor during the reign of his successor, under similar circumstances to those attending the Royal George in 1782—a dispensation that mysteriously appears to overhang a majority of the ocean-braving constructions which, in defiance of every religious sailor's superstition that the lumber he treads is naturally female, are christened by a masculine or neutral title. In the year 1769, Mark Isambard Brunel, the Edison of his age, as his son was the Ericsson of that following, permitted himself to be born at Hacqueville; near Rouen, France, went to school, to sea, and into politics; compromised himself in the latter profession, and went to America in 1794, where he surveyed the canal now connecting Lake Champlain with the Hudson River at Albany, N. Y. There he turned architect, then returned to Europe, settled, married, and was knighted in England. He occupied eighteen years of his life in building an unproductive tunnel beneath the river Thames at London; invented a method of shuffling cards without using the hands, and several other devices for dispensing with labor, which, upon completion, were abandoned from economical motives. On his decease, his son and heir, I. K. Brunel, whose practical experience in the Thames Tunnel job, where his biographers assert he had occasion more than once to save his life by swimming, qualified him to tread in his father's shoes, took up his trade. Brunel, Jr., having demonstrated by costly experiments, to the successful proof, but thorough exasperation, of his moneyed backers, that his father's theory for employing carbonic acid gas as a motive power was practicable enough, but too expensive for anything but the dissipation of a millionaire's income, settled down to the profession of engineering science, in which he did as well as his advantages of education enabled him. Like all men in advance of their time, when he considered himself the victim of arbitrary capitalists ignoring the bent of his genius, he did his best work in accordance with their stipulations. He designed the Great Western, the first steamship (paddle-wheel) ever built to cross the Atlantic; and the Great Britain, the original ocean screw steamer. Flushed with these successes, Brunel procured pecuniary support from speculative fools, who, dazzled by the glittering statistical array that can be adduced in support of any chimerical venture, the inventor's repute, and their unbaked experience, imagined that the alluring Orient was ready to yield, like over-ripe fruit, to their shadowy grasp; and tainted as he evidently was with hereditary mania, Brunel resolved to seize the illusionary immortality that he fondly imagined to be within his reach.

There was not much the matter with the brain of Brunel, Jr., but that little was enough; a competent railroad surveyor, a good bridge builder, he needed to be held within bounds when handling other people's funds; for the man's ambition would have lead him to undertake to bridge the Atlantic. He met with the speculators required in this very instance of the constructors of the Great Eastern. This monstrous ship has been described so often, that it would be a cruelty to our readers to inflict the story upon them again.

Natural Gas the Fuel of the Future.—The house of the near future will have no fireplace, steam pipes, chimneys, or flues. Wood, coal oil, and other forms of fuel are about to disappear altogether in places having factories. Gas has become so cheap that already it is supplanting fuels. A single jet fairly heats a small room in cold weather. It is a well known fact that gas throws off no smoke, soot, or dirt. In a brazier filled with chunks of colored glass, and several jets placed beneath, the glass soon became heated sufficiently to thoroughly warm a room 10x30 feet in size. This design does away with the necessity for chimneys, since there is no smoke; the ventilation may be had at the window. The heat may be raised or lowered by simply regulating the flow of gas. The colored glass gives all the appearance of fire; there are black pieces to represent coal, red chunks for flames, yellowish white glass for white heat, blue glass for blue flames, and hues for all the remaining colors of spectrum. Invention already is displacing the present fuels for furnaces and cooking ranges and glass, doing away with delay and such disagreeable objects as ashes, kindling wood, etc. It has only been within the past few years that natural gas has been utilized to any extent, in either Pennsylvania, New York or Ohio. Yet its existence has been known since the early part of the century. As far back as 1821, gas was struck in Fredonia, Chautauqua county, N. Y., and was used to illuminate the village inn when Lafayette passed through the place some three years later. Not a single oil well of the many that have been sunk in Pennsylvania has been entirely devoid of gas, but even this frequent contact with what now seems destined to be the fuel of the future bore no fruit of any importance until within the past few years. It had been used in comparatively small quantities previous to the fall of 1884, but it was not until that time that the fuel gave any indication of the important role it was afterward to fill. At first ignored, then experimented with, natural gas has been finally so widely adopted that to-day, in the single city of Pittsburgh, it displaces daily 10,000 tons of coal, and has resulted in building cities in Ohio and the removal thereto of the glass making industries of the United States. The change from the solid to the gaseous fuel has been made so rapidly, and has effected such marked results in both the processes of manufacture and the product, that it is no exaggeration to say that the eyes of the entire industrial world are turned with envious admiration upon the cities and neighborhoods blessed with so unique and valuable a fuel. The regions in which natural gas is found are for the most part coincident with the formations producing petroleum. This, however, is not always the case; and it is worthy of notice that some districts which were but indifferent oil-producers are now famous in gas records. The gas driller, therefore, usually confines himself to the regions known to have produced oil, but the selection of the particular location for a well within these limits appears to be eminently fanciful. The more scientific generally select a spot either on the anticlinal or synclinal axis of the formation, giving preference to the former position. Almost all rock formations have some inclination to the horizon, and the constant change of this inclination produces a series of waves, the crests of which are known as anticlines, and the troughs as synclines. Many drillers suppose that the gas seeks the anticlines and the oil the synclines, but others, equally long-headed, discard entirely all theory of this kind, and drill wherever it may be most convenient or where other operators have already demonstrated the existence of gas. It will surprise many of our readers to know that the divining rod, that superstitious relic of the middle ages, is still frequently called upon to relieve the operator of the trouble of a rational decision. The site having been selected, the ordinary oil-drilling outfit is employed to sink a hole of about six inches in diameter until the gas is reached. In the neighborhood of Pittsburgh, this is usually found at a depth of 1,300 to 1,500 feet, in what is known as the Third Oil Sand, a sandstone of the Devonian period. Where the gas comes from originally is an open question. When the driller strikes gas, he is not left in any doubt of the event, for if the well be one of any strength, the gas manifests itself by sending the drill and its attachments into the air, often to a height of a hundred feet or more. The most prolific wells are appropriately called "roarers." During the progress of the drilling, the well is lined with iron piping. Occasionally this is also blown out, but as a rule the gas satisfies itself with ejecting the drill. When the first rush of gas has thrown everything movable out of its way, the workmen can approach, and chain the giant to his work. The plant at the well is much simpler than one would suppose. An elbow joint connects the projecting end of the well piping with a pipe leading to a strong sheet-iron tank. This collects the salt water brought up with the gas. Ordinarily, about half a barrel accumulates in twenty four hours. A safety valve, a pressure indicator, and a blow-off complete the outfit. When the pressure exceeds a prescribed limit, the valve opens, and the gas escapes into the blow-off. This is usually 30 feet high or more, and the gas issuing from the top is either ignited or permitted to escape into the atmosphere. The pipe line leading from the tank to the city is of course placed underground. Beyond a little wooden house, the blow-off, and a derrick, the gas farms differ little in appearance from those producing less valuable crops. The pressure of the gas at the wells varies considerably. It is generally between 100 and 325 pounds. As much as 750 pounds per square inch has been measured, and in many cases the actual pressure is even greater than this, but, as a rule, it is not permitted to much exceed 20 atmospheres in any receiver or pipe. The best investment for parties of small means that we know of is in town lots in North Baltimore, Ohio. It is on the main line of the B. & O. Railroad and the center of the oil and natural gas discoveries in Ohio. Property is bound to double in value. For further information, address, W. A. Rhodes, North Baltimore, Ohio.

Hints on House Building.—Gas pipes should be run with a continuous fall towards the meter, and no low places. The gas meter should be set in a cool place, to keep it from registering against you; but if a "water meter," it should be protected from freezing. Cupboards, wardrobes, bookcases, etc., generally afford receptacles for dust on their tops. This may be avoided by carrying them clear up to the ceiling. When this is not done, their tops should be sheeted over flush with the highest line of their cornices, so that there may be no sunken lodging-place for dust. Furring spaces between the furring and the outer walls should be stopped off at each floor line with brick and mortar "fire stops;" and the same with hollow interior partition walls. Soil pipes should never have T branches; always curves, or Y branches. Water pipes should be run in a continuous grade, and have a stop and waste cock at the lowest point, so as to be entirely emptied when desired.

Furnaces should have as few joints as possible, and the iron fire-pot is better lined with fire-brick. There should be no damper in the smoke pipe; but the ash-door should shut air-tight when desired. There should be provision for the evaporation of water in the hot-air pipe. "Air boxes" should never be of wood. All air boxes should be accessible from one end to the other, to clean them of dust, cobwebs, insects, etc. Horizontal hot-air flues should not be over 15 feet long. Parapets should be provided with impervious coping-stones to keep water from descending through the walls. Sewer pipes should not be so large as to be difficult to flush. The oval sections (point down) are the best. Soil-pipes should have a connection with the upper air, of the full diameter of the pipe to be ventilated. Stationary wash-tubs of wood are apt to get soaked up with organic matter and filth. Stationary washstands in bedrooms should have small traps; underneath each should be a leaden tray to protect ceilings in case of leakage, breakage or accidental overflow. This tray should have an overflow, and this overflow should be trapped, if connected with the foul-pipe system (which it should *not* be if possible to arrange it otherwise). Flues should have a smooth parging or lining, or they will be apt to draw with difficulty. Gas pipes of insufficient diameter cause the flames to burn with unsteady, dim light. Made ground is seldom fit for immediate building; and never for other than isolated structures. Ashes, street-sweepings, garbage, rotten vegetation, and house refuse are unfit filling for low ground on which it is intended to build. Cobble pavements are admirably adapted to soaking-up and afterwards emitting unwholesome matters. Asphalt has none of this fault. Wood is pernicious in this respect. "Gullies" in cellar floors should be properly trapped; and this does *not* mean that they shall have bell-traps nor siphon-traps with shallow water-seal. Cellar windows should be movable to let in air, and should have painted wire-screens to keep out cats, rats, etc. New walls are always damp. Window sills should project well out beyond the walls, and should be grooved underneath so as to throw the water clear of the walls. Cracks in floors, between the boards, help the accumulation of dirt and dust, and may harbor vermin. Narrow boards of course have narrower interstitial cracks than wide boards do. "Secret nailing" is best where it can be afforded. Hot-air flues should never be carried close to unprotected woodwork. Electric bells, when properly put up and cared for, are a great convenience in a house; but when they don't work, they are about as aggravating as the law allows. Cheap push-buttons cause a great deal of annoyance. Silver-plated faucets and trimmings blacken with illuminating and sewer gases. Nickel-plating is perhaps a less pleasing white, but is cheaper and does not discolor readily. Windows are in most respects a great blessing; but there may be too much of a good thing. It is unreasonable to expect that one grate or stove or furnace can heat a whole county. Don't attempt it. If you have too many windows on the "cold side" of a house, give them double sashes (*not* double panes), and "weather-strip" them. Unpainted trimmings should be of hardwood. Yellow pine finishes up well. Butternut is brighter than walnut. Cherry makes a room cheerful. Walnut is dull and dismal.

The Forests of the World.—The rapid exhaustion of the forests of the world, and more particularly of the once great reserves of timber in the United States and Canada, renders it inevitable that, in a very few years indeed, iron must supersede wood for a variety of uses. The drain upon the world's resources in timber is prodigious. Every year 92,000,000 railway sleepers are used in America alone, while to supply firewood for the whole of the States, fourteen times the quantity of wood consumed by the railways is annually

required. At the computation of the most recent statistics there were 441,000,000 of acres of woodland in the United States; but since over 50,000,000 of acres are cut down yearly, this great area of timber will be non-existent in less than twenty years, unless replanting upon a very extensive scale be at once undertaken. Already efforts are being made in this direction, and not long since some 4,000,000 of saplings were planted in a single day in Kansas and the neighboring States. But since the daily consumption is even greater than this, it is obvious that the work of replanting must be undertaken systematically if it is to keep pace, even approximately, with the destruction. In France and Germany, where the forests are national property, forestry has been elevated to the status of an exact science; but the timber lands of those countries are small indeed compared with those in the United States.

A Church Built from a Single Tree.—A redwood tree furnished all the timber for the Baptist church in Santa Rosa, one of the largest church edifices in the country. The interior of the building is finished in wood, there being no plastered walls. Sixty thousand shingles were made from the tree after enough was taken for the church. Another redwood tree, cut near Murphy's Mill, about ten years ago, furnished shingles that required the constant labor of two industrious men for two years before the tree was used up.

Trees That Sink.—Of the more than four hundred species of trees found in the United States there are said to be sixteen species whose perfectly dry wood will sink in water. The heaviest of these is the black ironwood of southern Florida, which is more than thirty per cent. heavier than water. Of the others, the best known are the lignum vitæ and mangrove; another is a small oak found in the mountains of western Texas, southern New Mexico, and Arizona, and westward to Colorado, at an elevation of 5,000 to 10,000 feet.

Artificial Wood.—You can produce an artificial fire and waterproof wood in the following manner. More or less finely divided wood shavings, straw, tan, etc., singly or mixed, are moistened with a weak solution of zinc chloride of about 1·026 sp. gr., and allowed to dry. They are then treated with a basic solution of magnesium chloride of 1·725 to 1·793 sp. gr., and pressed into moulds. The materials remain ten to twelve hours under pressure, during which time they harden while becoming heated. After being dried for several days in a warm, airy place, they are placed for ten or twelve hours into a strong solution of zinc chloride of about 1·205 sp. gr., and finally dried again. The product is stated to be workable like hardwood, and to be capable of taking a fine polish after being tooled. It is fireproof and inpermeable to water, and weak acid or alkaline solutions, and not affected by the humidity of the atmosphere, being well suited to decorative purposes, as it will not warp and fly like wood, but retain its form.

How to Stain Wood.—The following are recipes for staining wood, which are used in large establishments with great success: Light Walnut—Dissolve 3 oz. permanganate of potash in six pints of water, and paint the wood twice with the solution. After the solution has been left on the wood for from five to ten minutes, the wood is rinsed, dried, oiled, and finally polished. Light Mahogany—1 oz. finely cut alkanet root, 2 ozs. powdered aloe, and 2 ozs. powdered dragon's blood are digested with 26 ozs. of strong spirits of wine in a corked bottle, and left in a moderately warm place for four days. The solution is then filtered off, and the clear filtrate is ready for use. The wood which is to be stained is first passed through nitric acid, then dried, painted over with the alcoholic extract, dried, oiled and polished. Dark Walnut.—3 ozs. permanganate of potash are dissolved in six pints of water, and the wood is painted twice with this solution. After five minutes the wood is washed, and grained with acetate of iron (the ordinary iron liquor of the dyer) at 20° Tw. Dry, oil and polish as usual. Gray—1 oz. nitrate of silver is dissolved in 45 ozs. water, and the wood painted twice with the solution; afterwards the wood is submitted to the action of hydrochloric acid, and finally washed with ammonia. It is then dried in a dark place, oiled and polished. This is said to give remarkably good results on beech, pitch pine and poplar. Black—7 ozs. logwood are boiled with three pints of water, filtered, and the filtrate mixed with a solution containing 1 oz. of sulphate of copper (blue copperas). The mixture is left to clear, and the clear liquor decanted while still hot. The wood is placed in this liquor for twenty-four hours; it is then exposed to the air for twenty-four hours, and afterwards passed through a hot bath of nitrate of iron of 6° Tw. If the black, after this treatment, should not be sufficiently developed, the wood has to be passed again through the first logwood bath.

The Highest Chimney in the World.—The highest chimney in the world is said to be that recently completed at the lead mines in Mechernich. It is 134 meters (439 ft. 6 in.) high, was commenced in 1884, and was carried up 23 meters before the frost set in; building was again resumed on the 14th of last April, and it was completed last September. The foundation, which is of dressed stone, is square, measuring 11 meters (33 ft.) on each side, and is 3·50 meters (11 ft. 6 in.) deep; the base is also square, and is carried up 10 meters (33 ft.) above the ground. The chimney-stack is of circular section, 7·50 meters (24 ft. 6 in.) diameter at the bottom, and tapering to 3·50 meters diameter (11 ft. 6 in.) at the top, and is 120·50 meters (395 ft.) high.

How to Measure Round Tanks.—Square the diameter of the tank, and multiply by ·7854, which gives the area; then multiply area by depth of tank, and the cubic contents will be found. Allow 6¼ gallons for each cubic foot.

The Largest Buildings in the World.—Where is the largest building in the world situated? The answer to this question must depend upon what the term "building" is held to represent. The Great Wall of China, 1,280 miles in length, wide enough to allow six horsemen to ride abreast along it, and with an average height of 20 ft., may fairly be called a building; so, too, may be called the Great Pyramid of Egypt. The question, however, was not meant to include such works as these. Some have supposed that the Vatican at Rome, with its eight grand staircases, 200 smaller staircases, 20 courts, and 11,000 apartments, is the largest building in the world; but surely this is a collection of palaces rather than a single building. The same objection applies to the famous monastery of the Escurial in the province of Madrid, with its seven towers, fifteen gateways, and 12,000 windows and doors, and to many other vast piles. For the largest single building extant, we must look to St. Peter's at Rome, within which our great cathedral, St. Paul's, could easily stand. St. Peter's occupies a space of 240,000 sq. ft., its front is 400 ft. broad, rising to a height of 180 ft.; the length of the interior is 600 ft., its breadth 442 ft. It is capable of holding 54,000 people, while its piazza, in its widest limits, holds 624,000. It is only by degrees that one is able to realize its vast size. St. Peter's holds 54,000 persons; Milan Cathedral, 37,000; St. Paul's, Rome, 32,000; St. Paul's, London, 25,600; St. Petronio, Bologna, 24,400; Florence Cathedral, 24,300; Antwerp Cathedral, 24,000; St. Sophia, Constantinople, 23,000; Notre Dame, Paris, 21,000; Pisa Cathedral, 13,000; St. Stephen's, Vienna, 12,400; Auditorium, Chicago, 12,000; St. Mark's, Venice, 7,000.

The Biggest Bell in the World.—There is a bell in the Temple of Clars, at Kinto, Japan, which is larger than the great bell of Moscow, or any other. It is covered with Chinese and Sanskrit characters which Japanese scholars have not yet succeeded in translating. There is no record of its casting. Its height is 24 ft., and at the rim it has a thickness of 16 in. It has no clapper, but is struck on the outside by a kind of wooden battering-ram. We are unable to obtain any more exact particulars as to the dimensions of this bell in order to determine whether or no it really does excel the "Monarch" of Moscow, which weighs about 193 tons, is 19 ft. 3 in. in height, 60 ft. 9 in. in circumference, and 2 ft. thick. There is another huge bell at Moscow, and those at Amazapoora, in Burmah, and at Pekin are far bigger than any we have in this country. Our biggest bell is "Great Paul," which was cast at Loughborough in 1881, and which weighs 17½ tons. Taking purity, volume, and correctness of note into account, it is probably the finest bell in Europe.

The Oldest Cities in the World.—They are the following:—Argos, Athens and Thebes, in Greece; Crotona and Rome, in Italy; Cadiz and Saguntum, in Spain; Constantinople, in Turkey, and Marseilles, in France, which was founded by a colony of Greeks 580 B. C. The age of these cities varies from twenty-four to twenty-seven centuries.

How to Manufacture Oil of Apple, or Essence of Apple.—The essence of apple is composed of aldehyde 2 parts; chloroform, acetic ether and nitrous ether and oxalic acid each 1 part; glycerin 4 parts; amyl valerianice ther 10 parts.

A Formula for the Manufacture of Artificial Cider.—Imitation cider consists of 25 gallons soft water, 25 pounds New Orleans sugar; 1 pint yeast; two pounds tartaric acid. Put all the ingredients into a clean cask, and stir them up well after standing twenty-four hours with the bung out. Then bung the cask up tight, add 3 gallons spirits, and let it stand forty-eight hours, after which time it will be ready for use. Champagne cider can be prepared by taking 10 gallons of cider, old and clear. Put this in a strong, iron-bound cask pitched inside (like beer casks); add 2½ pints clarified white plain syrup; then dissolve in it 5 ounces tartaric acid; keep the bung ready in hand, then add 7½ ounces of potassium bicarbonate; bung it as quickly and as well as possible.

Recipe for Making Instantaneous Ink and Stain Extractor.—Take of chloride of lime 1 pound, thoroughly pulverized, and 4 quarts soft water. The foregoing must be thoroughly shaken when first put together. It is required to stand twenty-four hours to dissolve the chloride of lime; then strain through a cotton cloth, after which add a teaspoonful of acetic acid to every ounce of the chloride of lime water.

Wood, which is a more unyielding material, acts with tremendous force when wetted, and advantage has been taken of this fact in splitting blocks of granite. This process is largely adopted in Dartmoor. After a mass of granite has been rent from the mountain by blasting, it is measured in every direction to see how best to divide it into smaller blocks. These are traced out by straight lines on the surface, and a series of holes are drilled at short intervals along this line. Wedges of dry wood are then tightly driven into the holes and wetted, and the combined action of the swelling wood splits the block in the direction required, and without any destructive violence. The same process is then carried out upon the other faces, and the roughly-shapen block finished with the hammer and chisel.

The Weight and Value of a Cubic Foot of Solid Gold or Silver.—A cubic foot of gold weighs about 19,300 ounces, and gold is worth $20.67 per ounce.   Silver is worth $1.29 per ounce, and a cubic foot weighs 10,500 ounces.   Consequently the cubic foot of gold would be worth $398,931, and the silver $13,545.

To Remove Spots on Brass.—Sulphuric acid will remove spots from brass that will not yield to oxalic acid.   It may be applied with a brush, but great care must be taken that no drop of the acid shall come in contact with the clothes or skin, as it is ruinous to garments and cuticle.   Bath brick or rottenstone may be used for polishing.

A Formula to Make a Good Shoe Dressing.—Gum shellac, $\frac{1}{2}$ pound; alcohol, 3 quarts; dissolve, and add camphor, $1\frac{1}{2}$ ounces; lampblack, 2 ounces.   The foregoing will be found to give an excellent gloss, and is especially adapted to any leather, the surface of which is roughened by wear.

Receipts for Dyeing Cotton Fabric Red, Blue and Ecru.—Red :   Muriate of tin, two-thirds cupful, add water to cover goods ; raise to boiling heat ; put in goods one hour; stir often ; take out, empty kettle, put in clean water with Nicaragua wood one pound ; steep one-half hour at hand heat, then put in goods and increase heat one hour, not boiling.   Air goods, and dip one hour as before.   Wash without soap.   Blue : For three pounds goods, blue vitriol 4 ounces ; boil few minutes, then dip goods three hours; then pass them through strong lime water.   Ecru : Continue the foregoing operation for blue by passing the goods through a solution of prussiate of potash.

MOTION OF WAVES.—The progressive motion of a wave on the water exactly corresponds in speed with that of a pendulum whose length is equal to the breadth of the wave; the same law, gravity, governs both.

LIGHT OF THE SUN.—A photometric experiment of Huygens, resumed by Wollaston, a short time before his death, teaches us that 20,000 stars the same size as Sirius, the most brilliant in the firmament, would need to be agglomerated to shed upon our globe a light equal to that of the sun.

Land Cultivation in Japan.—The entire arable land of the Japanese empire is officially put at only 11,215,000 acres ; but it is so fertile and thoroughly cultivated that it feeds a population of 37,000,000, about that of France.   Rice is one of the principal crops, and of this some 200,-000,000 bushels are raised annually.

Old London Bridge.—As early as the year 978 there was a wooden bridge where London bridge now stands.   This was replaced by another in 1014, and another in 1209.   The present London bridge was erected in 1831, and may be considered the oldest existing bridge over the river.

The Shortest Method of Removing Silver from Plated Ware Before Replating.—Dip the article in nitric acid ; this will remove the silver.

A Formula for White Metal.—Copper, 69.8 parts; nickel, 19.8 parts; zinc, 5.5 parts; cadmium, 4.7 parts.   It takes a fine polish.

Curiosities of Metal Working.—At a recent meeting of scientific men, a speaker produced an anklet worn by East Indian women.   This is a flat curb chain about one inch broad, with the links very close, and weighing about ten or twelve ounces.   It is composed of a species of brass composed of copper and lead, without any trace of silver, zinc, or tin.   Such anklets are sold for a few pence, and they are cast all at once, complete as an endless chain.   The links show no sign of having been united in any way.   How it was possible to produce such a casting as this passed his comprehension, and he hoped that some one who had seen them made would explain the nature of the process.   From the East much that was curious in metallurgical art came.   Cast-iron was, he believed, first made purposely in China.   It was, however, frequently produced unintentionally, when wrought-iron was made direct from the ore in little furnaces about as big as a chimney-pot.   It was found among the cinders and ash of the coarcoal-fire in grains or globules, which were not only like shot, but were actually used as shot by the natives.   He showed what he believed was the only specimen in England of this cast-iron, in a bottle.   He next referred to the celebrated Damascene blades of Indian swords, and explained that these blades were an intimate mixture of wrought-iron and hard steel, which must have required great skill, time and patience for its production.   One patern, in particular, known as "Mary's Ladder," showed wonderful finish and accuracy.   Concerning the tempering of these blades little was known ; but it was stated that it was affected by a long-continued hammering, or rather tapping, of the blade while cold.

How Many Tons of Coal a Large Steamship Consumes in a Day.—"Ocean steamers are large consumers of coal.   The Orient line, with their fleet of ships running to Australia every two weeks, may be mentioned.   The steamship Austral went from London to Sydney in thirty-five days, and consumed on the voyage 3,641 tons of coal ; Her coal bunkers hold 2,750 tons.   The steamship Oregon consumes over 330 tons per day on her passage from Liverpool to New York ; her bunkers will hold nearly 4,000 tons.   The Stirling Castle last year brought home in one cargo 2,200 tons of tea, and consumed 2,800 tons of coal in doing so.   Immense stocks of coal are kept at various coaling stations.   St. Vincent, Madeira, Port Said, Singapore and others ; the reserve at the latter place is about 20,000 tons.   It is remarkable with what rapidity these steamers are coaled ; for instance, the Orient steamship last year took in over 1,100 tons at Port Said in five hours."

What a Man Eats.—A French statistician has just ascertained that a human being of either sex who is a moderate eater and who lives to be 70 years old consumes during his life a quantity of food which would fill twenty ordinary railway baggage cars.   A "good eater," however, may require as many as thirty.

An Australian Railway Viaduct.—The Werribee Viaduct, in the colony of Victoria, is the longest work of the kind in Australia.   The structure consists of lattice-girder work.   It is 1,290 feet in length, and runs to a height of 125 feet above the level of the Werribee river.   The viaduct has fifteen spans each of 60 feet, and thirteen spans of 30 feet.   The total cost of the bridge was £600,-000.

The Sharpening of Tools.—Instead of oil, which thickens and smears the stone, a mixture of glycerine and spirit is recommended.   The proportions of the composition vary according to the class of tool to be sharpened.   One with a relatively large surface is best sharpened with a clear fluid, three parts of glycerine being mixed with one part of spirit.   A graver having a small cutting surface only requires a small pressure on the stone, and in such cases the glycerine should be mixed with only two or three drops of spirit.

Recipes for Plumbers.—Chloride of zinc, so much used in soldering iron, has, besides its corrosive qualities, the drawback of being unwholesome when used for soldering the iron tins employed to can fruit, vegetables and other foods. A soldering mixture has been found which is free from these defects. It is made by mixing one pound of lactic acid with one pound of glycerine and eight pounds of water. A wooden tank may be rendered capable of withstanding the effects of nitric or sulphuric acids by the following methods:—Cover the inside with paraffin; go over the inside with a sadiron heated to the temperature used in ironing clothes. Melt the paraffin under the iron so as to drive it into the wood as much as possible, then with a cooler iron melt on a coat thick enough to completely cover the wood. For brassing small articles: To one quart water add half an ounce each of sulphate copper and protochloride of tin. Stir the articles in the solution until the desired color is obtained. Use the sulphate of copper alone for a copper color. A good cement for celluloid is made from one part shellac dissolved in one part of spirit of camphor and three to four parts of ninety per cent. alcohol. The cement should be applied warm, and the broken parts securely held together until the solvent has entirely evaporated. Tin and tin alloys, after careful cleansing from oxide and grease, are handsomely and permanently bronzed if brushed over with a solution of one part of sulphate of copper (bluestone) and one part of sulphate of iron (copperas) in twenty parts of water. When this has dried, the surface should be brushed with a solution of one part of acetate of copper (verdigris) in acetic acid. After several applications and dryings of the last named, the surface is polished with a soft brush and bloodstone powder. The raised portions are then rubbed off with soft leather moistened with wax in turpentine, followed by a rubbing with dry leather.

Protecting Water-Pipes Against Frost.—A device has been brought forward for protecting water-pipes against freezing, the arrangement being based upon the fact that water in motion will remain liquid at a lower temperature than water at rest. One end of a copper rod, placed outside the building, is secured to a bracket, and the other end is attached to one arm of a weighted elbow lever; to the other arm of the lever is secured a rod which passes into the building and operates a valve in the water-pipe. By means of turn buckles the length of the copper rod can be adjusted so that before the temperature reaches the point at which there would be danger of the water in the pipes freezing the valve will be opened to allow a flow of water; beyond this point the valve opening will increase and the flow become more rapid as the cold becomes more intense, and as the temperature rises the valve is closed. This plan sets up a current in the pipes, which replaces the water as it grows cold by the warmer water from the main.

Destructive Work of Barnacles.—Unless some paint can be found which is proof against barnacles, it may be necessary to sheath steel vessels with an alloy of copper. An attempt has been made to cover the hulls with anti-corrosive paint and cover this with an outside coat which should resist the attack of barnacles. Somehow the barnacles eat their way through the paint and attach themselves to the hull. The vast item of expense attached to the dry-docking of steel ships makes this matter a not unimportant one. The barnacles interfere greatly with the speed of a vessel, and in a cruiser speed is of prime importance. They attach themselves in an incredibly short time to a steel hull, and it is not long before their effect can be noted by a comparison of the reading of the log.

How to Frost Glass.—Two ounces of spirits of salts, two ounces of oil of vitriol, one ounce of sulphate of copper, one ounce of gum arabic, mixed together and dabbed on with a brush; or this:—Dab your squares regularly over with putty; when dry go over them again—the imitation will be executed. Or this:—Mix Epsom salts with porter and apply it with a brush. Or this one:—Grind and mix white lead in three-fourths of boiled oil, and one-fourth of spirits of turpentine, and, to give the mixture a very drying quality, add sufficient quantities of burnt white vitriol and sugar of lead. The color must be made exceedingly thin, and put on the panes of glass with a large painting-brush in as even a manner as possible. When a number of the panes are thus painted take a dry duster, quite new, dab the ends of the bristles on the glass in quick succession till you give it a uniform appearance; repeat this operation till the work appears very soft, and it will then appear like ground glass. When the windows require fresh painting, get the old coat off first by using strong pearlash water.

How to Preserve Posts.—Wood can be made to last longer than iron in the ground, if prepared according to the following receipe:—Take boiled linseed oil and stir in pulverized coal to the consistency of paint. Put a coat of this over the timber, and there is not a man that will live to see it rot.

What Diamond Dyes and Paints Are Made of.—Solutions of the aniline colors.

What the Ingredients Are of Soapine and Pearline.—They consist of partly effloresced sal soda mixed with half its weight of soda ash. Some makers add a little yellow soap, coarsely powdered, to disguise the appearance, and others a little carbonate of ammonium or borax.

How Many Thousand Feet of Natural Gas are Equal in Heat-Creating Power to One Ton Anthracite Coal.—About 40,000 cubic feet.

SUSTAINING POWER OF ICE.

The sustaining power of ice at various degrees of thickness is given in the following paragraphs:

At a thickness of two inches, will support a man.

At a thickness of four inches, will support man on horseback.

At a thickness of six inches, will support teams with moderate loads.

At a thickness of eight inches, will support heavy loads.

At a thickness of ten inches, will support 1,000 pounds to the square foot.

THE EXPANSIVE POWER OF WATER.

It is a well known, but not less remarkable fact, that if the tip of an exceedingly small tube be dipped into water, the water will rise spontaneously in the tube throughout its whole length. This may be shown in a variety of ways; for instance, when a piece of sponge, or sugar, or cotton is just allowed to touch water, these substances being all composed of numberless little tubes, draw up the water, and the whole of the piece becomes wet. It is said to *suck up* or *imbibe* the moisture. We see the same wonderful action going on in nature in the rising of the sap through the small tubes or pores of the wood, whereby the leaves and upper portions of the plant derive nourishment from the ground.

This strange action is called "capillary," from the resemblance the minute tubes bear to a hair, the Latin of which is *capillus*. It is, moreover, singular that the absorption of the water takes place with great force. If a dry sponge be enclosed tightly in a vessel, it will expand when wetted, with sufficient force to burst it, unless very strong.

London Water Supply.—The quantity of water consumed in London amounts to about 145,000,000 gallons a day. If this quantity could be collected together, it would form a lake 700 yards long, 200 wide, and with a uniform depth of 20 feet.

A Protection for Embankments.—Engineers often have considerable trouble with the loose soil of newly-made embankments, so apt to slip or be washed away before they are covered with vegetation. According to a French railway engineer, the best plan is to sow the banks with the double poppy. Several months elapse before grasses and clovers develop their feeble roots, but the double poppy germinates in a few days, and in a fortnight has grown sufficiently to afford some protection to the slope, while at the end of three or four months the roots, which are ten or twelve inches in length, are found to have interlaced so as to retain the earth far more firmly than those of any grass or grain. Although the double poppy is an annual, it sows itself after the first year.

A Cheap Concrete.—A kind of concrete made without cement is composed of 8 parts of sand, gravel and pebbles, 1 part of burnt and powdered common earth, 1 part of pulverized clinkers and cinders, and 1½ parts of unslacked hydraulic lime. These materials are thoroughly incorporated while dry into a homogeneous mixture, which is then wetted up and well beaten. The result of this is a hard and solid mass, which sets almost immediately, becoming exceedingly strong after a few days. It may be made still stronger by the addition of a small proportion—say 1 part—of cement.

Marking Tools.—To mark tools, first cover the article to be marked with a thin coating of tallow or beeswax, and with a sharp instrument write the name in the tallow. Clear with a feather, fill the letters with nitric acid, let it remain from one to ten minutes, then dip in water and run off, and the marks will be etched into the steel or iron.

How to Prevent Chisel Handles Splitting.—All carpenters know how soon the butt-end of chisel handles split when daily exposed to the blow of a mallet or hammer. A remedy suggested by a Brooklyn man consists simply of sawing or cutting off the round end of the handle so as to make it flat, and attaching by a few nails on the top of it two discs of sole leather, so that the end becomes similar to the heel of the boot. The two thicknesses of leather will prevent all further splitting, and if, in the course of time, they expand and overlap the wood of the handle, they are simply trimmed off all around.

The Largest Wheel of Its Kind Ever Made in the World.—The greatest wheel of its kind in the world, a very wonder in mechanism, was built for the Calumet and Hecla Mining Company of Lake Superior, Mich., for the purpose of lifting and discharging the "tailings," a waste from the copper mines, into the lake. Its diameter is 54 feet; weight in active operation, 200 tons. Its extreme dimensions are 54 feet in diameter. Some idea of its enormous capacity can be formed from the fact that it receives and elevates sufficient sand every twenty-four hours to cover an acre of ground a foot deep. It is armed on its outer edge with 432 teeth, 4.71 inches pitch and 18 inches face. The gear segments, eighteen in number, are made of gun iron, and the teeth are machine-cut, epicycloidal in form. It took two of the most perfect machines in the world 100 days and nights to cut the teeth alone, and the finish is as smooth as glass. The wheel is driven by a pinion of gun iron containing 33 teeth of equal pitch and face and runs at a speed of 600 feet per minute at the inner edge, where it is equipped with 448 steel buckets that lift the "tailings" as the machine revolves and discharges them into launders that carry them into the lake. The shaft of the wheel is of gun iron, and its journals are 22 inches in diameter by 3 feet 4 inches long. The shaft is made in three sections and is 30 inches in diameter in the center. At a first glance the great wheel looks like an exaggerated bicycle wheel, and it is constructed much on the same principle, with straining rods that run to centers cast on the outer sections of the shaft. The steel buckets on either side of the gear are each 4 feet 5½ inches long and 21 inches deep, and the combined lifting capacity of the 448, running at a speed of 600 feet per minute, will be 3,000,000 gallons of water and 2,000 tons of sand every twenty-four hours. The mammoth wheel is supported on two massive adjustable pedestals of cast iron weighing twelve tons each, and its cost at the copper mines before making a single revolution, $100,000.

Strength of Brick Walls.—The question of strength of brick walls is often discussed, and differences of opinion expressed. The following is one of the rules given:—For first-class buildings, with good workmanship, the general average should not exceed a greater number of feet in height than three times its thickness of wall in inches, and the length not to exceed double the height, without lateral supports of walls, buttresses, etc., as follows for safety:

THICKNESS.	SAFE HEIGHT.	LENGTH.
8½ inch walls	25 feet.	50 feet.
13 "	40 "	80 "
17 "	55 "	110 "
22 "	66 "	130 "
26 "	78 "	150 "

Where the lengths must exceed these proportions, as in depots, warehouses, etc., the thickness should be increased, or lateral braces instituted as frequently as practicable.

Qualities of Building Stone.—The principal qualities of a good building stone are—(1) Strength, (2) hardness, (3) durability, (4) appearance, (5) facility for working. There are also other minor points; but stone possessing one or more of the above qualities, according to the purpose for which it is required, may be regarded as good for that purpose.

Strength of Stone.—Stone should only be subjected to a compressive strain. It is occasionally subject to a cross strain, as in lintels over doors and windows; these are, however, contrary to the true principles of construction, and should not be allowed except a strong relieving arch is turned over them. The strength of stone in compression is about 120 tons per square foot for the weakest stones, and about 750 tons per square foot for the strongest. No stones are, however, subjected to anything like this amount of compressive force; in the largest buildings it does not amount to more than twelve or fourteen tons per square foot.

Hardness of Stone.—This is of more importance than its strength, especially in pavements or steps, where it is subject to great wear; also in plinths and quoins of buildings where it is desired to preserve a good face and sharp arris. The order of strength and hardness of stone is—(1) Basalt, (2) granite, (3) limestone, (4) sandstone. Granite, seinite, and gneiss take the first place for strength, hardness and durability, but they will not stand a high temperature. "Stones which are of a fine, uniform grain, compact texture and deep color are the strongest; and when the grain, color, and texture are the same, those are the strongest which are the heaviest; but otherwise the strength does not increase with the specific gravity." Great hardness is objectionable when the stone has to be worked with a chisel, owing to the labor required to work it. Hard stones, also, generally wear smooth, and become polished, which makes them unsuitable for some purposes. Brittleness is a defect which frequently accompanies hardness, particularly in coarse-grained stones; it prevents them from being worked to a true surface, and from receiving a smooth edge at the angles. Workmen call those hard stones which can only be sawn into slabs by the grit saw, and those soft which can be separated by a common saw.

Expansion of Stone by Heat.—Rocks are expanded by heat and contracted by cooling. Variation in temperature thus causes some building stones to alternately expand and contract, and this prevents the joints of masonry from remaining close and tight. In the United States with an annual thermometric range of more than 90 deg. Fah., this difficulty led to some experiments on the amount of expansion and contraction in different kinds of building stones. It was found that in fine-grained granite the rate of expansion was .000004825 for every degree Fah. of increment of heat; in white crystalline marble it was .000005668; and in red sandstone .000009532, or about twice as much as in granite. In Western America, where the climate is remarkably dry and clear, the thermometer often gives a range of more than 80 deg. in twenty-four hours. This great difference of temperature produces a strain so great that it causes rocks to crack or peel off in skins or irregular pieces, or in some cases, it disintegrates them into sand. Dr. Livingstone found in Africa (12 deg. S. lat., 34 deg. E. long.) that surfaces of rock which during the day were heated up to 137 deg. Fah. cooled so rapidly by radiation at night that unable to stand the strain of contraction, they split and threw off sharp angular fragments from a few ounces to 100 lbs. or 200 lbs. in weight. According to data obtained from Adie "Trans. Roy. Soc. Edin.," xiii., p. 366, and Totten the expansion of ordinary rocks ranges from about 2.47 to 9.63 millionths for 1 deg. Fah.

BLUNDERS AND ABSURDITIES IN ART.

In looking over some collections of old pictures, it is surprising what extraordinary anachornisms, blunders, and absurdities are often discoverable.

In the gallery of the convent of Jesuits at Lisbon, there is a picture representing Adam in paradise, dressed in blue breeches with silver buckles, and Eve with a striped petticoat. In the distance appears a procession of Capuchin monks bearing the cross.

In a country church in Holland there is a painting representing the sacrifice of Isaac, in which the painter has depicted Abraham with a blunderbus in his hand, ready to shoot his son. A similar edifice in Spain has a picture of the same incident, in which the patriarch is armed with a pistol.

At Windsor there is a painting by Antonio Verrio, in which the artist has introduced the portraits of himself, Sir Godfrey Kneller, and May, the surveyor of the works of that period, all in long periwigs, as spectators of Christ healing the sick.

A painter of Toledo, having to represent the three wise men of the East coming to worship on the nativity of Christ, depicted three Arabian or Indian kings, two of them white and one black, and all of them in the posture of kneeling. The position of the legs of each figure not being very distinct, he inadvertently painted three black feet for the negro king, and three also between the two white kings; and he did not discover his error until the picture was hung up in the cathedral.

In another picture of the Adoration of the Magi, which was in the Houghton Hall collection, the painter, Brughel, had introduced a multitude of little figures, finished off with true Dutch exactitude, but one was accoutred in boots and spurs, and another was handing in, as a present, a little model of a Dutch ship.

The same collection contained a painting of the stoning of Stephen, the martyr, by Le Sœur, in which the saint was attired in the habit of a Roman Catholic priest at high mass.

A picture by Rubens, in the Luxembourg, represents the Virgin Mary in council, with two cardinals and the god Mercury assisting in her deliberations.

A STOPPAGE OF THE FALLS OF NIAGARA.

The following remarkable account of the stoppage of Niagara Falls, appeared in the *Niagara Mail* at the time of the occurrence: "That mysterious personage, the oldest inhabitant, has no recollection of so singular an occurrence as took place at the Falls on the 30th of March, 1847. The 'six hundred and twenty thousand tons of water each minute' nearly ceased to flow, and dwindled away into the appearance of a mere milldam. The rapids above the falls disappeared, leaving scarcely enough on the American side to turn a grindstone. Ladies and gentlemen rode in carriages one-third of the way across the river towards the Canada shore, over solid rock as smooth as a kitchen floor. The *Iris* says: 'Table Rock, with some two hundred yards more, was left dry; islands and places where the foot of man never dared to tread have been visited, flags placed upon some, and mementoes brought away. This unexpected event is attempted to be accounted for by an accumulation of ice at the lower extremity of Fort Erie, which formed a sort of dam between Fort Erie and Buffalo.'"

WONDERS OF MINUTE WORKMANSHIP.

In the twentieth year of Queen Elizabeth, a blacksmith named Mark Scaliot, made a lock consisting of eleven pieces of iron, steel and brass, all which, together with a key to it, weighed but one grain of gold. He also made a chain of gold, consisting of forty-three links, and, having fastened this to the before-mentioned lock and key, he put the chain about the neck of a flea, which drew them all with ease. All these together, lock and key, chain and flea, weighed only one grain and a half.

Oswaldus Norhingerus, who was more famous even than Scaliot for his minute contrivances, is said to have made 1,600 dishes of turned ivory, all perfect and complete in every part, yet so small, thin and slender, that all of them were included at once in a cup turned out of a pepper-corn of the common size. Johannes Shad, of Mitelbrach, carried this wonderful work with him to Rome, and showed it to Pope Paul V., who saw and counted them all by the help of a pair of spectacles. They were so little as to be almost invisible to the eye.

Johannes Ferrarius, a Jesuit, had in his posession cannons of wood, with their carriages, wheels, and all other military furniture, all of which were also contained in a pepper-corn of the ordinary size.

An artist, named Claudius Gallus, made for Hippolytus d'Este, Cardinal of Ferrara, representations of sundry birds setting on the tops of trees, which, by hydraulic art and secret conveyance of water through the trunks and branches of the trees, were made to sing and clap their wings; but, at the sudden appearance of an owl out of a bush of the same artifice, they immediately became all mute and silent.

CURIOUS DISSECTION OF THE OLD AND NEW TESTAMENTS.

SHOWING THE NUMBER OF BOOKS, CHAPTERS, VERSES, WORDS, LETTERS, ETC.

In the Old Testament.		In the New Testament.		Total.
Books......	39 ..	Books......	27 ..	66
Chapters...	929 ..	Chapters...	260 ..	1,189
Verses.....	23,214 ..	Verses.....	7,959 ..	31,173
Words.....	592,439 ..	Words.....	281,258 ..	773,697
Letters.....	2,728,100 ..	Letters.....	838,380 ..	3,566,480

Apocrypha—chapters, 183; verses, 6,081; words, 152,185.

The middle chapter and the least in the Bible is Psalm cxvii.

The middle verse is the 8th of Psalm cxviii.

The middle line is in 16th verse, 4th chapter, 2 Chronicles.

The word *and* occurs in the Old Testament 35,543 times; in the New Testament, 10,684 times.

The word *Jehovah* occurs 6,855 times.

OLD TESTAMENT.

The middle book is Proverbs.

The middle chapter is Job xxix.

The middle verse would be in the 2d of Chronicles, 20th chapter, between the 17th and 18th verses.

The least verse is the 1st of Chronicles, 1st chapter, and 1st verse.

NEW TESTAMENT.

The middle book is 2 Thessalonians.

The middle chapter is between the 13th and 14th of Romans.

The middle verse is the 17th of Acts xvii.

The shortest verse is the 35th of John xi.

The 21st verse of the 7th chapter of Ezra contains all the letters of the alphabet.

The 19th chapter of 2 Kings, and the 37th of Isaiah, are alike.

It is stated that the above calculation took three years to complete.

REMARKABLE INSCRIPTION.

The following singular inscription is to be seen carved on a tomb situated at the entrance of the church of San Salvador, in the city of Oviedo. The explanation is that the tomb was erected by a king named Silo, and the inscription is so written that it can be read 270 ways by beginning with the large S in the center. The words are Latin, "Silo princeps fecit."

```
T I C E F S P E C N C E P S F E C I T
I C E F S P E C N I N C E P S F E C I
C E F S P E C N I R I N C E P S F E C
E F S P E C N I R P R I N C E P S F E
F S P E C N I R P O P R I N C E P S F
S P E C N I R P O L O P R I N C E P S
P E C N I R P O L I L O P R I N C E P
E E N I R P O L I S I L O P R I N C E
P E C N I R P O L I L O P R I N C E P
S P E C N I R P O L O P R I N C E P S
F S P E C N I R P O P R I N C E P S F
E F S P E C N I R P R I N C E P S F E
C E F S P E C N I R I N C E P S F E C
I C E F S P E C N I N C E P S F E C I
T I C E F S P E C N C E P S F E C I T
```

Besides this singular inscription, the letters H. S. E. S. S. T. T. L. are also carved on the tomb, but of these no explanation is given. Silo, Prince of Oviedo, or King of the Asturias, succeeded Aurelius in 774, and died in 785. He was, therefore, a contemporary of Charlemagne. No doubt the above inscription was the composition of some ingenious and learned Spanish monk.

CURIOUS CALCULATIONS.

CONSUMPTION OF AIR IN ACTIVITY AND REPOSE.

Dr. Radclyffe Hall makes the following interesting statement with regard to the amount of air we consume in repose, and at different degrees of activity: When still, we use 500 cubic inches of air in a minute; if we walk at the rate of one mile an hour, we use 800; two miles, 1,000; three miles an hour, 1,600; four miles an hour, 2,300. If we run at six miles an hour, we use 3,000 cubic inches; trotting a horse, 1,750; cantering, 1,500.

THE VALUE OF LABOR.

Cast iron of the value of £1 sterling is worth, converted into ordinary machinery, £4; in larger ornamented work, £45; in buckles and similar kinds of fancy work, £600; in neck chains, £1,300. Bar iron of the value of £1 sterling is worth, in the form of knives, £36; needles, £70; penknife blades, £950; polished bottons and buckles, £890; balance springs of watches, £5,000.

INTEREST OF MONEY.

Dr. Price, in the second edition of his "Observations on Reversionary Payments," says: "It is well known to what prodigious sums money improved for some time at compound interest will increase. A penny so improved from our Saviour's birth, as to double itself every fourteen years—or, what is nearly the same, put out at five per cent. compound interest at our Saviour's birth—would by this time have increased to more money than could be contained in 150 millions of globes, each equal to the earth in magnitude, and all solid gold. A shilling, put out at six per cent. compound interest would, in the same time, have increased to a greater sum in gold than the whole solar system could hold, supposing it a sphere equal in diameter to the diameter of Saturn's orbit. And the earth is to such a sphere as half a square foot, or a quarto page, to the whole surface of the earth."

WONDERS OF SCIENCE.

A grain of gold has been found by Muncke to admit of being divided into *ninety-five thousand millions of visible parts;* that is, by the aid of a microscope magnifying one thousand times. A sovereign is thus capable of division into ten millions of millions of visible particles, being ten thousand times as many such parttcles as there are men, women and children in all the world.

SPONTANEOUS COMBUSTION.—Liebig, in his "Familiar Letters on Chemistry," has proved the unsoundness of spontaneous combustion. Yet Dr. Lindley gives nineteen instances of something akin, or the rapid ignition of the human body by contact with flame as a consequence of the saturation of its tissues by alcohol.

VIBRATIONS OF THE AIR.—If a person stand beneath a railway girder-bridge with an open umbrella over his head, when a train is passing, the vibration of the air will be distinctly felt in the hand which grasps the umbrella, because the outspread surface collects and concentrates the waves into the focus of the handle.

THE EARTH'S CENTER.—All bodies weigh less the further removed they are from the center of the earth. A block of stone weighing 700 pounds upon the sea-shore, will weigh only 699 pounds if carried up a mountain three miles high. A pendulum oscillates more quickly at the poles than at the equator, because the earth is flatter by twenty-six miles at the poles—that is, the "bob" of the pendulum is that much nearer the earth's center, and therefore heavier, and so swings more quickly.